Politics in Britain

An Introduction

Politics in Britain

An Introduction

Colin Leys

Heinemann Educational Books

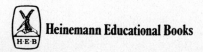

Heinemann Educational Books Ltd
22 Bedford Square, London WC1B 3HH
LONDON EDINBURGH MELBOURNE AUCKLAND
HONG KONG SINGAPORE KUALA LUMPUR NEW DELHI
IBADAN NAIROBI JOHANNESBURG
EXETER (NH) KINGSTON PORT OF SPAIN

First published 1983
Reprinted 1984

British Library Cataloguing in Publication Data

Leys, Colin
Politics in Britain.
1. Great Britain – Politics and government – 1964–
I. Title
320.941 JN231

ISBN 0-435-83492-4
ISBN 0-435-83493-2 PBK

Phototypesetting by Georgia Origination, Liverpool
Printed and bound in Great Britain by
Biddles Ltd, Guildford and King's Lynn

Contents

Preface

This book was written because there seemed to be a need for a general introduction to politics in Britain which would focus on what the layman well understands to be at stake there, namely the fate of capitalist industrialism, liberal democracy, and the socialist alternative. I am conscious of some of its shortcomings and also of some serious omissions, especially the absence of any systematic discussion of Britain's foreign relations. This topic has been omitted partly from considerations of length, and partly because of the difficulty of the task of integrating the relevant literature into the general analysis, a task which, however, needs to be undertaken. I hope none the less that the book will be useful to students and others who are concerned about Britain's future.

As far as possible, events and data have been covered to the end of 1981. A very brief review of events in 1982 has been added in an epilogue.

I am very grateful to several friends and colleagues for help and encouragement: Dennison Moore, Louise McAllister, Teddy Brett, Patrick Seyd, John Dearlove, Chantal Mouffe and Leo Panitch. I would also like to thank Ian Gough for allowing me to use statistics prepared by him in Table 13.1; Lewis Minkin for permission to base Figure 10.1 and Table 10.1 on pages 10 and 377 of his book, *The Labour Party Conference* (Manchester University Press, 1980); and Andrew Gamble for permission to quote several passages from the last chapter of his book *Britain in Decline* (Macmillan, 1981) – a work which deals trenchantly with much of the ground covered in Part I of this book. Inevitably a book such as this one owes a heavy debt to the work of other authors, as the footnotes show; and I would like particularly to mention the work of Tom Nairn, to whose penetrating ideas I found myself constantly, if sometimes reluctantly, returning. I am also glad to acknowledge the support of the Advisory Research Committee of Queen's University and the Social Science and Humanities Research Council of Canada, and to express my appreciation of the efficiency and kindness of Mrs Bernice Gallagher and Miss Margot Cameron who typed the drafts.

List of Tables and Figures

PART I

1

British Politics and Political Science

The dominant post-war tradition of texts on British politics defined politics in a distinctive way. What they discussed was not so much politics as the institutions through which a particular segment of political life – parliamentary party competition and the conduct of government – is carried on. What is more, these institutions were to a large extent not so much critically analysed as celebrated – even though, from the 1960s onwards, the celebration was increasingly tinged with doubt and anxiety.

The basis of this tradition was the political standpoint from which most of these books were written – the standpoint of the political 'establishment' of MPs, civil servants, judges, journalists, media commentators and others – which the authors of these books shared. Politics, from this point of view, is what goes on in the arenas in which, broadly speaking, the political establishment play leading, controlling, managing roles. Among the large reaches of politics excluded from this definition are the activities of the workers, towards whom the establishment feel a sincere condescension, mingled with irritation and some hostility for the part which the workers have played in calling into question the viability of the economy on which the parliamentary and governmental system depends.*

* Condescension towards the leaders of trade unions, with their limited education and shiny suits, is seldom far below the surface: see for instance, Richard Rose, *Politics in England*, Little Brown, Boston 1980, p. 230: 'as picturesquely described by Ernest Bevin, the Labour Party grew out of the bowels of the trade union movement'. Michael Frayn caught the angle of vision perfectly in his satirical essay, 'A Perfect Strike': 'It shouldn't be an unofficial strike, needless to say, because the public knows that if it had any justification at all, it would have been taken up by responsible trade union leaders. But that's not to say it should be official – it confirms the public's worst fears about union leaders to see them irresponsibly recommending strike action just when they seemed to be adopting a sensible and cooperative attitude. I feel sure, too, that strikers have suffered in the past by unfavourable comparison on television with the employers' representatives. Somehow, the employers have always seemed better dressed; they've shown more signs of having a public school education and a good accent. Is this simply poor personnel selection on the strikers' part? Or does it suggest some deeper failing?' (in R. M. Blackburn and A. Cockburn (eds.), *The Incompatibles*, Penguin, Harmondsworth 1967, p. 161).

In spite of this irritation and hostility, however, few authors of political textbooks thought to broaden their conception of politics so as to include the activities of the workers, let alone considered the bearing of these activities on the development and fate of the political system, or reconsidered the bearing of the system on the fate of the workers.

By contrast this book seeks to make such issues central. It interprets British politics as referring to the contemporary struggles of the British people as a whole to determine their historical fate. It also assumes that the chief purpose of studying politics is to play a more effective part in politics. For this purpose it seems important that political knowledge should be as reliable as possible, which in turn implies the need for a definite and appropriate method of enquiry. In particular, it is necessary to understand politics as part of the wider social whole, and also to understand it as a historical process. Perhaps surprisingly, these aims offend against certain rules that have been established in orthodox 'political science'.

Commitment and Objectivity

Many 'political scientists' subscribe to the doctrine of 'value freedom' according to which the student of politics should try to put aside his or her commitments, in order to be able to look at the facts objectively, instead of seeing only what he or she wants to see.*

Even for someone with definite political ends in view this sounds like good advice, but it is in fact misleading.

The essential mistake involved is that 'facts' do not exist 'out there', waiting to be 'seen'. There *is* an observable reality; but the concepts we employ in observing it help to determine what, given the reality, the 'facts' are held to be. If we look at Whitehall, using the concept of 'elites', we will tend to arrive at different facts from someone who uses the concept of 'classes'. Being objective, then, cannot be a question of 'ridding oneself of preconceptions' (we cannot look at the world and see 'facts', without prior concepts), but is a matter of not cheating – not refusing to see what one's own (pre-)conceptions suggest reality is like; and, certainly, seeing if other people's conceptions make better sense of it.

But is this more likely to happen if one has no commitments, or if they are weak? There seems no reason to think so. Bias may lead to correct conclusions, as well as to false ones; and Hugh Stretton argues rather convincingly that a strong commitment to some particular social goal will (other things being equal) make a social researcher more anxious to be

* The doctrine of 'value free' social science is attributed to Max Weber, especially in his speech 'Science as a Vocation' (H. H. Gerth and C. Wright Mills, eds., *From Max Weber*, Routledge, London 1952, pp. 129–56), although it is doubtful if Weber can be interpreted in this way.

right than one who is indifferent to the practical implications of what he or she is studying.[1] Of course, other things may not be equal; commitment may be accompanied by a blind zeal which swamps the scientific impulse. In practice, however, so-called 'value free' research has not been notable for its objectivity, nor committed research for the lack of it.

In any case, no-one is free from commitments, least of all in politics, and they are never 'set aside'. The most 'value free' text has a standpoint – the author's location in society, in terms of culture, education, occupation, gender, class, nationality etc. – which affects and colours how he or she defines politics, what kinds of explanation are pursued or excluded, and so on. A few examples of books on British politics will illustrate this point.

Professor Richard Rose's *Politics in England* (written mainly for North American students) is perhaps the clearest example of a value-free text, in intention at least.[2] It defines British politics as electoral party politics, conceived of as a complex piece of machinery. The task of the student is to understand *how* it works – its different working parts, its varying modes of operation, etc. (e.g.: 'the political scientist concentrates on asking who or what makes policy'); not *why* the machine is constructed in the way it is, let alone what it produces and what it does not produce, or who benefits and who loses as a result of the machine being so constructed.

For example, the 1980 edition makes the following points about Mrs Thatcher: She was one of four women cabinet ministers between 1964 and 1979, and the first woman Prime Minister; she first took office after winning an election, in which her opinion poll rating was lower than that of her opponent, Mr Callaghan; she aimed to be an 'active' Prime Minister; her father was active in local politics; her cabinet contained few businessmen and three Peers. This completes the information offered about Mrs Thatcher. The radical change in the Conservative Party's direction which her election as leader in 1975 represented, its profound significance for the internal polarisation of both major parties under the growing stress of the economic crisis, are not mentioned, let alone studied.

The fundamental reason for this curious principle of selection is that Rose was not studying politics with a view to changing anything, but playing an academic game called 'comparative politics' (the gist of which, as Bernard Crick aptly remarked, is that 'what cannot sensibly be compared can usefully be contrasted') – and, moreover, playing it by American rules. These rules not only define politics very narrowly, as electoral and pressure-group competition between 'elites', but also restrict explanation to a very narrow role (why a machine works as it does calls for a wider explanation than the question of how it works). The rules also call for information to be presented as if it were all capable of being explained as manifestations of established generalisations or laws based on observed behavioural regularities. Hence it is to be given mainly in the present tense (e.g., 'Members of Parliament are much more likely than voters to differ along party lines': 'Because British government is party government, control of the party promises control of the government') and, where possible, in a quantitative form, as a sign that it is (or might be) explicable as an instance of such laws.

The result is curious. Rose's book is full of information (some of it intriguing, such as that thirteen per cent of English people claim to know enough French to read a French newspaper, or that the Queen worships as an Anglican in England but as a Presbyterian in Scotland); but it is hardly an introduction to British *politics*. Besides almost wholly avoiding the *content* of contemporary politics – what it is or may be about, what interests and issues are at stake – it even defines politics narrowly as machinery. Trade unions, in particular, are only discussed as elements of the Labour Party, and as 'pressure groups', not as organisations of the working class; and industrial struggle is not discussed at all, even though it was directly or indirectly responsible for the fall of every government in the 1970s (Labour in 1970, Conservatives in 1974 and Labour in 1979).

Another consequence of reducing 'politics' to political machinery is that machinery can to a large extent be treated as unchanging. History enters into politics conceived in this way only as a 'constraint' which limits the choices of a country's 'governors'; the historical forces actually at work, the historically-determined options confronting not just 'governors', but the whole people, are not discussed, since for Rose the purpose of studying politics is not to be able to engage in making history. An ahistorical view of politics is thus linked with the doctrine of 'value freedom'. From time to time Rose makes it clear that his position is free from party zeal (he evidently does not wish to be thought of as one of those 'writers with strong left-wing or right-wing views' who 'criticise the established Conservative and Labour Parties for not offering voters a wide enough political choice').[3]

One effect of this apparent detachment is to make potentially disturbing issues seem dull. Racism, for example, played a crucial role in British politics from the mid-1960s onwards. By reducing it to the status of a problem of 'political management' ('how few coloured immigrants should be admitted to Britain in the coming years, and how much (or how little) government should do to promote good race relations within England') it can be made to seem almost tiresome.[4] Another effect of this approach is to play down the question of whether the conclusions drawn are valid, or the judgements arrived at sound. They are not meant to stand the test of practice, so much as to be items in examination questions. As a result, in spite of the author's preoccupation with facts, the book contains a remarkable number of judgements that are, to say the least, debatable.*

And, of course, the appearance of detachment is deceptive. Party-neutrality is not value-neutrality. Behind the facade of 'value freedom' there is often, as in Rose's case, a strong 'establishment' outlook, as may readily be seen from the book's *obiter dicta*, especially on economic policy, its notable tenderness towards senior civil servants, and the absence from its pages – except as 'machine-readable' data – of ordinary people.[5] The 'elite' understanding of British politics conveyed by Rose shows that the slogan of value freedom is not innocent.

Most British authors have been sceptical about the doctrine of value freedom but they have almost all adopted the same narrow definition of British politics, and held broadly the same view of it. A good example is Professor John Mackintosh, a Labour MP from 1966 until his untimely death in 1978. Mackintosh's view of politics is much more real, especially when he is drawing on his experience as a frustrated back-bencher. Yet, in spite of the title of his book *The Government and Politics of Britain*, 'politics' enters into it only in the form of party politics, and only in so far as it affects the 'system' of government – the Prime Minister, state and citizen, parliament, Whitehall, local government – which is his central concern.[6] 'The first objective for a student of politics', Mackintosh declared, 'is to try and discover where power lies within the system'. He concluded that by 1977 none of the political parties' current concerns, which reflected the concerns of the voters, implied any clear direction of change for 'the system' but had to do with 'the product of government, the level of taxes, welfare benefits and wages, the degree of unemployment and the standards of the public services' – with all of which, strange as it seems, Mackintosh was not greatly concerned.[7] There are plenty of glimpses of party politics in his book, but no description, let alone analysis, of the forces that animate them. Mackintosh *is* concerned about what happens – but only what happens to the 'system of government', which is implicitly or explicitly assumed to have value in its own right. In other words, British politics is defined as the British system of representative democracy.

So, although as an MP Mackintosh was sensitive to party differences

* For example, the statement that there was only very limited competition between the major parties in the 1970s (p. 278); that 'special advisers' in government departments have proved a success (p. 73); that there were two million members of parties in 1979 (p. 177); that the British economy 'improved' between 1976 and 1978 (p. 26). These examples are *not* evidence of poor scholarship. The point is that it does not matter sufficiently for the purposes for which Rose's book is written whether these judgements are right. If you want to know the real potential of the Labour Party for making major social changes, it matters a great deal whether its individual membership is 600,000 or 150,000 (as even sympathetic observers thought most likely in 1978). But if you want a figure to deploy in the game of 'measuring' involvement in national politics, Rose's figure of about 400,000 will do.

and took distinctive positions in relation to them, his book was intended less for those who want to engage in politics in order to change the world than for those who were being inducted into the British educated elite and who needed to know how 'the system' presently worked, and if possible in what ways it was changing, so as to be able to take their places *in* it – as civil servants, journalists, teachers, managers, or even elected councillors or MPs. Consequently his pessimistic conclusions – to the effect that the system is drifting in a broadly undemocratic and bureaucratic direction – are rather vaguely formulated and the causes are not systematically explored. They are tacitly seen as lying outside the purview of a text of this kind. They are simply a part of what the next generation of the political elite must be prepared to cope with in its prime task of *managing* the system.

Different as they are in many ways, Rose and Mackintosh have one thing in common: an underlying 'pluralist' conception of politics. This is the counterpart of their restricted conception of politics as the electoral competition between the parties, and the relations between Whitehall and 'pressure groups'. The core of the 'system' is seen as an essentially neutral apparatus which a multitude or 'plurality' of groups seek to influence or control. Even though Mackintosh was a Labour MP his book does not present politics as essentially a struggle between the interests of labour and capital, or the 'political system' as having been shaped (as it undoubtedly has) by the needs of capital in its effort to constrain, deflect or absorb the political power of the working class.

This conception of politics marks a significant difference between these two authors and our last example, Peter Calvocoressi's *The British Experience 1945–75*. Although the title makes no such claims, Calvocoressi's book does offer an introduction – and a sophisticated and engagingly written one at that – to modern British politics – or at least to the *policies* that have resulted from these politics.[8] Again significantly, it is an historical essay, even though its focus is hardly less recent than that of the two 'political science' texts we have discussed; also significantly, a great deal of it is about economics. Calvocoressi feels no inhibitions about discussing centrally what is central to politics in modern Britain (he is not playing 'political science'). Nor does he hesitate in identifying the major forces at work in British politics today, seeing here an evident continuity with the past – capital and labour, employers and unions, property and the people. Moreover Calvocoressi thinks that the purpose of studying politics is to influence them.

At the same time, his standpoint entails certain limitations. It is the standpoint of the middle class liberal intellectual (prone to Latin tags and elegant historical digressions) with social-democratic sympathies. Calvocoressi identifies himself with what he sees as an historic trend towards a 'caring' society – which, he holds, is the essence of socialism. On the other hand, he distances himself a little from those who have, in his words, sought most actively to serve as the 'national conscience', feeling that it is 'foolhardy' to give precedence to social outlays over industrial recovery; Britain must, he implies, reverse its priorities here – temporarily, no doubt. But, equally, he does not identify himself with the interests of capital (especially not with financial capital, for which he entertains a particular dislike).* From this standpoint above the fray he sees a need to transcend the 'crude conflict' between labour and capital by means of 'a more fruitful partnership between employers and employed' which must come from giving workers 'more responsibility and involvement' (but not, apparently, ownership).[9] His analysis does not, unfortunately, provide many clues as to how to realise this old liberal dream of making the capitalist lion lie down with the labour lamb (or vice versa).

Thus, in spite of the historical and practical dimension which makes Calvocoressi's book a true study of politics, his standpoint separates him from both of the main protagonists in the struggles he records; with the result that although he very much wants his work to make it possible for the British people to achieve both prosperity and social justice, he fails to suggest how it might be done.† Calvocoressi is far from lacking the knowledge to make this analysis, but his standpoint, outside the forces actually capable of acting on events, disinclines him to take it up. The gap at the centre of his analysis corresponds to the gap between him and each of the broad interests or social forces in whose hands the fate of the country ultimately lies.

And so Calvocoressi, whose account of 'what happened' is in many ways outstanding, is also reduced to celebration – though of the British people, not 'the system'. The British are congratulated for being a 'steady people', who have neither panicked nor 'bolted after precipitate panacæas', whose 'democratic instincts remain intact'.‡ With these reassuring thoughts Cal-

* Calvocoressi has been a publisher – a branch of capital which likes to think that it is animated by loftier motives than profit.

† '. . . the causes of the failures can be analysed and understood. The account of the thirty years presented in this book will not be accepted by everybody in all its details, but broadly speaking this is what happened and broadly speaking this is why, and – most important of all – British people can grasp the essentials and wish to do so. They are serious, intelligent and reasonably well educated people' (p. 252). Here we once again see the link between an author's standpoint and his ability to analyse politics. Calvocoressi is not playing an academic game, yet his chapter on 'Politics' as such is in some ways the least political in his book, being concerned with the governmental and constitutional machinery: in short, 'the system'. Although throughout the chapters on *policies* the protagonists – Conservative and Labour, employers and unions, the CBI, the Treasury and the TUC – come and go, when it comes to dealing explicitly with 'politics', what we are offered is not an analysis of the springs of their actions, the logic of the development of their comings and goings.

‡ Although Britain also, apparently, 'prefers the few to the many' (p. 177).

vocoressi joins ranks with the many intellectuals whose ultimate reaction to the crisis has been to find solace in the intangible qualities of British life and character.

To sum up: every author's standpoint is reflected in a framework of concepts which determines what are the facts that the author sees, what is defined as politics, what is seen as needing explanation and what kinds of explanation count. Given this, the problem of objectivity cannot be solved by not having a standpoint but only by adopting one which requires objective knowledge and by trying to work out a conceptual framework capable of yielding it.

Politics, Economy and Society

One of the peculiarities of most general books on British politics is that politics are discussed largely in isolation from the economy and (to a lesser extent) the society. The reasons for this are ultimately political. The separation of social studies into separate 'sciences' was part of the broader movement, begun in the 1920s, to give the study of society a 'professional' status by disengaging it from partisanship. The separation of 'political science' from 'economics' and 'sociology' only made sense if you could define separate spheres of activity in such a way that they were, in fact, largely uninfluenced by each other. This is one of the reasons why the political scientists' definition of politics tends to confine it to the machinery of the 'political system'; and this in turn only makes sense if the purpose of being a political scientist is not primarily to acquire knowledge useful for engaging in political struggles. For anyone who does want such knowledge, the separation of the study of politics from that of economics or social change of all kinds is as absurd as the restriction of the meaning of 'politics' to its machinery.

Most general political 'science' books on Britain implicitly recognise this by devoting a chapter or two to what they call the 'social context' or 'foundations' of British politics. The idea here is that the 'political system' does not actually stand quite alone; it is flanked by a 'social system', and sometimes also by an 'economic system'. Interestingly enough, the relation between these 'systems' and the 'political system' always seems to be unidirectional – the political system is influenced by the social system (by linguistic or regional differences, the 'class structure', 'culture', etc.) or by the economic system (the level of prosperity, the distribution of wealth, and so on) but not the other way round.* This is not so surprising when one considers that in order to examine the effects which the 'political

* In the numerous books and articles on the analysis of politics in terms of 'systems' the 'outputs' of the 'political system' are always supposed to be of equal importance with the 'inputs' but the best that can be said of this literature is that it is inutterably jejune.

system' has on the other 'systems' one must begin with an analysis of the political forces operating in it – their character, strengths, aims and tendencies – which has been ruled out of the proper purview of political science.

This is even true of those political scientists who go well beyond a perfunctory treatment of the 'social context' (a serious treatment of the 'economic context' by a political scientist writing on Britain does not yet exist). Professor Jean Blondel, for example, wrote a model text, *Voters, Parties and Leaders: The Social Fabric of British Politics*, which showed in detail how party activists, MPs and civil servants are drawn from different strata of the population, and what difference this makes to the way they behave.[10] Yet Blondel did not suggest what effects this had on the *outcomes* of politics – for instance, on the way the population was distributed into different strata – but stopped short at the effects it had on political *mechanics*. For instance, a chapter entitled 'Politicians' showing how differing social backgrounds were reflected in differing political opinions within and between the parties in parliament did not go on to discuss what implications this might have had for the political issues at stake in Britain in the mid-1970s (the last edition was published in 1974). Instead, Blondel concluded with a discussion of what sort of careers MPs could typically expect to follow. The view of politics, and the purpose of studying it, which produces this effect, is revealed in Blondel's closing sentences:

> Britain has now come to face some of the most serious economic and social long-term problems which she has had to meet for perhaps a century: in this the parties will have to provide a lead – and on this lead much of the future of the political system will depend. If . . . the lead is provided, Britain will once more have proved the strength of her political and social system, and she will once more leave sociologists and students of politics with ample scope for prolonged meditations.[11]

It is not enough, then, to recognise that politics does not take place in a vacuum – that it is related to the economy and to society, as the language of 'systems' acknowledges; a radical break with this whole way of looking at the matter is required. Politics is indeed distinguishable from economics and social life – but it cannot be understood as a distinct 'field' of activity, occurring in a separate realm or region of its own. It needs to be grasped, rather, as an aspect of all social relations (including economic relations), as the aspect of conflict and struggle. It is present in the workplace just as much as it is in elections, and is equally, if less obviously, active in the school system, the courts, the police, the pattern of housing, the scale and distribution of social services, the tax system – not to mention the structure of the family and the whole realm of 'culture'.

Does this mean, then, that elections, parliament, and party government are also merely aspects of economics, social structure and culture? This would certainly be a severe over-simplification, but a more fruitful one than the conventional view – that these are the arenas where politics more or less exclusively 'occurs'.

Such a view may seem to make the study of British politics impossibly complex. It is certainly hard to comprehend the complexity of any social whole, especially one as large and as ancient as Britain's, even if we are only seeking a provisional, practical understanding of some of its central features. But there is no reason for presuming that this complexity is impenetrable.

History

Politics, besides being seen as an aspect of the social whole, must obviously have a strong historical dimension. This does not mean that political generalisations are impossible. Political struggles in different times and places do resemble each other in many respects but each is a unique blend of elements derived from what has gone before, determining what can be done in the present and hence what may eventuate in the future. We need knowledge which embodies the lessons to be gained from studying the unique pattern of development of the particular country's politics on which we want to have some effect.

But this is not an argument for politics being studied *as* history. Historians are trying to understand the past: we want to understand the past in order to analyse the present and influence the future. Historical knowledge is indispensable to the study of politics, but not a substitute for it. It must be combined with knowledge of the present which can be acquired by various means not available to historians, including taking part in politics, and with comparative knowledge, based on the analysis of similarities and differences between various contemporary situations. Our conceptual framework must permit the combination of these different kinds of knowledge. Ahistorical approaches (the kind signalised by being written largely in the present tense) cannot hope to grasp what is happening, what questions have been historically posed, or what developments are possible. On the other hand, a purely historical understanding, that is not systematically integrated with knowledge of other contemporary situations, or of the dynamics of the immediate situation in which we are involved, is liable to be inconclusive (Calvocoressi is a case in point). The relation between historiography and the sort of knowledge called for here is indicated by Pierre Vilar in a discussion of Marx's own relation to history:

> In 1854 Marx received from the *New York Tribune* a request for some articles on a recent Spanish *pronunciamento* – the very archetype of a banal 'event'. What

> did he do? *He learned Spanish* . . . Soon he was reading Lope and Calděron and at last he could write to Engels – 'now I'm in the middle of Don Quixote!' The great and good Spanish anarchist militant Anselmo Lorenzo was astonished by Marx's Hispanic culture when he met him in 1871; admiring, if somewhat outclassed, he described it as 'bourgeois'. Nevertheless, in his series of articles of 1854–6, Marx had given an historical vision of Spain of which only the 20th century has been able to appreciate the full lessons – one which encompassed all the major features of Spanish history, without a single absurdity, and which in certain judgements on the War of Independence has yet to be improved upon. There was a genius at work here, admittedly. But also his method . . . In order to write about one military escapade he did not 'write a history of Spain'; but he thought it necessary to *think Spain historically.*[12]

A relevant contemporary example is the series of essays written in the early 1960s by Perry Anderson and Tom Nairn, the best known of which is Anderson's 'Origins of the Present Crisis' – 'a sustained attempt to develop a coherent historical account of British society', as E. P. Thompson called it.[13] What Anderson and Nairn proposed was a new understanding of the long-term formation of the class of capital and the working class in Britain, the corresponding peculiarities of the British state and the distinctive features of the British version of bourgeois ideology, all of which were brought together to explain both the long-term decline of the British economy, and the peculiar paralysis which inhibited either a left or a right response (see Chapter 3). Even sympathetic critics found some of the authors' judgements sweeping and questionable, yet it is hard to deny that these essays set the agenda for much of the whole contemporary debate about the nature and causes of the British crisis. It could even be argued that Anderson and Nairn grasped and articulated the existence of a crisis in a way that has hardly been surpassed almost two decades later. The important point to note, however, is that their intention was not to write the history of the previous three hundred years, but to quarry it, using new concepts and asking different questions, for information which would help explain the *present* crisis. They wanted to 'think' the present crisis 'historically'.

The Role of Ideas

What is one to make of the role of ideas in politics? The changes that have occurred in British political ideas since 1945 have been remarkable. In the 1950s, for instance, both major parties publicly supported full employment and a steady improvement in social services. By 1980, however, the Conservatives had openly, and the Labour Party tacitly, abandoned both of these commitments. Similarly, in 1950, Fascism was still something which the most popular war in modern British history had been fought to destroy. But by the 1970s neo-fascists were politically active in most large cities in Britain. In 1950 a 'Marxist' was either a communist – i.e., a member of the Communist Party of Great Britain – or, possibly, of an obscure Trotskyist group – in either case, the representative of a politically-irrelevant tendency. But by 1980, 'Marxism' of some sort was quite commonplace among politically conscious students and people of broadly 'radical' persuasions everywhere.

What produced these far-reaching shifts in ideas, and how did they in turn affect political developments? We will not get much help in answering these questions from the concept of 'political culture' adopted by the behaviouralists. 'Political culture' is defined by Rose as 'those values, beliefs and emotions which give meaning to politics.' 'Political culture' is usually treated as something possessed in common by whole populations; and although it is generally presented as exercising a large (if vague) determining effect on political life, it seldom seems to have any determinants of its own. It plays much the same explanatory role in this sort of political science that the concept of 'national character' played in an earlier literature.

A more useful concept is that of ideology.[14] What is meant by ideology here is any set of social ideas that becomes part of the operative assumptions of the political practice of a particular social group – whether a majority or a minority. For this to happen, at least two requirements have to be met. The ideas must be to some extent effective: that is, they must correspond to some degree to people's practical experience. Secondly, the social origins of the ideas must be lost to view. For example, liberalism was historically the product of the rise of new propertied classes from the seventeenth century onwards, corresponding to their needs and to the reality of the new social order they were creating. Considered in abstraction from these origins (which systematisation by philosophers such as Locke made possible) liberalism had a wider and more compelling appeal than it would have had if its class origins had remained apparent. And so long as the political interests of the new middle classes and the workers could be reconciled within it, liberalism was able to achieve an ascendancy which is still formidable. But this ascendancy was never total, and new conflicts arose to undermine it. Irish colonialism generated nationalist ideas, the rise of organised labour generated socialist ideas, the backlash of imperialism generated racist ideas. Each of these subsequently achieved a measure of influence, wider or narrower and of longer or shorter duration, according to the effects of economic and social changes and the course of political struggles in which these ideas themselves played significant roles. Undoubtedly, this is an intangible and complex area of enquiry.[15]

It is difficult to know, in general, what determines the emergence of particular systems of ideas, and why some and not others succeed in penetrating the practical consciousness of important segments of the population. But there is no doubt that this process plays a crucial part in politics, not least in the rhythm of the development and resolution of crises which is such a prominent aspect of modern British politics.

Method and Standpoint

The methodological ideas just discussed – focusing on the social totality, trying to think the present historically, and seeking the social origins and the effects of ideas – contradict the tenets of much orthodox political science, and not by chance. They are among the methodological tenets of the materialist interpretation of history. But the theoretical basis of historical materialism, or Marxism, has itself never been more in dispute than now; and in following some of its methodological precepts no claim is being advanced for the theoretical or predictive achievements of historical materialism in general (although these are undoubtedly more impressive than vulgar anti-Marxism understands). It is rather that these ideas seem necessary in order to make sense of what has been happening. The reader must decide how useful is the system of concepts employed – and, perhaps, whether it deserves any less to be considered 'scientific' than other conceptual frameworks which others have not hesitated to call political 'science'.

As for the standpoint of this book, its aim is to be democratic and socialist. Maintaining this standpoint consistently is difficult, yet the more one contemplates the British situation today, the harder it becomes to avoid the conclusion that a fundamental choice between democracy and authoritarianism, and between some form of socialism and an increasingly unproductive capitalism, is being posed. At the least, we must seek an understanding relevant to that choice.

At the same time, this understanding must be concerned with the present for its own sake, as well as with the future. What E. P. Thompson said of historians applies at least as strongly to students of contemporary politics:

> ... history cannot be compared to a tunnel through which an express races until it brings its freight of passengers out into sunlit plains. Or, if it can be, then generation upon generation of passengers are born, live in the dark, and die while the train is still within the tunnel. An historian must surely be more interested than the teleologists allow him to be in the quality of life, the sufferings and satisfactions, of those who live and die in unredeemed time... surely any mature view of history (or of contemporary actuality) must in some way combine evaluations of both kinds – of men as consumers of their own mortal existence and as producers of a future, of men as individuals and as historical agents, of men being and becoming?[16]

It is a truism that the goals people struggle for are seldom achieved, at least not in their lifetimes, and not in the form they hope for. On the other hand, people are constantly striving for future goals. It should not be too much to ask that studies of politics should reflect the pathos and drama of both aspects of the human condition, though it often seems to be.

2

Britain in Crisis

A hundred and fifty years ago, when the industrial revolution was at its height, people in Britain had no doubt that the country was in the grip of powerful forces which were drastically changing its economic, social and political structure. The breathtaking accumulation of wealth, the dramatic expansion of the industrial towns, impressed themselves on contemporary observers as 'great and extraordinary facts', 'almost miraculous', 'unparalleled in the history of the world'.[1] By 1840, the industrial revolution was almost universally recognised as 'probably the most important event in world history, at any rate since the invention of agriculture and cities'.[2] And later generations have had no difficulty in recognising that the industrial revolution also produced a new class of capital, and a new working class, or that the relationship between these classes had become, by the end of the nineteenth century, the central axis of British political life.

It is also well recognised now that from about 1870 the revolutionary forces which wrought these astonishing changes slackened in Britain, while gathering strength in Germany, the USA, Belgium and subsequently elsewhere. It was not just that other countries also became industrialised, eventually reducing the British share of world trade and world production to one more in keeping with her population size (from nearly 25% at the end of the 1920s – the peak – to about 14% by 1945).[3] From the moment that foreign industrial competition began to be seriously felt, contemporaries became aware that Britain could not meet it, in one field after another. Had it not been for the growing volume of imports paid for out of profits and interest on British overseas investment and lending, and for the advantages which British exports enjoyed in empire markets (Tables 2.1, 2.2), the relative decline of Britain's economic power would have been much more rapid, and might well have produced a

Table 2.1 How overseas investment income offsets Britain's trade deficit (1831–1931)

	(£ millions)				Proportion of visible trade gap covered by overseas investment earnings
	Balance of visible trade	Overseas investment earnings	'Invisible' trade	Current account balance	
1821	− 78.1	+ 3.9	+ 13.1	− 1.1	21.5%
1851	− 22.6	+ 10.4	+ 22.6	+ 8.0	46.0%
1871	− 46.0	+ 39.5	+ 82.4	+ 66.9	85.8%
1891	−122.1	+ 94.3	+ 99.6	+ 67.0	77.2%
1911	−121.2	+177.3	+146.8	+190.9	146.2%
1931	−407	+170	+134	− 37	41.7%

Source: B. R. Mitchell and P. Deane, *Abstract of British Historical Statistics*, Cambridge University Press, Cambridge 1962, pp. 333–5 (with bullion and specie movements excluded).

Table 2.2 Shares of major British exports going to empire markets (1870–1934)

	%						
	1870	*1880*	*1890*	*1900*	*1913*	*1929*	*1934*
Textiles	26.6	36.8	37.2	39.9	43.9	42.2	44.2
Iron & iron goods	21.7	31.2	33.5	36.7	48.2	51.4	55.3
Machinery	19.0	18.3	24.6	22.3	32.5	43.5	51.2
Locomotives	16.0	67.5	27.8	49.5	58.6	43.8	65.3

Source: W. Schlote, *British Overseas Trade from 1700 to the 1930s*, Blackwell, Oxford 1952, pp. 166–7.

social and political crisis severe enough to lead to a radical reconstruction of the economy in an atmosphere of national emergency.[4]

As it was, Britain's relative decline was protracted. It was only towards the end of the last, and greatest, upswing in the world cycle of capital accumulation (i.e., the long boom which ended in 1970) that her real weakness became fully apparent. Britain's manufacturing competitiveness was now shrinking below the level needed to maintain the real level of national income, to the point where one sector of industry after another was driven out of business without significant new sectors arising to take their place (Table 2.3). The resulting trade deficit was closed by periodic 'packages' of deflationary economic policies to curb the demand for imports and, theoretically, to encourage exports, although this served to aggravate the

Table 2.3 Some effects of Britain's declining manufacturing competitiveness (1951–1980)

	1951	*1961*	*1971*	*1974*	*1975*	*1976*	*1977*	*1978*	*1979*	*1980*
British share of world exports (%)	21.9	16.4	10.9	8.8	9.3	8.7	9.3	9.5	9.7	10.2
Foreign share of domestic sales of manufactures (%)	n.a.	n.a.	18	23	22	23	24.1	24	25.5	25.8
Foreign share of domestic sales of vehicles (%)	0	n.a.	12*	23	26	29	34	36	41	41
Real personal disposable income (Index: 1975 = 100)	53	73	88	101	100	99	95	106	114	115
Unemployed (millions)	.214	.376	.775	.605	.921	1.274	1.378	1.376	1.307	1.665

* excluding tractors and motorcycles.

Sources: *National Institute Economic Review*, *Economic Trends*, *Monthly Digest of Statistics*, *Department of Employment Gazette*.

growing unemployment arising from industrial closures. Living standards finally stopped growing and then, after a brief recovery in 1978–80, declined, to the accompaniment of many signs of social strain.

There is, however, a striking contrast between the general readiness to recognise the revolutionary social forces which made Britain into an industrial capitalist country, and the general reluctance to recognise these same forces at work when their action is, so to speak, negative. The logic which propelled the new classes of capital and labour onto the front of the political stage as the agents of Britain's world economic and political dominance is now, through these same agents, driving Britain towards a different, less comfortable, destiny. People readily acknowledge that in the nineteenth century politics was about the coming to power of the capitalist class, and the reconstruction of the entire framework of economic policy, fiscal policy, educational policy, the national and local state structure, culture, etc., in conformity with the interests of that class. The same people, however, find it difficult to entertain the possibility that the time may have come when politics is about the necessity of a comparable upheaval. Yet while this thought may be unwelcome, it is not unthinkable. Just as the nineteenth century was a period of radical reconstruction, based on the triumphs of British capital, the late twentieth century may well also be a period of far-reaching social and political change, based on its defeats.

In the mid-1960s, the predominant view was that Britain's problems could be solved by extensive reforms – in the way the government 'managed' the economy, in fiscal policy, in the internal organisation of the civil service, in education, in the organisation of corporate industrial capital, and so on. This idea, which Harold Wilson so successfully articulated when he was elected to the Labour Party leadership in 1963, had been thoroughly discredited by the end of his first administration in 1970 (though just why these reforms were either impracticable, or irrelevant, is seldom explained).

Following this disappointment the anxiety increasingly felt by political commentators expressed itself in several alternative forms. One was to suggest that the British are, after all, a non-materialistic people, who prefer the 'quality of life' to high living-standards, so that after a period of adjustment they will be content to live more modestly and things can go on much as before. If growth proved 'a will o' the wisp' it would indeed be comforting if the workers proved relatively satisfied, as Calvocoressi suggested, with 'pottering about in their gardens and watching football', while the middle classes were predominantly occupied with 'music, theatre, art exhibitions, rescue archaeology and buying and borrowing books'.[5] Another reaction was to celebrate industrial decline itself. It was positively good, according to the American journalist Bernard Nossiter, that Britain's dark satanic mills should close; instead, the British people would turn more and more to selling to foreigners *services* in the provision of which, as a nation, they have special skills.[6]

These ideas are – unfortunately perhaps – unrealistic,* but they do betray these authors' real anxiety: if the major classes, and perhaps especially the workers, who have less margin for sacrifice, are not content with non-material things, and if the 'de-industrialisation' of Britain continues, then the moderation, gradualism and civility which they see as the pre-eminent virtues of British politics are unlikely to survive. In other words, the political struggle may enter a very different phase. And this is, indeed, the central issue of contemporary British politics, which makes the study of British politics important not just for the British alone, but for any capitalist industrialised country which falls too far behind in the industrial race.

To understand this we must try to understand the causes and nature of the 'crisis'. What is the 'logic of relationships' which for more than a century has been pushing Britain steadily towards the margin of survival in the world of industrial competition? Since unlike, say, Australia or Canada, Britain cannot export primary commodities (with the short-run exception of oil), or even feed her own population, she must (*pace* Nossiter's vision of a nation of producers of television shows or hand-crafted pottery) export manufactured goods. At the end of the so-called de-industrialisation process there lies, for most of the population, nothing but unemployment and growing poverty. And as most of the population cannot be relied upon (*pace* Calvocoressi) to potter contentedly in their gardens while this occurs, the process of 'de-industrialisation' implies a general political crisis.

One reason why so many people continued for so long to celebrate the British political system, rather than analyse the new circumstances which have undermined it, is possibly a reluctance to believe that what has happened elsewhere could happen in Britain. For the new circumstances in which Britain finds herself are less novel than many people like to suppose. A process of economic 'involution' and political polarisation,

* The main reasons why a switch of resources to services is not a solution to Britain's economic problem are: 1. Services are on a much smaller scale than manufacturing. For instance, to offset a drop in Britain's share of world manufacturing exports of one percentage point in 1976, Britain's share of world exports of services would have had to increase by 3.3 percentage points – from 9.7% to 13% of the world total, an increase of more than a third. 2. The world market for services cannot be expected to grow very fast and Britain already has a large share of it. 3. The services which earn foreign exchange mostly do not employ many people (tourism is an important exception but for obvious reasons has some finite limits to its growth). Most of the increase in service *employment* since the 1960s has been in non-traded (i.e., public sector) services. (See J. R. Sargent, 'UK Performance in Services', in F. Blackaby (ed.), *De-Industrialisation*, Heinemann/NIESR, London 1979, and T. Sheriff, *A Deindustrialised Britain?*, Fabian Research Series 341, London 1979.)

culminating in authoritarian regimes more or less heavily reliant on terror, occurred in successive countries in Latin America in the 1960s and 1970s, and notably in Chile and Uruguay in 1973, both of which had long democratic traditions. It would be superficial to draw too close a parallel with the experience of these countries*; but it is equally superficial (if very British) to suppose that Britain could never undergo its own version of this fate, that for Britain something will always turn up.

The belief that 'something will turn up' seemed, of course, to be almost miraculously confirmed by the discoveries of oil in the North Sea, starting in 1968, followed by massive increases in the world-market price of oil. By 1980 North Sea production was already equivalent to all Britain's oil requirements. Yet by this time North Sea oil was also just beginning to be seen as at best a modest economic blessing, and at worst as an economic disaster. No major industrial reconstruction financed by oil revenues, or linked to oil technology, had yet been put in hand or was even being seriously planned. The exchange value of sterling rose sharply because of the strong overall balance of payments caused by oil exports (and savings on oil imports). This made manufactured exports dearer, and imports cheaper. The result was to accelerate the closure rate of British manufacturing companies. Now North Sea oil was 'killing our industry'.[7]

But North Sea oil had warded off a *political* crisis. In 1979, the deficit on Britain's visible trade account (the gap between the cost of imported goods and the value of exported goods) was £3.2 billion, in spite of oil production worth about £6 billion. Without North Sea oil output, the visible trade deficit might well have been £5 billion and the overall balance of payments could have been in deficit to the tune of some £4.5 billion.[8] This would have led at once to a payments crisis and – by one means or another – to a very drastic reduction of national consumption. Admittedly these figures are abstractions. No deficit of that magnitude would have been allowed to build up. Long before it was reached, more modest cuts would have been imposed. Yet, on this point, the behaviour of the Callaghan government in the year 1976 is extremely instructive.

At that stage, North Sea oil production was only worth £0.9 billion per annum, and the overall visible balance of trade deficit for 1976 was about £3.9 billion.[9] There was a flight of capital out of sterling. To halt the fall in the value of the pound, the government turned to the International Monetary Fund for a loan. The conditions attached to this loan (like all IMF loans) involved severe cuts in government spending and, therefore,

* Yet Chile and Uruguay, together with Argentina, had relatively high per capita incomes by world standards immediately after the Second World War; Uruguay had had constitutional democratic government from 1903, and Chile from 1932. After two decades of economic stagnation or regression, and mounting political crisis, the military seized power and made these countries bywords for barbarity.

in public consumption. There was strong opposition to it within the Labour Party. But Denis Healey, then Chancellor of the Exchequer, said that the alternative would be 'policies so severe that they would lead to riots in the streets' – i.e., so severe as to jeopardise the government's ability to govern at all. The IMF loan was repaid early, by April 1979 – partly out of government revenues from North Sea oil – by which time oil production had also largely closed the visible trade deficit in goods other than oil, which by 1979 had risen to £2.4 billion.[10]

So North Sea oil, whatever its long-run economic effects, tided the existing party-parliamentary political system over a reef on which it might well have foundered in the late 1970s. Thanks to North Sea oil, the belief that the politics of the 1950s could somehow be restored was still surprisingly widespread among British political commentators in the early 1980s;* even though oil output would eventually decline from the late 1980s onwards, by which time, unless a radical reconstruction of manufacturing industry had been put in hand, the balance of payments gap would have to be closed by cuts in living standards even larger than those that had so alarmed the government in 1976.

The Concept of Crisis

Part of the reason for the widespread unwillingness to confront the reality of the crisis was perhaps that the word itself had been so overworked in the course of the previous two decades. As Tom Nairn remarked, with only slight exaggeration, 'since 1910 it has all been "crisis", save for those few years in the fifties when we had it so good (a slogan invented, characteristically, just when it had become plain that the post-war UK boom was over and we would soon be back to crisis as usual)'.[11] Can the concept of crisis be given a reasonably clear and precise meaning?

The most systematic recent attempt to do this was made by Jürgen Habermas.[12] Borrowing (cautiously) from systems theory, Habermas tried to establish a model of society which would allow us to understand a social crisis in the sense in which medicine understands a crisis in an illness (as a turning-point at which the patient either recovers or dies) or dramatic criticism understands a crisis in the life of a character – the principal difference being that, there, the crisis is experienced as such, and consciously (though not necessarily rationally) participated in by the character concerned, a dimension of obvious relevance to social crises.

* Those who were converted to monetarism could perhaps be considered to have become convinced of the 'impossibility of going on in the old way', but many of these soon became disillusioned by the economic policy failures of Thatcherism and turned back with renewed enthusiasm to the idea of a 'centre option'. It is hard to believe that this would have seemed plausible by 1981 had Britain's short-term problems not been so greatly alleviated by North Sea oil.

A major difficulty faced by all attempts to apply systems theory to social life is that the 'boundaries' of social organisms are not precise. It is seldom easy to know whether a society has changed in such a fundamental way that we must say that the old society has been *replaced* by a new one. Habermas suggested that this problem could be solved by focusing on the 'constitutive tradition' of a society; usually, at least in retrospect, its members know when the tradition that gives it its identity has been broken (e.g., post-revolutionary French society represented a definite break from the old regime). Such breaks, Habermas argued, occur when a society ceases to be able to learn how to deal with changes (external or internal) which threaten to break its constitutive tradition. The capacity of a society to learn is given by the way in which its general principles of organisation determine (a) its control over 'outer nature' (i.e., its scientific, technological and organisational capacity) and (b) its 'integration of inner nature' (roughly, the aptitudes, values, personality types, etc., which are fostered by it).

On this model, Liberal (competitive) capitalist societies evolve from crisis to crisis. This is because their principle of social organisation leads periodically to economic slumps which put in question the key social relations on which they are based – private ownership and the class system. 'Organised' or state-regulated capitalism has learned how to prevent production crises by means of a state economic sector, state economic planning, the substitution of bureaucratic for democratic decision-making, and 'corporatist' wage-fixing. But the tendency to economic crisis that is inherent in any system of production for profit remains. But now it is manifested in the form of fiscal crises, or crises of economic planning; or as crises of administrative capacity ('rationality crises'); or as 'legitimation crises' (when the state has difficulty in justifying new policies necessitated by the new tasks it must take on); or as 'motivation crises' (due to the erosion of traditional values necessary to the maintenance of capitalism – for instance traditional family values).

Habermas's discussion succeeds in giving some precision to the concept of social crisis. As he points out, the fact that a 'crisis consciousness' develops does not mean that a society is objectively in a crisis. He sets out, however, a plausible model of the way in which objective changes may put in question the survival of society as its members recognise it. In the case of Britain, both elements are discernible: a general sense of crisis, at least among the middle classes from the late 1960s onwards, and a variety of indicators of at least severe deficiencies of production, administrative capacity, legitimation and motivation.

But the model does not help to explain why crises occur *where* and *when* they do. The tendencies it outlines are generic to all advanced capitalist countries. Why has Britain entered into a general crisis (combining most of Habermas's 'crisis tendencies') when most other advanced capitalist countries have not? To explain this, a historical analysis of the specific sources of the crisis in Britain is needed. Moreover, in Britain's case it is not an underlying tendency to overproduction, but to under-productivity, that is central. Habermas's model is, in fact, a checklist of possible sources of crisis in advanced capitalist countries in general. While it has some relevance to Britain, it does not seem to touch on what is most distinctive about the one advanced capitalist country which had actually entered a general crisis at the time Habermas was writing.

An alternative approach to the analysis of crises is that of Antonio Gramsci, who defined a general or 'organic' crisis (a 'crisis of authority' or 'crisis of the state') as a dissolution of the ideology that secures the consent of the mass of the population to the existing order.[13] In Gramsci's view, philosophy, a more or less coherent and critical system of ideas, becomes an ideology when it becomes an 'implicit premise' of men's practical lives, reflected in their language, 'commonsense' (what people see as being 'the way things are') and 'popular religion' or folklore (popular articles of faith, precepts for living). A philosophy that expresses the interests of the ruling class (for example the 'possessive individualism' of English liberal philosophy) becomes an ideology and binds the masses to the established order when it penetrates popular consciousness in this way. A 'crisis of the state' occurs when this cement breaks down, when 'the great masses have become detached from their traditional ideologies, and no longer believe what they used to believe...'[14]

> ...the content of the crisis is the ruling class's hegemony, which occurs either because the ruling class has failed in some major undertaking for which it has requested, or forcibly extracted, the consent of the broad masses (war, for example), or because huge masses... have passed suddenly from a state of political passivity to a certain activity, and put forward demands which taken together, albeit not organically formulated, add up to a revolution. A 'crisis of authority' is spoken of: this is precisely the crisis of hegemony, or general crisis of the State.[15]

At this point the 'historic bloc' of social classes that was once bound together by a unifying ideology under the leadership of the ruling class dissolves and must be either reconstructed or replaced through a fresh political initiative. The old dominant class, Gramsci suggests, is the first to respond, and generally restores control by means of a new philosophy, new men and new programmes; but an opportunity also arises to prevent this, to create a new 'historic bloc' under the leadership of a new, more popular alliance of classes.

Gramsci does not offer a theory of why organic crises occur, although the examples he gives in the passage cited above apply rather well to Britain, the first to the 1970s (after fifteen years in which successive governments had failed to produce the economic recovery for which they had repeatedly sought wage restraints, and imposed deflations), and the second to the period before 1914 (when the labour movement had moved out of its passive attachment to liberalism). But what Gramsci does is to make the concept of *general* crisis historically concrete. What is at stake is not a passive and intangible 'constitutive tradition' but an actively-constructed ideological hegemony, that can be both analysed and contested.

This idea (which underlies the work of Anderson and Nairn referred to in the previous chapter) allows us to make a preliminary clarification of the British situation as follows. Britain has known two general crises in the twentieth century, one before 1914, and a second which began in the 1960s and is still unresolved. The causes of these crises must be established by historical analysis: it will be argued that they are fundamentally the same.

The more specific crises – budget crises, sterling crises, and the like – which precede and accompany these general crises, are 'steering' problems which are perceived as crises by those specifically concerned with them (in the Treasury or the banking system, for example) when it is realised that they cannot be resolved by the adjustment mechanisms available but will require other, politically-expensive policy changes, such as new taxes, redistribution of wealth, or deflation. They are seen as crises to the extent that the dominant class realises that these costs represent a long-term threat to their hegemony. The distinction between crises in specific sectors and general or organic crises is obscured by media hyperbole; but it must be kept clearly in view if the dynamics of the contemporary general crisis in Britain are to be understood.

Britain's Recurring Crises

Essential as a first step is to recognise that the current crisis is not the first of its kind. The 'vast, insanely repetitious literature of self-censure and prophecy' which has poured forth ever since the 'sterling crisis' of 1961 and shattered the complacency of the 'affluent years' of the previous decade has made the problem seem novel. But it has all happened before, and a comparison of the recent literature with that of the earlier crisis is instructive.

In the early 1960s the problem was largely defined by the Labour Party, which had by then been in opposition for ten years. Because the party was divided on the question of further public ownership the leadership sought an explanation and a solution within the framework of the 'mixed economy' as it already existed. The essence of the problem, according to Harold Wilson (elected leader of the party in 1963) was first, a lack of planned and state-directed industrial investment (thanks to the Tories' lack of interest in the technical problems of an advanced industrial economy); and second, incompetence in the management of much of the private sector (a management recruited largely on the basis of private education and connections, not on merit, and one ignorant of, and indifferent towards, science and technology). In fact, by 1964 there had been no significant change for nearly fifteen years in educational provision, central or local government organisation and recruitment, the conduct of parliamentary business, or the management of the economy. So, understandably, there was widespread enthusiasm for Wilson's proposed reforms.

The reforms were of two kinds: reforms which would directly attack the shortcomings of state economic management, such as the setting up of new growth-oriented Department of Economic Affairs to plan the economy (following the much-envied example of France); and reforms – especially in education and in the recruitment of civil servants – which would tend to put policy-making and management in the hands of technically proficient people, regardless of their social origins. The key idea in Wilson's diagnosis of the problem was *technology* – a cornucopia of new marvels, the benefits of which had been denied the British people by a lax government of over-privileged amateurs. In this spirit a wide range of reforms was put in hand after the Wilson government took office in 1964.

But by the end of the 1960s it was obvious that the diagnosis and the solution had been hopelessly shallow. Even if the state machine had been thoroughly 'modernised' and put exclusively in the hands of people with degrees in economics, science and engineering – and in reality the reforms attempted seemed frustratingly feeble – it now appeared very doubtful if the state could do much to solve the basic problems which the sixties had thrust on the public's attention. In spite of a National Plan, wage controls, subsidies, mergers and very large tax concessions, company profits declined by roughly 50% between 1964 and 1970, while inflation accelerated from 3.3% to 6%, unemployment rose from 1.5% to 2.6%, and days lost in strikes increased from 2.3 million to 10.9 million.[16]

Wilson's complaint that his government had been 'blown off course' only reinforced this impression.* Problems beyond the reach of any governmental machine – problems having to do with the structure of the economy, with the relationship between employers and unions, or with the collective national psychology ('the will to work', 'insularity', etc.) – now came to be seen as fundamental. The alternative prescription of the Conservative leader Edward Heath – that efficient management and a hard-working labour force could be secured only through the maximum

* Wilson used this expression in reference to the seamen's strike of May 1966, which he blamed for the government's economic difficulties. The phrase stuck because it captured both the sense of failure which attached to his whole administration, and his readiness to blame everything but his own policies.

exposure to market competition – expressed and reinforced this change of view, which soon came to be generally accepted. In fact, popular commentary ever since has remained fixed with mesmeric intensity on these apparently intractable 'attitudes'. The Labour Party blamed the bosses and the Conservatives blamed the workers, but most people thought that there were faults on both sides: the problem was that no-one could offer a convincing plan for eliminating them. The left wing of the Labour Party called for more state control of company policy-making, and more worker-control; the right wing of the Conservative Party called for reducing the role of the state and letting market forces 'slim down' the economy until only those firms remained which could survive internationally, and only those workers had jobs who were prepared to work as hard as their German or Japanese counterparts.

Most people doubted if either formula would lead to an industrial renaissance, but seemed to have no better ideas. Very few were willing to contemplate the possibility that any effective 'solution' to the economic problem might call for a fundamental political transformation. Those who did were the small extra-parliamentary left, who were committed to socialist revolution, and the more powerful emerging ultra-right, who publicly wondered if Britain was still 'governable' – i.e. if democracy might not have to be 'curtailed' in the interests of efficiency.

A more common reaction was to hanker after a political 'moratorium', a non-party interlude, conceived of either as an agreement to put the economy in the hands of some kind of technocratic elite, or as a 'government of national unity', an all-party coalition of patriots. The technocratic alternative was advocated by the Hudson Institute in its 1974 report, *The United Kingdom in 1980*, which urged that 'economic policy should become the province of a new national six-year plan under the ægis of the state [i.e., covering a period longer than the life of one parliament]; . . . we would stress an apolitical, or better still supra-political nature for this plan . . . '. The plan was to become

> the province of Britain's best economists and administrators and engineers, all serving the nation in a self-conscious spirit of ambition (for the country) and enterprise. Those working for the plan . . . should come in time to see themselves as a new elite – not an arrogant technocratic bureaucracy beyond political control, but one committed to the restructuring of Britain and to its regeneration . . . what we are asking, then, is that in a new spirit of practicality the best brains of Britain be put to the task of analysing the society's economic needs, articulating regional plans, industrial plans, and long-range goals for the country as a whole, in contrast to the drift, evasion and sentimentality that has characterized economics in Britain at least since 1945.[17]

The alternative of a 'government of national unity' was proposed in 1974 by the Liberal leader, Jeremy Thorpe, shortly before the defeat of the

Heath government, and again by right-wing Labour leaders in 1978 shortly before the defeat of the Callaghan government.

In all of this, history was repeating itself with some precision. After the Paris Fair of 1867 had shown that British industrial design was lagging seriously behind that of its new competitors in a disturbingly large number of fields, Matthew Arnold published a celebrated report, *Higher Schools and Universities in Germany*, which suggested that the proportion of the British population receiving higher education was less than half that of France or Prussia. There followed a series of educational commissions which confirmed the dramatic shortcomings of British education, and especially scientific education, and recommended extensive reforms. These recommendations went largely unheeded. In 1902 there were at most 1,500 chemists in British industry compared with 4,000 in German industry.[18] According to Hobsbawm, 'Britain in 1913 had only nine thousand university students compared to almost sixty thousand in Germany, . . . only 5 day students per ten thousand (in 1900) compared to almost 13 in the USA; . . . Germany produced nine thousand graduate engineers per year while in England and Wales only 350 graduated in *all* branches of science, technology and mathematics with first- and second-class honours, and few of these were qualified for research'.[19] Indeed, as late as in 1913 only 208,000 British children (roughly five per cent) received any secondary education whatever, let alone any higher education, technical or otherwise.

British exporters found themselves squeezed out of foreign markets, and as foreign manufacturers began to penetrate the British domestic market 'the newspapers were full of gloomy talk about Britain's stagnating exports, lost markets and technological obsolescence, contrasted with Germany's superiority in business methods, salesmanship and industrial research'.[20]

The immediate historical background also bore some striking similarities to the situation after 1960. Just as the 1939–45 war had left Britain in a sellers' market for manufactures for the next fifteen years, so overseas wars (the American civil war of 1860–65, and Prussia's wars with Denmark, Austria and France from 1864 to 1871) had temporarily injured American and French production, helping British suppliers and fostering complacency. The Great Depression of 1873 to 1896, however, curtailed demand just when German and American productivity was rising very rapidly. Again, there is an obvious parallel with German, French and Japanese productivity growth in the 1950s and 1960s, and the onset of the world depression in the 1970s. The resulting conflict between capital and labour, in which employers sought to cut wages and 'dilute' labour (introducing new equipment manned by less-skilled and lower-paid workers) also paralleled the industrial conflicts of the 1960s and 1970s.

The earlier situation likewise produced a 'vast literature of pessimism and alarm' (which eventually degenerated into a war hysteria against Germany).[21] In 1901–2 *The Times* ran a series of articles on 'The Crisis in British Industry' which foreshadowed all the complaints against the trade unions, as the chief cause of the crisis, that were to be made again (and not least in *The Times*) in the 1960s and 1970s; while a parallel literature – including the evidence given to a succession of commissions of inquiry from the 1880s onwards – pinpointed exactly the same shortcomings of British management that were also to be rediscovered half a century later.

The unions were charged with 'restriction of output' (later called restrictive practices), opposition to machinery (later called opposition to new technology), interference with management (later called interfering with management 'prerogatives'), interference with 'free' labour (later this was the question of the 'closed shop' and 'intimidation') and fomenting disputes (later attributed to 'agitators').

Manufacturers were charged – again, in the words of contemporaries – with having become 'too supine and easy-going', 'content to follow mechanically the lead given by their fathers'. It was said that they 'worked shorter hours, and they exerted themselves less to obtain new practical ideas than their fathers had done'. They were amateur: 'very often there is no planning at all; it is left to the operative and rule of thumb. Generally there is some planning of a rough and ready kind, but some of the most famous works in the country are in such a state of chaos that the stuff seems to be turned out by accident . . . There can be no doubt that the most serious cause of new methods and new machinery not being rapidly adopted is to be found in the general absence of accurate technical knowledge . . . on the part of the responsible chiefs of the majority of big printing houses . . . The capable man rising from below has much greater difficulties in his way (than in the USA), difficulties which are the result of centuries of prejudice and class interest.'[22]

These views, and others which were to become familiar again after 1961, were advocated most consistently by the so-called National Efficiency movement. Just as the would-be reformers of the 1960s looked enviously at France, the would-be reformers of the early 1900s looked at Germany, and also at Japan, both of which had defeated apparently much larger military opponents (Prussia had defeated Austria and France, Japan had defeated Russia), while Britain could hardly subdue the tiny Boer Republic in two-and-a-half years of spectacular military and logistical incompetence. The National Efficiency movement indicted not so much industry alone, as the national character: the lack of the dedication, purpose, plan, discipline, and thoroughness which the leaders of the movement felt were characteristic of the Germans and the Japanese. A fundamental change of 'attitudes' was called for; a drastic expansion of public education and a planned shift of emphasis from the humanities to science and technology, directly linked to industrial needs; an overhaul of the machinery of government, local and central; a reduction of the power of the cost-conscious Treasury, and measures to make government more dynamic; a professionally trained civil and military elite, drawn from the talented in all ranks of society, in place of an upper-class stratum of ill-educated amateurs.[23]

As if this comprehensive preview of the themes of the 1960s and 1970s were not enough, the National Efficiency movement also manifested impatience with the party politics that seemed to frustrate these rational and urgently needed changes. Where the Hudson Report of 1974 proposed a new 'responsible elite, ambitious for their country', the National Efficiency movement seventy years earlier called for political power to be shared with, if not given to, 'experts', and for the introduction of businessmen and business methods into public policy-making. The movement questioned whether party politics were even compatible with national survival. Like Jeremy Thorpe in 1974 and Roy Jenkins (the former Labour Chancellor) in 1979, Liberal leaders in the first decade of the century, who shared the National Efficiency outlook and who saw the improbability of realising any significant part of it under the regime of either major party, sought an 'all-party' peace-time National Government.

History rarely repeats itself with the almost derisive fidelity that we see here. What it tells us in unmistakable terms is that we are dealing with something *systemic* – a syndrome towards which the whole society is periodically driven by the pattern of forces at work within it. It is remarkable that those researchers who have been most anxious to ground social science on regularities have been so uninterested in this one.

In the years after 1900, Britain's industrial weakness led to a crisis that was social and political as well as economic: a crisis of defence strategy; a crisis of order in industrial relations; a challenge to the authority of the elected government by the right wing in the House of Lords, and in the officer corps of the army, over the issue of Home Rule for Ireland; and a challenge to its legitimacy by the direct-action wing of the Suffragette movement. This accumulating crisis was suspended by the outbreak of war in 1914. The war and inter-war years saw a series of adjustments and compromises which gave a new lease of life to the old system. But the underlying causes of the crisis were not removed. When one considers how much the world had altered by 1960 it is almost awe-inspiring to reflect how, in Britain, nothing essential seemed to have changed at all, either in the forces that led to crisis, or in the British people's perceptions of their situation.

Explaining Britain's Crises

What accounts for this relentless regression? To explain the present crisis is obviously to explain the manifestation of a tendency well over one hundred years old. This means that the explanation must be historical, and – since we are looking at the long-run behaviour of a whole society – must be based on a theory of the 'social whole'. But most of the theories of the crisis which have been advanced over the past twenty-five years have been neither.

A good example of an ahistorical explanation is the widely-accepted theory that Britain's problems have been caused by excessive overseas commitments, causing a perpetual balance of payments problem, leading to constant recourse to deflationary policies and hence underinvestment in manufacturing. This theory has many variants: one stresses the British predilection for overseas rather than domestic investment; another blames primarily overseas military commitments; and so on. Although these tendencies have played a part in Britain's economic problems, an historical perspective shows that they are secondary. Britain's relative decline set in long before there was a significant threat to the balance of payments, at a time when there was sufficient capital to support both domestic and overseas investment, and it continued after North Sea oil temporarily removed the threat to the balance of payments in 1980.

In general ahistorical theories always pose a new question in the process of answering one. If the balance of payments constraint, for example, is important, how did it arise? If British management is inefficient, how did it come to be inefficient? If the problem is that trade union organisation is heterogeneous and decentralised, why did it develop in that way, and why has it remained so? If government economic policy-making has been inept, what caused this and why does it continue?

Ahistorical theories usually also disregard the uniqueness of each social totality. Theories of Britain's problems are largely positivist; they rest on the general assumption that explanation consists in finding causal connections between social 'factors' that can be isolated and which, underneath the uneven flow of events, exist in all societies. A good example of the 'comparative method' used by positivists is cited by Anthony Peaker in his *Economic Growth in Modern Britain*.[24] In order to see whether the rate of economic growth was related to the level of investment, an OECD study plotted the average annual rate of growth for the period 1960 to 1970 against the average annual percentage of national income invested, for twenty countries. Britain had the lowest percentage of national income invested (16%) and the second lowest rate of growth (3%); West Germany had one of the highest levels of investment (23.5%) and one of the highest rates of growth (5%). But several countries had higher growth rates than West Germany, with much lower levels of investment, and Portugal, with a level of investment little higher than Britain's, had one of the highest rates of growth of all. There is a relationship between investment and growth, but it is not straightforward and is unreliable. To put it another way, in some countries raising investment seems to raise the growth rate, but in others it does not, or does so by very little. In the language of positivism, it is, then, the particular way investment combines with other 'factors' in each country which we need to know.

To take another example, from the late 1960s onwards it was fashionable to blame Britain's industrial weakness on the unions, and especially on strikes. Peaker also compared the level of strike activity in Britain with those of its principal trade competitors, and established that the number of strike days per 100,000 workers was not significantly higher in Britain. However, the hostility of unionised workers towards government policies of wage control at the end of the sixties was so obvious that Peaker felt it *had* to be relevant. Perhaps, he suggested, the absence of a class party, such as the socialist or communist parties of the continent, meant that in Britain the workers' 'strong proletarian spirit' could not be 'dissipated' through politics, and so was channelled through industrial confrontation, to the advantage of Britain's manufacturing competitors.[25] As so often, when positivist explanations fail, they are replaced by thinly-disguised restatements of establishment demonology.

In general, the basic presupposition of positivist explanations – that causes are knowable only from statistical relationships – rules out causes that are unique to particular places and particular periods of time. As a result, the economic literature, in particular, which is largely founded on this methodological prejudice, has been singularly unrewarding in diagnosing British problems.

Hobsbawm's Interpretation

A large step forward was taken in 1968 by Eric Hobsbawm. Hobsbawm proposed a theory which was above all historical, and the essence of which was that Britain's problems were – precisely – unique. On the other hand, Hobsbawm rejected the view that a satisfactory theory must be based on a conception of the social whole. For him, 'economic explanations of economic phenomena are to be preferred, if they are available'.[26] This was to lead to severe difficulties. The phenomenon of decline was not more economic than social or political, and Hobsbawm's attempt at disciplinary apartheid proved self-defeating.

His main thesis was that the circumstances which enabled Britain to be the first country to industrialise, and so gave her a unique advantage, proved a serious disadvantage when later industrialising countries, led by Germany and the USA, began to compete in world markets for manufactures, especially in the science-based, mass-consumption goods phase of the industrial revolution. Britain's primacy in the two earlier phases – the mechanisation of textile production, and the capital goods boom of the mid-nineteenth century – had been based, Hobsbawm argued, on imperial power, which opened up foreign markets for Britain by force of arms and secured abundant sources of raw materials and cheap foodstuffs abroad. It had also rested on the existence of an already proletarianised labour force, and a landowning class much more committed to trade and more involved in agricultural modernisation, as well as being much less socially exclusive, than its continental counterparts. These two features, in particular, fostered the rapid expansion of a stratum of manufacturing entrepreneurs, with few social pretensions, who could make common cause with large segments of the landed ruling class, who, themselves, also profited from, and increasingly participated in, the industrial revolution. The technology of the first phases of the industrial revolution was relatively simple: the capital barriers were relatively low, with the result that England's industrial supremacy rested, in fact, on a patchwork of small firms and plants, usually in family ownership, employing a largely unskilled and certainly ill-educated workforce.

When Britain began to face serious manufacturing competition these features of the economy which had facilitated its early start turned into liabilities. The large-scale, technologically advanced German and American chemical, steel and electrical goods plants, setting out to make new products for mass markets, had few British counterparts. British manufacturing was still heavily based on the old staples – cotton textiles, iron and steel, railway materials and steam engines. The switch to the new industrial products and new technology was difficult for firms without the necessary technical expertise or large capital resources. Smallness of scale also militated against adequate borrowing. Innovations were often unprofitable without complementary new inputs from other sectors, but these were also technically backward. Worst of all, the new competition coincided with the Great Depression of 1873 to 1896. The real value of British manufactured exports grew by only 1.6% per annum during these years while imports of manufactures grew by 4.5% per annum.[27]

British manufacturing was 'subjected to a terrible beating', but no drastic overhaul was put in hand, for two main reasons. One was that British capital had been invested abroad in growing quantities from about 1815 onwards, but especially after 1850. Indeed, by 1870 more was being invested abroad than in Britain.[28] On the other hand, from 1870 onwards more was received in interest on profits from abroad than was invested abroad. This income increasingly cushioned the balance of payments against the pressures of foreign manufacturing competition. Second, 'empire' markets absorbed British manufactures which could no longer be sold in the industrialised countries, so that the effect of the Great

Depression 'was, alas, not great enough to frighten British industry into really fundamental change'.[29]

After World War I, the oldest sectors of the economy progressively collapsed. The world-wide depression, culminating in the 'slump', was, in Britain, the story of the permanent contraction of these industries and the waste of the lives of the families who depended on them.

> The grimy, roaring, bleak industrial areas of the nineteenth century – in Northern England, Scotland and Wales – had never been very beautiful or comfortable, but they had been active and prosperous. Now all that remained was the grime, the bleakness, and the terrible silence of the factories and mines which did not work, the shipyards which were closed.[30]

The crisis of the thirties forced both business and government to take action. Free trade was abandoned, and a process of cartelisation and mergers was encouraged to give fewer, much larger firms protected shares of the home markets. But little structural or technological modernisation was put in hand. Instead, 'Britain became a non-competing country at home as well as abroad'.[31] This became painfully obvious in the 1960s when the technological and organisational weakness of British industry was once again exposed to foreign competition.

Hobsbawm's thesis – which is much richer than can be indicated in this bare outline – is thus that the fundamental cause of Britain's decline was the structural legacy of its early start, coupled with the proposition that 'in a capitalist economy (at all events in its nineteenth-century version) businessmen will be dynamic only insofar as this is rational by the criterion of the individual firm, which is to maximize its gains, minimize its losses, or possibly merely to maintain what it regards as a satisfactory long-term rate of profit'.[32] A radical reconstruction of the manufacturing economy will only be undertaken if this is rational for all, or at least the major, individual firms. But the existence of 'empire' markets, and after 1931 the existence of a protected home market, gave enough of them an easier alternative. What would have been collectively rational for all the firms in a sector was often not rational unless all acted in concert, which no mechanism existed to ensure as long as a traditionally 'adequate' profit could still be made on the basis of the old investment, and financial capital could find more profitable investment abroad.

It is a powerful and important argument. But is it as plausible as it looks? The most obvious question it raises concerns the mysterious failure of any government to intervene and become 'the pacemaker of change and the force driving the economy forward'.[33] Hobsbawm's explanation for this is that 'Britain, the first of all "developed" economies, found it hard to think in the terms which came so naturally to backward nations trying to catch up advanced ones, to poor ones trying to become rich, to ruined ones trying to rebuild, or even to those with a continuous tradition of technological pioneering.'[34]

But this is to ignore some rather major difficulties. For one thing, the wartime government of 1940–45 intervened successfully to reconstruct British agriculture to make it the most efficient in Europe. Why did this not extend to manufacturing, especially after the crisis had fully re-emerged in the 1970s? It is true that 'British socialists thought of the public sector as an engine for achieving a redistribution of incomes and a measure of social justice, or more vaguely (and in contrast to profit-making capitalism) a "public service" ' – rather than as an instrument for forcing necessary changes in the private sector.[35] But why did they think like this? Since the price of the failure of 'business' to modernise itself was largely paid by the working class, why did British socialists not come to think in other terms? And, more generally, why was the pressure on the economy not 'desperate enough' when unemployment was above ten per cent for so many of the years between the two World Wars?

Hobsbawm's answer seems to be that habits of *mind* learned in the early nineteenth century persisted for more than a hundred years after experience should have suggested scrapping them – a rather 'idealist' position for a Marxist historian. We surely need an explanation of the determinants of 'government' action – or inaction. This, in turn, obviously involves understanding how social classes form and organise themselves – what entities like 'business' actually are and how they are related to 'government,' through parties, elections, pressure groups, money, etc. – how such apparently influential political ideas as the Labour Party's view of the 'public sector' are formed and maintained, and how much independent effect they have. Further, such an explanation points to the need to distinguish 'governments' from the *state*, a much broader phenomenon, interacting with 'civil society' in a much more continuous and structured way than 'governments'.

Another set of puzzles arises from Hobsbawm's view – for which there is good evidence – that British businessmen were not always profit-maximisers. According to economic theory, both classical and Marxist, this should lead to bankruptcy. Why it did not, or not immediately, may be partly explained by such special factors as the availability of empire markets, but there is still a puzzle: why were many British businessmen content with less than the highest possible rates of return? It seems that many of them compared the cost of new investment with the cost of the capital they had already laid out, and chose to go on accepting the existing rate of return from past investment, rather than seek a higher rate of return by risking new capital outlays. This, or course, is contrary to capitalist rationality, which says that seeking the highest rate of return is the only long-term way to stay in business. If British capitalists often thought like this – which seems to be the case – it is very important to explain it, and such an explanation can hardly be confined to the sphere of economics. It is a question of why British capitalists thought in this way, while American, German, or Japanese capitalists did not.

To take one further problem in Hobsbawm's account, there were important conflicts within the class of property. The City of London regularly opposed manufacturing industry, for example, over the exchange value of sterling, the level of interest rates and free trade versus protection, as Hobsbawm points out. What determined the outcomes of these conflicts? Why were governments 'closer to the City than to industry'? Why did the re-establishment of overseas investments receive the priority it did after 1945, with a Labour government in office? The answers to these questions are not self-evident, nor are they to be found in the economic logic of capitalism alone.

Hobsbawm rightly rejects 'simple sociological explanations' of Britain's economic decline, but a purely economic explanation, however sophisticated, is also inadequate.[36] What is needed is to combine the primarily economic-historical analysis of Hobsbawm with primarily sociological, cultural and political analyses, such as those of Anderson and Nairn, so as to try to link the different aspects of the social whole. No brief outline can hope to deal adequately with the problem; but if we are to 'think British politics historically' the attempt needs to be made.

3

The First Crisis

Even if some of the structural constraints which Britain's early start imposed on her manufacturing sector seem less absolute than Hobsbawm implies, one thing is clear: speaking generally, British capitalist manufacturers never did compete successfully against other *capitalist* manufacturers. What they did was to overwhelm *pre-capitalist* production everywhere; and it was the comparative ease of this victory, rather than the commitment of capital to particular sectors, such as textiles or railways, or to particular forms of business organisation characteristic of early capitalism, that led to later problems.

Until the last years of the nineteenth century, British capital still depended very heavily on labour-intensive production, working long hours at a much more intensive pace than pre-capitalist manufacture.[1] British manufacturing employees were also concentrated in larger production units, subject to a more complex division of labour, producing more standardised products than non-capitalist producers. Their products *were* also technically more advanced, and they were increasingly assisted by power-driven machinery. But as Raphael Samuel has shown, the degree of mechanisation was quite modest, even in the most mechanised sectors, such as textiles and engineering. Growth in machine-production had led to the creation of innumerable new tasks performed by hand, and some of the most important industries, including coal, construction and agriculture, were barely mechanised at all. For instance, the expansion of coal output from about 40 million tons in 1855 to about 275 million in 1911 was accomplished by expanding the labour force from 200,000 to 1,200,000, helped by 70,000 pit ponies – that is, with virtually no increase in productivity.[2] To a large extent, British supremacy was still based on 'the formal subsumption of labour under capital': the replacement of independent artisan production by wage employment, but without a radical change in the labour process.

Other countries – notably Germany and the USA – could develop their own industries initially by protecting their internal markets against British goods. But to compete with Britain in world markets they had to leap-frog Britain's stage of industrial development by heavy expenditure on superior technology, new products, and new methods of marketing to generate demand for them ('capitalist production sui generis').[3]

It was when this began to happen – from the late 1860s onwards – that British manufacturers started to lose ground. In the last phase of the Great Depression (from 1891 to 1896) the problem began to assume major proportions, mainly in the form of a more or less rapid eclipse of British goods by German goods in prime markets. After 1892 Germany outstripped Britain as a supplier of manufactures to Eastern Europe and Greece, after 1894 to the Low Countries and Russia, and finally, after 1910, to Italy and France. Germany also built up a strong trade surplus with Britain itself and sold more finished manufactures than unfinished goods to Britain, while Britain's (smaller) exports to Germany contained more unfinished goods than manufactured products.[4] By 1910 the German shipping magnate and commercial leader, Albert Ballin, could comment:

> the British can really no longer compete with us, and if it were not for the large funds they have invested, and for the sums of money which reach the small mother-country from the dominions, their saturated and conservative habits of life would soon make them a 'quantité négligeable' as far as their competition with us in the world's markets is concerned.[5]

The years immediately before the Great War were experienced as years of crisis. Real wages fell, neither party had an answer to the industrial problem, and from 1910 onwards the authority of the state was increasingly rejected, by the Irish, by the Suffragettes, and by a growing minority of anarcho-syndicalists in the labour movement. The scale of industrial conflict rose to a pitch not equalled before or since – apart from the General Strike of 1926 – while in 1913, senior army officers questioned the government's authority to impose Home Rule on Ulster.

The outbreak of war superseded the crisis of authority. Only when the relief afforded by the two wars, income from foreign investments, empire markets and domestic protection had at length all been exhausted, did British industry finally confront its nemesis. The question remains, why was so little attempt made to reconstruct British industry when its competitive weakness first appeared? Why should the spate of official and unofficial enquiries and reports on industrial efficiency at the turn of the century have had so little effect?[6]

As Hobsbawm pointed out, other governments used the state as an engine of industrial growth. Why did British governments not do the same? And, while many industrial capitalists in Britain may have become so complacent, or so infected with pre-capitalist values, as to prefer modest and vulnerable profits to risk-taking for growth, it is hard to believe that all of them were like this; that, at a time when capital was abundant and cheap, the situation should not have been modified by the initiative of at least a few enterprising capitalists who would have seen the opportunity to borrow on a big scale, and to leap-frog both domestic and foreign competitors by moving into still more-advanced and capital-intensive production.[7]

Industrial Class Struggle

These questions lead directly into the politics and sociology of the class struggle. Sir Arthur Lewis comes close to the heart of the matter when he points out that, given that in 1913 British wages were about half the level of US wages, it should have been greatly to the advantage of British manufacturers to adopt American technology – if they could have got as much output from it as US manufacturers did. Yet, in those industries where American technology had been adopted (for instance the English boot and shoe industry, which converted to US-made machinery in the 1890s), British output was far lower.[8] Lewis comments:

> ... British entrepreneurs were under heavy pressure in the last quarter of the century since the economy had turned unprofitable. American methods were fairly widely known. If entrepreneurs had expected them to yield the same output in Britain as in the USA, they would most probably have adopted them.

In the last analysis, Lewis attributes the fact that they did not do so to the 'lower work pace of the British workers'. Given this, he says, 'it is easy to see that the main reason why the British employers did not adopt the American technology was that it was not as productive for them as it was for American employers'.[9] On the other hand, Lewis also notes that the American factory was much more rationally organised – 'a more "scientific" place than the British factory'. There is also the question of whether the rate of work of British workers was proportional to their fifty per cent lower wages. If British workers had agreed to work twice as hard, would they not have expected the employers to pay them twice as much?

The key to the perennial problem of which is the chicken and which the egg in the relationship between management and labour in Britain is the historical development of the political relationship between capital and labour at this moment of history. For a hundred years the profitability of British capital had depended primarily – though not, of course, exclusively – on the extraction of as much work as possible from the labour force, for as small a wage as possible. This had not prevented real wages from gradually rising, as productivity gradually improved after the mid-century and trade union organisation spread; but it had not generally been necessary to seek a solution to the problem of profitability by raising productivity through technological innovation. When trade was poor, employers sought wage cuts and resisted the reduction of working hours, rather than contemplate new investment. The natural consequence was growing defensive solidarity on the part of the workers.

When the industrial 'climacteric' of the 1890s arrived, after more than twenty years of depression, wage-cuts, lock-outs and strikes, workers and employers were moving rapidly towards a new phase of conflict. The employers organised themselves to try to break the power of the rapidly expanding trade union movement by means of lock-outs and court actions. A series of court judgements, culminating in the Taff Vale decision of 1901, stripped away much if not all of the financial and legal security that the unions were supposed to have been granted in the legislation of 1871–6. The employers succeeded, in the short run, in crushing the socialist militants in the unions and in curbing the duration and effectiveness of strikes ('the employers organised their forces, fought and won');[10] but they also finally precipitated the labour movement into forming its own political party, the Labour Party, and created new opportunities for the spread of socialist ideas.

If the labour movement had been crushed, matters would have been different. But after 1867 both Conservatives and Liberals depended on working-class votes, and no such conclusive defeat was ever possible or indeed contemplated. To a much greater extent than in Germany or the USA (where, said Arthur Shadwell in 1909, 'employers hate and dread the unions'), unions had an accepted place in British industry in spite of the struggles of the '80s and '90s. By 1911, 18% of the employed population were members of trade unions and manufacturers were having to deal with ever better organised employees. To secure from these workers, after thirty years of increasingly fierce conflict, American levels of output premissed on British wages, was politically out of the question. Whatever the rationality of this or that particular industrialist might incline him to do, the British working class was already too strong, and too antagonised, for the American (or German) option to be generally profitable. A complete transformation of political, social and ideological relations would have been necessary to break up the, by now, hardened pattern of capital–labour relations. But this was not 'practical politics' in the circumstances of the time.

The Contradictions of Party Politics

The main reason why this was not practical lay in the constraints imposed on the two major parties: both represented elements of capital, but both were now competing for the votes of the workers – a situation which resulted from the peculiar historical evolution of the British capitalist class. As Anderson and Nairn pointed out, the British capitalist class was formed by a fusion of the rising mercantile and industrial interest with the old landed interest. How this fusion should be interpreted theoretically is a matter of dispute. Anderson sees it as beginning with a struggle – the English Revolution – *within* the old landed aristocracy, between elements which were committed to capitalist accumulation (mainly in farming, but also in trade) and those which were not, and culminating in a decisive victory for the former: 'the landed aristocracy had, after a bitter internecine struggle, become its own capitalist class'.[11] This class of largely agrarian capitalists succeeded in keeping purely mercantile (and later, purely industrial) capital in a politically and socially subordinate position, which in Anderson's view accounts for the failure of British industry or governments to respond energetically to the industrial crisis from the 1890s onwards.

E. P. Thompson, on the other hand, considers that the fusion which occurred started earlier, and that while aristocratic *manners* prevailed, no distinctive aristocratic *interest* did, and so this cannot explain the failure of British capital to rationalise itself in the twentieth century.[12] Yet there is agreement that the English landed class not only increasingly became capitalist farmers, but also grew increasingly involved in mining ventures, railway-building, merchant banking, urban real estate investment and eventually, via the joint stock company, in the whole range of capitalist enterprise, including manufacturing; and that, for their part, 'new' men of wealth bought landed estates and sent their sons to be educated with the sons of the gentry at the new 'public' schools.

This fusion produced distinctive social, ideological and political results. The one that matters here is political. In the early nineteenth century neither the Whig nor the Tory parties, though dominated by landowners, excluded representatives of new wealth. Sir Robert Peel, the Tory leader, was the son of a self-made manufacturer, and Gladstone, a Peelite who became leader of the Liberals, was the son of a slave-owner. In addition, fear of revolution after 1879, and fear of English working-class strength after 1815, tended to drive new and old wealth together politically. The result was that both political parties came to represent broadly the same class, the class of property.

So long as only the propertied class had votes, this was not inconvenient. It allowed conflicting elements and tendencies within the class of property – commercial, financial, agricultural, manufacturing, professional, high church, dissent, pro-temperance and pro-publican, pro-imperial and 'little England' – to find organisational expression. But when the vote had to be extended in 1867 and 1884 (producing an electorate sixty per cent of whom were workers) this arrangement became highly problematic. To win elections the parties had to compete for working-class votes. They could only continue to serve the interests of property if they could find a way to combine them with the interests of the workers.

This imposed tremendous strains on the party leaders, torn between the class demands of their main supporters and the need to win votes. The difficulty was more acute for the Liberals, who saw themselves as the natural party of the workers, but their difficulty was made immeasurably worse by the Irish problem.

In Ireland colonial oppression and underdevelopment had produced an irreversible popular commitment to nationalism, while in Britain the increasingly powerful working class could no longer be denied the vote. Because of the Act of Union it was difficult, if not impossible, to withhold any extension of the franchise from Ireland and this permitted the Irish nationalists to capture 86 seats at Westminster in the elections of 1885, and thus to hold the balance of power between Liberals and Conservatives. From then on they could either be repressed, at increasing risk to liberal values throughout the United Kingdom, and probably at increasing economic cost; or 'home rule' for Ireland, as demanded by the nationalists, was ultimately inescapable. Gladstone recognised this and chose to preserve liberal values by accepting home rule. The anti-home rule or 'unionist' section of the Liberal Party, including Joseph Chamberlain and a number of his radical supporters, left the party and allied themselves with the Conservatives. A significant body of electors followed them. The Liberals paid the price of being excluded from power (thanks to Conservative control of the House of Lords, rather than to electoral unpopularity alone, it must be said) for the best part of twenty years (the Conservatives were in office from 1886 to 1892 and 1895 to 1905).

During that time the Liberals could accomplish nothing for the British working class, while the Conservatives were under correspondingly less compulsion to accomplish anything for them, and showed increasingly little interest in doing so. Eventually – and reluctantly – the majority of the trade union leadership became convinced that they must seek independent representation for labour in parliament, and the Labour Representation Committee was established in 1900.

The more creative politicians of both parties at this time sought to re-attach the workers to capital in ways that might conceivably have facilitated economic modernisation. Joseph Chamberlain, from the Conservative and Unionist side, advocated social reforms financed out of tariff revenue, and Lloyd-George, for the Liberals, promoted social reforms financed out of taxes on wealth. Chamberlain's campaign for protection was the more relevant to the needs of British manufacturing. His scheme of 'tariff reform' would have ended half-a-century of free trade and reserved the British home market – still second only to that of the USA – for British manufactures; though in view of the failure of British companies to undertake radical investment programmes when protection was finally re-introduced in the 1930s it seems rather unlikely that Chamberlain's project contained the seeds of a radical restructuring of British industrial capital. In any case the electorate consistently rejected protection until 1931. No wonder that the 'National Efficiency' school dreamed of an all-party government which would entrust economic policy to 'experts'.

Class, State and Culture

The distinctive way in which capitalism was established in Britain also gave rise to other factors. Two in particular are often cited: the special role of the City of London, and the specific nature of the British state.

Britain's dominance in world trade and its role as a source of international loan capital had made the City of London the pre-eminent banking, exchange, shipping and insurance centre of the world before the First World War. This gave it exceptional influence with the Treasury. The City was also where large fortunes were most likely to be made, and where old landed families were more prone to establish an interest.[13] As a result, the City of London, and the wider financial and commercial interests with which it was linked, were much better connected to the Conservative Party – which after 1886 drew into its ranks nearly all the landed interest, and after 1914 virtually all other capital as well. Thanks to the decline of the Liberals after 1918, this influence undoubtedly played an important part in the preference subsequently given to free trade and a strong pound over the needs of British manufacturing.*

As for the state, it was *structured* in a fashion that reflected the originality of the bourgeois revolution in Britain.[14] Unlike countries where state power had to be used to achieve the 'forced' industrial growth necessary to catch up with Britain, in Britain many features of the pre-capitalist state were carried over into the nineteenth century and beyond. The common element, Nairn suggests, was the 'representative patrician' nature of the state apparatus: it was to an exceptional degree *composed of* the landed class itself, serving as magistrates, and supplying both the members of parliament and the leading policy-makers in the principal departments of state.

* Why the City's influence should have continued to dominate even post-war Labour governments' policies is a more complex question (see Chapters 4, 5, 9 and 11). In 1977, for example, the Labour Prime Minister, James Callaghan, in a secret meeting with two other cabinet ministers, the Permanent Secretary of the Treasury and the Governor of the Bank of England, decided to let sterling appreciate in spite of the adverse consequences this would have for manufactured exports (B. Sedgemore, *The Secret Constitution*, Hodder and Stoughton, London 1980, pp. 14–15).

This remained the case after the introduction of entrance examinations for all grades of the whole civil service from 1870 onwards, which was a house-cleaning operation *within* the traditional upper class based in London. Recruitment was now from those of its sons who could demonstrate the necessary ability. John Vincent remarks:

> The canons of Peelite administration might as well have been applied to another planet for all the provinces knew of them. If people in Sheffield were affected at all by competitive examinations for the Civil Service or abolition of purchase in the army, it was through their sense of justice, not of interest.[15]

As the state apparatus expanded, recruitment to it was developed on class lines; policy making remained the preserve of Oxford and Cambridge graduates who had received a classical education in public schools – schools originally created, it should be remembered, to *remove* 'the sons of shopkeepers from the taint of trade', not to interest them in trade. The state apparatus was thus not merely organisationally ill-adapted to become an agent of industrial reconstruction, but had a trained incapacity for that task.* The national preoccupation with industrial decline was articulated by independent researchers and publicists like Shadwell, Hobson and Williams, and taken up by editors and some MPs; it does not seem to have greatly exercised Whitehall.†

These cultural tendencies also affected the manufacturing class directly, as both contemporary and later critics remarked. Manufacturers were not only themselves largely ignorant of science, they were indifferent to the importance of investing in it. They employed relatively few scientists or engineers, and rarely gave those they did employ great influence in company policy; nor did they demand a major expansion of scientific and technical education. The effects were plain to every British visitor to German factories, where not only was the entire enterprise organised so as to take the most rational advantage of recent knowledge, but the technical training of the workers was strongly stressed:

> ... A deputation of employers and workmen went to the Continent in 1895 to visit German and Belgian iron and steel industries. They sought an explanation for the successful progress of these competitive plants, and what they learned must have been to many little short of startling. In Germany it was shown how much greater was the care taken to give the rank and file of men sound technical

* As late as 1890 the Board of Trade was not considered a senior cabinet office, and political offices such as the Secretaryships of the Board of Education and Local Government, which were crucial to any industrial reconstruction, were even less well paid or prestigious.

† A significant contrast is provided by Whitehall's keen interest in the health of the working class considered as potential army recruits, which led to an otherwise uncharacteristic early policy of providing meals for working-class schoolchildren before the Great War.

> education, while young men of special promise were even sent to technical colleges for several years of study at the expense of their employers. The consequence was that the German manufacturers had the advantage of employing a body of men who thoroughly understood the technique of their work.[16]

In the same spirit, the Germans invested heavily in their sales forces, understanding the need to create new markets for new products, in contrast to 'the glaring scarcity of British commercial travellers, and the ineffective endeavours to supply their place by lavish distribution of prices and catalogues – generally printed only in English.'[17]

The class of manufacturing owner-managers, though never composed of more than a 'minute fraction' of wholly self-made men, had once energetically propagated the *myth* of the self-made man and condemned the aristocratic ideal as idle and parasitic.[18] By 1900, after three generations of success, middle-class education and social acceptance, they had compromised significantly with aristocratic culture and had acquired a prevailing conservatism and complacency about their long-established business methods.[19] This even included a tendency, especially startling to Americans, to enforce a socially-determined upper limit on workers' pay lest workers might cease to 'know their place', even if paying more might have secured a more than compensating increase in output.[20]

The Crisis in Ideology

The way in which economic interest, political alignments and cultural orientations interacted so as to preclude any effective response to the onset of economic decline was complex. For instance, although the interest of the City lay in free trade against protection, 'it remained firmly Conservative; in contrast Lancashire and the West Riding reverted to their traditional liberalism in the wake of [the Conservative Party's commitment to] Tariff Reform – which was designed to benefit British manufacturing'.[21] The City, which had attached itself to the Conservative Party in its imperialist phase during the 1880s, maintained this attachment after 1903 in spite of Chamberlain's conversion of the party rank and file to protection, relying on its great influence with the party leadership and the Treasury to resist this move. Similarly, even though increasing competitive pressure from abroad and the growing strength of organised labour were pushing the cotton manufacturers towards the Conservative Party, they chose to remain loyal to the Liberals and to the cause of free trade, on which the textile industry's fortunes had been built for sixty years.

This is a good example of the need to distinguish between the different chronological rhythms peculiar to different aspects of political life. The attachment of the cotton-manufacturers to the Liberal cause proved extraordinarily enduring, thanks to their identification with free trade (the banner under which they had finally imposed their interests against those of the landed classes in the 1840s) and with the party which had expressed so many of their distinctive values – the right to religious dissent, temperance, economy and utility – for half a century. Conversely, the attachment of the City of London to the Conservatives, though quite recent and owing little to specific Conservative doctrines or policies, also proved remarkably strong. Chamberlain's Tariff Reform programme might have been expected to push the textile interest towards the Conservatives, and the City back to the Liberals, but their actual behaviour corresponded to a different logic, operating at the level of ideas and attitudes.

In fact, the first crisis was also a general crisis of ideology: tariff reform, socialism, women's emancipation and Irish nationalism simultaneously assaulted the orthodoxies of free trade, private property, male supremacy and English chauvinism. The list of dissonant themes could easily be extended: it signifies a crisis of 'hegemony' – a crisis of confidence in ideas which had hitherto provided all classes with their general understanding of the 'way things (naturally) were'.

These hitherto prevailing ideas were liberal ideas. The basis of their dominance had been laid down by about 1850, after free trade had triumphed over protection and ushered in half-a-century of reform aimed at completing the transformation of the corrupt and parasitical old state apparatus into one serviceable for a market-oriented industrialising society. But, simultaneously, the state began to soften the impact of industrialism on the working class. During the previous twenty-five years, the political consciousness of the workers had progressed rather rapidly through three phases – beginning with backward-looking efforts to reverse the catastrophic impact on their lives of 'political economy' (as the new doctrine of the market was known), followed by a phase of enthusiasm for the Owenite vision of replacing capitalism by a giant workers' co-operative, and ending with the campaign for the People's Charter – a mass political movement with an increasingly class-conscious left wing. This last development was accelerated by a decade of depressed trade and by bad harvests.

Eventually the state authorities' confidence that they could maintain control declined to a critical level. The adoption of Free Trade eased the confrontation by reducing food prices. The lifting of the previous ban on machinery exports in 1842, and measures to make it easier to export capital, permitted the profit rate to be increased without intensifying the exploitation of industrial workers. In this situation a start could be made in regulating factory safety (in 1844) and limiting working hours (in 1847); then the franchise was extended to workers (in 1867 and 1884) and legal protection was given to trade unions (in 1871 and 1875–6). Finally, elementary education was extended to workers' children (in 1870 and 1876) and some of the worst abuses in the sale of food and drugs and in workers' housing and sanitation began to be brought under control (in 1875).

The main vehicle of this liberalisation was the Liberal Party; but the Conservatives under Disraeli were also forced to conform to it, under pain of being permanently excluded from power, so that it was the Conservatives who carried out both the franchise extension of 1867 and the social reforms of 1875. The *political* logic of liberalism could then be summed up as regulating capitalism, to secure the class co-operation needed to make the extension of democracy safe for private property. This strategy was a complete success. In 1848 in London 150,000 special constables had been enrolled, troops and artillery dispersed at strategic points, and civil servants armed, to confront the workers massing at Kennington for what proved to be the last Chartist rally. In 1868 the same workers – or their sons – voted for the first time, and most of them voted Liberal.

The acceptance of liberalism, the creed of the new middle class, by both the working class and the landed class during these years – its emergence as a 'hegemonic' ideology – rested on the degree of convergence which government policy succeeded in establishing between life as people experienced it, and life as liberal doctrine painted it. Good harvests in the 1850s, and slowly rising productivity in most sectors of the economy, reinforced the prospect of accommodation with industrial capitalism which the regulation of hours and safety held out to the workers.

In place of the Chartist agitation with its 'physical force' wing and revolutionary undercurrents, led largely by self-employed tradesmen and artisans outside the authority structure of the factory, there emerged the 'new model' craft unions of the 'labour aristocracy', the foremen and pacemakers in the factories.[22] These new unions were dedicated to 'responsible' bargaining, looked on strike action as evidence of failure, and acted much more as self-financing insurance societies to protect their members against sickness and unemployment than as fighting organisations. This corresponded perfectly to the new liberal conception of industrial class society, and for two crucial generations after 1850 the leaders of the 'new model' unions also served as new models of working-class life – thrifty, sober, religious, cautious and respectable. It was these men whose leadership led Gladstone to pronounce the workers 'fit to come within the pale of the constitution' and who mostly rewarded his confidence by supporting the Liberal Party.

Working-class militancy was not completely extinguished after 1848; the extension of the franchise after 1867 was also due to revived mass-agitation, and militancy was to appear again in renewed industrial struggles throughout the Great Depression. But for thirty years after 1848 it was subordinated to class-collaboration. During this formative period the basis of 'labourism' (the defence and advancement of the interests of labour within capitalism, as opposed to socialism, which looks to the replacement of capitalism) was laid. By the end of this period labourism had acquired a specific electoral form, the 'Lib–Lab' alliance, whereby the leading trade unionists endorsed the Liberals in return for the adoption of a number of representatives of 'labour' as Liberal candidates, and the inclusion of some 'Lib–Lab' MPs in Liberal governments.*

The 'hegemony' of liberalism would have been impossible without the reforms introduced from the 1840s to the 1870s. Through them working men (if not women) were assured such benefits as the cheapest possible food (through free trade), a measure of protection from the crudest forms of exploitation at work and degradation at home, freedom to defend their interests against employers, a degree of protection in the courts, and an equal voice in elections. In these important respects, life appeared to be as liberal doctrine described it and to offer the prospect of modest but progressive improvement for the conscientious and hard-working breadwinner. This in turn sustained the 'popular religion' of self-improvement within the framework of working class culture – the friendly society, the 'Co-op' shop, the colliery choir, the working men's club, the chapel and the pub.

But while reforms made the ideological hegemony of liberalism possible, it did not come about spontaneously. As John Foster showed in his remarkable study of Oldham, the reforms were accompanied by energetic efforts on the part of local employers and property owners, the national parties, the press, Sunday school organisers, Orange Lodge leaders and the like, to re-establish their cultural authority over the working class. It is this which explains the *speed* with which the working class not merely abandoned the militant radicalism of the Chartist movement, but positively embraced the liberal creed. In 1855 an ex-radical in Oldham replied to a speech by Bronterre O'Brien, the former Chartist leader, in the following remarkable terms:

> Mr O'Brien had told them that their conditions were as bad or worse than Russian serfs, but he would ask him to point to a page in history where Russian serfs could meet and discuss public questions as they were doing that night (hear, hear and cheers) – where Russian serfs could eat white bread and good and wholesome food. Mr O'Brien might talk about the slavery and depression of the people in this country, but when the time had come for their freedom they would get it. Look at the enlightenment they could obtain by a liberal

* The first Lib–Lab MPs were elected in 1874. The first Lib–Lab MP to join a Liberal government was Henry Broadhurst in 1885; the first Lib–Lab cabinet member was John Burns in 1905.

> press, and by the right of public meeting obtained by their brave and noble fathers (cheers).[23]

But by 1900 the hold of these ideas over the workers had been severely weakened. The Great Depression had undermined their foundations in many ways. Class collaboration in industry was called in question when, over a twenty-year period, employers responded to falling profit-rates by cutting wages and employees responded by rising levels of industrial action. It was even more fatally damaged when the courts, responding to the employers' offensive, began to strip away the trade union rights which had appeared to be enshrined in the legislation of 1870 and 1875–6. From 1889 onwards the ascendancy of the craft unions and their 'Lib–Lab' leaders began to be challenged by the new mass-membership unions of unskilled workers, unions which were much more responsive to the socialist propaganda of the Social Democratic Federation (formed in 1883), the Socialist League (1884), the Fabian Society (also 1884), Robert Blatchford's newspaper *Clarion* (founded in 1891) and the Independent Labour party (founded in 1893).

Events were soon to show that the ideal of class collaboration was too strongly embedded in the consciousness of most labour leaders to be easily or quickly displaced by socialism. But they rejected the Liberals' idea of the basis for such collaboration. They wanted a state which would redress the inequality of power in industrial relations and provide workers with social security and social services, and they no longer trusted the Liberal Party to achieve this – an attitude which the Liberals' record in office after 1906 did little to change. The social legislation which they introduced – including schemes for old age pensions, national health insurance and unemployment insurance – was too limited in scope and conceded too slowly to cause the labour leaders any second thoughts about the necessity of an independent party of labour.

As for Ireland, the basis for the ascendancy of liberalism never existed there. The franchise simply gave the Catholic majority means to express their rejection of a system of alien rule that had been illiberal in essence from the first. Similarly with feminism; middle-class women agitating against discrimination in law (especially concerning prostitution and marriage) and in education, and working-class women organising for the first time against 'sweated' labour, found that there was still a paling round the constitution and that they were outside it. Liberalism was thus called in question by workers (especially the unskilled majority), the Catholic Irish and an articulate and determined minority of women. By 1910 'liberal England' was already dying.[24]

There was a conservative response to the crisis of liberal hegemony – the ideology of imperialism. Although primarily identified with the Conservative Party, imperialism captured an important wing of the Liberals, and some leading socialists too. It appealed to the insular, xenophobic and chauvinist (including anti-Irish) elements in British popular culture. It asserted the existence of a national interest above the interests of class, and a national destiny to govern inferior races. The 'aristocratic, amateur and normatively agrarian' social ideals of the imperialists received an enormous reinforcement from the popular success of imperialism as a political strategy down to 1900, especially in the public schools, which prospered and multiplied as never before. As Anderson pointed out, imperialism gave a new lease of life to the most archaic elements in the culture of the British capitalist class, just when their disappearance seemed overdue:

> ... with the agrarian depression of 1870s, the traditional economic base of the landowning class lapsed. Thus, just at the moment when the atavistic values of the landed aristocracy appeared mortally threatened, imperialism rescued and reinforced them.[25]

The ideology of imperialism temporarily eclipsed that of liberalism, rather than displaced it, but it seriously aggravated the problems of the economy. It reinforced the external and trading orientation of the state, and tended to perpetuate industrial weakness by securing temporary export refuges in empire markets. (It no doubt also reinforced the passion of the middle-class for creating as much social distance as possible between themselves and the workers, which expressed itself in ideas such as that already referred to of a 'proper' ceiling on workers' wages, and which still astonishes foreign observers of shopfloor relations in Britain today.) Liberalism rested on economic prosperity. Imperialism helped to undermine that prosperity. After the Great War liberal ideas progressively ceased to be the ruling ideas of Britain.

The crisis was resolved by the War, which suspended internal conflicts, allowing national unity to be reasserted as the supreme value and at the same time clearing the way for compromises that had been unattainable in peacetime – votes for women over 30, independence for a partitioned Ireland, a grudging recognition that the power of organised labour necessitated granting at least some consultative status on economic issues to the leadership of the Trades Union Congress. The defeat of Germany and the imposition of war reparations, the retention of empire markets and continued receipts of overseas income gave British industry a respite and permitted the growth of new, science-based consumer industries like those already developed in Germany and the USA. But the causes of the crisis remained, in the structure and social relations of British industry, the nature of the class forces developed in the previous century, and the character of the British state. The advent of a new crisis was only a matter of time.

4

Labour and the New Political Order

The second crisis was separated from the first by four decades. Two world wars and a decade of slump had effected far-reaching changes in the economy, the parties, the state and social life. New 'science-based' industries had been established and they provided some compensation for the continued decline of the old staples of textiles, coal-mining and shipbuilding. The new consumer-goods industries were concentrated in the Midlands and the South-East. London became, for the first time in its history, a major industrial centre.*

Private and public suburban development, based on new urban road-transport systems, drastically altered the geography of work and leisure. The Victorian slums of London, Glasgow, Nottingham and elsewhere had at last been largely cleared. Radio increasingly displaced newspapers, and was in turn increasingly displaced by television, as the popular source of news. Labour shortages in the two wars, and the rapid growth of semi-skilled non-manual work, had drawn women back into the productive labour force on a large scale. Secondary education of some sort had belatedly become universal and university education virtually free. There was full employment and a comprehensive system of social security. People could be forgiven for supposing that the economic problems that had caused such anxiety at the turn of the century had vanished along with horse-drawn traffic and Liberal governments. The ascension of Queen

* And perhaps for the last time. 'Over the past decade London's manufacturing industry has declined far more rapidly than in the country as a whole. Between 1971 and 1982, jobs in London's manufacturing industry fell from 1.2 million to 660,000, a fall of 44%, compared to a national decline of 25%. This decline has been especially concentrated in parts of inner London, though under the impact of the recession it is now spreading throughout the capital (paper given by Michael Ward, Chairman of the GLC Industry and Employment Committee to a seminar on public/private co-operation of the Chartered Institute of Public Finance and Accountancy, 21 June 1982).

Elizabeth II to the throne in 1952 was greeted as the dawn of a new Elizabethan Age. In reality, it was the prelude to the final crisis of the age of Victoria.

Yet, for those who looked there were plenty of signs already between the wars that the new industries suffered from similar weaknesses to those of the older ones: the problem seemed to be social or political, not simply one of obsolete economic sectors alone. Britain's share of the expanding world market for new products such as electrical goods, cars, radios and scientific equipment fell, while the shares of the USA, the Netherlands, Germany, Canada, Sweden and Switzerland rose. A contemporary observer wrote:

> Today what is really important and significant in England is not the depression of the depressed industries, but the relatively small progress made by the relatively prosperous. It is the growing, not the decaying, which require watching.[1]

Moreover, Britain did not suffer from any special handicaps which could explain this relative failure as being due to adverse external forces:

> Disorder and prosperity, depreciating and appreciating exchanges, tariffs and dumping, subsidies and prohibitions may all in fact have proved damaging; but there must surely have been some special reason connected with the *internal* economy which rendered them more disastrous to the United Kingdom than to other countries.[2]

The protective tariff established in Britain after 1931, and state encouragement for mergers during the 1930s, did not help matters. The new cartels took advantage of protection to raise prices but not to modernise. 'Britain became a non-competing country at home as well as abroad'.[3] The Second World War postponed the consequences by removing the Axis economies from the world market for nearly fifteen years. On the other hand, it also wiped out Britain's overseas investments. After the war, exports had to cover more than 80% of imports, rather than the mere 55% of pre-war days when interest and dividends from overseas investments were still abundant. Moreover, the post-war General Agreement on Tariffs and Trade progressively reduced the permitted level of protection of Britain's home and colonial markets, while British exporters' informal advantages in the latter were eroded by the process of decolonisation. By 1960, Britain's prosperity was no longer underpinned by advantages accumulated from the nineteenth century. Once foreign competition revived, British industry would suffer a relentless economic contraction unless and until its productivity could be raised to match that of its chief competitors.

The years after 1914 had been used not to modernise the economy, so much as to construct a new political order, with a new dominant ideology, which preserved the old social and economic order in all essentials. As a result, when the special conditions affecting international competition in manufactures ended, at the beginning of the 1960s, the economy was no more able than before to meet the competition from more efficient economies, and the country moved steadily towards a new crisis.

The key element in the new political order was the incorporation of the labour movement – both the trade unions and the Labour Party – into the state. From the time of the First World War, trade union leaders began to be accorded (however grudgingly, and as far as possible only symbolically) recognition as a legitimate and substantial political force. The terms of this recognition were that they should confine themselves to purely industrial questions and pursue industrial aims 'responsibly': i.e., that they should accept the legitimacy (and by implication the permanence) of the private ownership of industry. Similarly, the Labour Party, emerging in 1923 as the second largest party in parliament, was entrusted with the government of Britain's privately-owned economy – on condition that in office it showed no inclination to get rid of it.

Economic and political conditions in the inter-war years allowed this modification to the political order to be undertaken with a minimum of risk. The unions, though much stronger as a result of the war, were constrained by chronic unemployment, and the Labour Party, though twice winning enough seats to form a government (in 1923–24 and 1929–31), never had an overall parliamentary majority, and could therefore be dismissed from office by the combined votes of Conservative and Liberal MPs if it showed signs of adopting policies dangerous to private property.

After an initial period (1918–22), during which the wartime coalition of Conservatives and Liberals was prolonged into peacetime, the Liberal Party, having split into two factions around the rival leaders Lloyd-George and Asquith, declined to a parliamentary rump. Those elements of capital which had so far remained loyal to the Liberals now transferred their allegiance to the Conservatives as the only party still capable of resisting socialism. The Conservative leadership, however, understood that the only safe way to do this was to oblige the labour movement to renounce socialism in the sense of anything but the pursuit of moderate reforms within capitalism.

Fortunately for them, the Labour Party's leader Ramsay MacDonald had long advocated this, although he also talked in vague rhetoric of a socialist future. Like the Fabians, who saw the problem as one of 'educating the ruling class to socialism', MacDonald's idea of socialism involved above all a convergence of opinion between workers and the middle class on the necessity of a regulated, humanised and 'mixed' economy, with 'municipal socialism' (enterprises run by local government, plus local social services) at the base, and central government planning and some state-owned industry at the top, leading to a progressive decline of class differences. Socialism, he argued, would appeal to the rich as well as the poor,

> because it brings order where there is now chaos, organisation where there is now confusion, law where there is now anarchy, justice where there is now injustice. Socialism marks the growth of society, not the uprising of a class. The consciousness which it seeks to quicken is not one of economic class solidarity, but one of social unity and growth towards organic wholeness.[4]

And although a left wing of the party strongly disagreed, believing that socialism meant confronting a fundamental conflict of interest between capital and the working class, most trade union leaders and most of their members tended to agree with MacDonald, if more prosaically. In practice, they believed in pressing for further reforms within capitalism, and maintaining the Labour Party in parliament as an instrument for this purpose. They therefore backed MacDonald in his efforts to allay the fears of those middle-class voters who had hitherto voted Liberal and whose support he considered essential on both philosophical and practical grounds. From the first he determined on an ostentatiously 'moderate' and 'constitutional' line by opposing the party's militant wing (whom he called 'our wild men'), publicly abjuring the use of industrial action for political ends, and when first in office in 1924, demonstrating that the party was 'responsible' by proposing no socialist measures or administrative innovations.

This policy came to a head in 1926, when the party was again in opposition. The TUC called a General Strike in support of the coalminers' resistance to wage cuts of up to 40%. The Labour Party leadership supported the strike ambiguously and reluctantly, the TUC retreated, the general strike was called off unconditionally after only nine days and the miners' strike was eventually broken. The Conservatives passed a Trade Disputes Act in 1927 which outlawed 'sympathetic' strikes and the TUC formally resolved to revert to the policy of collaboration with employers which had been begun during the war. The second minority Labour government of 1929–31 (again led by MacDonald) conformed to the same logic, seeking to win long-term electoral support by confining itself to very limited reforms which Liberal MPs would support.

This strategy was momentarily called in question by the ignominious end of the 1929–31 Labour government, when MacDonald agreed to head a so-called National Government, consisting almost exclusively of Conservatives and Liberals, to implement cuts in social security payments that his own party and the TUC had rejected. In the subsequent election of October 1931 Labour's parliamentary representation was reduced to 52 seats – almost back to the level of 1906. The Labour party conference now resolved not to take office again without proposing 'definite socialist legislation' on which it would stand or fall. For the moment this change of policy seemed fairly academic. In the 1935 election the Labour vote recovered, but not its share of seats, and the slump weakened the trade unions still further.

The situation changed rapidly, however, with the coming of the second World War. Full employment restored union membership, and the need for national unity dictated that the Labour Party should be brought into the wartime coalition on much more equal terms than in 1916. Key ministries were held by Labour leaders, including Ernest Bevin, General Secretary of the biggest union, the Transport and General Workers Union. The popular mobilisation required by total war also meant that extremes of inequality, and the persistent unemployment of the inter-war years, had to be repudiated. Popular aspirations for a more secure, and above all 'fairer' society now had to be reckoned with. Years of socialist propaganda, and the threat of fascism, had converted a wide segment of middle-class opinion to the need for change. Keynes's strategy of regulating effective demand so as to maintain high levels of employment suggested that social-democratic policies were compatible with capitalism and might even be necessary for its survival, and the success of the war economy seemed to prove that it was practicable. The new political order, incorporating the labour movement, thus eventually led to a general acceptance of many of the main tenets of social democracy: that capitalism could and should be made acceptable to 'ordinary people' by being regulated, humanised, and made to support a comprehensive system of social security.

This was the basis of Labour's 'landslide' victory in the first post-war election of July 1945, on a programme of public ownership of a number of key industries and a new system of state-provided social welfare. But the scope of the consensus was limited, even on the Labour side. The fiasco of 1931 had really convinced the party's leaders that when they next took office they must be effective, not that they must be socialist, and four years of coalition government during the war had reinforced this view. They actually opposed the resolution of the 1944 Annual Conference which committed the Labour Party to a package of specific measures of nationalisation, although unlike later Labour leaders they accepted it when it was overwhelmingly passed on a vote.

Similar reservations were felt among the trade union leadership. The unions had lost almost half their members between 1921 and 1934 and, with over two million unemployed throughout most of the 1930s, they had been able to do little more than try to minimise wage cuts for those remaining in jobs. Full employment during and after the war restored union membership, and real wages rose substantially, but the union leaders had been deeply scarred by the Depression and opposed any measures that might jeopardise the prosperity of the remaining private enterprise sector. Most of them were more hostile to communism than to capitalism (Ernest Bevin, who became Foreign Secretary in 1945, was one of the most militant champions of the Cold War). Experience with the wartime system of economic controls had shown that unemployment could be avoided, and upon this they were determined to insist. They were also committed to nationalising those industries which in private ownership could no longer pay the employees a living wage. But there was no inclination to go further; nor – on the other hand – did many trade union leaders envisage the possibility that full employment might strengthen the working class to the point where capital's profitability might be fatally eroded.

The Labour leadership thus saw themselves as having a mandate not for socialism, but for the ideals of the war years – full employment, social security and 'fair shares'. This permitted the progressive wing of the Conservative Party to embark on a campaign to convince their own diehards that it was both safe and essential to accept the new order. Their success led to a 'consensus' on the main elements in Labour's social-democratic package to which all parties adhered, in broad terms, until the end of the 1950s.

Implementing the Consensus 1945–51

The Labour Prime Minister Clement Attlee – 'a very modest little man, with a great deal to be modest about', Churchill is supposed to have said – was well suited to the task that he and his senior colleagues had set themselves, having served as party leader since 1933 and as Deputy Prime Minister in the wartime coalition. His government inherited three major assets from the war. First, the plan put forward in 1942 by the Liberal economist Sir William Beveridge, providing for universal insurance against sickness, old age, widowhood and unemployment, and for family allowances. The 'Beveridge Plan' gave concrete expression to what most people wanted. Beveridge himself energetically promoted it and, in spite of Churchill's opposition, many Conservatives became persuaded of its political necessity. Support was also overwhelming for the Labour government's National Health Act of 1946, enabling it to be carried in spite of opposition from a majority of doctors. Second, the government inherited an elaborate framework of wartime economic controls, from state allocation of raw materials to manufacturers to the direction of workers into jobs, and including the rationing of food and clothes and the control of all prices and rents. This allowed the government to manage the transition from military to civilian production without significant unemployment or economic dislocation. Third, the government inherited a vast, unfilled international demand for virtually anything Britain could export.

The party's 1945 pledges were rapidly redeemed. With regard to nationalisation the Bank of England, the coal-mines, the railway and canal companies, the power and gas companies and all road haulage were transferred to public ownership by 1948. Most of the iron and steel companies were also 'nationalised' in an Act of 1949, but in this case the strength of the industry's opposition to the measure (many steel companies, unlike the coal-mines and the railways, were still profitable) combined with reviving Conservative Party morale and faltering purpose in the cabinet to delay the implementation of the Act until 1951. Shortly afterwards (in October 1951) the Conservatives returned to power and in 1953 legislated for the companies to be sold back to their former owners.

The effect of the nationalisation measures was that, in 1950, nationalised industries produced roughly twenty per cent of total GDP, and employed nine per cent of the workforce. This gave the state an important measure of direct influence in the economy through the investment, pricing and employment policies of these industries.

However, the long-run political implications were two-edged. First, nearly all the industries nationalised, including many of the steel companies, were declining industries, and most were victims of long-standing neglect by their former owners. The compensation awarded to the former owners was probably excessive. Certainly neither the railways nor the coal-mines were able both to service the compensation debt, and to find from profits the investment funds needed in order to stay competitive; they could not break even 'taking one year with another' as the legislation envisaged. The problem grew worse, especially after 1951, as successive governments limited the nationalised industries' ability to borrow for investment, and directed the railways, the Electricity Board and the Coal Board to keep down their prices, and the state-owned airlines to buy expensive British-made aircraft. The result was that nationalised industries became identified in the public mind with 'loss-making', which was in turn ascribed to inefficiency, and were then forced to become more 'productive' by drastically contracting.

Second, the nationalised industries were placed under the control of public corporations appointed by the relevant minister and drawn predominantly from the former private boards of management. Consumer councils were set up, but these were not elective either, and had no powers. In short, 'nationalisation' was not 'socialisation'. So far from acquiring a new sense of identification with the state, the workers in the nationalised industries found themselves prime targets of successive governments' attempts to control wages, since the state could, as their employer, apply downward pressure on their wages without passing special legislation. From the mid-1950s to the 1960s the incomes of public sector employees, including most nationalised industry workers, grew more slowly than the incomes of workers in the private sector.

Third, the Conservatives, aided by large anti-nationalisation advertising expenditures by the private sector, made 'nationalisation' the focus of an intense ideological campaign to limit any further socialist advance.[5] This campaign was successful. The record of performance of the nationalised industries, within the constraints imposed on them by the Labour legislation of 1946–9 and the subsequent policies of Conservative governments, provided no basis for the development of popular support. Opinion polls registered a steady loss of public support for nationalisation, to the point where, in 1959, the Labour leader Hugh Gaitskell sought, though unsuccessfully, to expunge from the party's constitution any further commitment to nationalisation. Down to 1979 the Labour Party never subsequently returned in practice to the view that the 'common ownership of the means of production' was a valid objective in its own right.

The other half of the Labour government's programme was the establishment of the 'welfare state' through family allowances (introduced in 1945) and the National Insurance Act of 1946, which provided against loss of livelihood from unemployment, sickness, industrial injury, maternity, death of the breadwinner or retirement, and through the National Health Act (also of 1946) which made medical services freely available to all. These were pioneering reforms, ahead of all other western countries at the time.

They too, however, had some serious limitations, the most important being their undemocratic character. The new services were administered by civil servants; there was no attempt to involve the public directly in their provision. They were administered bureaucratically, however valuable they were, and when, later, the service provided gradually declined, members of the public were slow to realise what was happening, and then did not feel personally responsible, or capable of getting things put right. The result was that thirty years on (by the early 1970s) the percentage of national income spent on social services in Britain was below that of the other West European industrial countries, while the absolute level of spending per capita was very much lower still.[6] A second weakness was that the contributory element in the funding of both National Insurance and the National Health Service was a flat rate, which fell most heavily on the poor. Combined with a not-particularly-redistributive tax system, the effect was that 'the "welfare state" provide[d] for wage earners to finance the bulk of their own social security. Redistribution between classes [was] very limited'.[7]

The fact that the tax system was not very redistributive contradicts a still popular myth, strongly propagated until well into the 1970s, that the post-war Labour government also brought about a great reduction in income inequality. Between 1938 and 1949, the share of total personal income received by the richest one per cent of the population fell from about 15% to about 10% but this resulted from wartime tax changes; after 1949, only a minor further reduction in post-tax income inequality occurred; the income share of the poorest 50% scarcely changed at all.*

In fact, the Attlee government was quite orthodox in its economic policies. Any temptation it might have felt to be otherwise was curbed by its need to close the massive balance of payments gap (caused by the loss of income from foreign assets sold to finance the war, and by pent-up demand for raw material imports) before an American loan for post-war reconstruction was exhausted in 1949. It was able to do this only by imposing an extreme 'austerity' programme on the population (continuing to ration food, clothing and other necessities), by a big devaluation of the pound in 1949, and by securing the unions' agreement to exercise restraint in wage demands from early 1948 until September 1950. The balance of payments deficit on current account (i.e., in traded goods and services) was closed in 1949.

By that time, however, the government's energy, as well as its will to further reform, had been exhausted. Although the Labour vote rose substantially in the election of 1950 (to 13.2 million from 12 million in 1945), the Conservative vote recovered to 12.5 million (see Table 5.1). Labour's big majorities in urban working-class constituencies meant that it had more 'wasted' votes, and its majority in parliament fell to five seats. The leadership was divided over the rearmament programme called for by the USA after the outbreak of the Korean war. The political initiative was allowed to pass back to the Conservatives, who won a majority of 20 seats in the election of October 1951.

The Age of Affluence 1951–60

The Conservatives were to hold power for thirteen years, until 1964, winning three successive elections (1951, 1955 and 1959), a political feat without precedent.† This was made possible by the equally unprecedented rate of economic growth which was maintained throughout the 1950s. Output rose about 35% between 1951 and 1961; real average earnings by some 2.7% a year. This was fundamentally due to the 'long boom',

* The figures may overstate the redistribution that did occur: see the 7th Report of the Royal Commission on the Distribution of Income and Wealth (Cmnd 7595 of 1977), p. 7.

† The Liberals had won the successive elections of January–February 1906, January–February 1910 and December 1910, but in the two 1910 elections they failed to win overall majorities, whereas the Conservatives increased their majority in both 1955 and 1959.

the world-wide upturn in the accumulation cycle which lasted from the 1940s until the late 1960s. It was also due to the temporary absence from world markets of the export production of the economies most severely dislocated by the war – the German, Italian, French and Japanese.

Thanks to this, the Conservatives were able to preside over years of rising wages and relatively high profits (over the decade as a whole profit rates were approximately 15.5%.)[8] This made it easier for them to accept Labour's social-democratic legacy, including the 'mixed economy' – a label which suggested a change in its basically capitalist nature which had not in fact occurred – and the 'welfare state'. Nothing was added to either, but with only a few exceptions – notably the steel industry, and the profitable parts of the road haulage industry – there was no attempt to put the clock back. Thanks to the boom, too, unemployment remained minimal (at no time was it above two per cent between 1951 and 1964), and the Conservatives proved as eager to avoid industrial conflict as any Labour government – in fact, almost more so. Their claim was that the good times were due to the merits of private enterprise – capitalism had overcome its former limitations, and the Conservatives had shed their indifference to the interests of labour. Harold Macmillan, who became Conservative leader and Prime Minister in 1957, campaigned in 1959 on the slogan 'Life's better with the Conservatives. Don't let Labour ruin it'.* The voters were enjoying the new 'life style' of cars, television, household appliances and package holidays in Spain, which their rising incomes made possible. They were helped to make up their minds politically by 'give-away' budgets before the elections of 1955 and 1959. The Conservatives ended the decade with an overall parliamentary majority of 100.

Upon his retirement in 1955 Atlee was succeeded as Labour leader by Hugh Gaitskell, an Oxford economist who believed strongly that the mission of the Labour party was to humanise capitalist society, not to reform it out of existence.[9] Gaitskell was also influenced by Labour party theorists and sociologists who believed that the class struggle as it had existed for more than a century and a half was now over, and that the workers were becoming middle-class in outlook as they grew richer. Mark Abrams' book, *Must Labour Lose?*, argued that it must, so long as it remained the party of nationalisation, which was no longer popular; while Tony Crosland, in *The Future of Socialism*, held out the vision of a prosperous capitalist economy paying for an increasingly generous, enlightened and meritocratic welfare state.

Gaitskell threw his influence against all proposals for further nationalisation. His attempt to expunge Clause 4 of the party's constitution (which

* Churchill retired in 1955 and was succeeded by the Foreign Secretary Sir Anthony Eden. Eden resigned in 1957 after the fiasco of the Anglo-French attack on the Suez Canal.

commits the party to 'common ownership' of the means of production) was defeated by a combination of the party's left-wing with 'traditionalists' who were not keen on further nationalisation but (like the German Social Democrats in the famous 'Bernstein debate' at the turn of the century) were fearful of the consequences that such a symbolic renunciation of socialism might have for party morale. This struggle, and a parallel left–right struggle in 1960–1 over the issue of nuclear disarmament, worked to the Conservatives' electoral advantage.

In spite of the atmosphere of prosperity, the 1950s were later seen as years of fatal illusion, in which the Conservative government maintained an international posture beyond Britain's reduced means and ignored the growing relative weakness of the British economy. Britain's rate of growth, while high by her own historical standards, was no longer high enough. At the same time as Britain's output rose by 35%, between 1951 and 1961, France's rose by nearly 100%, Germany's and Italy's by 200%, and Japan's by 400%. This was not just a question of the other countries starting from a smaller base. Their growth rates rested on very high rates of investment and productivity growth. Between 1955 and 1965, as their manufacturing production began to return to world markets, the British share of world manufacturing exports fell from 20% to 4%.[9] Thanks to a simultaneous fall in the prices of raw material imports, the balance of payments remained positive for most of the decade, but vulnerability to speculation against sterling (due to the financial markets' recognition of Britain's growing relative industrial weakness) led to packages of deflationary measures in both 1955 and 1957 – the 'stops' of the 'stop-go' cycle, as the Conservatives' alternation between deflation and expansion came to be called.

Given the weakening industrial base, Conservative policies during the 1950s became more and more unrealistic. Leaving economic policy to a succession of six different Chancellors of the Exchequer, none of them with economic training, the Conservatives pursued international policies based on the idea that Britain was still a 'first-class' power. These policies included the maintenance of British forces in the Far East and in Germany, and the effort to maintain an independent British nuclear weapons system. The average level of defence spending throughout the decade was close to nine per cent of GNP, compared to the three to five per cent of Britain's main economic competitors. From the same illusion flowed the costly and futile attempt to overthrow Egypt's President Nasser by the attack on the Suez Canal in 1956, and the initial, short-sighted and possibly disastrous decision not to join the European Common Market at its formation in 1958. Few would now dispute the judgement of Samuel Brittan that this great-power illusion was

> the common factor behind our failure to join the European movement when we could have got in on our own terms, the crippling of the economy in the Korean armament drive, the failure to fund the sterling balances after the war, the long delay in rethinking both the international role of sterling and its exchange parity, the investment of large resources in a series of military and aerospace projects, many of which had to be cancelled before completion, and the growth of overseas defence commitments . . . [10]

Reality did begin to force itself on the attention of the Conservatives before the end of the decade. In 1959 Macmillan recognised the strength of African nationalism and appointed a Colonial Secretary, Iain MacLeod, who was willing and competent to arrange a rapid programme of transition to independence. Formally, at least, the British Empire was liquidated. Macmillan also accepted that it had become impossible for Britain to finance an independent nuclear missile system and that she must therefore buy one from the USA (with the obvious political dependence which this involved). In 1961, following the same logic, and with strong encouragement from the Americans, he accepted the need for a realistic alternative to the increasingly unreliable 'sterling area' as the basis for British commerce, and belatedly sought admission to the European Common Market (only to be rebuffed by de Gaulle).

These were radical departures from traditional Conservative interests and attitudes. It would have taken exceptional management and good luck to have induced the party, already humiliated by Suez, to accept them in the way that it had previously accepted the domestic legacy of the Attlee government. Even so, it might have been possible, had the economy been strong enough to sustain a new national role for Britain as one of Europe's prosperous middle-rank powers. But the 'consensus' years had diverted attention from the underlying causes of the country's industrial deficiencies.

As a result a second crisis began, and led, like the first, to a steady deterioration in the authority of governments and the state, and to a progressive weakening of popular support for the dominant ideas of the political order built up over the previous four decades. For twenty years after 1945 the Conservatives had not dared, and mostly had not wished, to advocate restoring high unemployment, dismantling the welfare state or ending public ownership of the principal nationalised industries; any more than the Labour Party had seriously advocated any significant extension of public ownership or new measures of popular control of industry. Over the next twenty years, this consensus disappeared, and a new political order had to be created again.

5

The Paralysis of Social Democracy

From 1961 onwards British politics became dominated once more by the country's economic problems. Britain's share of world exports of manufactures fell persistently (from 15.7% in 1961 to 9.5% in 1978), while foreign manufactures increasingly penetrated the British domestic market, reaching 25.6% of total domestic sales (nearly 60%, in the case of car sales) by mid-1979. The overall rate of profit (before tax) fell from 14.2% in 1960 to 4.7% in 1978. Investment remained static, falling farther and farther behind the levels of competing economies abroad. By 1978, productivity in manufacturing was little over half that of the German level.

The immediate result was a succession of increasingly severe 'sterling crises'. As the relative decline of exports and growth of imports kept tending to push the current account into deficit, holders of sterling speculated against the pound, reasoning that a devaluation would be needed to close the gap, and hoping to make a profit by forcing the authorities into it. Governments – Conservative until 1964, then Labour – resisted this, by using their reserves of foreign exchange to buy pounds, and by deflating the economy so as to reduce the level of demand for imports. This aggravated the unemployment which was already being caused by the closure of unsuccessful companies. As a result, between 1961 and 1979 manufacturing employment fell by 20% – a loss of 2.1 m jobs. Whole sectors of manufacturing disappeared – from motorcyles (in which Britain in 1950 had led the world) to a large part of the home appliances sector – while others such as shipbuilding, cars and even steel were threatened. Unemployment rose from 0.3 million (1.5%) to 1.4 million (7%) in 1978. Managing output rose only slowly in the 1960s, and hardly rose at all in the 1970s. Inequality was rediscovered, with a vengeance. By the early

1970s it turned out that some twenty-three per cent of the population were too poor to take a full part in the normal life of the community.[1]

Workers – the unionised rank and file – were not prepared to accept unemployment and downward pressure on wages without a struggle, and thanks to the 'affluent' fifties, when sometimes more job vacancies were recorded than job-seekers, they had become well-placed to resist. In return for sustained production, management, especially in engineering, had conceded a substantial measure of shop-floor influence over the labour process. This influence was channelled through the shop stewards, directly elected by the workers in each 'shop'. As the 1960s progressed, rank and file resistance, enforced through 'unofficial' – i.e. non union-endorsed – strikes, usually lasting less than three days and often only a few hours, came to account for ninety-five per cent of all strikes. Thanks to this, real wages of manual workers still increased on average by 2.5% a year throughout the 1960s, only a little below the 2.7% achieved in the 1950s.[2] Manufacturing companies could not pass all this on in price increases because foreign firms, with superior productivity, were underselling them. As a result, investment fell further and further behind the levels achieved in competing economies. Although governments – most notably the Labour government of 1964–70 – provided subsidies, resulting in some increase in investment (financed, in effect, out of revenues from personal income tax), the results were not impressive.

The failure of successive governments to reverse these trends led to a marked loss of electoral support for the two major parties. In the 1959 election the Labour and Conservative parties between them had taken 93.2% of the vote; by October 1974 their combined share of the vote was down to 75%, or only 55% of the total electorate (see Table 5.1). This reflected more than loss of confidence in the parties' leaderships. The social-democratic values to which even the Conservatives had subscribed during the 1950s were losing some of their authority. The parties themselves, faced with the intractable problem of economic decline, became increasingly polarised. Political currents previously considered 'extreme' – the market-oriented doctrines of the 'new right' and the more radical socialist views of the 'Labour left' – gained ground in the parties outside parliament, and in the case of the Conservatives, captured control inside the parliamentary party as well in 1975. The authoritarian strand in the Conservative Party became more pronounced; the narrowly parliamentary approach of the Labour leadership was increasingly rejected by the party's activists. Outside Northern Ireland there were no outright challenges to constitutional authority comparable to those of 1910–14; but the state increasingly prepared for them.

Table 5.1 The decline in the major parties' vote (1945–1979)

	Percentage of votes cast			Labour and Conservative vote as percentage of electorate				
	Labour	Conservatives	Others	Lab	+	Con	=	Total
1945	47.8	39.8	11.8	36.1	+	29.8	=	65.9
1950	46.1	43.5	10.4	39.8	+	37.7	=	77.5
1951	48.8	48.0	3.2	40.2	+	39.6	=	79.8
1955	46.4	49.7	3.9	35.6	+	38.2	=	73.8
1959	43.8	49.4	6.8	34.5	+	38.7	=	73.2
1964	44.1	43.4	12.5	34.0	+	33.4	=	67.4
1966	47.9	41.9	9.7	36.1	+	31.7	=	67.8
1970	43.0	46.4	10.7	31.0	+	33.3	=	64.3
1974 (Feb)	37.1	37.9	25.0	29.1	+	29.9	=	59.0
1974 (Oct)	39.2	35.8	25.0	28.7	+	26.2	=	54.9
1979	36.9	43.9	19.2	27.9	+	33.3	=	61.2

New Aspects

Few people saw the crisis in such a serious light, even by 1981. This was partly because of the time span which separated this crisis from the earlier one, making it hard to recognise it as a recurrence of an old syndrome, and partly because of some novel aspects.

The most obvious of these was that after 1970 the British crisis was compounded by a worldwide accumulation crisis. The reasons for the end of the long post-war boom are complex. The exhaustion of the impulse of technological innovation provoked by the Second World War is usually considered a basic, underlying cause. The advent of Japanese competition in all the most advanced sectors of production also cut into accumulation in the USA and Europe. Spare capacity emerged, and spare investible funds, leading to a strong movement of manufacturing capital towards cheap-labour, anti-union regimes such as Taiwan and Brazil. This aggravated the problem of maintaining growth rates in Europe and the USA, a problem further exacerbated by the oil-price increases after 1973. By the end of the 1970s virtually all the industrialised economies were experiencing reduced growth rates, rising unemployment, inflation and in some cases balance of payments problems as well. What distinguishes the British experience, however, and underlines more clearly than anything else its 'endogenous' nature, is that in Britain the new crisis had already begun in the 1960s – a decade of unparalleled prosperity for the rest of the industrialised world. The worldwide accumulation crisis of the 1970s did not cause the British crisis, it only made it worse.

Another novel aspect of the crisis was the changed nature of manufacturing capital in Britain. It had become extremely centralised, and to a very significant extent internationalised. In 1910, the largest hundred manufacturing companies had accounted for less than 15% of total output. By 1970 they accounted for about 50%, and by 1980, about 60%.[3] Fifty of these same hundred companies were multinational, and fifty accounted for more than a quarter of Britain's visible exports.[4] By 1979 American-owned firms alone accounted for 19.5% of Britain's visible exports, and 31% of all British exports were transactions between different branches of single companies – i.e., intra-firm transactions.[5] At the same time, British multinational companies owned a disproportionately large share of world assets, and made a third of their profits from overseas operations.

As Stuart Holland pointed out, the rise of this 'meso-economic' sector (in-between the 'macro-economic' level of the whole economy and the 'micro-economic' level of the individual firm) rendered obsolete a good deal of conventional wisdom about state economic management. Profit-accounting, transfer pricing and the sheer scale and complexity of the operations of the major companies make them almost impossible to inspect, monitor or police. A large part of the manufacturing sector had become increasingly immune to state efforts to control prices, to regulate the supply of credit, to tax corporate profits, or to affect economic growth by exchange rate changes. Much of the failure of successive governments in the 1960s and 1970s to accomplish any of their economic goals was due to more fundamental causes, but some of it was due to the growing difficulty which any government would have experienced in controlling an economy which had increasingly become a mere 'location' in the global division of labour of corporate manufacturing empires – and an increasingly unattractive one.

> There is a crucial contradiction between the fact that Britain ranks first in the European top 500 with 140 firms yet has an economic performance lower than and worse than any of our main European competitors. The reason lies substantially in the extent to which such leading multinationals have written Britain off as the main location for their expansion, and are shunting investment and jobs in modern industry abroad.[6]

This affected both Labour and Conservative governments in different ways. Labour governments seeking more control over private-sector investment policies, for example, could find themselves either ultimately impotent in face of corporate control over markets, information and investment funds; or, if they were to make determined efforts to break this control, they could face a crisis of 'business confidence', and a threatened or actual capital flight.*

* A well-publicised threat of a capital flight was that of Pilkingtons, the glass manufacturers, after the October 1974 elections. Private investment abroad during the years 1975–1978 inclusive was equal to 31% of gross investment in Britain by industrial and commercial companies.

Conservative governments, on the other hand, seeking to strengthen 'market forces', would find that this tended to accelerate the decline of the already too weak *national* (as opposed to multinational) sector of the British economy. Yet, without a national economy, a national party of capital risks the loss of its electoral base. The fact that the Conservative Party's representation in the House of Commons after the 1979 election was overwhelmingly concentrated in constituencies south of the Trent was a painful reminder of this.*

Yet – and here was the most striking novelty of the new crisis – the state itself had enormously expanded. In 1910 total state expenditure had been 12.7% of GDP. By 1975 it was 57.9% (including transfer spending). By 1977, the public sector (central and local government and public enterprises) employed almost thirty per cent of the labour force.

The expansion of the state, combined with the growth of monopoly in the private sector, accounted for a good deal of the inflation that accompanied the stagnation of output. Since hyper-inflation on Israeli or Chilean lines was judged socially and politically unacceptable, even Labour governments hesitated to try to use the state as an instrument of further economic expansion. The scale of state employment also complicated the problem of wage levels in general. Wage demands in the state sector encountered only the political limits set by governments' will to resist, and by the mid-1970s this will had been weakened. At the same time, the greatly enlarged state seemed no more suited or inclined than it had ever been to initiate and carry through a radical reconstruction of the economy.

Perceptions of the Crisis

These new features of the crisis, and the extensive changes that had occurred since the First World War, made it hard for people to recognise it for what it was. As a result, they ran through the gamut of the earlier diagnoses, as if discovering them for the first time: trade union restrictive practices and strikes, amateurism and conservativism in management, technical and scientific backwardness, poor design and poor salesmanship, inadequate scale of production, party competition for votes, excessive overseas investment, an overvalued pound.[7] Some of the diagnoses were new. For instance, the tendency to blame excessive overseas investment, an overvalued pound or the 'stop-go' oscillations of government policy reflected a much greater realisation of the conflict of interest between manufacturing and financial or commercial interests than had existed sixty

* The Conservatives won only 75 (32%) of the 235 seats in Northern England and Scotland, the lowest share in any general election won by the Conservatives since 1951; conversely, they won 186 (85%) of the 219 seats in England south of the Midlands, excluding London (see D. Butler and A. Sloman, *British Political Facts*, Macmillan, London 1980, p. 213).

years before. Another new diagnosis was that there were 'too few producers', i.e., too many state employees – a version of the neo-conservative reaction to the growth of the state.[8]

By now it should not be necessary to belabour the point that most of these diagnoses are not wrong – on the contrary most of them are essentially correct. For example, a comparative study of British and foreign automobile production by the government's Central Policy Review staff in 1975 suggested that relative to US and European plants British plants were overmanned. But, it added, 'even when manning levels are virtually identical and the capital equipment, model involved and plant layout are the same, the output of production lines in Britain is about half of that of continental plants'. The report seemed to imply that the fault lay with the workers: 'In other words, with the same power at his elbow and doing the same job as the British worker, a continental car assembly worker normally produces twice as much as his British counterpart'.[9] In fact, capital per employee in the British car industry as a whole was much lower than in Europe or the USA, and British plants were also too numerous, and produced too many engine types and a poorly balanced range of models. Another study showed that American-managed firms in Britain were more profitable than equivalent British-managed firms.[10] The truth was that management was less competent *and* – partly because of this – workers worked less efficiently (and perhaps less hard) than elsewhere. No one factor, or a few factors taken in isolation, contain the key to the problem. It can only be understood as the consequence of a total historical process.

By the 1960s, the relationship between capital and labour in Britain had been modified in many ways, but not in essentials: on the one hand, a class of capital still deeply attached to many pre-capitalist values, and on the other, an organised working class deeply sceptical of any suggestion that any advantage that they might concede to the employers would actually advance their own long-term interests. What was new in the 1960s was that the workers had acquired the strength to resist any increase in the level of exploitation, when such an increase had finally become essential.

To maintain its existing competitiveness – let alone, improve it – in face of rapidly rising productivity in other countries, big increases in the productivity of British manufacturing were required. This implied massive increases in investment. *The Times*, in 1973, suggested £20 billion. But whatever the figure, the implication was for investment on an unprecedented scale. This in turn implied the need for vast increases in profits. Would the workers be willing to leave these to the shareholders? In any case, part of these sums would have to come from profits on the basis of existing investment levels, i.e., by tax changes in favour of profits.

The conditions which permitted capital in Germany, France or Japan to impose an initially high level of exploitation (i.e., the gap between value added and wages) on the workforce did not exist in Britain – even if British management had had the necessary technical and managerial sophistication. British workers were too well organised, and they were no longer much impressed by the 'work ethic' which had been so assiduously preached to them in the nineteenth century (any more than British management seemed to have been, at least since the turn of the century). As the President of the National Union of Mineworkers, Joe Gormley, put it to the 1979 Labour Party Conference: 'The British people were not made to work' – a sentiment rather unlikely to have been expressed by his opposite number in Germany, the USA or Japan.

On the other hand, the British working class in the 1960s was no more ready to vote for a party seriously committed to an entirely new economic order than it had ever been. Whatever dreams it may once have entertained of building a transformed, egalitarian society – such as the Owenite movement of the 1830s had envisaged, for instance – had long been forgotten. The working-class consciousness which emerged after the defeats of the early nineteenth century was 'corporate', not 'hegemonic': it was consciousness of the distinct interests of the workers as workers – as at most an historic *underclass*. This remained broadly true in the 1960s.[11] So the contradictions between the need of capital to move to a higher level of exploitation, and the determination of workers to prevent this, presented itself as something to be resolved within the existing political framework defined by the Conservative and Labour parties. It took two decades to discover that this was impossible.

State-led Modernisation – the Wilson Reforms

Harold Wilson, who became Labour leader in 1963, had opposed Gaitskell's efforts to delete Clause 4 from the party's constitution. This maintained his reputation as a man of the left, but his grounds were pragmatic, if not cynical:

> We were being asked to take Genesis out of the bible. You don't have to be a fundamentalist to say that Genesis is a part of the bible.[12]

Wilson consistently resisted efforts to commit the party to new measures of public ownership. Instead, he laid stress on modernisation and technology within the existing 'mixed economy'. Wilson attacked the Conservatives as a party led by aristocratic amateurs, ignorant of the scientific and technological requirements of the modern world, who had presided for 'thirteen wasted years' over an economy whose management cadres were similarly recruited on the basis of class and connections, not merit; without planning, without reform, without keeping up with the times. Instead, he offered a vision of a society run by its men of talent. In a much-quoted speech to the Labour Party Conference in October 1963, after his election as Party leader, he said:

> We are redefining and we are re-stating our socialism in terms of the scientific revolution... the Britain that is going to be forged in the white heat of this revolution will be no place for restrictive practices or out-dated methods on either side of industry.[13]

The passage illustrates very well the thrust of Wilson's appeal – to 'both sides of industry' against incompetence, not to the working class against capital. Wilson understood that the consensus was endangered by industrial weakness. He offered to do what was necessary to remedy it. He answered the need to reassure people that, after all, 'no one need be defeated in the class war because no war was being fought. Capitalism could provide affluence for the working class while at the same time preserving the gains of the well-to-do'.[14] In the October 1964 election, the Labour Party campaign based on this theme at last secured electoral victory – though with only the barest majority of four seats.

Wilson's analysis of the economic problem was that it was due to a lack of central planning based on a commitment to growth (the French planning system was particularly identified as a model); to production on too small a scale; and to a generally archaic structure of state policy-making and business management, hostile to innovation and closed to lower-class talent. Promising to accomplish more in a hundred days than the Conservatives had done in thirteen years, Wilson quickly set in motion a comprehensive set of reforms. He established a new Department of Economic Affairs, charged with producing a National (five-year) Plan and promoting long-term economic growth, to offset the 'dead hand' of the Treasury, with its traditional preoccupation with short-term policy, balancing the books and maintaining the value of sterling; an Industrial Reconstruction Corporation, with substantial funds to subsidise corporate mergers; fiscal policies designed to encourage high levels of investment; and a wide range of institutional reforms designed to modernise the structure of the state.

These included reforms of the civil service, based on the report of a commission of inquiry (the Fulton Commission) which recommended the abolition of the hierarchy of 'classes' into which the policy-making cadre had been divided at the turn of the century, and measures to permit 'specialists' – technically-trained officials – to rise into the senior ranks. There were also measures to replace the separate grammar, secondary modern and technical school system of secondary education by all-ability 'comprehensive' high schools; and to break the older universities' status monopoly by sharply increasing the number of degree-granting institutions, including the former Colleges of Advanced Technology (which became universities), the Polytechnics and the Teacher Training Colleges. Parliament was also to be reformed, to give new standing committees oversight of policy-making in government departments; an Ombudsman, rejected by the Macmillan government, was established in 1967; the Official Secrets Act was to be amended, in the interests of more 'open' (and hence more efficient) government; and a major review of local government organisation was begun.

The same spirit of innovation was shown in social policy. Besides re-establishing traditional Labour priorities (for instance, by restoring the priority in house-building to one favouring publicly-owned housing for rent, over private-sector housing for sale) the government introduced a capital gains tax (long since established elsewhere) and a separate corporation tax, and planned for the introduction of income-related pensions based on graduated contributions. All in all, it was a stunning contrast with the era of Churchill and Macmillan. Early in 1966, in spite of the multiple economic difficulties which had been encountered, Wilson called an election, correctly judging that people had been convinced that his government understood the problems facing the country and had an effective formula for tackling them. In that election, in March 1966, Labour's majority (which had fallen from four seats to one through a by-election defeat) was increased to 96.

But the voters were to be disappointed. The economic measures – especially the tax relief and subsidies to industry, and the programme of mergers promoted by the Industrial Reorganisation Corporation – did not lead to an increase in productivity relative to Britain's competitors. It is doubtful if these measures – or any measures that did not touch the central relationships between capital and labour – could have achieved much. But they were never really given a chance. To succeed, they needed a climate of expansion. This was the core assumption of the National Plan produced by the new Department of Economic Affairs in September 1965. It assumed a target rate of growth of four per cent per annum, resulting in a 25% increase in national output between 1964 and 1970. But by the time the Plan was published, the economy was being fiercely deflated in order to prevent a new sterling crisis forcing a devaluation of the pound. In fact the government spent its entire period in office cutting back domestic demand, not expanding it. Output grew by 14%, not 25%; and gross investment grew by 20%, not the 38% forecast in the Plan, so that there was no question of increased productivity relative to other countries from this source.[15] In fact, British productivity grew 30% between 1963 and 1970, French and German 50%, and Japanese over 100% (Table 5.2).

The immediate reason for this failure was the attempt to maintain the exchange rate of the pound on an industrial base that had already become too weak to support it. When Labour took office in 1964, the exchange rate

Table 5.2 Output per person-hour in manufacturing (1963–1970) (1963 = 100)

	1963	*1964*	*1965*	*1966*	*1967*	*1968*	*1969*	*1970*
Japan	100	111	118	129	151	170	196	223
France	100	107	111	118	124	133	148	157
Germany	100	110	113	116	126	137	144	147
UK	100	106	110	114	118	125	127	131
Canada	100	106	110	114	118	125	129	131
USA	100	104	107	110	112	115	118	122

Source: *National Institute Economic Review*, Statistical Appendices.

was still US $2.80, the rate fixed in 1949. But Labour also inherited a current account deficit of £402 million in the balance of payments (the visible trade deficit was £545 million, offset by a surplus of £143 million in 'invisibles' – earnings from shipping, banking, insurance services, etc.). If this gap was not closed, a devaluation would be inevitable. Foreign holders of sterling, seeing the new government's first budget (which fulfilled election pledges to improve the level of social security benefits), judged that it would not cut back home demand enough to close the balance of payments gap, and a flight from sterling began.

The US government urged Wilson not to devalue the pound, fearing that it would force a devaluation of the dollar as well. Wilson, in any case, seems to have thought that the 1949 devaluation had hurt the Labour Party's image as an 'effective' manager of the economy, and was opposed to a further devaluation. In his conviction that bad economic management by the Conservatives was such an important part of the problem, he failed to realise – as did most of his ministers and advisers – the seriousness of the underlying weakness of British manufacturing. There followed a series of piecemeal efforts to defend the pound by borrowing. When this did not work, the government was forced to deflate. Finally, in 1967, it was forced to devalue anyway (from US $2.80 to US $2.40 – a 15% drop); and then, in order to ensure that this was not challenged by further speculation, still further deflation was required.

The result was a disaster. The 'technological revolution', which – if it was to be more than rhetoric – depended on accelerated economic growth, was still-born. Planning, in the words of one of the National Plan's authors, was 'many months dead already, or murdered' by the end of 1966.[16] The 'pace-making' Department of Economic Affairs itself was abolished in 1969. A large foreign debt had been incurred in the futile defence of the pound, which had to be repaid before revenues could be applied to the increasingly massive task of economic reconstruction. The other social goals of the government suffered equally. The comprehensivisation of schools had to be tackled without building any new schools. The hospital service, starved under the Conservatives – not a single new hospital had been built in their thirteen years in office – continued to be starved.

Most serious of all, from a political point of view, the government set itself to try to save company profitability, and to satisfy its foreign creditors, by curbing wage increases. In the years from 1948 to 1950 the Labour government had secured voluntary wage restraint from the union leadership. Now, expectations were very different, and the unions had less control over their members. After an attempt to rely on voluntary agreement in 1964, legislation was passed in 1965 (partly in response to American pressure) to give the government powers to delay any wage settlements that exceeded a permitted 'norm'. In 1966, the powers were extended to permit the imposition of a general wage-freeze, followed by legal ceilings on all wage increases. Finally, in 1968, seeing that these controls could not be maintained, Wilson proposed legislation on American and Canadian lines, which would, in effect, have outlawed unofficial strikes and compelled the balloting of union members before strikes could be held, on pain of heavy financial penalties against the unions.

Throughout all this the unions, aware that price controls (which had also been instituted) were ineffectual, and that dividends, too, were barely curtailed in practice, grew more and more resistant.[17] In 1969 they finally threatened to withdraw their support from the government if the new proposals (embodied in a White Paper called *In Place of Strife*) were taken any further. Wilson and the minister responsible, Barbara Castle, were forced to retreat. The contradiction between the Labour Party's legitimacy as a representative of the interests of labour, and the Wilson government's attempt to try to save British manufacturing capital, was thus brought into the open.

The attempt to deal with the economic crisis by deflation and wage controls not only cost the Labour Party votes; it also led to a politicisation of industrial struggle. Nine per cent more working days were lost in the sixties than in the fifties, though this was nothing compared to what was to follow in the seventies (Table 5.3). The industrial front acquired a new political salience; the Wilson government, as it was drawn deeper and deeper into the defence of British capital, found itself more and more frustrated by the unwillingness of the workers to make the sacrifices asked of them. A succession of Councils, Commissions and Boards, appointed (at five-figure salaries) to pronounce on the 'justice' or otherwise of workers' pay claims for sums in the order of £100 or so a year, succeeded only in disposing of any lingering illusion that wages were determined in some 'natural' fashion. In the 1960s the workers lost some of the

Table 5.3 Working days lost in strikes 1951–1980

Year	*1951*	*1952*	*1953*	*1954*	*1955*	*1956*	*1957*	*1958*	*1959*	*1960*
Million days	1.7	1.8	2.2	2.4	3.8	2.1	8.4	3.5	5.3	3.0
Year	*1961*	*1962*	*1963*	*1964*	*1965*	*1966*	*1967*	*1968*	*1969*	*1970*
Million days	3.0	5.8	1.8	2.3	2.9	2.4	2.8	4.7	6.8	11.0
Year	*1971*	*1972*	*1973*	*1974*	*1975*	*1976*	*1977*	*1978*	*1979*	*1980*
Million days	13.6	23.9	7.2	14.7	6.0	3.3	10.1	9.4	29.5	12.0

Source: *Monthly Digest of Statistics*, CSO, London.

'profoundly attractive innocence' which Professor Chapman had found in them only a few years before.[18]

The Labour government's eventual subordination of all its other goals to the defence of the capitalist economy led to the emergence of new political forces. The student movement, growing out of the nuclear disarmament campaign and opposition to the government's support for the American war in Vietnam, challenged the whole range of established attitudes, and helped the development of new left-wing organisations, both reformist and revolutionary. Left-wing intellectuals, alienated from the Labour Party, joined more radical groups such as the International Socialists or the International Marxist Group, or the women's movement.

At the other political pole there was the growth of racism. Starting in the mid-1950s, a rapid influx of immigrants from the West Indies, southern Asia and East Africa occurred. By 1970 1.2 million British people were of 'new Commonwealth and Pakistan' origin. Conservative and Labour leaders allowed themselves to be frightened by racist agitation into competing with each other to demonstrate their readiness to cut down the flow, passing the Commonwealth Immigration Acts of 1962 and 1968. This in turn encouraged the activities of the neo-fascist groups who, in 1966, formed the National Front.

Another development which compounded the crisis was the collapse of authority in Northern Ireland. The system of social, political and economic subordination of the Catholic minority by the Protestant majority in the six counties of Ulster had been connived at for over forty years by Labour as well as Conservative governments. The social-democratic consensus stopped short at the Irish Channel. On the other hand the provisions of the welfare state, which had been gladly adopted by the

Unionist government in Belfast (since it was subsidised from Whitehall), had made the Catholics less insecure, and given new educational opportunities to their children. In 1968, partly inspired by the civil rights movement in the USA, the Northern Ireland Civil Rights Association, largely led by educated Catholics challenged the status quo by demanding equal rights for all, including Catholics. The challenge was met by repression, leading to the intervention of the British army and to a revival of Irish Republican Army activity in the province, inaugurating what quickly became a bitter and intractable new phase in Ireland's two centuries-old civil and colonial war.

The crisis in Ulster was not a result of the crisis in the economy, but was closely linked to it. Belfast had participated in the earliest stages of the industrial revolution and was now particularly affected by the decline of old staple industries such as shipbuilding and textiles. Unemployment in Northern Ireland was the highest of any region of the United Kingdom, and it affected Catholics most. The Catholic challenge to Protestant domination, especially in the form of discrimination in state employment and housing, reflected this. And the weakness of the British economy precluded any attempt to resolve the problem by large-scale industrial investment programmes.

There were also significant centrifugal tendencies in Scotland and Wales. In England the decline in support for Labour and Conservatives was matched by a revival of support for the Liberals, but in Wales, and especially in Scotland, it was the nationalist parties which chiefly gained (see Table 11.1). By the late 1970s the nationalist trend was to play a fateful part in breaking up the post-war political order.

Unable to deal with the economic crisis at home, the government also found itself less and less able to act effectively abroad. The most dramatic example of this was its inability to impose its will on Ian Smith and the white settlers in Rhodesia when they made their Unilateral Declaration of Independence in 1965. At that time Labour had a majority of three in the House of Commons, and with no financial leeway Wilson could not have intervened militarily even if he had wished to. Instead, he made the mistake of boasting that economic sanctions would bring down the illegal regime in 'weeks rather than months', while Smith, knowing this boast to be empty, refused the various face-saving compromises which Wilson subsequently offered. Both men, however, underrated the long-run strength of the Zimbabwean liberation movement, which eventually settled the issue by force of arms in 1980.

Wilson's general foreign policy differed little from Macmillan's. In 1968 the decision was finally taken to withdraw all British troops 'east of Suez'. As the timing shows, it was a decision taken on financial grounds, not as an end in itself. And in 1967, Wilson (reversing his position as Macmillan had done earlier) made his own application to join the European Common Market. This, however, de Gaulle vetoed once again in May 1968, maintaining that Britain was not yet ready to become a member of the European community. In retrospect, it is hard to fault this judgement, especially since Wilson's unswerving support for US policy in Vietnam made it only too clear that Britain's so-called 'special relationship' with the USA had become simply that of a client.

There were redeeming elements in the record of the Wilson years. The laws covering divorce and abortion were liberalised, capital punishment was abolished, and the well-intentioned attempt to promote 'equality of educational esteem' through the comprehensivisation of secondary schools was pursued. There was also an expansion of university education (which, exceptionally, was maintained against the general trend of spending cuts). Not everything ended in failure. It was true that unemployment was rising, but for those in employment the end of wage controls and the defeat of the proposed new law to curtail strike action led to a recovery in wages in 1969–70 which substantially made good the relative losses imposed by controls in the previous years. And from the point of view of the City of London, the government's deflationary policies had finally closed the balance of payments' gap.

Labour's defeat in the June 1970 election was, in fact, by no means a foregone conclusion. Shortly before the election the opinion polls suggested that Labour would win. But the gap between the government's economic performance and its promises was too wide. Wilson's rhetoric about harnessing science to socialism had proved too hollow. Labour party membership had declined precipitously. At the last moment, opinion turned away from the general line of continuity with the past, which Wilson had maintained, and towards the 'new conservatism' propounded by the Conservative leader Edward Heath.

6

Into the New Crisis

After the Conservative Party's defeat in the 1964 election many party activists and MPs felt that, in effect, Wilson's charge that it was led by an amateur, backward-looking elite contained an uncomfortable element of truth. There was a growing distrust of the party's traditionally upper-class leadership – the 'magic circle', the former Colonial Secretary Iain Macleod called them – including Macmillan himself, and his successor Sir Alec Douglas-Home.* It was decided that from now on the leader would be elected by the Conservative MPs. Home stood aside and in the election held in August 1965 the choice fell on Edward Heath.

Health, like Wilson, had been President of the Board of Trade. He had also been Macmillan's negotiator in the abortive Common Market application from 1961 to 1963, and was very much a 'European' and a 'technocrat'. Like Wilson too, 'Heath's abiding commitment was to the ideology of growth'.[1] But where Wilson hoped to achieve modernisation through active state intervention, Heath sought it through competition – through reducing state intervention, curbing monopolies, allowing the market to weed out backwardness and reward innovation.

The later sixties also saw a more fundamental right-wing movement than Heath's 'competition policy' gaining ground inside the Conservative Party. Enoch Powell, Heath's 'shadow minister' for health, shared his enthusiasm for the market and for cutting back the state, but went much farther in calling for denationalisation, an end to state intervention in industrial disputes, and strict control of the money supply to control inflation. He also combined this with a nationalist campaign against entry into the EEC, and a racist campaign against immigrants, both of which

* Home became Prime Minister and leader of the party in 1963 on the basis of advice tendered to the Queen by Macmillan (when he resigned from ill-health) after informal consultations within the party leadership.

proved popular themes. In 1968 Heath dismissed him from the shadow cabinet for his most notorious speech, a veiled invocation of racial violence ('As I look ahead, I am filled with foreboding. Like the Roman, I seem to see "the River Tiber foaming with much blood".')* But the new monetarist, nationalist, racist rejection of the post-war consensus which Powell expressed found a keen response on the authoritarian right wing of the party. These currents converged with Heath's more limited 'competition policy' at a pre-election strategy conference at the Selsdon Park Hotel in Croydon in January 1970 which committed the party to many of the 'new right' policies, including the abolition of universal social security payments and legislation to curtail trade union powers. Wilson commented: 'Selsdon Man is designing a system of society for the ruthless and the pushing, the uncaring . . . his message to the rest is: "you're out on your own"'.[2]

The story of the next decade is the story of how at first Selsdon Man was defeated, because the consensus had not yet been weakened enough, and of how from 1974 to 1979 the consensus was then further eroded in a second unsuccessful attempt by Wilson and his successor, James Callaghan, to rescue Britain's competitive position without challenging the balance of power between capital and labour. Finally, the way was opened for a new, much more radical Conservative attempt to break with the past under the leadership of Margaret Thatcher.

The Heath Initiatives 1970–74

Heath's strategy was straightforward. Having prepared the ground with de Gaulle's successor, Pompidou, he reapplied for admission to the EEC in 1971. Also in 1971, to prevent the inevitable 'sterling crisis' choking off his strategy for economic expansion, he abandoned the fixed exchange-rate and allowed the pound to 'float', thus reducing sterling's role as an international reserve currency, and overcoming one of de Gaulle's former objections to British entry. Britain finally entered the EEC in 1973.

Secondly, he set about dismantling much of the apparatus of state economic intervention created during the Wilson years – the Prices and Incomes Board, the Industrial Reorganisation Corporation, the system of investment grants. Thirdly, the budgets introduced by the Conservative Chancellor, Anthony Barber, during the government's first eighteen months shifted the burden of taxation substantially away from companies and the richer tax payers and onto the working class – to the tune of about £2 billion, or some 12% of total revenue. Combined with a reduction in the subsidy given to council house rents (under the Housing Finance Act

* Andrew Gamble notes that Powell received 105,000 letters of congratulations within a few days of this speech (*The Conservative Nation*, Routledge and Kegan Paul, London 1974, p. 121).

1972) and an increase in the charges made for medical care, the class character of the new fiscal policy was unmistakable. It helped to restore declining company post-tax profits, and was supposed to restore incentives to entrepreneurship.

But it also exacerbated the unions' hostility to the fourth main element of the Heath programme, the Industrial Relations Act of 1971. This Act, which came into force in 1972, introduced the North American pattern of legal regulation of industrial conflict by imposing punitive financial sanctions on registered unions whose members took industrial action other than by prescribed procedures. These provided for compulsory 'cooling-off' periods and strike ballots before strikes could be called, and imposed severe penalties for taking industrial action against an employer while an existing contract was in force. Unions were free not to register under the Act, but then they lost their legal immunity from civil actions by employers for breaches of contract. Under the Act, unofficial strikes became either illegal or vulnerable to civil suits; so did 'sympathetic' strikes, the ultimate expression of the solidarity which was the British labour movement's historic source of strength.*

The government's idea was that, having altered the balance of power in favour of employers, it should stand aside from industrial relations and let the 'law of supply and demand' determine the level of wages. It therefore began by abruptly terminating the consultative arrangements between Downing Street and Congress House (the TUC headquarters) which had been established since the war. On the other hand, as a major employer, it set itself to resist all wage claims by public-sector workers above the level it considered in line with the growth of productivity.

But the labour movement's massive opposition to the Industrial Relations Act became the prime cause of the Heath government's eventual defeat. The Trades Union Congress advised all its member unions not to register under the Act and expelled thirty-two small unions which did so. The militancy displayed against the Act was due partly to the comprehensive nature of the threat – the unions were in no doubt that if the Act prevailed, the balance of advantage would shift decisively to the employers – and partly to the build-up of rank and file confidence, expectations and organisational experience during the previous two decades. Militancy had been increased by the Wilson government's wage controls, rising inflation, and was now intensified by the Heath government's fiscal policies (especially by measures directly affecting workers, such as increased council-house rents, increased charges for school meals and cuts in subventions to areas of high unemployment).

* Sympathetic strikes had been banned by the Trades Disputes Act of 1927 passed by the Conservative government after the General Strike in the previous year. Repealing the 1927 Act had been one of the first acts of the Attlee government in 1946.

The outcome of this struggle showed that, when the unions and their members were united, they were stronger than the government. In a strike in January and February 1972 – just before the 1971 Industrial Relations Act came into force – the mine workers forced the government to concede a wage increase three times as big as the Coal Board's 'final' offer. This strike also revealed extensive public sympathy for the miners – a sign of life still left in the 'consensus' which was to cost Heath dearly two years later. Similar confrontations with the railwaymen and the dockers later in 1972 – the latter bringing the country to the verge of a general strike – in effect made the Industrial Relations Act a dead letter within three months of its introduction. A year later, the Director-General of the Confederation of British Industries, Campbell Adamson, publicly condemned the Act as having been responsible for the drastic deterioration in industrial relations which had marked the Heath years.

The strength of the labour movement forced a radical shift in policy. Heath's strategy called for an economic expansion if 'market forces' were to produce the investment boom needed to bring about a radical improvement in productivity. But expansion would be jeopardised if large wage increases led to rapidly rising prices, rather than increased profits and investment. The strikes in the first half of 1972 showed that the Industrial Relations Act was powerless to prevent this. In the summer of 1972, therefore, the TUC leadership was suddenly recalled to Whitehall for discussions on a new voluntary policy of wage restraint. When these discussions failed, the most comprehensive system of legal wage controls yet seen was enacted by parliament in November, 1972. This was a dramatic departure from the philosopy of the market. It was also keenly resented by the unions, contrasting as it did with the spectacular gains awarded to the well-to-do in the Barber budgets of the previous two years.

There now began a dramatic convergence of forces, each indicative of a different side of the contradiction in which the Heath strategy was caught. Internationally, the long boom came to an end in 1970. Competition in world markets for manufactured goods became more intense, and exports harder to sell. 'Hot' money flowed into commodity markets, pushing up commodity prices and causing a sharp increase in Britain's import bill and hence aggravating an inflation already accelerated by expansionary budgets. Retail prices rose on average by 8.4% a year from 1969 to 1973, twice the rate of the preceding four years, adding to the price of exports. The expansion also sucked in imports on an unprecedented scale.

The combined result was a haemorrhage in the balance of payments. The 'visible' balance moved from a surplus of £261 million in 1971 (inherited from Wilson's deflationary policies) to a deficit of £722 million in 1972. This was cushioned by an 'invisibles' surplus of £875 million, to leave a modest overall current surplus. To avoid having to halt the economic expansion needed to defend a fixed exchange-rate against speculative selling, the pound had been 'floated'. But in 1973 the visible balance showed a deficit of £2,383 million (only half of which was due to the increase in oil prices following the Egypt-Israel war in October), and the overall current balance was just under £1 billion in deficit. Even with a floating exchange rate, there could now be no question of further expansion. That November, an emergency deflationary budget was introduced. The 'dash for freedom' was over.

Meantime the government was chagrined to find that manufacturers failed to respond to its policies by increasing investment. Real manufacturing investment in each of the years of the Heath government stayed more or less constant, at a level slightly below that of the last years of the Wilson government. As Heath complained to the Institute of Directors in 1973:

> The curse of British industry is that it has never anticipated demand. When we came in we were told there weren't sufficient inducements to invest. So we provided the inducements. Then we were told people were scared of balance of payments difficulties leading to stop-go. So we floated the pound. Then we were told of fears of inflation and now we're dealing with that. And still you aren't investing enough[3]

But companies voted with their profits, and it was not a vote of confidence in the Heath strategy. Between 1970 and 1973 the volume of direct investment abroad tripled.

Even the policy of cutting back the state had to be abandoned. The Conservatives had particularly set their face against using the state to subsidise failing concerns. The 'competition policy' dictated that inefficient companies should be weeded out to make way for efficient ones. But the government's celebrated commitment 'to gear its policies to the great majority of the people, who are not lame ducks' was broken, in 1971, by the decision to salvage Rolls Royce by nationalising it. In face of the lack of response by industry, the government also felt obliged to return to a system of investment grants and, in 1972, established an Industrial Development Executive, which bore a striking resemblance to Wilson's Industrial Reorganisation Corporation, abolished in 1970.

Heath's U-turn, back to the essential strategies of the sixties, resulted, ultimately, from the fact that the electorate was not ready to accept the consequences which a consistent application of 'social market doctrine' to British conditions would have entailed – namely, an industrial recession on a scale not witnessed since the 1930s. Heath himself was also unwilling to accept these consequences (as his subsequent attacks on Thatcher's economic policies demonstrated). When confronted by serious political or social costs, his attempt to revert to the 'corporatist' approach of the previous decade (i.e. seeking to secure union compliance in wage controls through their incorporation with business representatives in consultative economic policy machinery) reflected his strictly qualified commitment to the new conservative creed.

The Egypt–Israel War of October 1973 (which led to a doubling and later quadrupling, of the price of oil) coincided with the start of Stage 3 of the government's wage control programme, which set a ceiling of seven per cent on wage settlements for the coming year. In November the coal-miners, judging that the sudden improvement in the prospects for coal (relative to oil) presented a unique opportunity for them to recover some of the ground in pay which they had lost in relation to other skilled workers since 1946, began an overtime ban to enforce pay claims of between 22 and 46 per cent (depending on the category of worker). Heath responded by declaring a state of emergency under which a variety of measures were taken to conserve coal stocks, culminating at the New Year in a national three-day working week. The TUC nervously sought a compromise, but the miners pressed on and voted for a strike, whereupon Heath called an election for February 1974.

Opinion poll evidence suggested a good deal of public scepticism about the need for this confrontation. What the election result indicated above all was a lack of enthusiasm for both the Conservative and the Labour parties, both of which lost votes, while 6 million votes (19%) went to the Liberals, and 600,000 to the Scottish National Party (22% of the Scottish vote). Labour won four more seats than the Conservatives, but had no overall majority. The Liberals, however, declined to keep the Conservatives in office. Heath was obliged to resign and Wilson returned to office as leader of a minority government with Liberal support.

Heath remained leader of the Conservatives for another year. But after losing twenty more seats in the election of October 1974 (called by Wilson in an attempt to secure a parliamentary majority) he paid the penalty by being replaced by Margaret Thatcher, his former Minister of Education, in a leadership contest in February 1975.

Thatcher's victory was seen at the time in largely personal terms – particularly as a revenge by back-benchers offended by Heath's notorious aloofness – as well as an instance of the well-established rule that Tory leaders may not lose more than one election. Heath had lost three, including the election of 1966. But the right wing of the Conservative party in parliament were also opting for a leader who represented a more aggressive brand of right-wing Conservatism, reflecting more faithfully the prejudices on hanging, race, 'communism in the unions', 'welfare scroungers' and the like, which were entertained by their suburban supporters – and, as Thatcher herself shrewdly understood, by large numbers of workers too. Under the Wilson–Callaghan administrations which followed her election as leader, the remaining credit of the social-democratic consensus dwindled still further, while the Conservative Party was being prepared, under Thatcher's leadership, for a right-wing initiative more doctrinaire, radical and unpredictable in its outcome than anything in the party's previous history. Selsdon Woman was to prove a great deal more deadly than Selsdon Man.

The 'Social Contract' 1974–79

Wilson, in contrast to Heath, had retained his leadership of the Labour Party after the 1970 defeat without serious challenge. Responding to the industrial militancy of the rank and file of the party and unions, the 1971 party conference had adopted a more far-reaching programme than anything it had entertained since 1945, including 'a socialist plan of production, based on public ownership, with minimum compensation, of the commanding heights of the economy'.[4] At Wilson's insistence this was later watered-down by the National Executive, although the tone of party statements remained radical. The 1974 manifesto pledged 'a fundamental and irreversible shift in the balance of power and wealth in favour of working people and their families'. Nationalisation, however, was promised only for shipbuilding, the aircraft industry and the docks (all ailing sectors). The private sector was otherwise to be brought within the ambit of state-planning, only by means of selective share purchases by a National Enterprise Board, and by 'Planning Agreements' between the state and individual large companies. The party also proposed to introduce a measure of 'industrial democracy' in the largest firms.

Tony Benn, who had become the leading spokesman of the party's left wing, declared at the party's 1972 conference: 'the crisis that we inherit when we come to power will be the occasion for fundamental change and not the excuse for postponing it'. But the party was not converted to this view, and when Wilson took office again in February 1974 it had not come to power. It was a minority government, holding office with Liberal and Nationalist party support. It was also a government confronted with a catastrophic balance of payments deficit, inflation accelerating towards twenty per cent and the pent-up frustration of a labour movement more mobilised than ever before – but not, for the most part, any more committed than before to fundamental social and economic change. Wilson, for his part, was as committed as ever to the view that the only realistic goal for Labour was to find an agreed basis for reviving the ailing capitalist economy. The immediate problem was that organised labour was not willing to see profits restored at its expense without any quid pro quo. Heath had deliberately abandoned the institutionalised and regular consultation between the state and the leaderships of organised labour and capital that had been so characteristic of the later fifties and sixties. Wilson now made Labour's special ability to repair the government's relationship with the unions the cornerstone of his policy and of his electoral appeal.

The key phrase in this exercise was the 'social contract', adopted by the party and the TUC to denote the set of understandings between the state, capital and labour on the basis of which the state could look for the labour movement's co-operation with its policies, and which Heath was charged with having destroyed. Wilson undertook to repair the 'social contract' so that the voluntary support of the unions could then be obtained for a new 'incomes policy.'

The immediate necessity was to settle the miners' strike. This was done by accepting the recommendations of the Pay Board, to which Heath had sent the miners' claim before the election, and which gave the miners what they had asked for. The restoration of the 'social contract' was then put in hand. First, trade union rights were restored by a Trade Unions and Industrial Relations Act which repealed the 1971 Industrial Relations Act, and extended the principle of the closed shop, and an Employment Protection Act, aimed at improving job security by tightening up on unfair dismissal and providing compensation paid by the employer for many categories of redundant worker. A commission was also set up (the Bullock Commission) to make recommendations for 'industrial democracy'.

Second, the 'social wage' – collectively-consumed services and social security benefits – was to be increased. The 1972 Housing Finance Act which had raised council-house rents was repealed; state pensions and widows' benefits were raised and better indexed against inflation; the tax burden was shifted (slightly) back toward the rich; and price controls were established and prices of some essential foods subsidised. The government later undertook to increase the 'social wage' each year in real terms.

Third, a National Enterprise Board was established to invest public funds in companies in profitable sectors; the nationalisation of shipbuilding and aircraft production was embarked upon. 'Planning Agreements' with the largest firms, covering their employment and investment plans, were to be made by the Department of Industry, headed by Benn.

Having outlined this strategy for securing trade union co-operation and state-directed industrial recovery, Wilson called an election in October. The result was equivocal. The Labour vote actually fell slightly, but the Conservative vote fell further, by 1.4 million, and the Liberals also suffered a setback (see Table 5.1.). Labour emerged with an overall majority of three seats, too small for a reliable 'working' majority. But in an effort to head off the Scottish National Party's challenge in Scotland (a traditional Labour stronghold) the party had promised to legislate for a

Scottish Assembly with devolved powers. The SNP, with 30% of the Scottish vote in October, and 11 MPs, calculated that an Assembly could be used as a stepping stone towards real independence, and so decided to support the government. The Welsh Nationalists, with three MPs, and the Liberals with 13, also gave qualified support.* The government could govern, on this basis – if it could resolve the immediate economic crisis.

By the end of 1974 the rate of inflation was 23%, and over the twelve months from July 1974 to July 1975 it rose to more than 26%. Over the same period earnings rose nearly 28%. Meantime the current balance of payments deficit for 1974 was no less that £3.6 billion (on visible trade alone it was £5.2 billion, offset by a surplus of £1.6 billion on invisible trade). The deficit was covered partly by the inflow of funds for investment by foreign companies in the North Sea oilfields, and partly by short-term foreign loans. By May 1975, however, it was clear that a final crisis was not far off. Labour's claim to be able to deliver union cooperation in stabilising the economy was now to be tested.

The initiative was taken by the one man who had the real authority to do so, Jack Jones, leader of the two million workers in the Transport and General Workers Union. He proposed a voluntary agreement to restrict wage claims in 1975–6 to a flat rate maximum of £6 per week, with no increase in incomes over £8,500 per annum – an agreement that would hurt the lowest-paid workers least. This was accepted by the government and the TUC and implemented with remarkable fidelity. (To anticipate, it was followed by a further agreement for 1976–7, to limit claims to a maximum increase of 4½% or £4 per week, and in 1977–8, although the unions declined to enter into any further agreement, many of them conformed in practice to the government's wish for a ceiling of ten per cent. Estimates of the effects of this restraint vary, but it is generally agreed that over the years 1975–7, manual workers as a whole experienced a cut in real income of between seven and eight per cent compared with 1974; a loss which was largely made up, however, in 1978.)

On this basis Wilson hoped to get some industrial recovery, and foreign support for interim measures to cover the balance of payments deficit. But this was too optimistic. For one thing the world trade recession (after a temporary revival in 1971–3) severely limited the prospect of any recovery of exports. Secondly, the level of public consumption implied in the social contract was higher than foreign creditors thought the economy could afford. Thirdly, there was a general loss of 'business confidence', focused largely on Benn, the left-wing Secretary of State for Industry.

To meet these reservations, the government introduced deflationary

* The offer extended to Wales too, although Welsh opinion was much less strongly nationalist (see Chapter 11).

measures in November 1974, and began to redistribute the tax burden away from company profits again. In June 1975, taking advantage of a national referendum decision in favour of remaining in the EEC (on somewhat modified terms), Wilson also removed Benn, who had led the campaign for a 'no' vote, from the Department of Industry to the Department of Energy. This spelled the end of any attempt to use the National Enterprise Board or Planning Agreements to extend public ownership or public participation in the economic policy-making of the large-firm ('meso-economic') sector. The only novel elements in Labour's approach to the industrial crisis were thus abandoned in favour of the familiar and self-destructive policy of deflation, just as the National Plan had been abandoned in 1965–6.

In March 1976, Wilson retired, professing himself confident that things were on course for a recovery, and was succeeded as leader and Prime Minister by his Foreign Secretary, James Callaghan. But by this time it was clear that foreign capital was not yet convinced that the balance of payments gap would be closed, and a movement out of sterling began which took the value of the pound down from US $2.02 in January 1976 to US $1.63 in September (it had been US $2.60 at the end of 1971). A devaluation on this scale entailed all sorts of new and intractable problems. To reverse it by a corresponding scale of deflation would, thought Callaghan and the Chancellor of the Exchequer, Denis Healey, court political instability (see Chapter 2, p. 23). The only remaining option – short of abandoning the capitalist system and declaring the whole economy public property, which could not have been further from their thoughts – was to seek a transitional foreign loan. In June 1976, a $5 billion loan was obtained from foreign central banks, but for only six months.

By September, with $1.5 billion of this loan used up, the government accepted the need to seek a longer-term loan from the International Monetary Fund, even though this would inevitably entail drastic deflationary policies;[5] At the same time, the government lost its parliamentary majority as a result of a series of by-elections. From now on, it presided over a programme of ever more severe deflation, sustained in office only by the SNP for the sake of the Scotland Bill, and by the Liberals for the sake of electoral 'credibility' as a party able to influence events – a strategy which eventually led in March 1977 to an official 'pact' between Callaghan and the Liberal leader, David Steel.

From this point onwards, the Callaghan government's policy was almost entirely subordinated to the deflationary goals set by the IMF, although Healey also became convinced of their necessity. By 1978/9 total government spending had risen eleven per cent over the 1973/4 level; but this was largely due to increased spending on debt interest, unemployment pay (the number of people unemployed had risen from 600,000 in 1974 to

1.5 million in 1978), and subsidies to employers to maintain employment. Plans to expand provision in other fields were cut back, and in some areas spending was reduced below 1973–4 levels.[6] The 'social wage' also stagnated, increasing by only 0.3% in real terms over the whole period 1974–9. The National Enterprise Board made no acquisitions except to prevent various large enterprises, such as Ferranti and British Leyland, from collapsing with the consequent loss of large numbers of jobs and long-term industrial capacity. The only Planning Agreements concluded were with the Chrysler Corporation, at the time of the government's attempt to induce the company, by a large loan, not to close its Scottish subsidiary in 1975 – and with the National Coal Board! The Bullock Commission's recommendations in 1977 for a system of trade union representation on the boards of directors of all large firms were strenuously opposed by the CBI and later dropped by the government.

As for industrial recovery, it was further away than ever. British exports continued to expand more slowly than the volume of world trade; British productivity continued to rise more slowly than that of France, Germany or Japan. Manufacturing output fell by 6% in 1974–5 and rose by only 4.4% from 1975 to 1979. By the end of the decade 'de-industrialisation' had become a large and ominous reality. In Northern Ireland, which had passed under direct rule from Whitehall in 1972, nothing could be done, except, possibly, with massive expenditures, but these were out of the question. Likewise, nothing was done about the scandal of racial discrimination in jobs, housing and in other fields.[7] The only clear accomplishments of these years were, first, that the Labour government approached the end of this decade, like the last, with its inherited balance of payments deficit more or less eliminated – partly thanks to the level of deflation (i.e., unemployment and idle plant leading to fewer imports), and partly because of rapidly growing North Sea oil production; and second, that inflation had eventually fallen back to 9½, little more than its pre-1974 level. The situation had been stabilised – but at the cost of a more or less complete social stasis.

It now fell to the unions, for the third time in a decade, to destroy the fragile (and increasingly opportunistic) political balance. The patience of many workers – especially the lower-paid – was wearing thin. The recovery which had been so often promised in return for their sacrifices seemed more remote than ever. In 1978, the TUC refused Callaghan's request for a fourth year of wage restraint. In September, when all commentators judged that he would be well advised to call an election, he instead called for a new wage ceiling of five per cent, a call which was rejected by the Labour Party Conference. Meanwhile the workers at Ford (UK), which had declared profits for 1977 of £246 million, judging (not unreasonably) that most of this would not be invested in Britain but would be remitted to Detroit, demanded a wage increase of thirty per cent. After a strike lasting seventeen weeks, they accepted nineteen per cent. The dam now broke in a series of large-scale strikes throughout what also proved to be one of the coldest winters in living memory. The low-paid public sector unions were particularly involved, from ambulance drivers to street-cleaners and school janitors. The snow lay in Regent Street, with no one to clear it away. Rubbish accumulating in normally wholesome districts was not collected. Schools were closed.

While the 'winter of discontent' continued, referenda were held in Scotland and Wales on the proposed devolution of powers from Westminster. Opponents of devolution inside the Labour Party had joined with Conservatives to amend the Scotland Bill to the effect that unless at least 40% of the whole Scottish electorate voted 'yes', the government would not be bound to establish a Scottish Assembly. On 1 March 1979 52% of those voting voted 'yes', but they constituted only 33% of the electorate, and Callaghan reasonably judged that this did not warrant implementing the devolution scheme. The SNP members of parliament vented their frustration by deciding to support a motion of no confidence moved by Margaret Thatcher later in March. The Liberals had also abandoned the 'pact' with Labour in 1978 after Labour MPs had voted against the use of proportional representation for elections to the European Parliament (which Liberals had seen as an important precedent for a future change in the British electoral system). So the vote of no confidence was carried against the government and an election was called for May.

Thatcher, aided by a media campaign which suggested mounting middle-class hysteria, attacked the unions and argued, effectively enough, that Labour's claim to be able to secure union wage restraint was empty. The state, she declared, was a rigid, overgrown and parasitic obstacle to economic recovery, not an instrument of prosperity or welfare. She promised to cut income tax as well as state spending and adopted a position on immigration that was seen by some as explicitly racist. The result was a massive swing of 2.2 million votes to the Conservatives (including an 18% swing among skilled manual workers), producing a Conservative majority of 41. The SNP paid the price of their pique, being reduced from 11 MPs to two. In the accelerating development of the crisis, the moment of 'Thatcherism' had arrived.

The New Conservative Project of Margaret Thatcher

The failure of the 'social contract' as a basis for economic recovery had finally driven British politics towards a radical realignment. For the first time the leadership of a major party was committed to a project which went to the heart of the relationship between capital and labour. Thatcher had long subscribed to the individualist, anti-state, anti-union, anti-egalitarian views of her party's right wing. Shortly before her election as leader she also adopted the 'social market' and monetarist economic doctrines to which her friend and counsellor Sir Keith Joseph had recently been converted. Unlike the 'competition policy' of Edward Heath, Thatcher's vision meant abandoning, as fast as electoral considerations allowed, the welfare state; effecting the decisive reduction in trade union power from which Heath had drawn back after the failure of his 1971 Industrial Relations Act; and overcoming social and cultural resistance to a new order based on hard work, inequality, and the firm imposition of authority in the workshop and in the streets, by means of 'firm government' and an ideological crusade lasting, if necessary, for a decade or more. Whether realistic or not, the new strategy had a coherent logic. Unlike Heath, its proponents were not only ready to accept the social costs of restoring 'incentives' by creating mass unemployment, but judged that the public could be persuaded to accept them too.

The ideological movement which 'Thatcherism' represented was as important as its economic policies, and perhaps more so. Some observers argued that its long-run significance would be primarily in the extent to which it succeeded in completing the break-up of the amalgam of ideas which composed the post-war social-democratic consensus (Fabian faith in the state, Keynesian commitment to full employment, and Liberal commitment to social security); and only secondarily in what it achieved through economic policies in office.[8] The campaign to link the pro-market, anti-state doctrines of Thatcherism to popular Conservative themes such as the call for 'law and order' versus 'crime' and 'terrorism', 'the family' versus 'vandalism' or 'permissiveness', 'hard work' versus 'welfare scroungers', and so on – certainly gave it more popular appeal than the Labour Left's advocacy of the Alternative Economic Strategy (see pages 96–97) which had no such 'populist' dimension.

Moreover, the 'consensus' values which it attacked had already been seriously undermined. The Labour Party could no longer deliver material rewards to the workers when in office; the credibility of the Fabian, full-employment welfare state had been seriously undermined. The state which people encountered as school parents or state employees, or when they were retired, unemployed, or sick, often seemed patronising, bureaucratic and mean, rather than an instrument of the popular will. The working class itself had been undergoing some profound changes, too, as we shall see in Chapters 7 and 8. The 'common style of proletarian life' of the 1930s and '40s, with which the welfare state had been so intimately linked, had begun to break up. For both these reasons commitment to the 'welfare state' was no longer 'second nature', as it had been for the previous generation. It was no longer unthinkable for workers to be hostile to the state; it was even possible for Thatcher to win an election on a platform explicitly *attacking* equality.

But in the short run the internal contradictions of Thatcherism as a strategy of economic management and reconstruction seemed liable to offset whatever ideological appeal it might possess. It is hard to compress into a short formula the policies of the Thatcher government from 1979 to 1981, since they aimed at a comprehensive re-ordering of government priorities, public attitudes and the political and industrial balance of power. Their common source of inspiration was 'neo-liberalism' – replacing the welfare state by the incentives of the market far more systematically and comprehensively than anything attempted by Heath in the early 1970s. At least three major themes are discernible – 'monetarism', 'supply-side economics', and what may be called 'class-war politics'. 'Monetarism' refers to the idea that the principal economic task of the state should be to keep the growth in the supply of money in line with the growth of output. This done, inflation must eventually disappear. In particular, if workers demand, and receive, wage increases larger than the increases in output they produce, their employers will be unable to finance this by borrowing, and workers will be laid off until wage settlements are in line with productivity. 'Supply-side economics' refers to the view that the obstacles to growth do not lie with limited demand, as Keynesian thinking was supposed to assume, but in factors inhibiting the supply of goods – such as too large a public sector 'crowding out' the private sector (by creating shortages of labour or capital, or by taxing away the incentive to make profits) or trade unions' restrictive practices. 'Class-war politics' (not, of course, a term used by the supporters of Thatcherism) refers to the redistribution of class power in a wide variety of spheres, from industrial relations to education and health services.

These ideas converged in specific policies, especially in public-spending cuts, which were intended (a) to reduce the money supply by reducing state borrowing (the Public Sector Borrowing Requirement, or PSBR); (b) to reduce the share of the state and increase the share of the private sector in total spending; and (c) generally to reduce the 'social wage' – collective consumption – which was more important to wage-workers than to the middle classes.

The main measures implemented in the years 1979 to 1981 were:

1 *Public spending cuts* Thatcher sought cuts of £8 billion, or roughly ten per cent, in total government spending over three years. £7 billions' worth of cuts (except in defence spending, which was supposed to rise by three per cent per annum in real terms) had been imposed by early 1981. The cuts fell on road-building, house-building, and nationalised industry investment of all kinds. They

also fell on recurrent expenditure and were meant to lead to reductions in central and local government employment as well as employment in the nationalised industries. Nationalised industries were instructed to 'break even' within two years.

2 *'Privatisation'* Forty-nine per cent of the government's shares of British Petroleum were sold, and a majority of the shares in Cable and Wireless; plans were announced for selling minority shareholdings in British Airways, and in the British National Oil Corporation. The National Enterprise Board with its collection of former 'lame ducks' was run down as far as possible; nationalised industries were instructed to sell off various assets, such as the urban real estate owned, for example, by British Rail on or near its main line stations. Council house tenants were given the right to buy their houses at a 30% discount on the 1980 market price, thus fulfilling the Conservative aim of a 'property-owning democracy'.

3 *Money Supply* The money supply was set to rise at well below the current rate of inflation by cutting the PSBR and raising the Minimum Lending Rate to the unprecedented level of 17% from November 1979 to June 1980.

4 *Fiscal Policy* The June 1979 budget of Sir Geoffrey Howe cut income tax, as promised in the election campaign, but sharply increased the Value Added Tax (indirect taxation). The resulting overall tax reduction was large for those in the top income brackets, but negligible for those in the lowest.

5 *Industrial Relations* The Employment Act of 1980 banned 'flying pickets' (the importation of union pickets from other work-sites) and sympathetic strikes, and restricted 'secondary action' and the closed shop. The government dropped all consultation with the TUC and (with one exception – see below, p. 95) made a great show of refusing to be drawn – at least not openly – into industrial disputes. The days when 'both sides' in major disputes expected to be summoned to discussions at 10 Downing Street were over.

6 *Social Policies* 'Comprehensivisation' of the remaining grammar and secondary modern schools was halted. Funds were provided to local authorities to pay for selected pupils to attend private schools. Private medical care was encouraged. Charges for services under the National Health Service were increased. Police and military pay was dramatically raised.

The most immediate results of Thatcherism in practice were a spectacular deflation, combined with a sharp *increase* in the rate of monetary inflation (from 11% in May 1979 to 22% in the second quarter of 1980), a sharp *increase* in the growth of the money supply, a *growth* of the state's share of GDP, and even a *rise* in the level of taxation. These results – the precise opposite of what Thatcher had promised – flowed from three main contradictions in the programme: the contradictions inherent in monetarism as a strategy of deflation, the contradictions of market doctrine, and the contradiction between the government's commitment to neo-liberalism and its attachment to privilege.

The fundamental contradiction of monetarism lay in its only partially-acknowledged aim of reducing trade union power by means of a level of deflation which would drastically increase unemployment. This was dictated by the discouraging example of Heath's experience in 1972–4, when he tried to curb union power by comprehensive legislation. But coming on the heels of three years of expenditure cuts by the Labour Chancellor, Healey, and in the midst of a world depression, the result was a national slump. Officially-recorded unemployment rose from 1.6 million (over six per cent) in 1979 to nearly 3 million (12 per cent) by December 1981, almost a million more than the government had predicted a year earlier. (In fact, even the official figure was about a million less than the real total, ignoring, as it did, those, mainly women, who were available for work but did not register as unemployed; the true rate of unemployment was 16 per cent).[9]

Unemployment on this scale meant a large drop in home demand, declining profits and a record level of bankruptcies. GDP fell by five per cent between May 1979 and December 1981. Manufacturing output fell 15% in 1980 alone. Like all its predecessors, the government talked constantly about the recovery to come in a year or two, but even its warmest sympathisers found this hard to envisage.[10] As output contracted, government spending on unemployment rose, with the result that the state's share of GDP was three per cent higher in 1981 than it had been in 1978–9, with a parallel surge in the growth of the money supply. By 1981 the burden of financing unemployment had reached the point where the prospect of tax cuts, which had been a major part of the Conservative election campaign in 1979, was dwindling.* Inflation had also been increased, first by a big shift to indirect taxation and then by the price increases imposed by the nationalised industries as a result of the government's anti-subsidy policy.† The problem was that a deflation sufficient to

* In March 1980 the Treasury had forecast scope for tax cuts of £2.9 bn. in 1982–3, and £4.1 bn. in 1983–4. In March 1981 – these forecasts had fallen to £1 bn. and £2 bn. respectively – less than the personal tax *increases* of 1980 and 1981. The March 1982 Budget for 1982–3 arguably did not reduce taxation at all, but redistributed it from employers to employees.

† In the six months ending in March 1981 the prices of food, clothing and household goods rose by only 2%: the prices of coal, electricity, gas, etc., rose 27% (W. Eltis in the *Sunday Times*, 8 March 1981). By the end of 1981, however, the rate of inflation was still higher than it had been in May 1979.

achieve the government's *political* goals (in relation to the unions) severely damaged the economy's remaining productive potential, as well as leading to other consequences which flatly contradicted the beliefs of monetarism.

There were two main contradictions in 'market doctrine'. In the first place, the economy was not a system of perfect competition, so that 'market forces' did not produce the results theoretically ascribed to them. This was immediately noticeable in the public sector, where spending cuts led to reduced services, but not to greatly reduced staff. It was also obvious that small business could not play the regenerative role in manufacturing which Thatcherite theory assigned to it; it tended to be the large corporations which could both weather deflation on this scale and develop market-leading innovations.

Secondly, there was a serious contradiction between the Thatcher government's dependence on a *national* economic regeneration, and the *international* nature of the market to which it looked for the forces to bring about efficiency. For instance, international market forces in the production of cars pointed to a drastic contraction of British production, beginning with the elimination of British Leyland, the only significant British-owned producer remaining of those that had been taken over by the state as 'lame ducks' under the Wilson government in 1975. Faced with its imminent collapse, the government found itself agreeing to very large additional state funding as a lesser evil than that of allowing a work-force estimated at up to 700,000 (including suppliers, dealers, etc.) to be added to the social security bill.

The contradiction between neo-liberalism and the government's attachment to privilege was revealed in its lack of interest in a radical reform of the state and 'civil society' – the private social and economic framework of British life. The notorious inefficiences of British life, from the secretive and ineffectual system of state economic policy-making to the archaic systems of taxation, banking, and law, the insanely slow and costly system of real-estate conveyance, and an educational system as spectacularly inadequate in its day as it had been in 1900 – such spheres were not objects of Mrs Thatcher's concern.* She distrusted the civil service, the universities and the BBC for their past attachment to the social-democratic consensus, but her 'populism' stopped short of a radical assault on the

* At a time when the Danish government sought to ensure mass competence in the use of electronic calculators by issuing them free to every school child, and the Japanese government's long-term aim was to give every member of the population higher education, in Britain only 30% of manual workers had any vocational qualifications (compared with 60% in Germany); only 13% of the age-group were in higher education (compared with 19% in Germany and 39% in Japan); and nearly one adult in three could not divide 65 by 5 (results of a survey carried out for the Cockroft Committee on the teaching of mathematics, reported in *The Times*, 27 Jan 1982). Meantime the Thatcher government was reducing by 20,000 (8%) the number of students to be admitted to university from 1982–3.

structures on which the establishment's power rested, perhaps because she and the middle class were too attached to them.

Some of these contradictions converged in a policy crisis in November 1980, when some limited U-turns were executed. A £4 billion commitment was made to preserving the state-owned steel industry from extinction, and a £1.1 billion commitment to British Leyland. These measures were followed in February 1981 by a dramatic government retreat in face of a threatened mineworkers' strike. The issue here was a proposal to accelerate the National Coal Board's programme of pit closures, primarily in order to cut back coal production which, thanks to the big drop in demand for energy resulting from deflation, was leading to the accumulation of costly excess stocks. The National Union of Mineworkers threatened to strike. The government agreed to abandon the accelerated closure programme and to find an unspecified sum (at least £70 million) for the National Coal Board to cover its losses on excess production. Meantime, frustrated by the scale of public sector pay increases in 1979–80, the government announced a ceiling of six per cent on public sector pay increases, to be enforced through 'cash limits', for 1980–1 – in other words, public sector wage controls.

The rest of 1981 saw no relief from the government's policy failures, but no change of basic policy either, apart from a modest reduction of interest rates. The level of strikes had fallen to the lowest point since 1976, which was not unconnected with the fact that unemployment, close to four million and still rising, was costing the unions a loss of some 10,000 members every week. The balance of payments was also stronger than ever, thanks to the degree of deflation and the contribution of North Sea oil output. Manufacturing productivity had risen, but largely due to the closure of marginal plants and to lay-offs. In fact, it seemed that the rise was no greater than in earlier recessions, while manufacturing investment was down by a quarter (below the rate of replacement). Thus, government claims that a radical transformation was in progress rested almost wholly on the view that reduced manning and improved work practices induced by deflation would continue into reflation and *then* be matched by large investments.[11] But even the most optimistic of the serious forecasting models expected only minimal growth over the next four years, and a further increase in unemployment.[12] The government blamed the world recession but most indicators were worse for Britain than for other industrial countries.* There was no doubt that the deflation caused by monetarist policies – the maintenance of a high exchange rate, high interest rates and a drastic reduction in the 'true' level of government

* There was also a very large increase in the outflow of funds into investment abroad – a net flow of £8 billion in the eighteen months from January 1980 to June 1981.

borrowing (i.e., borrowing other than that required to pay for the extra unemployment created) – had made matters substantially worse. Government spokesmen still talked of a future recovery on a 'leaner, fitter' industrial base, but few commentators were convinced.

Yet – it was doubtful how many people cared. The most remarkable feature of the situation at the end of 1981 was that, in spite of real unemployment of 16% (20% or more in many cities), in spite of real cuts in personal incomes for the majority of those still in work (due partly to wage settlements below the rate of inflation and partly to increased taxation of all but the richest), and in spite of the growing conviction, even among commentators who had been attracted to monetarism, that the government's policies had, if anything, made industrial recovery less rather than more likely, the 'neo-conservative' mood remained strong. In 1979 Thatcher had campaigned strongly on the themes of opposition to the welfare state, support for private rather than collective consumption, competition and inequality. Research by the Institute for Economic Affairs (a right-wing 'think tank') had shown these ideas to be quite popular among former Labour voters, especially skilled manual workers, and it was indeed this group who swung most strongly to the Conservatives. Two-and-a-half years later there was little sign that these social attitudes had changed.

Moreover the Conservatives' electoral prospects were by no means hopeless. This was partly thanks to divisions within the Labour Party, and the formation of the SDP which drew support from Labour as well as from Conservatives in the opinion polls. But these developments themselves were due to the crisis. The Conservatives had proved that savage deflation, on the scale of the 1930s, no longer carried an automatic electoral penalty as had formerly been believed. The 'moderates' in the Conservative leadership who argued in the autumn of 1981 that the level of deflation being inflicted could destroy the party had not yet been shown – in any obvious way – to be correct. That the new Conservative project contained the germs of an industrial renaissance seemed improbable. But it was not out of the question that it foreshadowed a durable change in the mode of defence of the capitalist social and political order in Britain.

The Labour Left Alternative

When the new right came to power in the Conservative Party an opposite tendency was gaining ground in the Labour Party, but less decisively. The failures of the Wilson government in the sixties, and the militancy of the union rank and file, led to the adoption of much more radical policies by party conferences after the 1970 defeat. Out of these emerged an 'Alternative Economic Strategy' which gradually crystallised as the left's response to the crisis of the economy. The essential elements were economic expansion, led by increased state expenditure; a reduced working week of 35 hours, to spread employment; nationalisation of some 25 major companies and all banks, and planning agreements (reinforced by industrial democracy) for the rest of the large-firm sector; and import controls, to permit expansion to take place without precipitating a new balance of payments crisis (most observers agreed that British manufacturing was now so weak that even the large contribution of North Sea oil would not be enough to avert a payments problem in any large-scale reflation). Prices would also be controlled, but not wages. Most of the strategy's supporters also advocated withdrawal from the EEC in order to recover the freedom of action necessary to implement this strategy. This latter argument had been defeated in the 1975 referendum, and Wilson and Healey had also abandoned the other elements of the strategy; but it became common ground for the various 'left' tendencies in the party and was reasserted by a large majority at the 1979 Party Conference.

Among its many problems the most obvious was that the strategy assumed that a Labour government would be able to secure from the private sector (by competition from 'selectively' nationalised firms, by state control of investment funds and by planning agreements plus worker representatives on boards of directors) what the private sector had not given to Heath – namely, massive new investment. Moreover, this would be expected to happen in the context of controlled prices and, presumably, revived trade union strength. As critics to the left of the Labour Party pointed out, this seemed to assume away the problem caused by lack of 'business confidence' in the past. Only experience could show whether this was wishful thinking, and whether the strategy really implied going beyond a state-led mixed economy to a wholly state-owned, socialist economy – and whether political support for this could be secured.

Down to 1981, however, its advocates inside the Labour party were less concerned with such problems, critical as they were, than with the problem of how to ensure that any such alternative strategy would ever be put to the test of experience – how to ensure that, in future, a Labour government would not abandon radical strategies adopted by the party conference. Seeing the history of the party as a series of such 'betrayals', the Labour left – its ranks swollen by a new influx into the party of activists, including Marxists of various tendencies – concentrated most of its energy after 1975 on a struggle to make the parliamentary wing of the party more effectively responsible to the party outside parliament. In this they were aided by a growing impatience among many trade union activists. In 1979 the Conference finally endorsed two of the three internal reforms for which the left had been pressing: the National Executive would have final control over the content of election manifestos (rather than the leader alone); and Labour MPs would be required to submit to 'reselection' by their constituency parties between general elections. In September 1980 the Conference also decided that the Party leader himself would no longer be chosen by the Labour Members of Parliament, but would be elected by an electoral college in which constituency and union representatives would also take part. The precise formula for the electoral college was to be determined at a special conference at Wembley in January 1981.

Faced with this development, in October 1980 Callaghan announced his retirement, with a view to allowing a 'moderate' leader to be chosen under the existing rules. The leading candidate was Denis Healey, the former Chancellor of the Exchequer, whose choicest invective was apt to be reserved for the party's left wing (they must, he said, be 'out of their tiny Chinese minds'). MPs hesitated to plunge the party into the struggle which this intransigence portended and chose instead Michael Foot. Foot was a former leader of the party's left-wing Tribune Group, lukewarm towards the EEC, committed to unilateral nuclear disarmament, and broadly sympathetic to the Alternative Economic Strategy. On the other hand he was a strong 'parliamentarian' who was not closely identified with the left's drive for extra-parliamentary control. Before the Wembley special Conference the National Executive adopted Foot's compromise proposal for an electoral college for the leadership, in which half the delegates would be MPs. But the Conference supported a formula which gave forty per cent of the delegates to the unions and only thirty per cent each to the MPs and to representatives of the constituency parties.

The stage was set for a trial of strength between left and right within the party. The reselection process led to the readoption of most sitting Labour MPs, including those on the right wing of the party, except in cases where there was also a history of personal animosity between the MP and the local party, often due to the MP's neglect of the constituency. Much more dramatic was the decision by Tony Benn to contest the annual election for the Deputy Leadership (a purely symbolic office held by Denis Healey), an election which was covered by the new electoral college rules. Benn was narrowly defeated, after a bruising campaign lasting through the summer of 1981.

A 'Centre' Option

But the struggle between left and right had meantime precipitated a breakaway by four former ministers on the right of the party (Roy Jenkins, Shirley Williams, David Owen and Bill Rodgers) who formed the Social Democratic Party in March 1981. By the end of the year it had been joined by 26 Labour MPs, including some whose reselection prospects were doubtful, and one Conservative. It had also gained a new MP as a result of Shirley Williams's decisive victory in a by-election in November. At the end of the year the Alliance of the SDP and the Liberal Party was attracting substantially more support in opinion polls than either the Conservatives or the Labour Party. Some of this support was undoubtedly ephemeral but the new 'centre' force could not be ignored.*

Its significance was that the major parties were being pushed by the crisis away from the 'middle ground' which they had occupied in practice – and since 1950 largely in rhetoric too – for forty years. 'Moderate' MPs of both parties shrank from the implications of this; they wanted to bring their parties back to the middle ground. The possibility of occupying the middle ground with a new party, or a coalition of parties including the Liberals, was more attractive to centrist Labour MPs, who were becoming a minority in the party at large, than to Conservative MPs whose party was in some ways less dependent on its extra-parliamentary organisation, and who did not believe that it would continue to be dominated by Thatcherism.

The electoral prospects of the new Social Democratic Party were problematic, in spite of the evidence of support in opinion polls. Even more problematic were the party's prospects of dealing with the, by now, overwhelming problems of the economy. The Social Democrats' strategy could apparently be summarised as 'a planned mixed economy', an 'incomes policy' (i.e., wage controls) and 'social egalitarianism' – which in so far as it was clear, seemed to be very much the formula followed to so little purpose by the Labour party under Wilson and Callaghan for two decades.† In spite of the nostalgia for the old consensus among many voters and most of the press (whose initial reception of the new party as a prophylactic against the return of a 'Bennite' Labour government bordered on rapture), the relevance of the SDP to the accelerating logic of the British crisis seemed modest.

The essence of the problem was that the political 'middle ground' required a competitive manufacturing sector to sustain it. The reason why the Labour and Conservative parties were being driven off the middle ground was that they had been unable to resurrect this base. That a new party could re-occupy the middle ground, without a formula for re-establishing the necessary industrial foundation, was in the longer run implausible.

* In February 1981 before the party was officially launched between 36% and 39% of people polled said they would support it (ORC poll reported in *The Times*, 9 February 1981). By December 1981 43% of people said they would vote for SDP, Liberal or Alliance candidates if an election were held the next day. Two months later this figure had fallen to 33% (*Sunday Times*, 7 February 1982).

† An unkind reviewer of Shirley Williams's book, *Politics is for People*, writing in *The Economist* of 18 April, 1981, described her vision of the future revealed there as 'Harold Wilson's "white heat of technology" gone vegetarian'.

Liberal Democracy in Question

As the familiar outlines of the party system began to fray under the pressure of the crisis, liberal-democratic politics itself came under threat. The threat was not from the revolutionary left, which had negligible influence and no force at its disposal, nor from the far right, at least in its party-political forms. It came from the state itself; an erosion of civil liberties, a curtailment of effective democratic control, an extension of police powers of suveillance and social control, a redefinition as 'subversive' of previously tolerated forms of dissent and protest.[13] The whole of the army's infantry had been trained in the military control of the civilian population through the campaign in Northern Ireland; the police had been regrouped for political control purposes; and improbable figures toyed with ideas of coups.* It is always difficult to know how seriously to take tendencies of this kind. But it was no longer wholly absurd to ask the question, 'Would a "Left Labour" government be permitted to carry through the Alternative Economic Strategy – let alone a comprehensive nationalisation?' It was no more absurd, at any rate, than to imagine that such a Labour government might come to power. It was, in short, no longer possible to take civil liberties and democratic institutions entirely for granted. Every turn of the screw of economic contraction put them under fresh strain.

* In 1968 the newspaper boss, Cecil King, had touted the idea of a coup against the Wilson government, with Lord Mountbatten as figurehead. In 1974 a retired army officer, General Walker, openly recruited a private army for a possible confrontation with the unions. According to a former security service agent Thatcher's closest political adviser, Airey Neave, MP, discussed with him and other former agents before the 1979 election plans for an undercover 'army of resistance' to prevent Tony Benn from ever becoming Prime Minister (*New Statesman*, 20 February 1981). Neave was assassinated by a group calling itself the Irish National Liberation Army just before polling day.

PART II

7

Capital and Labour

> You know, the shareholders have got the money to buy shares. We haven't got it. So I suppose they have to have them' (worker at ChemCo).[1]

The warp and weft of British society consists of the relations between the owners and the non-owners of its productive resources. These relations are fundamental to the formation and nature of classes and parties, and are implicit in almost every sphere of culture, sacred and profane. But the way classes, parties and culture are based on and refract the relation between capital and labour is complex. This chapter seeks to outline the basic relationship at its most direct and simple level.

Three broad phases of development in the relation between capital and labour can be distinguished: the phase of competitive industrial capitalism, from the late eighteenth century till about 1870; the phase of monopoly capitalism, from about 1870 till about 1930; and from about 1930 onwards, the phase of organised or state-managed capitalism, a phase which includes, from the 1950s onwards especially, the development of multinational production. While it would be wrong to ascribe exceptional importance to any one of these phases, the earlier phases were politically formative, and so it is necessary to pay some attention to them even though contemporary British capitalism exhibits so many differences.

The first phase is important because it was the first, because it was very prolonged, and because it was in certain respects *limited*. Manufacturing capital, employing wage labour directly, developed rapidly – industrial output increased sevenfold between 1800 and 1900 – yet in 1900 non-agricultural production (which included a good deal of essentially pre-industrial activity) still accounted for only 40% of the total national income, compared with 23% in 1800.

Throughout this time a large share of the profits from manufacturing was siphoned off for investment abroad. The vast holdings of overseas assets owned by British capitalists at the end of the century had been built

Table 7.1 Composition of the National Income (1801–1955)

		Agriculture, Forestry and Fishing (%)	Mining, Manufacturing and Building (%)	Trade and Transport (%)	Rent of Dwellings (%)	Others (%)
Great Britain	*1801*	33	23	17	5	22
	1851	20	34	19	8	19
	1901	6	40	23	8	23
	1924	5	40	30	6	19
United Kingdom	*1935*	4	38	30	6	22
	1955	5	48	24	3	20

Source: B. R. Mitchell and P. Deane, *Abstract of British Historical Statistics*, Cambridge University Press, 1962, and B. R. Mitchell and H. Jones, *Second Abstract of British Historical Statistics 1971*.

up largely from the earnings of British manufacturing, especially before 1875.[2]

The urban working class came into being in the same prolonged and qualified process. By 1830, E. P. Thompson has argued, it was already 'made' (or rather, it had already 'made itself' through its resistance to exploitation and repression).[3] Yet in 1831, 28% of all families were still engaged in agriculture; factory work proper was still largely confined to textiles and the north; divisions among workers based on religion, race (the Irish), income and skill, were severe, and prevailing ideas of how to remedy the workers' ills were confused and often impractical.

By 1870 artisanal self-employment was rapidly giving way to wage labour in all sectors, and the Great Depression of 1873 to 1896 accelerated the elimination of agriculture as a major area of employment (by 1901 it accounted for only 8.4% of all employees). However, the small family-firm, using relatively primitive technology, remained a characteristic form of industrial capital, and the highly differentiated workforce was still, in its majority, non-industrial. This was the situation when the formation of capital and labour into organised antagonists entered its decisive stage during the Great Depression, amid bitter struggles which were to leave a permanent mark on the organisation and attitudes of both.

Capital took refuge increasingly in monopoly – in empire markets, in tariffs, and in mergers and cartels – and at the same time employers organised in order to overcome union opposition to wage cuts and the 'dilution' of labour. Concentration of capital accelerated, as the depression eliminated weaker firms and bigger firms found themselves better placed to secure a degree of monopoly, which in turn favoured their growth at the expense of others. The older industrial sectors stagnated and finally began to contract, but not without protracted struggles in which the employees, organised into federations in particular sectors (such as coalmining), tried to survive by weakening the unions and cutting wages – struggles which dominated industrial relations before and after the Great War. The workers, in reply, organised themselves in large 'general' unions (embracing a great variety of occupations in a wide range of industries) with a strongly defensive ethic of class solidarity.

These structures survived into the third, and still continuing, phase with relatively few essential changes. In the period of 'organised' capitalism the oldest economic sectors contracted drastically and in key instances were nationalised (coalmining, railways, steel and shipbuilding). 'White collar', 'service industry' and state employment expanded, leading to changes in the balance of power within the trade union movement but not, on the whole, to changed organisation or strategies. Trade unions followed the concentration of capital with a merger movement of their own, especially from the mid-1960s onwards; but they were not able to match capital's shift to the internationalisation of production. Capital became increasingly able to move production from one part of the world to another, independently of the geographical pattern of demand for products, and to determine independently where profits should appear to accrue; but trade unions developed no significant corresponding powers. These changes had, of course, important political implications.

The Elements of Capital

The most significant recent changes within capital are the sharp increase in concentration, the emergence of new sectors and the decline of older ones, and internationalisation. In manufacturing alone, the largest hundred firms, which accounted for 16% of net output in 1909, accounted for 42% in 1975; and 100 firms owned 79% of the net assets of all quoted commercial and industrial firms.[4] From the point of view of labour, four out of five workers now worked for firms with over 100 employees; less than a quarter of a million worked for firms with fewer than 20 employees. The 'meso-economic sector' was now paramount. Growth of investment and profits was greatest in the food, drink and tobacco sector, and in services and shipping. Not only did the old 'staple' industries decline, but all manufacturing began to decline relative to other sectors even before the dramatic de-industrialisation of the 1970s. The process of internationalisation was very rapid after 1950. By 1979, 31% of British exports were 'intra-firm' transactions and British manufacturing and commercial companies were making over ten per cent of their income abroad. Eighty-two per cent of all exports were due to multinational companies (of which two-fifths were foreign-owned).[5]

Throughout these developments, however, one crucial feature of British capital remained constant – the dominance of financial and commercial capital. The special position of banking and merchant capital arose from their historical priority and their role in the export-based expansion of industry. The export trade was financed by merchant capital and depended on the power of the state, which was financed by banking capital through the public debt. As manufacturing industry expanded, so did the importance of banking and trade; sterling became the supreme international trading currency and London the centre of attraction for foreign investors and borrowers. The City of London, where the banks and insurance, shipping and trading companies were concentrated, became 'the most cosmopolitan element in British society' whose 'wealth and culture wore down the reluctance of the British upper classes to accept even the upper echelons of the Haute Juiverie'.[6] A job in the City – dealing largely with one's social equals and having no direct contact with production – became socially acceptable in a way that industrial management never did, or at least not until the age of the giant firm.

This reinforced the external orientation of British economic policy. The City's interest lay in maintaining a strong pound and freedom of movement for capital, and policies such as protection, devaluation and exchange controls, designed to assist industry, were consistently resisted. In the struggle over tariff reform, after 1902, the City had plenty of allies (in the trade and transport sectors, and among the working classes, who feared increases in food prices), but its later victories are more remarkable. In 1925 Britain went back on the gold standard at the 1914 rate of exchange; this seriously overvalued the pound and sounded the death-knell for many shipyards and textile mills as well as for a large part of the coal industry (still the largest single industry in terms of employment). Even new and relatively efficient manufacturing sectors were severely handicapped.

Bankers' lack of 'confidence' also destroyed not only the second, unlamented Labour government of 1931, but also the only production-oriented economic solution proposed (apart from Mosley's Fascism) for the economic problem at this time, namely, the Macmillan Committee's proposals for making banks become long-term equity investors in manufacturing on German lines.[7] After the Second World War the City's desire to restore British foreign investments and maintain sterling as an international reserve currency led to a persistently overvalued pound and to large outflows of investment overseas at times when domestic investment was increasingly inadequate.* Eventually, as we have seen, the desperate

* 'Official estimates of private long-term investment by Britain in the period 1946–64 gave a cumulative total in the overseas sterling area of £2,900 m, or two-thirds of the total outflow of British private long-term capital, and £1,900 m in the rest of the world put together. This investment in the sterling area was equivalent in money terms to the pre-war accumulation of British investment of the previous hundred years' (S. Strange, *Sterling and British Policy*, Oxford University Press, Oxford 1971, pp. 66–7).

condition of manufacturing forced a change and sterling was 'floated' in 1972. By this time, however, the whole international monetary system was in a state of flux and the City had discovered that when most currencies were 'floating', including the pound, it could still make money as an international financial centre dealing in many other trading currencies.

But the other differences of interest between the City and industrial capital remained. After 1979, for example, the City adopted the tenets of monetarism with an enthusiasm based partly on its anxiety to cut inflation and maintain the value of sterling, but also on the fact that high interest rates, which formed a necessary element of monetarist policy, brought profits to the banks and attracted more foreign capital to London. In 1980 a sharp conflict arose, between manufacturing industry and the City over interest rates. The Director-General of the Confederation of British Industry, Sir Terence Beckett, publicly criticised Mrs Thatcher for maintaining interest rates at a level that was threatening many manufacturers' survival. Though he was rebuked by some 'loyalist' business spokesmen, the government made a compromise reduction in interest rates in the March 1981 budget, and introduced a retroactive tax on some of the banks' windfall profits. This clearly revealed the conflict; but the overall effect of the Thatcher policies (including the lifting of all exchange controls), while theoretically designed to rejuvenate manufacturing, was to consolidate the City's dominance.

Given the relatively limited weight of the interests represented by the City in the economy as a whole (see Table 7.2), it may well seem unreasonable to explain the City's dominance over industry exclusively in terms of its special position in the social structure. In fact, organisational factors also came into play. The Bank of England, though nationalised in 1946, retains its real autonomy, and represents the City's views to the Treasury more intimately and effectively than the CBI represents the views of manufacturing industry. Moreover, the dependence of successive governments on foreign loans when dealing with chronic balance of payments deficits reinforced the City's views. At times like 1966–7, or 1976, foreign bankers' confidence was seen as holding the key to short-term political

Table 7.2 Shares of Gross Domestic Product (1959–1979)

	% of GDP		
	1959	*1969*	*1979*
Insurance, banking finance and business services	3.0	6.8	9.0
Distributive trades	12.6	10.6	10.5
Manufacturing	35.6	33.0	27.9

Source: *Annual Abstracts of Statistics*, HMSO, London.

survival, and before North Sea oil came on stream this dependence was such that deference to City opinion tended to become axiomatic for Treasury policy-makers.

By 1981 it almost seemed that the City's dominance had become self-perpetuating. By then it was clear that British industry needed radical re-construction and very large injections of investment funds. Revenues from North Sea production, and its contribution to the balance of payments, appeared to afford an opportunity to provide both. But, by this time, the key sectors of industry were owned by multinationals which were unlikely to make the long-term investment that was needed in a country which was a political 'trouble spot'; the non-oil balance of payments deficit was now so wide that oil production only covered it in conditions of severe deflation; and the revenues from oil production were largely committed to paying for unemployment and for tax reductions for the well-to-do.

What is striking, as one reflects on this pattern of events, is not just the strength of banking and commercial capital in determining policy, but also the political weakness of manufacturing capital. As its position deteriorated, so its opposition to policies oriented towards the interests of finance and trade stiffened, but it was notably unsuccessful in proposing a convincing industrial strategy of its own. With the exception of Chamberlain's imperial project the leaders of British manufacturing industry have not conceived of a *political* order in which productive capital would set state policy and dominate the national culture.[8] They have been more influenced by fear – fear of competition, fear of labour, and fear of the state. As Crouch commented in 1979,

> any move against the City would undoubtedly mean, in the British political context, increased government involvement in investment, probably with a significant trade-union role. Industrialists feel much less threatened by the City, responsive after all to capitalist interests, than by government (especially a Labour one) and union intervention in the issue – investment – that constitutes capital's main power base within society.[9]

In general, Crouch added,

> employers want a government which keeps out of industry (but bails out, on industry's terms, firms which get into difficulties); which does not allow the level of unemployment to get too low (but keeps the economy buoyant); which keeps control of trade unions and income growth (but does not get in employers' way when so doing)... The position adopted also varies with distance from the national centre [the CBI in London]. The inability of the centre to coordinate the periphery [i.e., the firms throughout the industrial areas of the country], but corresponding failure of the latter to generate any consistent strategy, is a mark of the irresolute position of British capital as it stands somewhere between liberalism and corporatism.[10]

This irresolution has probably been compounded by multinationalisation.

> The fact that the industrial sector is completely dominated by multinationals implies that it shares various immediate interests with finance, namely the desire to keep open the option of capital export, and has good reason to follow the City's lead in matters of industrial policy even if the consequence is erosion of the home base to some degree.[11]

It is even likely that, for many companies, the concept of a 'home-base' was losing much of its former significance.

Compared with the difference of interests between money and manufacturing capital, other divisions have been of modest importance. The unhappiness of small business in face of galloping concentration and the tendency of fiscal policy to be focused on the needs of big companies was an important factor in the emergence of Thatcherism. It led to panegyrics for small business at Conservative Party conferences, and to various measures of relief for small business in the budgets of 1979–81. It was very doubtful, however, if this would slow down the growth in the weight and influence of large companies. Another cleavage exists between nationalised and private industries. There were some notable instances of nationalised industry chairmen resisting government policies designed to subordinate their interests to those of the private sector. But, on the whole, publicly-owned capital was run just like (and as a support for) private capital (see Chapter 13).*

The Organisation of Capital

Capital was represented by five main types of organisation of capital: employers' federations; industrial and trade associations; the Bank of England; the Confederation of British Industry; and a cluster of research, propaganda and espionage organisations.

Employers' federations date back to the days of the Great Depression of 1873–96 and the attempt to defeat the trade unions. Periodically this endeavour is revived, a recent example being the unsuccessful attempt by the Engineering Employers' Federation to defeat the Amalgamated Union of Engineering Workers in a two-month confrontation in the late summer of 1979. But the federations lost their prime purpose when the unions won financial security under the Trade Disputes Act of 1906. Their effectiveness was further undermined by the growth of plant-level bargaining,

* An instance of the first of these points was the resignation in 1980 of the Post Office chairman, Sir William Barlow, over the government's hiving-off of its profitable communication services to private enterprise, while preventing the Post Office from borrowing in the open market to maintain its own modernisation programme. As an instance of the second point, see the 'compromise' worked out within the Confederation of British Industry to allow the nationalised industries to belong to it: 'The nationalized industries are also members; they share in the framing of industrial relations policy but not in policy on the question of public ownership itself (enabling the CBI to maintain its strong hostility to nationalization)'.(!)[12]

which reflected the uneven ability of employers to pay a nationally-agreed wage, as well as the absence of industry-wide unions (see page 117). However, the federations played a significant part in the passage of the anti-union legislation of 1980–2, which went a long way to restore the legal advantages which employers had enjoyed over trade unions before 1906.

The Confederation of British Industry was formed in 1965 out of the former Federation of British Industry and the National Association of British Manufacturers, which had represented smaller companies. It was a merger strongly encouraged by the Wilson government and one which reflected the rapid advance of industrial concentration at that time. From the mid-1970s the CBI began to voice, with increasing urgency, the needs of industrial capital as a whole, and, in purely organisational terms, was well equipped to do so. With an annual budget of over £6 million it made constant representations to all the economic departments of state, collaborated with them in collecting economic statistics, and represented capital *vis-à-vis* labour on a large number of state advisory bodies. The weaknesses of the CBI – which, after all, presided over an industrial decline of unprecedented proportions in the years after its formation – sprang from the fundamental political shortcomings of British industrial capital, not from organisational inadequacy.

Even after 1979 the CBI refrained from attacking some policies, such as the maintenance of a high value for sterling, which handicapped British manufacturing exports and facilitated the penetration of the home market by foreign goods. CBI policy reflected the weight of the large multinational companies, of which a very important segment – notably the oil companies, and the manufacturers of 'packaged goods' with high import content, such as processed foods, for the home market – benefited from a strong pound. Similarly, the CBI declined to call for measures to oblige the banks to invest long term in manufacturing, or to prevent capital being invested abroad. The truth was, that the CBI reproduced within itself the structural peculiarities of British capital which lay at the heart of Britain's industrial problem. It did not act as a voice for the single-minded pursuit of policies to construct an internationally competitive industrial complex in Britain.

The most consistent political thrust of capital, in fact, was expressed as much by the cluster of propaganda and union-breaking organisations which it finances as it was by the CBI. These fell broadly into two categories. Research and propaganda organisations, such as the Institute of Directors, the Institute of Economic Affairs, the Institute for the Study of Conflict, AIMS (of Freedom and Enterprise) and the Freedom Association, provided ideological support through conferences, pamphlets and other media; collectively they played an important role in developing and popularising the 'new right' and 'social market' doctrines which gained ascendancy in the late 1970s. Espionage and 'union-busting' organisations included the Economic League, Common Cause and British United Industrialists. These specialised in blacklisting union activists, infiltrating unions, financing court proceedings against unions and the like. One estimate put the finances provided by capital to this last group of organisations at a level greater than the funds of the Conservative and Labour parties combined, in an election year.[13]

Labour

The nature and pattern of work, and hence of the workforce, altered with the changes in British capital. First, the workforce employed in farming went on declining until, by the end of the seventies, only 394,000 people, or just 1.7% of all employees, were on the land, compared with 1,386,000, or 8.4% in 1901. The virtual completion of the urbanisation process in Britain by 1900 helps to explain the peculiarly defensive solidarity of the British labour movement. By that time there was no agrarian alternative, in an economy which seemed decreasingly able to afford the workers a decent existence (no fewer than 2.3 million people emigrated over the decade and a half before the First World War). It was clear that most people's situation could be improved only through solidarity in struggles to change the existing framework. This understanding lasted until the 1950s.

Second, major changes occurred in the employment of women. Broadly speaking, married women, who had begun to be withdrawn from productive work by the beginning of the century, were drawn back into it (or forced back through economic pressure) in the two world wars and in the 1960s and 1970s. Meantime, single women moved out of domestic service (which in 1931 still accounted for 23% of all women in employment), partly into unskilled or semi-skilled manual work (especially in the new service industries), but above all into clerical work (which accounted for about 40% of all women workers by the end of the 1970s). By 1975, 55.5% of all women of working age worked, mainly in low-paid jobs, and accounted for 38% of the workforce.

Third, there was a marked decline in 'manual labour'. This needs to be treated with caution. Although the figures suggest that the proportion of men in manual work fell from 75% in 1921 to 61% in 1975 (and the proportion of women from 68% to 44% over the same period), a significant part of the change is really a change from one kind of manual work to another, which is classified as 'non-manual' for reasons that are ultimately ideological.[14] This is obvious in the case of women junior clerical workers, whose work is hardly less manual or more 'mental' than that of most skilled manual workers, yet who are classified as 'junior non-manual workers'. Much of the shift was due to the growth of work of this kind, and the final disappearance of still essentially pre-industrial forms of manual work, some of them very skilled, which were relics of the earlier years of capitalism. Most of the new non-manual jobs were hardly 'middle-class' occupations.[15] On the other hand, there *was* also an increase in the share of supervisory and semi-professional work; and even where the new 'non-manual' work was 'low level', the change was a real one and had ideological and political consequences. The new work might be no less tedious – in fact it might be more tedious – but it was often less exhausting and usually carried with it better working conditions and slightly higher status. Moreover, much manual work itself had become less dependent on strength. A workforce that is nearly half 'white collar' and predominantly employed by large organisations is a *different* workforce from one in which 70% were manual workers, working largely for small family-firms, many of them as, what the Victorians called, 'common labourers'.

Fourth, by 1978, 29.7% of all workers and 32.9% of all women workers were in the state sector. This was an ambivalent change. It freed an important segment of the workforce from direct dependence on private employment, yet at the same time increased the risk of divisions within the workforce, especially between workers paid out of taxes and those who

Table 7.3 Women in the workforce (1911–1971)

	Women in each category (%)		
	1911	*1951*	*1971*
Employers and proprietors	18.8	20.0	24.9
White collar workers	29.8	42.3	47.9
(a) managers and administrators	19.8	15.2	21.6
(b) higher professionals	6.0	8.3	9.9
(c) lower professionals and technicians	62.9	53.5	52.1
(d) foremen and inspectors	4.2	13.4	13.1
(e) clerks	21.4	60.2	73.2
(f) salesmen and shop assistants	35.2	51.6	59.8
Manual workers	30.5	26.1	29.4
(a) skilled	24.0	15.7	13.5
(b) semi-skilled	40.4	38.1	46.5
(c) unskilled	15.5	20.3	37.2
Total occupied population	29.6	30.8	36.5

Source: C. Hakim, *Occupational Segregation*, Department of Employment, 1979 (cited in A. Coote and B. Campbell, *Sweet Freedom*, Picador, London 1982, p. 77).

were not. The Thatcherite appeal to public resentment of the capitalist state could be, and was, extended to generate hostility between state and non-state employees.

On the other hand, as state employment expanded, workers in this sector were particularly exposed to the efforts of successive governments to curb wage increases. From the sixties some public-sector unions began to play the sort of militant role formerly played only by the big industrial private-sector unions (for instance, low-paid public sector workers played a large part in the 'winter of discontent' of 1978–9).

Fifth, and last, there were important changes in the level and distribution of incomes. After 1945 there was a large increase in average real earnings, which sharply distinguished this period from the preceding fifty years. The increase continued in the sixties and seventies, despite Britain's lagging productivity, partly thanks to trade union strength, and partly because people worked long hours.* At the same time, poverty 'reappeared'.

The reasons for the re-emergence of a distinct group, 'the poor', were complex, but several major components stand out. First, there were people who were dependent on state pensions or social security payments which were fixed at a grossly inadequate level, such as retired workers and their wives, widows, sick or disabled workers and their families, single-parent families (which accounted for five per cent of the population). Second, there were unemployed workers and their families – one in eight by 1981, very unevenly distributed between regions.† Third, there were workers in low-paid, often poorly unionised jobs, mainly in low-productivity sectors (such as catering, cleaning and distribution). What all these categories had in common was that incomes were so low that they depended on further 'supplementary benefits' provided by the state to bring them *up to* the official 'poverty level'.‡

Speaking generally, it is clear that the changes outlined here implied major alterations in the consciousness and internal relations of the working class, and the need for major developments in union organisation and strategy.

* Male manual workers, in particular, worked a lot of overtime in order to maintain their incomes, averaging 45.7 hours a week in 1978. Over a quarter of them worked more than 49 hours a week – longer hours, for much lower wages, than workers in other major EEC countries.

† For instance, in January 1981 unemployment was 6.8% in the South East, 11.3% in the West Midlands, 13.4% in Wales and 17.2% in Northern Ireland (seasonally unadjusted figures including school-unemployed). The crisis, experienced as a disaster in some industrial towns, was barely perceptible in some areas of the South and East Anglia.

‡ At the end of 1981, for example, unemployment benefit for a single person was worth 15.9% of average earnings for a male manual worker. Even in 1977, over a fifth of all households were living *mainly* on social security benefits; 18% of all households received less than 5% of their income from wages.

Before considering these issues, however, it is worth reflecting briefly on the nature of work, as it emerged in the age of organised, large-scale capitalism in the crucial industrial sector of the economy.

It is sobering to read the sociological evidence collected on this question, by Huw Beynon and his colleagues, in a pioneering series of studies in the sixties and seventies. What they consistently show is how, in spite of so many changes, so little seemed to have changed in essentials. This was not so hard to understand, perhaps, on the production line at Ford's Halewood factory in Liverpool, where the workers were under pressure to speed up the work, but with fewer workers ('reduced manning ratios'), and where nothing had been done to reduce the alienation for which assembly-line work is so notorious. But what of 'ChemCo', one of the most modern chemical plants in Britain, with a 'New Working Agreement' to raise productivity, with high wages by British standards – only 20% below Dutch and German wages in 1967 – and with a 'co-operative' trade-union branch? In the end the problem remained that 'nobody cared'. The work was still boring, noisy, sometimes dangerous and – for a surprising number of workers – often plain, muscular, heavy labour, that left you finished at 45.

> One worker – the only one at Riverside who refused to talk to us – summed up his job like this: 'It's f—— awful. Just do it. That's all. *Do it.*'[16]

But many didn't do it, as waste, absenteeism, and general underperformance at ChemCo showed.

Of course, there were many people in Britain, as elsewhere, who liked their work, not all of them in creative or materially advantageous occupations. But not many of these worked for the 'hundred or so gigantic corporations' on which Britain's economic welfare ultimately depended. Among those who did, few were socialists. Many more were concerned only with what they saw as an inevitable and interminable struggle to limit, wherever possible, the stress and unpleasantness of their work, and to maximise their wages and security. It was under these conditions, even when they seemed little different from those in similar plants elsewhere, that British management seemed by and large unable to match the competition. By 1981, unemployment had reduced militancy to a historically low level. But it was still difficult to imagine that it would not revive with any long-term industrial recovery.

The Organisation of Labour

By 1978, 13 million workers, or 55% of all employees, were members of trade unions; most of them voluntarily, some because it was a condition of employment under closed-shop agreements. The percentage was higher than in many other OECD countries, though lower than in Belgium,

Table 7.4 Percentage of all employees who were trade union members in 1978

UK	55
Sweden	80[1]
Belgium	76
Denmark	70–75
Ireland	65
Italy	60
W. Germany	42
Netherlands	37
Canada	31
France	28
USA	22

Note: [1] Data for 1980. W. Korpi (*The Working Class in Welfare Capitalism*, Routledge, London 1978), estimated that over 90% of non-agricultural employees were unionised in Sweden.

Sources: EEC, *Social Indicators for the EEC 1960–1978*, 1980; Labour Canada, *Directory of Labour Organizations in Canada*, 1980; Swedish Central Statistical Office, *Statistical Yearbook 1981*; Bureau of the Census, *Statistical Abstract of the United States 1981*.

Table 7.5 The twenty largest unions, 1982

Trade union	Membership (thousands)
Transport Workers (TGWU)	1,700
Engineers (AUEW)	1,020
Municipal Workers (GMWU)	866
Local Government (NALGO)	796
Public Employees (NUPE)	704
Shopworkers (USDAW)	438
Managerial Staff (ASTMS)	428
Electricians (EEPTU)	395
Builders (UCATT)	275
Miners (NUM)	250
Printers (SOGAT 82)	237
Health Workers (COHSE)	231
Teachers (NUT)	224
Civil Servants (CPSA)	210
Postmen (UCW)	202
Engineers (TASS)	186
Railwaymen (NUR)	160
Bank Staff (BIFU)	148
Printers (NGA)	136
Telecom Staff (POEU)	133

Source: *The Economist*, 11 September 1982.

Denmark, Sweden and Italy (see Table 7.4). The rate of unionisation among men (62%) was much higher than for women (38%). The unions were therefore strong, but not exceptionally so.

By 1979 the vast majority of trade unionists were concentrated in a few, very large unions. The union merger movement of the sixties and seventies had reduced the total number of unions and made the big unions bigger still, while new giant unions emerged in the public sector (NALGO and NUPE). Over eight million workers (63.5% of all trade unionists) belonged to 11 unions having over 250,000 members each; 10.6 million (80.8%) were in unions with 100,000 or more members (see Table 7.5).

These unions were overwhelmingly 'general'. At the end of the nineteenth century, when most of them took their modern form, British industrial capitalism was still in transition from using labour to do work which was still much like that of the pre-industrial era, to modern production based on constant revolutions in technology and hence in work. To organise the great majority of workers, who were still largely unskilled, and employed in a wide range of diverse trades and establishments, the new unions could not – unlike those formed in the 1850s and '60s – consist of workers possessing specific craft skills. The unskilled labourer's

> only chance ... was to recruit into one gigantic union all those who could possibly blackleg on him – in the last analysis every 'unskilled' man, woman or juvenile in the country; and thus to create a vast closed shop.[17]

On the other hand, the 'common labourer' *was* giving way to the partly-skilled, partly-specialised labourer, who could not, without loss, be replaced by a complete novice. So the general unions became, in fact, associations of 'quasi-industrial' unions in a great range of different industries, each local industrial branch enjoying a large measure of autonomy. Then, in the years 1906–14, renewed industrial conflict forced the general unions to organise, in addition, non-local 'trades' (categories of semi-skilled and skilled workers across the country) so that the unions became amalgamations of both 'quasi-industrial' and 'quasi-craft' unions. This process was greatly accelerated after 1918. Conversely, many of the skilled crafts which the earlier unions had organised were gradually displaced by technical change. The engineers' union, for example, originally a union of the 'labour aristocrats' of the steam-engine, gradually came to represent a much larger force of skilled and semi-skilled workers in the metal and machinery industries, through not before many semi-skilled workers in these industries had been organised into other, general unions.

As a result, no modern British union, with the exception of the mineworkers' union, is an industry-wide union covering all the workers in a single field of employment, and very few are still pure 'craft' unions. Most unions have members in many different sectors of the economy, and most plants have workers in several unions. The most characteristic effects of this are:

(a) Wages and conditions are not determined nationally. There are national agreements (made between the leaders of unions and the various employers' federations and associations), but these set only national minima; plant-level bargaining sets the rates and conditions applicable to the unions' members in each particular plant, at whatever levels the companies can afford and the local union negotiators can secure.
(b) In day-to-day industrial relations, each 'shop' or section of a factory has a shop steward, directly elected by the workers in that shop to represent them regardless of the different unions to which they may belong. Shop stewards are co-ordinated by 'convenors', and in the engineering industry, in particular, they constitute the effective voice of the organised workforce. In the mid-1960s the Donovan Commission found that there were about 350,000 shop stewards, operating 'below' the level of the unions' national, district and branch officials, and in many respects being more significant.[18]

The importance of the shop stewards was enhanced by a second distinctive feature of British trade unionism: its substantial freedom from legal regulation, which distinguished it sharply from the position of the unions in Germany, the USA and Canada, in particular. There was no such thing as either a statutory right to strike, or an illegal strike; if workers decided not to work, they simply stopped working. Nor was there any legally prescribed bargaining route, nor was a union prohibited from taking industrial action during the period of an existing agreement.* In short, union-management relations rested only on the relative strengths of the two sides – and their mutual dependence.

* Even those forms of union action which the Thatcher government made unlawful by the Employment Act of 1980 only gave the employer recourse to civil proceedings in a civil court – they did not make the unions or their members liable to prosecution in the criminal courts. The main forms of action made open to civil proceedings by employers by the 1980 Act were 'flying pickets' (i.e., participation in picketing by workers not employed at the place of work picketed, a measure used with exemplary effect in the 1972 miners' strike); and secondary action (i.e., action such as 'blacking' or refusing to handle the products of companies which are not involved in the dispute, unless as near customers or suppliers of the company where the dispute exists). The Act also made it actionable for a union to try to force anyone to join it under a closed shop agreement, and required 80% of the workforce to agree to any new closed shop being set up. The 1982 Employment Act represented a step nearer foreign practice, but did not go the whole way by any means.

This freedom from state control resulted from the Conservatives' and the Liberals' dependence on working-class votes at the peak of Britain's commercial and industrial supremacy in the 1870s. But its survival also reflected the exceptional solidarity of the British working class in the past. Every time that capital sought to reverse the liberalisation of industrial relations adopted at that time, it was eventually forced to return to it – with the Trade Disputes Acts of 1906 and 1946, the abandonment of the Wilson–Castle proposals in 1969, and the repeal, in 1974, of the 1971 Industrial Relations Act. It remained to be seen whether this would also hold true of the Conservative legislation of 1980 and 1982.

In the boom of the 1950s, labour was scarce, wages rose and so did union membership. In engineering, especially, workers wrested from management an unprecedentedly large measure of control over the labour process, significantly reducing 'management prerogatives' – the 'principles that are at stake when the foreman starts to allocate work and the steward retorts "Hang on a minute. *You* tell us what's to be done and *we'll* decide who does it"'.[19]

This was achieved mainly through 'unofficial' strike action, which (unlike the typical 'wildcat' strike in North America) was not illegal but unofficial, in the sense that union officials had not called for it. Unofficial strikes usually lasted for no more than a few days, but by the end of the 1960s they accounted for 95% of all strikes in Britain. It was because of the effectiveness of unofficial strikes that the Wilson and Heath governments both made unsuccessful attempts to change the law. In the end it was only the unemployment induced by the Thatcher government which reduced strike action, including unofficial strikes, to a substantially lower level.

The significance of strikes is debatable. Before 1979 it was commonplace to attribute Britain's economic problems to strikes, but a comparison with other countries does not support this unequivocally. Table 7.6 shows that more days were 'lost' through strikes in Britain than in most other EEC countries, but fewer than in the USA or Canada (where fewer, but much longer, strikes were the rule).

In any case, as Hyman has pointed out, the real cost of days 'lost' through strikes is dubious. Other costs fall when workers are on strike, and lost production is often largely made up when the strike is over. Absences from work due to strikes are modest compared with absences due to illness (10 million person-days compared with well over 310 million due to illness in 1977, for example); or with days lost from industrial accidents, which are often due – as is much of the illness – to inadequate safety precautions and poor working-conditions, not to mention the days lost because of management inefficiency, which are not recorded at all.[20]

It is also important to note that, even in the most militant years, most workers were not involved in any strikes at all (for instance, in the years 1971–3, 83% of all employees were not involved in any strike action.)[21] Strikes were largely confined to industries in trouble, where workers were faced with redundancies, speed-ups or declining pay relative to other sectors, such as the coal industry (which accounted for no less than three-quarters of all stoppages throughout the 1950s), the docks and motor-vehicle industries in the 1960s, and low-paid public sector workers in the late seventies. It is none the less clear that strike action in those years did limit the ability of particular sectors of capital to solve their problems by increasing the rate of exploitation of the labour force, even if the low productivity of British industry cannot plausibly be blamed on strikes.

This fact underlay the intense hostility felt by capital towards the unions, a hostility reflected with growing intensity by the media from the mid-1960s onwards. The militancy of those years also meant that general programmes of wage control could not be made permanent, and that management generally lacked confidence that large increases in profits would follow from large-scale investments.

This situation gave rise to a widespread misunderstanding about the trade unions. Unions were widely judged to have 'too much power', whereas power lay with the unionised rank and file of a few industries where militancy and solidarity were at a high level, rather than with the unions themselves; the unions as such were in reality rather weak in several respects. Some commentators recognised this by urging legal changes to *strengthen* the unions by making them less democratic and giving more power to their bureaucracies, who were judged more 'responsible' (i.e., more inclined to fall in with the wishes of manage-

Table 7.6 Strikes in Britain and elsewhere (1970–1979)

	Working days lost through industrial disputes per 1,000 workers in mining, manufacturing, construction and transport		
	1970–79	*1970–74*	*1975–79*
Canada	1,840	1,724	1,965
Italy*	1,778	1,746	1,810
USA	1,211	1,380	1,042
UK	1,088	1,186	990
Belgium	489	520	458
France	312	300	324
W. Germany	92	92	92
Netherlands	82	118	38

* Includes gas, electricity and water

Source: Department of Employment, *Employment Gazette*, 89/1, January 1981, p. 28.

ment).* But even from a democratic standpoint the union structure inherited from the Victorian era contained major sources of weakness.

First, the organisation of 'general' unions did not correspond in a rational manner to the organisation of industry. This made it difficult for invidual unions to formulate and successfully advance long-term demands for the development of the various sectors in which their members worked. Second, although they were unencumbered by the expensive staffs of lawyers reuired for negotiations by unions in North America, they tended to lack staff who could formulate the more complex bargaining strategies of, for example, the Swedish unions; this was partly owing to the fact that union dues were kept low (about two-thirds the level of the European average as a share of workers' earnings) by the need felt by unions to remain competitive with other unions recruiting in the same industries. The demands of British unions have, in fact, been in many ways more limited than those advanced by unions in the other OECD countries. Third, for these reasons British unions did not respond as effectively as they might to some of the changes in the nature and pattern of work outlined above. Women, for instance, remained poorly represented even in unions in which a large proportion of the members were women, and the Equal Pay Act of 1970, though passed as a result of union pressure, had limited effects.†

The large numbers of new white-collar and state employees were mostly recruited into unions, but much less effectively recruited into the 'labour movement', as is shown by the fact that, by 1977, nearly half of the 11.7 million workers whose unions were affiliated to the TUC were not affiliated to the Labour Party which the TUC had originally created. The unions, and particularly the 'broad left' alliance of activists within them, did take up the causes of women, the unemployed, pensioners, young people and other underprivileged groups, but at the end of the 1970s the

* For instance Ben Hooberman, later a leading member of the SDP, wrote in 1974: 'In order to strengthen the powers of decision-making in unions it may be necessary to restrict elections to senior union officers. The officials who represent the middle management of the union could then be appointed on the basis of merit rather than elected on the grounds of popularity. Their terms of engagement could give them reasonable job security and compensation should they be dismissed or declared redundant. In this way, officials would become part of the permanent governing machine of the union and freed from the hazards of the electoral system. They would carry out decisions without hesitation and have an interest in communicating and commending to the members in their regions the policies adopted by elected officers of the union'. (*An Introduction to British Trade Unions*, Penguin, Harmondsworth 1974, p. 29).

† In 1978 only eight out of 65 members of the National Executive Committee of the National and Local Government Officers union, the fourth largest union in Britain, were women, although women accounted for forty per cent of the membership. In a sample of unions investigated by the TUC in 1975 a third of the members were women, but only three per cent of the unions' full-time officials were women. Women's gross hourly earnings rose from 63.1% of men's in 1970 to 73.0% in 1979.[22]

union movement as a whole could not yet be said to have become an effective expression of the changes that had occurred in the workforce in the preceding decades. The movement's inability to respond effectively to the unemployment and anti-union legislation of the early 1980s had a good deal to do with this fact.

The unions' co-ordinating body, the Trades Union Congress, though it enjoyed the strength that came from being a single centre (unlike the situation in several other European union movements), and had a competent secretariat, was not in a position to make good the basic weaknesses of the unions themselves. It could act only within the framework of a general consensus of its member unions' leaderships, and had no powers over member unions other than the power to expel (a power which could obviously only be used in exceptional circumstances). Its 37-member General Council, elected at annual TUC conferences and including most of the major trade union leaders, was none the less a very important political body; the labour movement as a whole could not be expected to accomplish much that the General Council was not prepared to support. It was the Council that had launched the General Strike on the 3rd May 1926, and called it off on the 12th. Later, refusal by the Council to support cuts in the 'dole' led to the collapse of the MacDonald government in 1931 and, in 1969, its opposition killed the Wilson–Castle proposals for industrial relations legislation and secured the eventual repeal of the Industrial Relations Act of 1971. The Council's attitude to the struggles within the Labour Party over the strategy to be adopted in the 1980s would be no less crucial, and in this context it was seriously handicapped in representing a movement whose organisation was in important respects archaic. The solidarity which had been the secret of the labour movement's strength in the past needed increasingly to be re-created on new lines to which the unions were still very imperfectly attuned.

The trade unions and the TUC were not the only organisations which represented the economic interests of labour. There were, besides, the Co-operative movement, which in 1979 still had 10.4 million members and 6.7% of all retail sales in Britain, though it was by then in serious financial difficulties; and other supportive organisations such as the Institute for Workers' Control and the Conference of Socialist Economists (policy research and educational associations). These bodies could play, however, at best a marginal and long-term role.

Capital and Labour: an Assessment

In the pluralists' universe, capital and labour are merely 'factors of production' which, along with a multitude of other interests, act as 'pressure groups' of relatively equal strength: if anything, 'labour' was considered to have become, at least before 1980, more powerful than 'business'. Yet, as Miliband pointed out, in capitalist society capital is necessarily dominant.[23] He identified three basic sources of this dominance:

1 capital's autonomous power of decision in the economy, based on its ownership and control of production and accumulated wealth, and the dependence of governments on 'business confidence' for investment, growth, and tax revenues;†
2 the strength which capital derives from its international character – the support given to it by foreign bankers, the IMF, and foreign governments; and
3 the social and financial advantages which capital enjoys – superior access to, and sympathy from, state officials and legislators, the ability to switch large financial resources into research, propaganda, the Conservative party, lock-outs, etc.†

Labour, on the other hand, lacks these advantages, including that of funds. (In spite of much disingenuous talk about the scale of trade-union bank balances, in 1979 they amounted to only £27 per trade union member, however impressive the figures might be made to appear by adding them all together.)[24] Labour also suffers from certain inherent limitations noted by Anderson.[25]

1 Trade unions are an intrinsic part of capitalist society; by their nature they 'both resist the given unequal distribution of income within the society by their wage demands, and ratify the principle of an unequal distribution by their existence . . .';

* In this connection the intensity of British capital's resistance to proposals for the industrial democracy is revealing. In 1973 the Labour Party promised to introduce a measure of industrial democracy when next returned to office. The majority report of the Bullock Committee (established by Wilson in 1975) recommended in 1977 in favour of giving workers and shareholders equal representation on the boards of directors of all companies employing 2,000 or more workers (some 738 companies in all at this time), with a smaller number of additional directors chosen from outside the company by the workers and shareholders' representatives jointly. The CBI representatives on the Committee dissented and the CBI refused to discuss the main issues further. The Callaghan government allowed the matter to die. The only move in this direction was taken experimentally by the Post Office, a public corporation, and this was terminated at the end of 1979 'at the request of the Chairman and all the non-worker directors' (*The Economist*, 23 Feb. 1980). It should be recalled that in West Germany, workers and shareholders have equal representation on boards which supervise the boards of directors of the largest firms (650 firms in 1976); in Norway, the workers elect a third of the directors of all companies with over 50 employees; in Sweden, the workers elect two directors of all companies with over 100 employees, and all decisions concerning the sale of the company, changes in production organisation, investments and most senior appointments are subject to negotiation with the unions.

† An interesting example of this was the proposal prepared by the CBI in 1979 (though subsequently abandoned) to establish a national 'strike fund' to provide collective coverage by the whole of industry to enable individual firms to resist strikes.

2 They have only one significant weapon, the passive, negative and sometimes unsuitably blunt weapon of the withdrawal of labour, compared with the many active, positive steps open to capital;
3 They are sectoral organisations, producing on their own only a 'corporate' consciousness (a consciousness of belonging to a particular economic group of workers, not to all workers at large) which not even their central body, the TUC, can easily transcend. As a result, labour tends to be more divided than capital.

But the root cause of labour's relative weakness is less organisational than ideological. It lies in the fact that 'capital' is ultimately the *system of relationships* which arises from the fact that most productive resources are owned by a very small minority of the population for whom most of the rest work.* This fact pervades every aspect of life (including the way in which the state-owned sector of production operates) and gives capital the advantage of being taken for granted, so that all actions that tend to conflict with the interests of capital are felt to be somehow improper, even by many of those involved in them.

The media – themselves largely part of private capital – play an important part in producing this effect, not least in the field of industrial relations itself, where television (watched by working-class adults for an average of 20 hours per week) presents 'both sides' but (a) unequally – more coverage, and much more sympathetic coverage, is given to the management side; and (b) in a way which, by adopting an apparently 'neutral' (and by implication authoritative) standpoint, endorses the idea

* The basic facts about the ownership of capital are often obscured by discussions which focus on the question of the distribution of 'wealth', as for instance in the report of the 1975 Royal Commission on the Distribution of Income and Wealth. Stating that it had 'no axe to grind' the Commission focused primarily on the question of how 'fair' the distribution of wealth in Britain was – a question which a decade of wage controls had made politically sensitive. The Commission defined wealth as 'marketable assets' and even went on to show that if rights to pensions were included, the poorest 80% of the population owned 45% of the national wealth. However, even if pension rights are disregarded, most of the marketable assets counted as wealth were items such as dwellings, consumer durables, and personal savings which the owners cannot use as *capital*, i.e., cannot use to enable them to employ other people for profit. The core of personally-owned *capital* consists of farms, forests and non-residential real estate, the assets of small businesses and above all the assets of limited liability companies. Five per cent of the population owned 80% of all company shares; one per cent owned 54%. A much wider group of people owned a few shares, but this only blurs the edges of the central reality that capital is largely owned, and wholly controlled, by about one per cent of the population for whom two-thirds of the rest work. The ownership of company shares by pension funds is sometimes held to qualify this and it is true that by 1975 nearly 17% of company shares were held by pension funds. But as Minns has shown, these funds are largely controlled by the banks and are managed in the interests of the companies concerned; there is no indication that they have been or will be used to change either the control or the distribution of ownership of capital (R. Minns, *Pension Funds and British Capitalism*, Heinemann, London 1980).

that there is a legitimate 'public' interest which the relationship between capital and labour serves.[26] This conception of neutrality endorses as natural the whole arrangement whereby most people are employees who must work for others. Media treatment of industrial relations in the 1960s and '70s, however, was not even consistently neutral in this sense; and this had something to do with the fact that the proportion of people willing to agree that 'the unions have too much power' rose from 54% in the middle of 1968 to 74% at the end of 1975 and that by the latter date even 66% of trade unionists were of the same opinion.[27]

But the ultimate source of the hegemony of capital is social relations themselves, the fact that most workers (including most trade union leaders) are socialised in homes where, for example, it is taken for granted that most of the children attend schools over which the parents have no control and which will prepare them to be wage workers; where the women expect to be paid less than the men, and to do the lion's share of the housework as well as their jobs; where the daily paper is a pro-business tabloid, and so on. The acceptance of capital, expressed in the quotation at the beginning of this chapter, originates in this experience, and is reflected and reinforced by the media.

8

Social Classes and British Politics

During the 'age of affluence' in the 1950s a rather strange argument was advanced, that this 'most class-ridden country under the sun' (as Orwell called it) was positively united by its class differences. The most characteristic example of this was held to be the 'deferential' working-class voter who voted for the Conservatives because he (or she) felt that the 'upper class' was bred to rule ('Breeding counts every time. I like to be set an example and have someone I can look up to').[1] In other words, British people were supposed to know their place in the class system and be satisfied with it. Less was heard of the merits of this amiable arrangement as the crisis unfolded after 1961. Still, the nature of the class system is far from obvious, and its political significance needs careful consideration.

The first essential is to establish what we mean by 'class'. Different ways of conceptualising classes have very different political implications. Even placing this chapter here, rather than after a discussion of political parties, has implications which may be questioned. For many writers, the existence of classes is simply a 'given' with which the parties must work, and so for them the social classes of Britain should naturally be described first (in so far as this is judged to be necessary at all).[2] But it is also possible to consider classes as at least partly the *products* of party competition, and as will be argued shortly, there are good reasons for doing so. 'Classes' are perhaps best thought of as expressing the constant *interaction* between socio-economic structure and political process, and between what is determined and what can be, and is, changed by human agency. This is a severe oversimplification; but it is less misleading than to present 'the class system' as something 'prior to' political parties. The significance of this chapter's location, between the discussion of the capital-labour relationship and the discussion of the parties, should be interpreted in this sense.

Conceptualising Social Classes

The word 'class' was first applied to British society when the industrial revolution began to produce large new categories of occupation which were unknown in the pre-industrial social order. Previously, there had been the gentry, and the 'common people', with merchants, bankers, clergymen, doctors, clerks, shopkeepers and the like constituting no more than well-understood qualifications to a social hierarchy still fundamentally based on land ownership. By the middle of the nineteenth century the new categories had become too important to be treated in this way. People spoke of the 'middle classes', those in-between the landed gentry and the common people. The word was first used in the plural and was extended to the 'labouring classes' by polite society only later.[3] The Conservative Party leader Lord Salisbury, for example, wrote to Joseph Chamberlain in 1886 that the Conservative Party's 'strongest ingredients' were 'the classes and the dependants of class' – meaning the propertied and their personal servant, tenants, clients, tradespeople, doctors, tutors, etc.[4] The reduction of the 'middle classes' to one 'middle class' and of the 'labouring classes' to one 'working class' in popular usage was the result of politics. It reflected the emergence of a labour movement which, by 1900, had developed an awareness of common interests uniting all wage-earners, and a corresponding tendency for all those who had any personal property to define themselves *out* of the 'working class' residentially, educationally and electorally.

So much for popular usage. Can we make anything more of the concept of class than a general descriptive category of this kind? The most common tendency has been to take popular usage and simply try to make it more precise. Society is seen as 'stratified', divided into layers according to different levels of esteem or status. These 'strata' are largely defined by occupation, and this is actually the meaning given to the term 'social class' in the censuses, producing a 'class structure' like that shown in Table 8.1.

Table 8.1 'Social classes' according to the Census, 1971

		heads of families (%)
Class I	Professional occupations	5.1
II	Intermediate occupations	20.0
III	Skilled non-manual occupations	11.9
IV	Skilled manual occupations	37.9
V	Partly skilled occupations	18.0
VI	Unskilled occupations	7.3
		100.0

Source: *Social Trends*, HMSO, London 1975, p. 11.

As Nichols says, we can regard this as 'the nearest thing we have to an official definition of "social class"'.[5] It is noteworthy that not only are the categories of this 'structure' based on an official judgement of the degrees of esteem to be attached to the various occupations, but as Nichols also points out, in this *class*ification, 'the owners of capital are lost to sight' – the 'class system' thus constructed completely *ignores* the capital-labour relationship.[6]

Still, this official judgement of degree of esteem is quite close to that which ordinary people make when asked by sociological investigators to rank occupations according to their status; and the main contribution of most sociologists to the question of social class in Britain has been to try to refine the criteria according to which the ranking is done. For instance, sociologists distinguish between so-called 'objective' bases of 'social class' – the 'factors' which determine what class people see themselves as belonging to – and the 'subjective images' which people have of themselves as belonging to a particular class. But the essence of the former is, everyone agrees, occupation. So, although for some purposes it is interesting to know that eleven out of twelve British people assign themselves to either the 'middle class' or the 'working class', it turns out that this is so strongly related to their occupational status that this serves as a proxy for 'self-assigned class' for most purposes. The data collected on this basis are not without value. Striking differences in people's conditions of life are revealed by classifying them in this way, as Table 8.2 shows.

Table 8.2 Differences of condition according to socio-economic group: 1975–1976

		%
	Chronic sickness Rate per 1000	16–19 age group* in full-time education
Professional	81	70
Employers and managers	127	40
Intermediate and Junior non-manual	158	42
Skilled manual and own-account non-professional	141	24
Semi-skilled manual and personal service	205	21
Unskilled manual	282	15

* Based on fathers' socio-economic group.

Note: The basis of this classification resembles, but is not identical with, the 'social classes' of the Census.

Source: *Social Trends* 1979, pp. 76, 135.

The same is true of people's party preferences. Using a slightly modified scale of occupational status, Butler and Stokes found that in 1963 the 'classes' so identified divided their allegiance between Conservative and Labour as shown in Table 8.3:

From the point of view of someone wishing to spread higher education more equally, or of a party organiser contemplating an election campaign, Tables 8.2 and 8.3 are useful starting-points. But, beyond that, two kinds of problem immediately arise.

1 What is the nature of the relationship? For example, do skilled manual workers tend to vote Labour because of its record of concern for them or because they are more unionised than other kinds of worker?
2 What determines what occupations there are, how people are distributed among them, and what rewards and status they carry?

Sociologists have done a great deal of work on the first of these two questions, but very little on the second. Yet when answers to the first question have been found, the second still needs to be answered. Otherwise, explaining anything in terms of 'classes' is not very helpful – it simply refers us to the occupational status structure, which itself remains unexplained.

For this reason anyone who wants to explain politics in terms of class needs a concept of class that belongs to a general theory of social change, as the Marxist concept of class is meant to do. The basic idea of Marx was that classes are constituted by the relations of production that are dominant in any given society – in a capitalist society, by the relations of ownership and control of the means of production that link the owners to the non-owners of capital. Marx failed to provide a definition of class, but Lenin defined it as follows:

> Classes are large groups of people which differ from each other by the place they occupy in a historically definite system of social production, by their relation (in most cases fixed and formulated in laws) to the means of production, by their role in the social organization of labour, and, consequently, by the dimensions and method of acquiring the share of social wealth that they obtain. Classes are groups of people one of which may appropriate the labour of another owing to the different places they occupy in the definite system of social economy.[8]

This definition is very general and does not particularly stress the aspect of antagonism between the principal classes which is so important in Marx's theory. It will serve, however, as an initial formulation. With this concept of class, classes appear as historical agents produced by the 'logic' of a specific economic and social system. Political action is then conceived of as expressing the interests which people see themselves as having by virtue

Table 8.3 Party self-image by occupational status, 1963

	Higher Managerial	Lower Managerial	Supervisory non-manual	Lower non-manual	Skilled manual	Unskilled manual
Percentage of total sample	(6.5)	(11.2)	(11.5)	(8.2)	(38.4)	(24.2)
Conservative	86%	81%	77%	61%	29%	25%
Labour	14	19	23	39	71	75
	100%	100%	100%	100%	100%	100%

Source: D. Butler and D. Stokes, *Political Change in Britain*, Second College Edition, St Martin's Press, New York 1976, pp. 49 and 53.

of their class membership, and the results of these actions in turn react back on the development of the economy and society. This may not be a valid theory; but it is the *kind* of theory needed if 'class' is to be a useful explanatory concept, rather than a purely empirical concept that merely accepts, without further enquiry, the 'stratification system' found to be operative in a given society at a given time – especially when this means adopting uncritically the language of everyday life, according to which, as Nichols wryly remarks, 'there is a "middle class", with a "working class" underneath, and – a sort of bald class structure this – nothing on top'.[9]

The role of class in British politics? Some theoretical questions.

The Marxist concept of class presents some immediate problems when applied to contemporary Britain. It ought, for instance, to be able to explain political developments by showing that people act as they do because of their class interests. But the Marxian concept does not seem to predict the political activities of many people in Britain, especially the many workers who support the Conservatives. A second major difficulty is that modern capitalism does not differentiate people as clearly into antagonistic classes, one exploiting and the other exploited, as Marx often seems to have assumed. The growth of a 'new' middle class (or new middle classes) of professional, technical, supervisory and especially state-employed salaried workers, who appear to be neither exploiting nor – except in a rather abstract sense – exploited, seems to cast further doubt on the utility of the Marxian concept of class for the study of British politics (or the politics of any other advanced capitalist society, for that matter). Each of these difficulties must be considered in turn.

The first problem was, in fact, recognised by Marx, who conceived of a class as coming into existence as a result of the development of a given mode of production, but acquiring 'class consciousness' only gradually in the course of struggles with another antagonistic class. Marx, however, tended to assume that these struggles would inevitably reveal more and more clearly to the exploited class where its class interest lay, and how it was necessary to make a political revolution in order to satisfy this interest. The development of the British working class, a third of whom, after two hundred years of capitalism, do not see themselves as having a class interest opposed to the capitalists, and hardly any of whom are revolutionary, obviously casts doubt on the usefulness of Marx's class concept for explaining British politics.

Theorists have sought to deal with this problem in one of two main ways. One approach, exemplified by Giddens, is to retain the idea that classes are constituted by the relations of production, but to see their political significance as varying greatly, according to other aspects of each country's historical experience.[10] Giddens refers to this as differing degrees of 'class structuration'. Thus, a working class, for example, is more 'structurated' the less individual social mobility there is into and out of it, because this makes the life experience of its members more homogeneous. This 'structuration' is also strengthened by the sharpness of the distinctions drawn at work between operatives and technicians, or between workers and supervisors, and by differences in income and related benefits, especially those which tend to reinforce the residential segregation of classes. An example of this would be the difficulty most British workers have experienced, historically, in getting mortgages, so reinforcing the tendency for them to be concentrated in rented 'council housing'. These considerations seem relevant to the differences found between Britain and the USA or Canada, for example, in respect to the salience and usefulness of 'class' as an explanation of political life. British classes are relatively more 'structurated'.

Giddens also argues that the reason why the British (or any other) working class has at most a 'labourist', and not a revolutionary, consciousness is that once the transition to capitalist society is complete, and the industrial and political relationship between labour and capital has been institutionalised, the working class no longer has any experience of alternative modes of production which could give it a sense that any other system of production is historically *possible*. That is why, according to Giddens, revolutionary consciousness was characteristic of the European working class only in the first half of the nineteenth century, ('the point of impact of post-feudalism and capitalist-industrialism'); and why it tends to develop nowadays among workers in 'backward' countries where the contrast or contradiction between the potential of capitalist production technology, and the pre-capitalist relations of production which still prevail, generates painful paradoxes and a powerful sense of the possibility (as well as the desirability) of radical change. In Giddens' view, therefore, Marx's concept of class is broadly sound, but his theory of social change needs revision: in advanced capitalist societies like Britain's, the working class is not impelled to see itself as irreconcilably opposed to the capitalist class or to envisage a revolutionary alternative to capitalist society.

This approach, with its rather fatalistic political implications (to the effect that things in Britain could hardly be otherwise, and that no radical change can be expected), has two main weaknesses. First, it does not account for differences *within* the British working class in respect of class or political consciousness; and second, it tends to assume that capitalism is a much more *stable* system of production than it in fact is. In reality, the short and long-term changes which are constantly occurring in the capital-labour relation, interacting with political leadership and organisation and the effects of ideological struggles, have affected the political significance of the class system in Britain in decisive ways. They have led to periods of confrontation and the spread of socialist ideas – including 'revolutionary' ideas of various kinds – as well as to periods of collaboration and consensus.

Recognition of these fluctuations has been one of the bases for the other approach to the problem of how far the Marxian concept of class can explain the realities of modern British politics. According to this view, while the economic division of labour and the relations of exploitation create classes, organisation and leadership are the key to their development as political 'agents'. Lenin adopted an extreme form of this doctrine at one point, arguing that a party of professional revolutionaries, including especially elements drawn from the 'bourgeois intelligentsia', was the decisive factor in determining whether a working class could progress beyond mere 'trade-union consciousness'.[11]

Lenin's view has been used to rationalise a long sequence of unsuccessful attempts at the revolutionary mobilisation of British workers since the formation of the Communist Party of Great Britain in 1920. Later theorists, however, have adopted a more democratic and nuanced position. A leading example here is Przeworski, who has traced the way in which all the social-democratic parties in Western Europe have, in effect, been forced by electoral competition to become merely reformist parties and, eventually, to convert their own supporters into supporters of the capitalist system.[12] Przeworski sees this as neither more nor less than a political victory, won in the course of a century, by the capitalist class over the working class: as he puts it, classes are *formed* (i.e., given specific forms, not brought into existence – capitalism does *that* of its own accord) through struggles *about* classes. These are struggles that determine what it means to be a worker and who will see themselves as workers: all political struggles are 'class struggles' in this sense, even if the protagonists do not see themselves as acting as members of a class or upholding class interests, let alone consciously trying to determine the long-run balance of class power by affecting people's consciousness of class.

This approach has the merit of being historical, and it allows for more possibility of radical change than Giddens' sociological-structural view (while not being wholly inconsistent with it). In Przeworski's view, 'labourism' (not to mention Conservative-voting) among British workers reflects a historic defeat which in new circumstances may be retrieved. It is not a 'generic' and permanent feature of capitalism as such. Przeworski is also well aware of the vulnerability of capitalism in general, and of individual national capitalist economies in particular, to crises. While he recognises that crises lead as easily to Fascism as to socialism (and perhaps more easily), he also points out that they are 'break' points in which the political significance of previous periods of class 'formation' is disclosed, and opportunities arise to form classes in new ways.[13] In other words, Przeworski modifies Marx's theory of the way classes affect policy, but not so much as to empty it permanently of all its original impact. In Przeworski's view, the interplay between the economic development of capitalism and the politics of capitalist countries such as Britain hinges on classes, but in a process of mutual interaction and with no predetermined outcomes.

What is attractive about this interpretation is that it retains the value of Marx's concept of class by keeping it located within a general theory of social change, but at the same time recognises that classes are the result, as well as the origin, of political action. The anonymous *Times* columnist understood this when he wrote the famous comment, that Disraeli 'discerned the Conservative working man as the sculptor perceives the angel prisoned in a block of marble'. Disraeli, in other words, saw the possibility of *forming* the British working class into what it is today (with largely conservative views and considerable Conservative Party sympathies) very much as Marx imagined that the communists would (in his phrase) 'form the proletariat into a class' of a very different kind.[14] It is a realistic and useful concept of class, and we shall broadly use it in what follows.

The 'New Middle Class'

There remains, however, the second major problem noted earlier, the significance of the growth of the 'new' middle class or classes. This is actually a broader issue than whether modern capitalism has generated a new class in-between the capitalists and the working class. Substantial differences of condition also exist between modern workers. For example, workers with technical qualifications employed in the control rooms of capital-intensive plants such 'ChemCo' have markedly different levels of income and conditions of work from those of most semi-skilled operatives, let alone most unskilled manual workers. These differences have led some European sociologists, such as Mallet, to write of a 'new working class' which they consider potentially a vanguard of social change. Other sociologists, contemplating the growth of 'white collar' state and service-industry employment, have seen this as evidence that part of the working class was being transformed into a 'middle class'.

Interpretations vary primarily according to whether or not one wants to retain the core Marxian idea that capitalism thrusts two principal classes into opposition to each other, and that this provides the long-term driving force of history. Giddens, as we have seen, rejects the last part of this theory and, consistent with this, considers that a 'basic three-class system' of an 'upper', 'middle' and 'lower' or 'working' class is 'generic to capitalist society'.[15] Just as he does not think that the conflict of interest between workers and the 'upper' class is enough to make the workers revolutionary, so he does not believe that the workers are, as Marx sometimes wrote, destined to become the 'vast majority'. Instead, the 'middle class' is more or less 'structurated' into a separate class with interests no more opposed to the capitalists' than to the workers'.

Marxist writers, by contrast, have tackled the problem in ways that stress the fundamental opposition between capital and labour, considering these 'new' elements as either actual or potential allies, or even members of the working class, in spite of their different conditions of work and life. All of these approaches focus attention on the relations of production, the ultimate basis of class, rather than on conditions of life, which they see as secondary.

Wright, for example, considers that besides the basic distinction between owning and not owning capital, which divides capitalists from workers, there is a continuum of authority, necessary for capitalist production, from senior managers to foremen (with technicians, scientists, accountants, merchandising staff and so on, in-between).[16] These people mostly own no capital, but because they exercise authority on behalf of the owners of capital they are placed in what Wright calls a 'contradictory class location', and whether they align themselves politically with the workers or with capitalists is decided by political organisation and struggle.

A similar approach is that of Carchedi. He sees such employees as non-capitalists who, however, spend part of their time exercising the 'global function of capital', which includes the design and planning of profitable production and sales, and the co-ordination of tasks, as well as the imposition of authority on the rest of the workforce.[17] The extent to which a job involves this function is a question of degree; when it contains a substantial element of the global function of capital, its occupant tends to be a member of a 'middle class'. This is reinforced when the rest of the job is 'non-productive' – that is to say, when it does not contribute to the production of commodities which sell at a profit, as is the case with most state workers and also (in the opinion of most theorists) of commercial workers such as bank employees or supermarket staff.*

A sales manager in a large company is the clearest example of this middle class. The significance of the difference between Carchedi and Wright comes out clearly in Carchedi's further insistence that the process

* But not employees of state commercial enterprises such as the National Coal Board, which do produce commodities for the market. The distinction between productive and unproductive labour turns on the labour theory of value; work is only 'productive' when it produces surplus value, and this is judged important for class analysis by theorists who think that only workers who do this will find themselves fully exposed to the pressure on their wages and hours which employers subject to capitalist competition are driven to try to exert. For an explanation of the distinction, see Ian Gough, 'Marx's Theory of Productive and Unproductive Labour' *New Left Review*, **76**, 1972, pp. 47–72.

of capitalist production involves a constant search for ways to reduce costs by substituting cheaper labour for more expensive labour. The resulting 'dequalification' of jobs, or 'deskilling' as it is often called (following Braverman), means that, over time, the new middle class is subject to a constant process of 'proletarianisation'.[18] A hundred years ago a 'clerk' was a position of considerable status reflecting relatively scarce skills. Today this position involves low-paid routine work. Twenty years ago computer programmers were scarce and relatively highly-paid. Today they are routine workers. Technical advance also constantly throws up new jobs of a 'middle-class' nature; Carchedi's point is that they are all vulnerable to this long-term erosion. According to him, the conditions of existence of the new middle class contain features which make it susceptible to alliance with the working class; white-collar unionisation of formerly 'middle-class' occupations such as bank employees and company technicians, and the growing militancy of such unions in the 1960s and 1970s, leading to their affiliation to the TUC, could be interpreted this way.

Yet another interpretation has been proposed by Lindsey. Lindsey distinguishes two sections of the working class, one involved in production and one in circulation, the latter being 'natural' allies of the former, with broadly similar conditions of work, wages, etc., but not subject to entirely similar pressures from capital, and hence less reliably militant. In addition, Lindsey identifies an 'ideological' class composed of people whose jobs involve 'reproducing' the capitalist system as a whole, especially by legitimating it ideologically – higher and middle-level bureaucrats, judges, court clerks, journalists and broadcasters, 'management' and even trade union bureaucrats. This class is tied to capital by its function, and Lindsey sees it as inherently hostile to the workers.[19]

Evidently, these different conceptualisations have different political implications. For instance, one writer whose work has influenced much of the debate, Nicos Poulantzas, proposed to treat only 'productive workers' as composing the working class; everyone else, from bank janitors to state hospital cleaners, belonged to the 'new petty bourgeoisie'.[20] This was because Poulantzas was strongly opposed to the policy of the French Communist Party at that time, of treating all categories of wage or salary-earner as if they were workers with identical interests. Lindsey's theory has similar intentions, insisting as it does that the 'ideological class' cannot become an ally of the working class.

We do not need to endorse any of these views. They have been reviewed here mainly in order to show that the facts will bear quite a variety of different interpretations. Contrary to the assertions of many writers, to insist that *a* middle class 'exists' in Britain is not an empirical observation, but a political or ideological statement.* So is the claim that there is no such thing as a middle class. What we have is the term 'middle class', which has a perfectly obvious historical origin in the transition from the pre-capitalist to capitalist society, being used today as a more or less unconscious weapon in the ongoing struggle between capital and labour, to try to attach to the side of capital the various segments of the population which the development of the economy and the state differentiate out from the old core of manual workers.

The theories mentioned above are less incompatible with each other than their authors sometimes seem to think; each of them contains important insights. It may even be possible to systematise them into a single theory, but this task lies beyond the scope of the present discussion. We will simply try to draw on these insights, and to use them in ways which are consistent, in discussing some questions about class that have great practical importance for British politics.

To sum up this part of the discussion, we conclude that it is first necessary to go beyond the empirically-observed fact that people in Britain think in class terms, and to try to establish a concept of class that will help explain political action. Such a concept can be found in Marxist theory, but it needs to be modified in order to detach it from some oversimplified and reductionist aspects of that theory. We have, then, two historically-formed classes – capitalist and working classes – plus a succession of new social categories, constantly produced by the development of capitalist production and the state, which popular usage, encouraged by empiricist social science, once again calls 'the middle class'. These categories are often subject to pressures, especially 'dequalification', which tend to polarise them towards the working class; but they are also the object of constant political and ideological efforts to maintain and consolidate their sense of being apart from the workers and attached to capital. Similar efforts are directed towards the workers in even the oldest of working-class occupations, affecting how far they see themselves as working class, and what this might mean for them politically. The relevance of some of these ideas for the British experience will be considered in what follows.

The Changing Connotations of Social Class in Britain

On the one hand, it is clear that the struggle between capital and labour, sometimes open, sometimes partly concealed, runs through all British political history for the past two hundred years or more, and that this

* For example, Butler and Stokes write as follows: 'In short, virtually everyone accepted the conventional class dichotomy between middle and working class. It is difficult not to see this as evidence of the acceptance of the view that British society is divided into two primary classes. This is much more than a sociologist's simplification; it seems to be deeply rooted in the mind of the ordinary British citizen.' (Butler and Stokes, *Political Change in Britain*, p. 46).

struggle has been reflected in popular perceptions of society as divided into classes with more or les conflicting interests. On the other hand, there is great variation in the extent to which people see a connection between class and politics (particularly politics defined as party politics). In the mid-1960s 86% of working-class Labour supporters saw party politics as being about class interests, whereas about 65% of 'middle class' Conservative supporters saw party politics as having no connnection with classes or class interests.[21] Such differences are partly due to class interest itself: it is understandable that people in professional, managerial occupations which pay well and enjoy high status should deny that their support for the Conservative Party reflects any class interest. It is also due to the effects of party propaganda. In so far as the Labour Party stressed its mission as a champion of working-class interests, working-class labour voters would tend to see politics in class terms.

In the late 1950s many sociologists, and many Labour Party strategists, considered that differences of *condition* between the classes were narrowing, or even disappearing, to the point where any such emphasis on working-class interests was becoming electorally risky. Working-class life, they thought, was becoming more and more like middle-class life. It was argued that the distribution of income and wealth had become much more equal; that social mobility was increasing (especially as a result of wider educational provision); that increased absolute levels of income were permitting workers to adopt 'middle-class' living patterns (cars, television sets, holidays in Spain); and that the growth of new 'middle-class' employment was in any case reducing the working class's weight in the electorate. In addition, it was argued, there was no real capitalist class left for the working class to oppose. Shareholding had become widely dispersed, and separated from management, which was salaried work and not directly animated by the thirst for profit.

The empirical refutation of most of these ideas, which was notably begun by Westergaard and consummated in his book with Resler, *Class in a Capitalist Society*, can only be summarised here in the briefest terms.[22] The distribution of income and wealth became more equal during both World Wars but since 1945 has changed only slightly. What little redistribution of income there was occurred wholly within the top half of the population, mostly within the top twenty per cent, and ceased altogether by 1970. Individual social mobility exists, but mostly across a limited range – from skilled manual work to supervisory work being the most typical example of upward movement across the politically-sensitive manual/non-manual divide. This mobility is in any event unequal – sons of higher-status fathers have more upward and less downward mobility than manual workers – and by no means significantly greater than it was in the past. The idea that wider access to higher education had changed matters was an illusion. In the first place, the scale of the improvement was minimal – in 1979 a manual worker's son still had only one-eleventh as much chance of entering university as the son of a professional man or a manager. Secondly, the post-war expansion of professional and managerial employment, which called for more people with higher educational qualifications, benefited mostly 'middle-class' children. In fact, expansion of educational provision turned out not to have improved the chances of workers' children reaching such positions in the slightest degree.[23] The argument that absolute increases in workers' incomes was leading to significant changes in their living patterns had some force, but invalid conclusions were drawn from it. For one thing, 'middle-class' living patterns were improving simultaneously – as workers bought houses and fridges, so the 'middle class' bought second homes and freezers. The gulf between manual workers' lives and those of non-manual workers, especially the higher-paid, remained clear and wide – not only in terms of a continuing and wide difference between manual workers' incomes and those of most non-manual workers, but also in terms of hours worked, the absence of any 'career' expectations for manual workers (especially their different 'earnings profile' with declining incomes in later life), shorter holidays, limited fringe benefits, harsher work discipline and dependence on union strength to keep their incomes rising.[24] Higher earnings did not permit many workers to adopt a truly 'middle-class' life-style, but only certain elements or imitations of it.

The argument that manual work was giving way to non-manual work was more persuasive, though apt to be exaggerated. Much less convincing was the argument about shareholding and management. Westergaard and Resler showed that company directors were the group of shareholders with the largest holdings of shares of any elite group; and the judgement of Giddens 'that an overall homogeneity of value and belief and a high degree of social solidarity, as manifest in interpersonal contacts, friendship and marriage ties, is more noticeable than any marked cleavages' between owners and managers, would now be broadly accepted.[25]

As for the workers, more and more of them were employed by large companies where they confronted only paid managers, not owners. In some situations this probably did tend to make them less militant (for example, many of the workers at 'ChemCo', while expressing hostility to management, also regarded them as deserving their position and rewards by virtue of their qualifications, and saw the shareholders as remote individuals bearing no responsibility for company policy). But in other situations – for example, the car industry – the separation of ownership from management had no 'moderating' effects; and as small, owner-managed firms tend to be less unionised, the trend towards big companies and the separation of ownership from management had other effects which tended to increase class-consciousness, at least in its 'corporate' or 'trade-union' form.

The announcement of the 'withering away' of class was, then, premature, to say the least. However, authors such as Westergaard, who did so much to demolish this fiction, tended to overstate the counter-argument. Although classes did not disappear, class relations were changing throughout the entire post-war period, in some respects radically. Some of the changes pointed out by the withering-away-of-class school were significant, although not in the way alleged. For example, the increase in the absolute real incomes of workers did not eliminate the distinction between manual workers and non-manual workers, but it did make manual workers feel richer. This had both negative and positive political effects. It encouraged a consumerist, leisure-oriented, 'privatised' and hence more individualistic outlook, which contributed to a decline in workers' interest in trade-union and party activity; on the other hand it was accompanied by a *rise* in trade-union membership, and, as we have seen, by growing rank-and-file power on the shop floor in some industries, and it raised expectations which mobilised people in support of new collective goals.

Yet, while real wages had risen, real poverty had also increased, and it grew rapidly worse as the crisis advanced. The proportion of the population living in poverty rose from 7.8% in 1953 to 14.2% in 1960. By 1976 the proportion living on or below the official poverty line (i.e., the level of income up to which Supplementary Benefits are paid) was 11.4%, and the proportion with incomes no more than 20% above this line – which most researchers in the field consider a more realistic measure of deprivation – was 18.6%.[26] This gave rise to a new and profound division within the working class, as most of those in work were gaining, while this growing minority fell into poverty.*

When we add together such changes – and the changes in the nature of work and the structure of the workforce outlined in Chapter 7 – we find,

* The following definition of poverty given by the Supplementary Benefits Commission deserves reproduction: 'Poverty, in urban, industrial countries like Britain, is a standard of living so low that it excludes and isolates people from the rest of the community. To keep out of poverty they must have an income which enables them to participate in the life of the community. They must be able, for example, to keep themselves reasonably fed, and well enough dressed to maintain their self respect and to attend interviews for jobs with confidence. Their homes must be reasonably warm; their children should not feel shamed by the quality of their clothing; the family must be able to visit relatives and give them something on their birthdays and at Christmas-time; they must be able to read newspapers and retain their television sets and their membership of trade unions and churches. And they must be able to live in a way, so far as possible, that public officials, doctors, teachers, landlords and others, treat them with the courtesy due to every member of the community.' (Cited by Coates and Silburn, *Poverty: The Forgotten Englishmen*, Penguin, Harmondsworth 1981, p. 257).

not the 'embourgeoisement' of the working class, but a kind of dissolution or decomposition. The old 'matrix' of working-class life, which had included an increasingly automatic allegiance to the Labour Party, was breaking up. The changes of the post-war years had not made the workers 'middle class' but they had weakened the ties of tradition and place which underpinned the traditional sense of what it was to *be* 'working class'.[27]

Fewer were manual workers (which in itself involved some changes in outlook) and more owned their own houses (over fifty per cent of skilled manual workers and foremen).[28] Combined with slum clearance, this meant that many fewer workers now lived in one of the old inner-city working-class districts with its close-knit community life revolving around the local football club, the local 'co-op', the local cinema, the local dance-hall and the local pub (or chapel). More had working wives, more owned cars and took holidays abroad. More worked for the state: this did not mean that they no longer needed trade unions to increase or maintain their wages, but their political context altered – they belonged to different unions, and when they were obliged to strike it often meant striking at the expense of other workers (as consumers of state services such as schools or hospitals or public transport), with divisive effects to which the unions often seemed insufficiently sensitive. Yet another new line of differentiation arose from immigration. An important minority of workers, mostly in low-paid employment, were now black, with different traditions and tastes, who were often the object of discrimination and the focus of racist agitation.

In other words, what had changed were many of the historical connotations of working-class life which had in the past furnished so many *badges*, by reference to which workers knew they were, and were known to be, members of the 'working class'. This was immensely important because it touched on what had hitherto been so distinctive about the British 'class system' – its *caste-like* character, the astonishing precision and fixity with which everyone was located in it by almost indelible signs of accent, dress and manner, imprinted on him or her by upbringing and experience.

This point must be briefly expanded, and brought together with the theoretical and historical interpretations offered earlier. What so impressed the North American visitor to Britain in the past was the pervasive and explicit recognition of class distinctions; what astonished the continental visitor was their prevailing acceptance. Historical circumstances in North America have led to a class system in which attributes of class origin play a comparatively inconspicuous role, leading to a degree of invisibility (low 'structuration' in Giddens' terms) which is reinforced by a powerful (dominant) class ideology that denies that classes exist. In

Britain, on the other hand, the new propertied classes of the early nineteenth century were most anxious to acquire the badges of rank of the existing, explicitly stratified pre-capitalist social order, which thus received a new lease of life. In contrast with France or Germany, the British working class, after the defeat of its earliest radical initiatives, never gave its allegiance to a radical or revolutionary party but moved from being the tail of (mainly) the Liberal Party to supporting 'labourism' and the Labour Party.

The explicit system of rank of the earlier agrarian social order was thus preserved, but infused with new content to form an unusually explicit system of class; while the antagonism which elsewhere accompanied a strong sense of class among the workers was, in Britain, unusually muted. The post-World War II years saw a change in both dimensions. The British working class lost a good many of its former class badges, together with some of its faith in labourism. These changes worked in combination to the advantage of the radical right in the 1970s. Although the old class system had helped to preserve an obsolescent economy and an archaic state, the labour movement had also drawn strength from a working-class solidarity based on the sharp cultural demarcation of class boundaries. The loosening of the bonds of the old working-class culture provided an opportunity to redefine the 'classness' of the workers most affected by these changes. The working class did not begin to 'wither away'. It began to break out of its traditional mould and became susceptible of being 'formed' again in new ways. The radical right – and some of those who later formed the Social Democratic Party – realised this.[29] The electoral victory of Thatcherism demonstrated the enormous importance of their perception that a fresh opportunity had arisen to create a new kind of 'conservative working man'. It was a victory – not necessarily permanent, but a victory all the same – in the struggle between classes, *about* classes.

Some similar changes also occurred among the 'middle classes'. They were affected in somewhat contradictory ways by changes such as the growing necessity for white-collar workers to unionise, the continued dequalification of various traditionally middle-class occupations, the dilution of formely high-status occupations (e.g., through the rapid expansion of the 'helping professions'), the encroachment of the working class on formerly middle-class preserves (driving, air travel, the grammar schools), and the effects of inflation. Such changes tended to polarise the middle classes, partly towards the labour movement, and partly towards anti-union and authoritarian positions. What changed least were the class associations of the capitalist class proper; their firm base in the public schools, the ancient universities, the army, the City, the Church of England, landownership and the honours system.

Class and Party

Writers on the relationship between class and party in Britain have mostly been experts on electoral behaviour, who have accepted the sociological concept of class and who see the relationship between the parties and classes as a kind of fishing competition in which the parties compete to see which one can pull the most votes out of each 'stratum' of an electorate seen as 'stratified' in a pre-given way. These writers also tend to define politics as party politics, and party politics as a series of election campaigns. This approach is not very illuminating, and at worst, is quite misleading.

Butler and Stokes, for example, subjected the data from a series of surveys of electors' party preferences in the 1960s to a sophisticated quantitative analysis under the title *Political Change in Britain*. It fell to another specialist on elections, Ivor Crewe, to point out that even within their limited conception of 'politics' Butler and Stokes had failed even to notice the most dramatic changes that had occurred in the period they studied: the decline in the proportion of the electorate voting for either of the two main parties, the fall in turn-out and the increasing volatility of support between the major parties (all of which are obvious *starting-points* for the analysis of political change pursued in this book).[30]

Crewe also showed that the model which Butler and Stokes had used to explain where their interest lay, namely in changes in the two major parties' shares of the vote, was invalidated by the decline that had occurred in support for both parties. For example, according to Butler and Stokes, the main determinant of voting is the strength of each individual voter's psychological identification with a given party, which is strongly inherited from one's parents and grows stronger over a lifetime. From this it ought to have followed that, as the electorate came to consist more and more of people who had known only the Conservative and Labour parties in office, and fewer of whose parents could have been Liberal voters, support for the two major parties would rise; whereas the precise opposite had occurred. Butler and Stokes, in fact, not only reduced the concept of class to a mere occupational category, but also reduced the concept of voting to a mere individual psychological reflex, largely independent of the course of the political struggle.

The sort of study of which their work is a leading example can illuminate some of the complex factors that enter into *every* election outcome – the effects of the death of older voters, the differing abstention rates of various categories of voter, differing patterns of vote switching, etc. It can also shed light on the relation between voting patterns and such things as trade-union membership, residence in a predominantly working-class constituency, and so on. But if one ignores almost entirely the political events and changing social forces in the context of which elections actually occur, one cannot explain what actually happens in elections, let alone shed any light on the real relationship between party and class.

It is not, therefore, in this literature that we can hope to find a useful analysis of the party–class relationship, even though not all elections specialists have such a narrow conception of politics. Because of their method (i.e., seeking to interpret statistical relationships between data on voting or statements of party support, and class 'indicators' such as occupation), all such studies use an empiricist, and ultimately ideological conception of class. For illumination on the relationship between class and party, the best sources by far remain historical treatments of party politics, some of which will be referred to in the following two chapters. However, a brief comment on the pitfalls involved may first be appropriate.

In a class society, political parties clearly express class interests, but the way they do so is complex. As we shall see in Chapter 9, the Conservative Party undoubtedly represents and defends the interests of capital against the interests of labour, but it would be a serious oversimplification, and underestimation, to call it *the party of* capital. Similarly, the Labour Party was formed to promote the interests of labour but it defined these interests not ony as including *everyone* who worked ('by hand or brain') but also – after 1926 if not before – as involving collaboration with capital. From its inception, the party was led mainly by professional men; it increasingly returned non-workers to parliament (especially after 1951); and, when in office from 1964 onwards, it accepted in practice the need to preserve profits at the expense of wages. So it is at least a serious oversimplification to call it 'the party of the working class' – even though it may continue to be seen in this light by the great majority of those who see themselves as 'working-class'. Any attempt to *reduce* parties to their 'class base' necessarily burkes these problems. How then should the relationship be understood?

Briefly, parties must first be distinguished from organisations which aim at defending the immediate perceived interests of particular groups (including classes or elements of classes). The point of a political party is to secure those interests by means of a much wider project.

> ... a party is not a trade union, not an employers' association, much less a professional association. A party's existence implies a transition from the defence of corporative* interests to the promotion of a specific project for

* The term 'corporative' derives from Gramsci: 'A tradesman does not join a political party in order to do business, nor an industrialist in order to produce more at a lower cost, nor a peasant to learn new methods of cultivation, even if some aspects of these demands of the tradesman, the industrialist or the peasant can find satisfaction in the party. For these purposes, within limits, there exists the professional association, in which the economic-corporate activity of the tradesman, industrialist or peasant is most suitably promoted. In the political party the elements of an economic social group [a class – C. L.] get beyond that moment of their historical development and become agents of more general activities of a national and international character' (*Selections from the Prison Notebooks*, ed. Q. Hoare and G. Nowell-Smith, Lawrence and Wishart, London, 1971, p. 16).

> society, and must be analysed in its direct relation to the question of power. Involved in a party is social space in its totality. A party undertakes not only the promotion of specific, multiple and heterogeneous interests, but also the reproduction of the totality of the social formation. In it unfolds the whole domain of hegemony, alliances and compromises.[31]

A party must, by its nature, formulate programmes for, and develop links with, numerous elements in society outside the class whose interests fundamentally inspire it.* These programmes and links may take a great variety of forms, depending on circumstances. In the last analysis a party's record in office discloses its 'class character' – i.e., the class interests it ultimately serves – but this must be interpreted with care. For example, did the Conservative Party's acceptance of the welfare state after 1951 show it to have acquired a working-class character? Did the Labour Party's economic policies from 1964 to 1970 mean that it had taken on a capitalist character? A proper analysis must be long-term, and have a necessary degree of sophistication.

Since a party must be concerned with 'the reproduction of the totality of the social formation', it must be ready on occasion to sacrifice some of the immediate economic interests of the social class or classes it represents. The occasions when parties do this are especially revealing. They show how the party leaders understand the party's *raison d'être*; what interests they judge to be central and what they consider ultimately dispensable. These moments are obviously fraught with danger for the leadership and can easily lead to personal defeats, as in the famous case of Peel's decision to repeal the Corn Laws in 1846. Another equally famous case, Roosevelt's adoption of the New Deal programme, turned out more fortunately for Roosevelt personally, though he was well aware of the risks:

> The rich may have thought that Roosevelt was betraying his class; but Roosevelt certainly supposed [reflecting in spring 1935, on the mounting opposition from business circles]... that his class was betraying him.[32]

Przeworski makes the same point in his summary of the dilemma of social democratic leaders as their programmes for a transition to socialism without revolution lead to economic crises:

> Faced with an economic crisis, threatened with loss of electoral support, concerned about the possibility of a fascist counter-revolution, social democrats abandon the project of a transition or at least pause to wait for more auspicious

* For example, the Conservative and Unionist Party leader Lord Salisbury had feared in 1903 that if Chamberlain converted the party to free trade it would 'be transformed into a Conservative party of the American or Colonial type, a party of manufacturers and *nouveaux riches*', which would be electorally perilous: see E. Halevy, *Imperialism and the Rise of Labour*, Benn, London, 1951, p. 326.

> times. They find the courage to explain to the working class that it is better to be exploited than to create a situation which contains the risk of turning against them. They refuse to stake their fortunes on a worsening of the crisis. They offer the compromise; they maintain and defend it.[33]

This does not mean that party leaders' judgements are correct. Mistakes are made and betrayals do occur. The point is rather that while parties do have objective relationships to classes of which party leaders are well aware, determining what these relations are is perhaps the most complex of all tasks of political analysis.

Secondly, in considering the relation between classes and parties, it is necessary to keep in view the point already made concerning the socially-constructed nature of class, remembering that classes are the objects of party competition, something 'produced' by parties, as well as something pre-given. It is true that classes *are* pre-given, both in the sense that the relations of production are what they are at any given moment, and in the sense that classes have a form and content given to them by previous 'class struggles'. But classes are also constantly being 're-produced' in new ways: materially, by economic and social changes which affect the occupational structure (e.g., the accelerated concentration of capital in the sixties or the de-industrialisation of the seventies), or people's living conditions (e.g., changing tax or housing policies); and ideologically, by policies and campaigns aimed at defining people in class terms in particular ways. The relationship between classes and parties is thus always a complex and dynamic process of interaction.

To anticipate briefly the following chapters, we may very schematically conceive of the relation between class and the major parties in Britain *before* 1960, as follows. Two-thirds of the manual workforce and their families had been successfully defined by the Labour Party and the trade unions, with the help of the distinctive character of working-class life, as members of the working class, committed to the Labour party as the party of the workers. And about twenty per cent of salaried, white-collar and professional workers had been defined as Labour supporters on the basis of the party's championship of social reform, modernisation, equality of educational opportunity, etc. Conversely, the Conservatives had succeeded in defining a significant minority of wage-workers as either 'deferential' Conservatives, or as aspirant 'middle-class' Conservatives, on the basis of the fact that the Conservative Party also, at that time, subscribed to the post-war consensus on full employment and 'welfare'.

After 1960, however, the consensus gradually ceased to be compatible with economic growth, while the changes in the nature of the labour force weakened both parties' definitional grip on their respective segments of it. Both manual workers and the 'new' middle class threw up elements outside the established definitions, while the 'old' middle class became more and more impatient with the concessions entailed by the consensus. The emphasis shifted from the *maintenance* of established class allegiances to the *redefinition* of classes and the articulation of new grounds for party allegiance. This shift was initiated by the Conservative Party, which far out-stripped the Labour Party in this respect during the 1970s. But if we look more closely at some of the new social forces to which the Conservative initiatives were in part a response, we can see that the picture is more complex. It was not just an altered relationship between parties and social classes, and not just an opportunity for the Conservatives, which the crisis produced.

Classes and Other Political Forces

From the mid-sixties onwards some new elements became politically important in Britain, as in other advanced industrial countries: for example the women's movement, the student movement, the movement against racism, the gay liberation movement, the ecological movement. People were mobilised, as women against sexual discrimination, as blacks against racism, as villagers against new motorways and as town-dwellers against 'developers', to a degree which at least matched their mobilisation as workers against exploitation. What is the relationship between social class, the historic origin and continuing basis of the parties, and these new political forces, which almost wholly ignored – and were largely ignored by – the major parties?

Some observers have been inclined to see the new movements as evidence that politics were ceasing to be 'class-determined', becoming instead a matter of plural competing interests unconnected with social class, although as the seventies unfolded this seemed less plausible. Others have seen them as reactions to the failure of party politics to secure an electoral consensus for the policies needed to resolve the crisis of capitalism, leading to more and more bureaucratic 'corporatist' forms of policy-making, reaching into more and more spheres of life.[34] Still others have seen the new groups and movements as evidence of the existence of generic conflict between state power as such and 'the people' – parallel to the conflict between classes but not reducible to it – a conflict which has become more acute as states have been forced to become larger and more bureaucratic.[35]

The most interesting analyses of this question turn on Gramsci's theory of hegemony. The ideological hegemony of the dominant class resulted, in Gramsci's view, from a process in which other groups had been actively enlisted in support of a general or national 'project' put forward by that class, in which they saw (or thought they saw) their own aspirations realised. This was more than a question of alliances; it involved a fusion of these different elements into an 'intellectual and moral unity'.[36] In the same way, Gramsci argued, the working class must establish its hegemony over various other social elements by putting forward policies, and a general conception of the future, which offered a genuine prospect of solving the varied problems they experienced and which brought them into conflict with the existing order.

From this standpoint, the emergence of new and radical political forces in Britain may be seen as evidence of the collapsing hegemony of the dominant class, which had either to be reconstructed or succumb to the counter-hegemony of opposing social forces. There are many indications that this theory is broadly correct. The 'Thatcherite' themes of family, law-and-order, racism, 'hard work' and the like appealed to popular reactions *against* these new movements, in language which tapped a large reservoir of traditional sentiment among ordinary people.[37] By contrast, the Labour Party's emphasis throughout the 1970s was almost wholly on economic issues of immediate concern to the workers as workers (with a strong bias towards male workers), and only very secondarily on issues such as personal security, racial or sexual emancipation or the environment. In short, the Labour Party did not respond as positively to these new movements as the Conservative Party responded negatively.*

In office, the Labour Party did pass laws in favour of equal pay for women (1970), against discrimination against women (1975), and against racial discrimination (1977), but in all of these it sought the line of least resistance between its own radical wing (and the demands of blacks and women) and the established order.[38] The legislation was weak and weakly enforced, and the party did not take up the broader, less economic issues raised by the blacks' or the women's movements, let alone those raised by the environmentalists, the students, the gays, or the nationalists – a failure which cost it dearly.

This is not to say that a successful new progressive alliance could be built out of these new materials; but the old alliance between the working class, organised in the labour movement, and the liberal-minded wing of the intelligentsia, which had been the basis of Labour's past successes, was no longer capable of achieving any further advance on the left,[39] whereas the potential of some of these new movements was considerable. The women's movement is the most striking case in point.

The subordination of women is as old as history and so, probably is the

* It was the Liberals, with their 'anti-class' philosophy, rather than the Labour Party, who engaged with some of the new issues by taking up 'community politics' – working with ratepayers' and tenants' associations and claimants' unions – for primarily tactical reasons in the early 1970s, and found that it paid some handsome dividends, leading to their having the largest number of seats on Liverpool City council in 1974 and a large share of the vote in local elections elsewhere. The National Front also engaged in 'community politics' of a different stripe, presenting the problems of the inner-city areas as being due to coloured immigration and the indifference of middle-class 'liberals' in city halls and at Westminster.

record of women's resistance. What was novel about the women's movement in Britain (and elsewhere) in the late 1970s was its scale, comprehensiveness and historical awareness, and its organisational versatility. These features seem to be linked to the fact that, by the late 1960s, women had a higher participation-rate in paid employment than at any previous time this century, and a higher level of education (inferior to men's as it still was) than at any previous time in British history – while, at the same time, women continued to suffer a comprehensive social, sexual, cultural, economic and political subordination. Feminist activists now directed their attack on this whole structure, while for many more women the practical struggle for legislative reform on equal pay and job opportunities gradually disclosed the inter-connectedness of all aspects of oppression. Women trade unionists, for example, found that the Equal Pay Act of 1970 (which made it illegal to pay women less than men for doing similar work) did not help so long as most women were confined to jobs that men did not do at all; and employers, sometimes with trade-union connivance, went to great lengths to segregate women's and men's work more thoroughly in the five years that they were allowed for making 'adjustments' between the passage of the Act in 1970 and its implementation in 1975.

> Equal pay was seen to be meaningless without equal opportunity [i.e., to hold 'men's' jobs]. Equal opportunity was seen to be meaningless unless women were given the chance to take their opportunities. To do so women needed equal education and training. They also needed the right to control their fertility, to choose when or whether to have a child. If they chose children, they needed paid maternity leave to protect their jobs and good child care facilities to enable them to continue work after having a child. To be equal meant being equal in terms of sick pay, pensions, social security and tax; it meant having the right to sign a hire purchase form without the husband's consent. In fact the logical argument led to the demand for equal citizenship.[40]

In 1981, it seemed to many people that the women's movement was destined for yet another eclipse. The trend to more equal pay had halted in 1977 and subsequently began to go into reverse.[41] Unemployment induced by the Thatcher policies eliminated women from jobs faster than men, partly because of the cuts in the public sector where so many women worked. These cuts also reduced or eliminated the few publicly-provided services which enabled mothers to work (day nurseries, nursery schools, cooked school meals). A strong Conservative campaign to revive the ideology of the family threatened to reverse the progress made in the previous decade in raising women's (and men's) consciousness of women's oppression and their right to equality.

But this reckoned without the width of the gap that had opened up between even official ideology and women's practical experience.

Documentation and analysis of their situation was improving rapidly and growing numbers of women were becoming aware of it and angry about it. Moreover the social basis of the ideology of motherhood as a vocation was being steadily eroded; the 'typical family' (of male breadwinner, wife and two children) so often referred to by judges, wage negotiators, and the drafters of social security regulations now accounted for only five per cent of all families! It seemed improbable that women would allow their new demands to lapse; and the same could be said for several of the other new movements that had developed in the sixties and seventies too.

The 'broad left' inside and outside the Labour Party had begun to realise that important as issues of employment and production were, they did not exhaust the urgent concerns which many people felt. They were also beginning to recognise that the demands of women, blacks, ecologists and others, while they were unlikely to be satisfied within the existing hierarchy of status and reward, would not be automatically satisfied under socialism either, *unless* socialism were explicitly defined so as to meet them. Some of them – for instance, the needs of many tenants and squatters and of many low-paid workers – had a clear basis in class relations. But more often there remained an important distinction between the needs people felt as workers and their needs as women, blacks, environmentalists, or whatever. Not all progressive demands can be reduced to class interests, and what is more, not all are necessarily compatible with the immediate 'corporate' interests of workers. To take two examples, real equality for women in pay and access to jobs would be likely to increase male unemployment in the short run, and pollution controls, too, can cost jobs.[42] The potential offered by the emerging social movements of the 1970s for a new and radical programme was very great, but to achieve it would call for a high order of political skill.

Conclusion

The distinctive features of the British class system can be identified only if we first clarify what we mean by 'class'. Having rejected the reduction of the concept of class to that of *stratum*, because it at best describes popular ideology at a particular moment, without enabling us to explain anything, we must face the difficulties involved in the alternative, Marxian concept of class. These difficulties can be partly resolved if we conceive of social classes as sets of 'places' in the relations of production. The way in which people actually experience and perceive classes and their place in them, however, is the result of political struggles which are largely about the existence, nature and significance of classes. Change is of the essence of both aspects – changes in the relations of production, and changes in the course of the class struggle.

The distinctive feature of the British class system can then be seen as lying in its archaic, caste-like character, the legacy of the distinctive and gradual path of Britain's transition to capitalism. In the post-World War II period the working class experienced a variety of changes, some of them far-reaching, in the associations of class that had characterised it for almost a century. The political *redefinition* or *re*-formation of the working class therefore became an important political issue. Some homogenisation of class-ranking also occurred within the 'middle class', though this was less significant.

To conceive classes in this way is also to recognise that political parties are not merely instruments (or manipulators) of 'pre-given' classes but are among the chief determinants of classes, at the same time as they are products of them. One of the most striking dimensions of this relationship from the mid-1960s onwards was the emergence of new political forces that were often linked to classes, but distinct from them. By the end of the 1970s, however, only the Conservatives had responded effectively to these new forces, in such a way as to re-attach a significant proportion of the working class to Conservatism – or more accurately, to the neo-Conservatism of the wing of the party led by Thatcher. It might prove a temporary attachment, in party terms, particularly since the Conservatives' economic policies had contradictory effects on the incomes and job security of so many workers; and the new social forces to which neo-Conservatism was a reaction had a potential for radical mobilisation which had still to be exploited. But the re-activation of traditional conservative themes was likely to leave a lasting mark on the consciousness of many workers, and had thus modified to a significant degree what the 'working class' *was* as it entered the 1980s.

PART III

9

The Conservative Party

Political parties are the natural victims of general crises. The Liberals succumbed – as a party of government, and for three decades as a significant political force – to the crisis of 1900–14. Neither the Conservatives nor the Labour Party were guaranteed to survive the crisis that set in in the sixties, and any description of their main features in 1981 must be more than usually provisional. The Conservative Party, moreover, has been poorly served by scholarship. Material on the party's leaders and doctrines is abundant, but critical studies of its social base and political economy are lamentably scarce. Within these limitations an attempt to understand this most powerful and resilient of all European conservative parties is indispensable.

'Conservative history is a microcosm of British public history as seen from the position of the ruler.'[1] That this should be so is one of the more remarkable facts of modern party politics. The Tory Party, out of which the modern Conservative Party, grew, was closely tied to landed property, which was fast being eclipsed as a significant source of wealth and power in Britain by the middle of the nineteenth century. The Conservatives succeeded in transforming themselves into a party – eventually *the* party – of industry and commerce, and then continued to dominate British politics even after the most proletarianised population in Europe (and, in trade-union terms, the most unified working class) had obtained the vote. The Conservatives were in office for 67 out of the 114 years between 1867 (when male urban workers were largely enfranchised) and 1981 – and for no less than 19 out of the 36 years since 1945, when the Labour Party came into its full electoral inheritance. What made this possible? And on the other hand, how could a party with such an exceptional capacity for survival none the less be in some danger of not surviving – at least as a major party of government – the crisis of the late twentieth century?

The Conservatives' Problem

It may be objected – many Conservatives would object – that the problem as we have posed it is a false one: that the Conservative Party represents the nation as a whole, not the interests of one class (as the Labour Party initially set out to do). The party's rhetoric has always claimed this; and it is a fact that a third of all manual workers have tended to vote Conservative, while more than half of all Labour supporters approve of Conservative policies more than Labour policies.[2]

However, the Conservative Party's history does not support this argument. We can follow the Tory Party's evolution into the modern Conservative Party under a succession of leaders – Peel, Disraeli, Salisbury and Baldwin, in particular – who declared more or less openly that the defence of property and the constitution which secured it was the party's prime task, and who saw the courting of the 'working man' as necessary for this purpose. The claim that, in doing so, the Conservative Party also served the interests of the workers, depends on a historic series of concessions: from the concession of cheap bread in 1846, to the acceptance of the Welfare State after 1951. Of course, if measures of this kind were substantial and regular enough it would be mere prejudice to describe them as 'concessions'. Samuel Beer, in fact, argued that whatever the Conservatives' original aim may have been, they should be regarded as having become not a class party which makes concessions to the underclass but *de facto* a party of compromise between competing class interests.[3]

But the record does not show the Conservatives to have taken any significant initiatives on behalf of the workers except in order to preserve the party's electoral position when it was acutely threatened. After the famous year 1875, in which Disraeli's government passed a series of measures to regulate and improve workers' living standards (at the expense of the still largely Liberal manufacturers and ratepayers), Conservative social legislation was conspicuously permissive rather than mandatory, and narrow in scope. The subsequent major advances in workers' social security, health provision, conditions of work and housing were all Liberal or Labour measures, usually opposed by the Conservatives.* The Conservatives' preference has always been to improve 'the condition of the people' by a general increase in prosperity, not by legislative reforms; in hard times, they have declared reform impracticable. Andrew Boyd's judgement must be accepted:

* The Education Acts of 1903 and 1944 could be considered exceptions, although the latter was very much the product of the wartime coalition government and was the work of R. A. Butler, one of the Conservative leaders most alert to the risk that the party could destroy itself by not coming to terms with the popular reaction to the slump and the democratisation of British life caused by the war.

> The Conservative party has a persisting unity denied to both the Labour and the Liberal parties. Its main purpose never changes: to preserve, as long as may be, a state of society in which private property and private enterprise may flourish.[4]

Or, in the characteristically uncompromising language of Enoch Powell in 1964 when he was still a leading Conservative:

> Whatever else the Conservative party stands for, unless it is the party of free choice, competition, and free enterprise, unless – I am not afraid of the word – it is the party of capitalism, then it has no formation in the contemporary world, then it has nothing to say to modern Britain.[5]

Securing the survival of capitalism in face of a well-organised working class majority has, then, been the Conservatives' central problem. As Rose remarks, 'if the Labour Party were as successful in winning working class votes as the Conservatives are in winning middle class votes, Labour . . . would have a permanent electoral majority'.[6] The question to be answered is how the Conservative Party has prevented this from happening.* Furthermore, the party has had to solve this problem while also dealing with changes, and not infrequently conflicts, within its base of support. This problem is shared to some extent by any political party, but it became particularly serious for the Conservatives once they had become a party of modern capitalism, which is by its nature subject to constant changes of form and content. The Conservatives had to adapt from being a party of landowners to being a party of competitive commercial capitalism, and then adapt again to being a party of giant bureaucratic corporations. This also called for flexibility, and as Harris observed,

> When Disraeli deserted what was left of the land of the squires, when Ulstermen stood opposed to King and Constitution, when the inter-war diehards went into battle in 1945 to refuse the price of the Second World War, it was certainly not a foregone conclusion that the party was capable of this 'flexibility'.[7]

The Elements of the Problem

Andrew Gamble proposed a relatively straightforward way of analysing the Conservatives' dilemma.[8] The party has a core of interests to defend and opinions to express – the interests and opinions of capital (manufacturing, commercial and financial) and the interests and opinions of the

* Of course this task does not have to be shouldered by the party alone. The power of private capital is (in Perry Anderson's words) 'polycentric'. It resides in the control of investment, in the ownership of newspapers and television companies, in its social influence within the state, and so on. None the less the ultimate guarantee that the interests of capital will be secure is that a party favourable to these interests is frequently in office; and down to the late 1970s, at least, the Conservatives have seen holding office as being very important in itself, important enough to justify the sometimes major concessions at the expense of property already referred to.

classes allied to capital (notably, the middle classes' interests in their personal property: houses, second homes, company cars, private education and private health-service arrangements, etc.). These are 'allied' classes, in the sense that they are not themselves the principal beneficiaries of Conservative policy, but they benefit in return for the support they give to the party. The Conservative Party must resolve the conflict that arises between these elements, and between them and the workers, in such a way as to maintain their active support. Gamble calls this the 'politics of support'.

Contrasted with the politics of support are what Gamble calls the 'politics of power'. This refers to the constraints and priorities imposed on any party in office by the requirements of economic production and national security. In a capitalist country, these requirements are 'at bottom . . . a compromise between the interests of capital in accumulation and its interests in political stability'. They call for a consistent set of policy objectives: for example, 'the maintenance of free trade, economy, and the gold standard, objects of British government for so long, comprised such a set of priorities'.[9] (Later, during the 'consensus' years, the maintenance of full employment, steady prices and a positive balance of payments comprised an alternative set.) Speaking generally, the 'politics of power' means, for the Conservatives, solving problems in ways that are compatible with the economic and political requirements of capital. These requirements are evolving and changing all the time. The party leadership must constantly reassess them and find new formulae for dealing with them.

At the same time these formulae must be congruent with parallel formulae for the politics of support. For example, one of the last acts of the Macmillan government in 1964 was to pass legislation abolishing Resale Price Maintenance, which in effect restored price competition in the retail trade in British manufactures. This was judged necessary in order to restore a measure of efficiency both in retailing and in manufacturing for the home market. However, its chief effect was to encourage retail outlets with high turnover and low margins, at the expense of many small retailers who were a mainstay of the Conservative Party's constituency associations. This was a case of the politics of power incurring costs in terms of the politics of support. By contrast, Mrs Thatcher's 1979 promise to cut personal income tax was seen as consistent with both the politics of support (appealing as it did to all tax-payers, and especially those with higher incomes) and the new politics of power to which she was committed – cutting state spending and enlarging the sphere of the market. (Whether it would prove a *successful* formula for the politics of power was another matter.)

Whereas the politics of power is focused on the state, the politics of support is focused on the 'nation' (to use Gamble's term) – the social classes and other elements into which society is divided. In practice the politics of support relates to the 'nation' in three main arenas – parliament, the party organisation, and elections – but especially the last two. The Conservative leadership must satisfy the elements which finance and run the party organisation, while at the same time trying to satisfy a majority of the electorate. As Gamble points out, meeting this last requirement involves a sophisticated reconciliation between the politics of power and the politics of support, because the party's supporters do not constitute an electoral majority. The rest of the votes the party needs must be won partly by real concessions, partly by psychological inducements (appeals to patriotism, racism, social deference, and the like) and partly by appearing to have a more credible or attractive politics of power than the opposing parties – what Gamble calls the party's 'electoral perspective'.

As a party dedicated to being in office, the Conservatives have always tended – at least until the late 1970s – to subordinate the politics of support to the politics of power, or at any rate tried to adapt their politics of support to what they saw as the necessities of the politics of power. Under Thatcher, these priorities began to alter. While stressing heavily themes such as law and order, hierarchy, and individual initiative, which have traditionally expressed the interests and outlook of the party's core of support, she was studiously vague about the party's policies for dealing with the problems of the economy – so much so that some observers were misled into expecting these policies to be *less* radical than those of Heath in the years 1970–72, because Heath had heavily emphasised the formulation of detailed policies in the years before 1970.[10]

An alternative interpretation, however, is that the priorities remained the same, but that Thatcher and her closest colleagues in the leadership entertained a radically different conception of the politics of power from Heath's. On the surface, their formulae for the politics of power appear similar: a smaller state, a reduction in union power, and reliance on competition and market forces to restore efficiency and encourage new investment. But in reality they were dissimilar. Thatcher had a very different understanding of the political parameters within which such a politics of power could or should operate. She was prepared to let the 'discipline of the market' work; she was prepared to accept the unpopularity this incurred (by the end of 1981 the Conservative Party's share of popular support had fallen to 23%);[11] she even seemed prepared to risk losing the next election. Unlike Heath, she conceived of a new order, for capital and labour alike, based on return to nineteenth-century values. She did not *subordinate* the politics of power to the politics of support – she had a vision of a new politics of power, and a new electoral perspective, resulting from a new 'neo-liberal' hegemony.

These contrasting interpretations reveal the limitations of any relatively simple analytic framework. Party management and leadership remain an art, not a science, with intuition and personality playing as important a part in success or failure as analysis and organisation. None the less, Gamble's model does throw a good deal of light on the successive transformations of Conservative policy and doctrines in modern times. For example, Joseph Chamberlain's campaign for tariff reform at the turn of the century is a case of a new politics of power (protection) and a new politics of support (social reform to be financed from import duties), but which failed because the conditions were not yet ripe for either. By the 1930s, however, a number of key relationships had changed: protectionism was becoming general throughout the world, and the Conservatives had inherited the support of those elements of manufacturing capital which had been attached to the Liberals thirty years earlier. The Labour Party had been discredited by the debacle of 1931, and so protectionism as a politics of power could now be complemented by a politics of support based not on social reform but on 'safety first' – retrenchment and preservation of the status quo.

It is not entirely far-fetched to see a parallel between this and the transition to 'Thatcherism'. Heath, like Joseph Chamberlain, proposed a politics of power whose time had not yet arrived. In the early 1970s capital was not yet ready to stand by the Conservative government in its confrontation with the trade unions nor, on the other hand, to invest in manufacturing so long as the industrial balance of power remained unchanged. Heath's politics of support were also inadequate. While his doctrine of efficiency and growth (especially in its Selsdon Park version) was in tune with the sentiments of the party's activists, his technocratic approach not only failed to stress the themes through which traditional Conservative values were expressed – law and order, inequality, the family, etc. – but also led him to execute a dramatic policy U-turn when his politics of power failed. The party's supporters were thus denied even the gratification of seeing the party confirm its reputation as the natural party of 'effective government'.

It fell to Thatcher to develop a politics of support appropriate to Heath's politics of power, and to implement the latter with the necessary faith and indifference to conventional wisdom. Also, the crisis was nearly ten years older when she took office, and the CBI, in spite of some misgivings, was now desperate enough to give her government continuing support in face of policy failures for which it would never have forgiven Heath.

Reference to the CBI's misgivings serves as a reminder that neither the 'politics of power' nor the 'politics of support' is synonymous with *policies* of power or support. On the contrary, although the Conservative Leader has, as we shall see, exceptional power, he or she must continually struggle to develop and maintain the chosen strategy and tactics in face of opposition not only from the party's natural opponents, but from among its own natural supporters, and even within its own ranks. In other words, *policies* of power and support are the outcome of the *politics* of power and support. These struggles are, typically, most visible and acute between the party's activists, far removed from the responsibilities of office, and the party's leadership, which comprises a large section of the parliamentary party. When the party is in power, about one Conservative MP in three is a holder of a government position – Minister, Junior Minister or unpaid Parliamentary Private Secretary to a Minister. When in opposition, an even larger proportion are ex-members or would-be members of government. They all tend to have a national view of politics, strongly influenced by the interplay between the politics of power and their assessment of the mood of the electorate – and especially the mood of those 'marginal' Conservative voters who are near the 'centre' of the national spectrum of opinion.

Back-bench MPs – particularly those with no experience of office, or no prospects of it – act as a sort of hinge between these two outlooks, and as a result back-benchers play a key organisational role in the party. Their support in the division lobby sustains the party leadership in office; their links to their constituencies make them sensitive to what their local party activists are saying.

A good example of this division of outlook occurred during the winter of 1980–1 when a series of cuts in services, flowing from the Thatcher government's spending cuts, culminated in a characteristically 'Tory' revolt. Conservative members of the House of Lords, from predominantly rural areas, declined to endorse the reduction of rural school-bus services, and some 32 Conservative MPs opposed or abstained from voting on a Budget clause which further raised the price of petrol (a measure which particularly affected rural voters, on whom the party increasingly depended).

Relative Autonomy

For the Conservative Party to be able to uphold the interests of capital in face of an enfranchised working-class majority is therefore a complex task, requiring, above all, a special kind of freedom for the party leadership in carrying it out. Until about 1970 this freedom was secured in two main ways – first, a finely-graduated social stratification within the party hierarchy, which insulated the leadership from its supporters; and second a unique degree of authority vested in the Leader.

The finely-graduated social stratification of the party was first pointed out by Jean Blondel. Drawing on a variety of sociological studies (mainly from the 1950s), he showed that as one moved up the hierarchy of the

Conservative Party – from members, to constituency association officers, to parliamentary candidates, to elected MPs and finally to the Cabinet – the social weight of the working class dropped, from a third of party members to zero in Conservative cabinets, by rather well-graduated stages.[12] Even more significantly, the weight of the 'lower middle class' (shopkeepers, teachers and the like, who accounted for around 16% of the electorate) made up over half the membership of the Conservative Party, but only about a quarter of the local party officers. More than half of these officers were drawn from what Blondel calls the 'well-to-do' (professional people, managers), who constituted only three or four per cent of the electorate. At the level of candidates and MPs the social composition became still more rarefied. The 'lower middle class' largely disappeared, and at each level the proportion who had been educated at public school rose. 'The higher one is in the educational and occupational scale, the more one is likely to get elected for a safe seat in the Conservative party'.[13] By the time the level of Conservative cabinets was reached, the proportion who had been to public school rose to about 85%, and the proportion from Eton alone to over a quarter. Over two thirds had been to Oxford or Cambridge.

The effect of this graduated social hierarchy was to *associate* the working class to some extent, and the lower-middle class very strongly, with the party's grass-roots organisation. The Conservatives have never claimed to know how many members they have; and, as pointed out by Blondel, Conservative constituency associations are associations, not local parties – i.e., they are primarily social clubs, groupings of conservative-minded people, and only seondarily electoral, let alone 'policy-proposing' organisations – so it is not of great moment what precise number of working-class people are members. Rough estimates suggest that some 3–400,000 working-class people do belong, with a tendency to be concentrated in towns with long-standing traditions of working-class Conservative affiliation (such as Glossop, near Manchester, where one of the early studies used by Blondel was carried out);[14] plus perhaps three-quarters of a million 'lower-middle class' people. These people provide the party's workers at elections, and they have some voice at the party's annual conferences; but much less than the local associations' officers, who are already predominantly drawn from higher income and status brackets, and are socially closer to the party's candidates and MPs. But even they are mostly at some social distance from those MPs who become Conservative ministers.

This graduated hierarchy, in other words, has permitted the leadership to appeal to a mass membership which has some basis in the working-class majority; to draw strength from the conservative passions of the lower middle class; but to enjoy an immunity, conferred by social distance and the respect for social status which is part of the Conservative tradition, from these passions when they run counter to the requirements of the politics of power.

This versatile social chain is matched by the unique organisational independence accorded to the party leader. The main elements of the party's organisation are as set out in Figure 9.1. The Conservative and

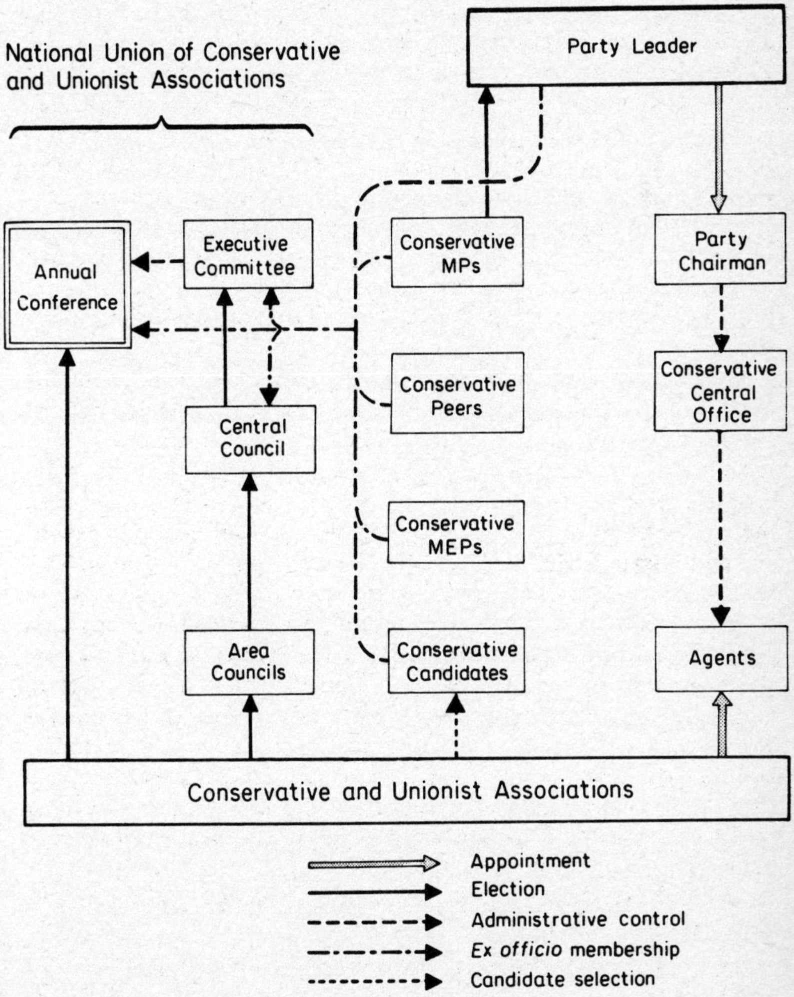

Figure 9.1 Conservative Party Organisation

Unionist constituency associations formally comprise the National Union of Conservative and Unionist Associations and elect the bulk of the 2,500–3,000 delegates who attend the annual Conservative Party Conference. This Conference, however, is also attended by the members of the Central Council of the National Association, which meets once a year in between the annual Party Conferences and includes all Conservative MPs, members of the European Parliament, peers, prospective parliamentary candidates and the senior officials of the Conservative Central Office. The Central Office is a purely professional organisation, the party's headquarters; the Conservative Research Department and Conservative Political Centre (policy-making and propaganda bodies, respectively) are attached to it, but its main business is formulating electoral strategy appointing and supervising parliamentary candidates, fund-raising, the appointment of agents in the constituencies, etc.

The Leader's formal position in all this is simple. Having been elected by the party's MPs, she (or he) holds office indefinitely until she resigns or is defeated at a subsequent leadership election. During this time, the Leader is subject to no formal constraint or control of any kind, either from the parliamentary party or from the National Association. The Director of the Central Office is answerable to the party Chairman, and both of them are appointed by the Leader, who also personally appoints the Director of the Conservative Research Department, the party's Vice-Chairman and Treasurer and other officers. The party's election manifestos, and all other policy statements, are the responsibility of the Leader alone.

This organisational apartheid is very visible at Annual Conferences of the party (i.e., of the National Union). The leadership on the Conference platform is neither elected by, nor is in any way answerable to, the party organisation represented by those on the conference floor.* The leadership seek the support of Conference – and usually get it, even when the mood is critical – but while leaders and supporters meet in Conference, they do not transact any business together. Annual Conferences pass resolutions, but the instances where these have been accepted by the leadership when they ran counter to what had previously been seen as dictated by the politics of power are so few as to be famous. One such instance was the pledge made by Harold Macmillan at the 1950 Conference to accept the target of 300,000 new houses a year as government policy (a pledge later redeemed in office).

These arrangements contrast sharply with the position of the Labour Party Leader, who even before the constitutional changes of 1980 and 1981 was formally bound by the policy resolutions of the Labour Party

* An attempt to give the membership some formal power was made in 1884, led by the Tory radical Lord Randolph Churchill, but it was deflected by the leadership.

Conference, and had to work with party officers elected by the Conference or appointed by the National Executive Committee, none of whom was responsible to him. In addition, the Conservative Leader enjoys the great power that goes with patronage – her power to appoint, and dismiss, all 130 or so members of any Conservative government.[15] The Leader is thus free to adopt, adapt or drop policies according to her or his judgement of the necessary balance to be struck between the politics of power and the politics of support, to an extent not found in any other party's constitution. This freedom is the second key to the famous 'pragmatism' which the Conservatives have shown over the century-and-a-half since Sir Robert Peel first articulated the modern concept of conservatism, of continuing to conserve what is essential by accepting change in what is not.

It is striking that, with so much power, Conservative Leaders have had a higher casualty rate than the leaders of other parties.[16] That is the price they have paid for not succeeding in fulfilling the party's goal of defending property to the satisfaction of their followers, above all by failing to maintain the party's hold on office. In the post-war period Churchill was untouchable because of his wartime position, and clung to office after he was no longer able to exercise it effectively; but Eden, Macmillan and Home were all forced to resign and Heath was forced to submit to re-election in circumstances which led to his defeat. The executioners of this law of failure are the Conservative MPs. This has become much clearer since Conservative MPs decided, in 1965, to elect Leaders directly, and, in 1975, to oblige Leaders to submit to an annual election when in opposition.

Before that, an informal process of criticism and control had been exercised by the back-benchers through the '1922 Committee', a semi-official organ of back-bench opinion.* The 1922 Committee could, in effect, force the Leader to take its views into account, or even to resign, by a sufficiently united and forceful expression of discontent. But it had no formal power, and a Leader determined to defend himself could always hope to deflect opposition by the appeal to rank, by the use of patronage and by his strategic control of the extra-parliamentary party machine.

It was to reduce the power of the 'magic circle' of rank and privilege in which previous leaders had moved that the Conservative back-benchers made these changes, making the Leader directly and visibly, not indirectly

* The 1922 Committee takes its name from a famous meeting of Conservative MPs which repudiated the decision of the party's Leader, Austen Chamberlain, to continue the coalition that the Liberal Leader Lloyd-George had maintained since the end of the 1914–18 war. The committee consists of all the Conservative MPs except the Leader when the party is in opposition; when the party is in office it consists only of back-benchers (the Whips attend but do not vote).

and invisibly, answerable to the party in the House of Commons. These changes reflected their feeling that the style of leadership that had served the party in the interval between 1918 and the second onset of the crisis must change. In the past, it had been said that the Conservative leader 'emerged'. In absence of a 'natural' leader – and the Conservatives had known only one (Churchill) in the twentieth century – the effect of this principle was to confer the leadership on 'sound' figures at the centre of the spectrum of party opinion.

In 1964, however, the 'emergence' of Lord Home, the least divisive of the contenders for the succession to Macmillan, produced a figure unattuned to the crumbling of the consensus, a hereditary peer with virtually no experience of the Commons and little interest in domestic affairs. In sharp contrast, the leadership election of the following year led to the choice of Heath, with his clear if over-intellectualised approach to the problem of reconstructing British capitalism. Heath's policy failures (the U-turns, the unsuccessful confrontation with the miners, the imposition of direct rule in Belfast, the unpopular EEC), culminating in two election defeats in 1974, prompted the back-benchers to move again – this time to take routine powers to terminate a leader's tenure by means of annual elections. As the political stakes rose, the Conservative Leader became more directly and visibly dependent on the parliamentary party.

Hegemony

While the relative autonomy of the Conservative Leader has been necessary for Conservative success, it is not the whole explanation. Why has one worker in three regularly tended to vote Conservative? What are the positive elements which tie a major section of the working class to the Conservative Party? One surprisingly simple answer is that workers tend to agree more with Conservative than with Labour policies. Though a majority vote Labour because they see it as the party most identified with their interests, even these workers tend to hold views more in line with Conservative policies (on, for instance, education, law and order, housing or foreign affairs). What accounts for this?

The answer must be sought in the 'naturalisation' of conservative ideas that results from the penetration of all social life by the capital–labour relationship discussed in Chapter 7. This is not primarily a matter of 'indoctrination'. On the contrary, the power of the ideas implicit in the capital–labour relationship springs largely from their being *self-taught*. Paul Willis's study of a comprehensive school in the Midlands in the mid-1970s showed, for example, that it was in their very rejection of the official culture of the school (with its stress on academic achievement and conformity to authority) that working-class boys *prepared themselves* for unskilled labouring jobs.[17] Their preparedness to accept a life of repetitive, low-paid work, and to accept as natural, or at least inevitable, that there should be such work and that they should do it, was largely the result of their own active contribution to a working-class *counter*-culture while still at school. To say that the existence of such work at one end of the scale, and of owners and managers at the other, is a 'fact of life' which is accepted as natural because 'that is the way it is', is to miss the active dimension through which – in the absence of an ideological counter-initiative – the 'victims' constantly *re-create* the social reality which victimises them. It was certainly true that the authority figures in these boys' lives – teachers, parents, police, future employers – also actively contributed, in a different way, to constructing the same social reality; and both processes continue throughout adult life.

The ideas which Willis recorded from the 'lads' at 'Hammertown Boys Comprehensive' already contained many quintessentially Conservative themes, such as the status of women, race, the value of physical labour, and the inevitability of the established order. And in another study of 'hippies' and a motorcycle 'gang', Willis noted how, with new experiences in adult life, the range of conservative political ideas expanded, even in these apparently 'deviant' working-class sub-cultures.[18] Nationalism, racism, the monarchy and even authority were positively endorsed.

The 'social-democratic' counter-culture of the labour movement was, by comparison, feeble, at least by the late 1970s; such vitality as it still possessed owed more to the residual effects of the 'people's war' and the sheer scale and omni-presence of the Welfare State than to any continuing effort by the Labour Party or the trade unions to develop an alternative conception of society among their members.

The Conservative Achievement 1945–70

The Conservative party therefore appeals to a population, including its working-class majority, which tends to be predisposed to respond to Conservative themes. Considered in this light, the success of the Labour Party in attracting the support of two-thirds of the working-class electorate could be said to need as much explanation as the success of the Conservative Party in retaining the support of the one-third. Yet this is also a somewhat misleading way of putting the matter. The fact that a majority of workers still tend to vote Labour in spite of having more or less Conservative views on many issues, shows that voting is not a matter of policy preferences alone; the structure of people's political attitudes is much more complex. It has been shown, for instance, that people change their views on specific questions to bring them more into line with the position adopted by 'their' party.[19] What this implies for the Conservative Party is the need to maintain an 'image' capable of *activating* the conservative predispositions of the mass electorate sufficiently to offset the strength of the Labour Party's 'image' as the party of the working class.

For almost a century the Conservatives found to hand major issues which enabled them to project such an image, using and constantly adapting a limited range of traditional themes: national unity (opposition to both regional and class division), national sovereignty, the Empire, the constitution (especially monarchy, parliament and the rule of law), the established Church, and last but not least, the 'conduct of the King's (or Queen's) government'. The Conservatives particularly stressed their 'competence' as the natural party of government, and particularly attacked the Labour Party as not merely based on 'narrow', 'sectional' (i.e., class) interests, but also as incompetent and unfit to be trusted with the affairs of state.

For the party leadership to continue to exploit these themes, while pursuing a politics of power adapted to the greatly altered circumstances following the Second World War, tested the mechanisms of adaptation outlined earlier to their limits, but with brilliant results. Two of the chief architects of what was then called the 'new Toryism', Macmillan and R. A. Butler, are excellent examples of the leadership's ability to pursue the politics of power it judges necessary while at the same time disengaging the party from declining social strata and recruiting new elements of future support. After 1945, 'a vital Conservative task was to recruit professional managers in modern industry and jettison the railway stockholders and the mine owners'.[20] To enable the leadership to come to terms with the expanded interventionist and welfare state, and the new nationalised-industry sector, Conservative MPs in touch with modern corporate enterprise had to replace rentiers, retired majors and landowners. The task was accomplished – gradually but thoroughly – by internal party reforms initiated after 1945. The 'new' type of Conservative MP, without large private means or a family political tradition, did not reach the ranks of the leadership until the mid-1960s, but this allowed the party to present a strong appearance of continuity with the past throughout the fifties.

As Ramsden has pointed out, the Conservatives were also helped to make this crucial transition – in effect, to come to terms with social democracy – by the fact that in the early 1950s, at least, much of the prewar context did not seem to have changed. Apart from India, the Empire was still intact; the army – so powerfully linked to the Empire and the Conservatives – was larger than it had ever previously been in peacetime; the higher civil service was still largely Conservative (or Liberal) in background and outlook, as were the professions, the Church of England, most of the press and virtually all of the management of industry.[21] Stability in these contexts allowed Macmillan not only to keep the party committed to the Welfare State, but to assert his own preference for inflation over unemployment by accepting the resignation of his whole Treasury team (the Chancellor of the Exchequer and junior ministers) in 1958 when they thought otherwise. (Macmillan characteristically dismissed the crisis as 'little local difficulties'.) Social services went on expanding under the Conservatives within the general lines laid down by Labour after the war. 'The Conservatives set out to prove themselves better managers of Social Democracy than the Labour Party, and aided by the long boom in the Western economy they succeeded beyond expectation'.[22]

This success in turn reinforced the party's image as the party of good government. By the end of the 1950s it was the Labour Party which was on the defensive, concerned that 'embourgeoisement' had made its own residual socialist commitments a liability rather than an asset among the working class. Exploiting this success, Macmillan also tackled the dismemberment of the empire (which Churchill had once declared himself 'not elected to preside over'), the application to enter the EEC, the abandonment of an independent nuclear capacity and the scaling down of the armed forces. Had the economy been capable of sustaining the growth of the 1950s, the Conservative Party might have survived without any more radical changes to become the dominant party of government of a prosperous middle-level European power in the last quarter of the twentieth century. But this was not to be.

The Crisis and the Conservatives

Writing in 1971 Nigel Harris observed that from the point of view of capital,

> Other things being equal, the Conservative Party could always be trusted. It might fumble, or cling to policies which aligned it with an earlier *status quo* rather than seek to accelerate the evolution of a future *status quo*, but at least it was free from those alarming adventures that occasionally afflicted Labour. Such calculations were possible provided Britain faced no crisis so great that its demands exceeded the limits of Conservative 'flexibility'. It was never necessary to create a new party of the *status quo* because the Conservatives could no longer fight the fight... And this was so because of the sheer stability of British society... The social schisms never became so wide that the Conservatives could not make some attempt to straddle them. The pursuit of 'balance' was never forced to give way entirely to the struggle for 'order'.[23]

After 1970, the crisis began to exceed these limits; a growing segment of Conservative opinion began to think that the party was no longer fighting the fight. They did not turn to a new party of order, however, but sought to change the Conservative party itself into such a party. The election of Thatcher as Leader and her general election victory in 1979 were large steps in this direction, though the resistance of the 'Tory' wing of the party was not definitively overcome, even by 1981. Meantime the emergence of the Liberal–SDP alliance, seeking to occupy the 'centre ground' vacated by the Conservatives, profoundly altered the electoral calculus.

The immediate occasion of the rise of the new right within the Conservative Party was what they perceived as the growing cost of seeking trade-union co-operation in the formulation and implementation of economic policy, a policy which had culminated in the concessions made to the unions under the 'Social Contract'. Not only did this policy seem to them to give the unions an unconscionable degree of power, it had also failed to halt the country's industrial decline. To put it in terms of Gamble's formulation, the politics of support became less and less consistent with the politics of power as Heath understood them from 1972 onwards. The mounting unrest on the Conservative back-benches was matched not only in the constituency associations – where the 'old-fashioned' right had always been strong, and where the abandonment of empire and the decline of British military power were particularly resented – but much more significantly elsewhere: for example, in the Confederation of British Industry – the organised voice of large-scale industry. There, the Director-General, after dismissing his Economic Director in 1973 for his monetarist opposition to Heath's policies, was himself obliged to quit his office in 1975, after which CBI policies swung firmly in a neo-liberal direction. [24] The fact that the civil service did not do likewise, and that the professions, the universities and the media were, by now, much less reliably Conservative (at least with a capital C) than they had been in the 1950s, heightened the sense of insecurity on the Conservative right.[25]

The electoral prospects of the party had also become increasingly bleak. Their share of the total vote cast had declined at every election since 1955, from nearly 50% in 1955 to under 36% in October 1974. Their grip on the all-important working-class voters had been weakening; some were abstaining, some were voting Liberal in England or Scottish Nationalist in Scotland, while in Northern Ireland the Unionists, bitterly resentful of Heath's imposition of direct rule in 1972, ended their historic alliance with the Conservatives after the February 1974 election. These losses damaged the Conservatives' image as the party of national unity as well as the party of good government. They had also surrendered sovereignty to the EEC – this, after giving up the empire.

In February 1974 Enoch Powell, a former Conservative Minister, left the party and called on voters to vote Labour because Labour was opposed to the EEC; and, in October 1974, he stood as a Unionist in the Northern Ireland seat of South Down to underscore his opposition to Heath's policy of seeking an 'all Ireland' solution to the conflict in Ulster. In Scotland, the SNP offered a substitute nationalism, and in the October 1974 election pushed the Conservatives into third place in terms of votes cast. In England, too, the far-right, racist National Front won an average of over three per cent of the poll in the seats it contested in 1970 and in the two elections of 1974.[26] While these votes were not all gained at the expense of the Conservatives, they represented a pool of voters with whom the Conservative right felt a good deal of sympathy and whose support they would have liked to have.

What all this implied was that the Conservatives' existing politics of power could not be justified in terms of electoral success. A new 'electoral perspective' was needed too. Thatcher's contribution was to see that the new politics of power proposed by 'social market' doctrine, combined with a new politics of support based on an attack on the 'consensus', could pay electoral dividends, and she demonstrated this dramatically in May 1979. The question posed by this historic election – in which the Conservatives achieved the largest electoral swing since 1945 – is whether it marked the conversion of the Conservative Party from a dominant party of government, surviving by occupying the centre ground, into a party of order, destined to retain power only so long as no centre ground existed.

In 1981 the answer to this question lay in the future, but some signs pointed to such a change. The new leadership election process made it less likely that the party would in future be led by patricians of the Macmillan type. The internal changes inaugurated after 1945 had eventually produced a significantly different parliamentary party: 'In the seventies, for the first time in its history, the Conservative Party ha[d] more MPs from grammar schools than from Eton and half of its MPs [were] occupied in business'.[27] The significance of this shift should not be exaggerated. The Tories, or 'wets' (as Thatcher called them), were still strong, particularly among the senior ranks of Conservative MPs, and by 1981 they were campaigning openly for a return to the 'middle road'. But the outlook of the new generation of MPs was more directly representative of the party's support base than it had been for some time.*

A similar shift also seemed to have occurred within the constituency associations. Although research is lacking, observers of Annual Conferences noted that the 'county' and professional middle-class element, which had tended to predominate among Conservative representatives in the past, had given way to the more aggressive accents of the lower-middle class. They also noted that the rapport between the Conference rank-and-file and the Leader (as opposed to her 'Tory' or 'wet' colleagues on the platform) was closer than at any time since 1945. Could the reduced formal autonomy of the leader have been paralleled by a process of social

* For example, in March 1973 the President of the CBI was invited to a meeting of 40 Conservative back-benchers 'to explain the CBI's reluctance to associate itself with the Conservative Party. The meeting was fairly heated, the back-benchers complaining that the CBI was cutting its links with its natural spokesmen in Parliament' (W. Grant and D. Marsh, *The CBI*, Hodder and Stoughton, London 1977, p. 114).

homogenisation in the constituency associations, thus reducing both elements of the 'insulation' which had been so important to the Conservatives' 'flexibility' in the past?

If so, the course set for the party by Thatcher might prove increasingly hard to reverse. The risks involved were signalised by the emergence of the SDP, whose popularity in opinion polls and at by-elections in 1981 implied that the Conservatives could conceivably be reduced to a permanent parliamentary minority. There was even a growing body of support within the party for proportional representation, which would almost certainly mean the end of purely Conservative governments in the future. It seemed that some Conservatives increasingly accepted that the party could no longer 'fight the fight' alone.* Thatcher herself was playing for higher stakes: to remain the dominant party of government in a country where 'business' could once again flourish, and where the public had returned to pre-social-democratic – if not pre-democratic – values.

* Or preferred this to fighting alone on Thatcher's strategy; the Conservative Action for Electoral Reform group was predominantly 'wet' in outlook.

10

The Labour Party and the Left

The crisis affected the Labour Party even more fundamentally than the Conservatives. By the end of the 1960s the left wing of the party in the constituencies and the trade unions, and a small group of Labour MPs, had become impatient with their traditional role as the 'conscience' of the party, prominent when the party was in opposition, but disregarded by the party's parliamentary leaders when in office. From 1972 onwards they began organising to commit the party to a more uncompromisingly socialist programme; after 1979 they also mobilised to change the party constitution so as to make the parliamentary leadership accountable to the party outside parliament.

By March 1981 the success of the 'Labour left's' campaign had precipitated a split; a small section of the parliamentary right wing, led by four ex-ministers, broke away to form a Social Democratic Party. By the end of the year, 25 sitting Labour MPs (and one Conservative) had joined the SDP, which in alliance with the Liberals had also won a spectacular by-election victory.[1] Labour's voting strongholds in the industrial cities might hold firm but there was a clear risk that the SDP–Liberal Alliance could prevent Labour from forming another majority government – especially if the Alliance found itself in a position to secure the adoption of proportional representation. If that happened, the Labour Party could be faced with an indefinitely long period in opposition; and in that case some trade unions, already weakened by unemployment and anti-union legislation, might wish to reduce or even sever their formal links with the Labour Party – links that still formed the bedrock of the party's financial, organisational and ideological support.

The Labour Party and the labour movement were tougher, denser social forces than recognised by the media (which eagerly followed – or promoted – the struggles within the Labour Party and the rise of the

SDP). They would not be easily separated from each other, or displaced from the centre of the political stage. But the risk that the crisis could effectively destroy the party was none the less real. To assess this risk a historical understanding of the situation is essential.

Labour in Politics: the Formative Years

In 1900 two socialist parties already existed in Britain, the Independent Labour Party (ILP), founded in 1893, and the Social Democratic Federation (SDF), formed in 1883. Unlike their counterparts in Germany and France, they had made very limited inroads into working-class political consciousness. The ILP ran 28 candidates in the 1895 election; all were defeated. The SDF, a Marxist party, ran three candidates in 1885, two in 1892 and four in 1895, all equally unsuccessfully. The leadership of the trade-union movement was overwhelmingly Liberal in allegiance and confined itself to trying to get a number of 'Liberal–Labour' representatives (not all of whom were workers) adopted as Liberal parliamentary candidates. In 1895 (the last election before the formation of the Labour Party) 24 'Lib–Labs' were adopted and nine were elected. To appreciate the extent to which the British labour movement was still subject to Liberal hegemony it is only necessary to recall that, by 1912, the German Social Democrats were the largest party in the Reichstag, while in 1910 the French Socialists and Socialist Radicals had 42% of the seats in the Chamber of Deputies.

As we saw in Chapter 3, the trade unions' reluctant decision to seek independent representation in parliament in order to protect their legal rights and their members' living standards was a response to the efforts of the employers, supported by the courts, to restore profitability by cutting wages during the Great Depression. In 1899, the Trades Union Congress agreed to form a Labour Representation Committee on which the ILP, the SDF and the Fabian Society were also represented. The 1900 election came too soon for the LRC to do more than return two MPs, but in the 1906 election 30 LRC candidates were successful, and joined with the 22 Lib–Lab MPs elected at the same time to form a 'Labour Party' in the House of Commons. After 1906 the LRC and the Labour MPs became known simply as the 'Labour Party', supported by the network of 'Trades Councils' developed by trade-union activists in most cities during the 1890s. But it was not until 1918 that a mass base of individual members was created in 'constituency parties' throughout the country, to complement the federal structure of 'affiliated' organisations built up by the LRC.

This delay reflected the limited conception of the LRC's founders: to establish in parliament an independent group of spokesmen for the interests of labour. The LRC rejected at the outset the SDF's proposal to make the achievement of socialism one of its objectives. The ILP, whose representative (Keir Hardie) concurred in this decision, had called itself an independent 'labour' party, not a socialist party, for the same reason: the workers did not yet support the idea of socialism. The ILP believed that once the workers supported an independent party of labour, support for socialism would grow out of the struggle for reforms. Meantime, the LRC's aims were confined to redressing the grievances of the workers within the existing order. This approach was reinforced by the Fabian Society, an organisation of middle-class intellectuals formed in 1884 and dedicated to Socialist reform through 'permeation', i.e. persuading the leadership of whatever party was in power to adopt Fabian policy. At first the Fabians' hopes were pinned on the progressive wing of the Liberal Party, but they soon recognised the potential of the new Labour Party and gave it increasing intellectual support.

The LRC was also greatly assisted by the award in 1901 of damages to the Taff Vale Railway against the Railway Servants' union after a strike, a ruling which put all trade-union funds at risk in industrial disputes. The number of strikes decreased, as support for the LRC rose. Three LRC candidates were elected at by-elections in 1903. The Liberal Party's Chief Whip recognised the danger and made a secret agreement with Ramsay MacDonald, the Secretary to the LRC, to avoid the LRC and the Liberal Party competing against each other in a number of working-class constituencies. The result in 1906 was a landslide victory for the Liberal Party combined with the remarkable success of 30 of the LRC's candidates. The Taff Vale judgement was promptly reversed by the Trades Disputes Act of 1906, which served as the legal basis of British trade union rights until the 1970s. The LRC's strategy seemed to be brilliantly vindicated.

But labourism did not remain unchallenged as the policy of the party for very long. The years of industrial conflict preceding the outbreak of the First World War generated demands for more radical change. This was reflected in the party's new constitution, adopted in 1918, whose famous Clause 4 stated that the party's object was 'to secure for the workers by hand or by brain the full fruits of their industry... upon the basis of the common ownership of the means of production'. But these words meant different things to different people. For most of the party's leadership, and probably most of its members, the party's new programme, *Labour and the New Social Order*, also adopted in 1918, was 'a Fabian blueprint for a more advanced, more regulated form of capitalism', rather than a formula for a radically different principle of social organisation, which it was taken to be by some socialists.[2] For, by 1918, the 'labourist' conception of the party had become strongly established, and had been reinforced by two other features of the original project: its parliamentarism, and the lack of a formal extra-parliamentary base for the party in parliament.

Parliamentarism, of course, was the essence of the original proposal. The task of the LRC was to secure parliamentary representation for 'labour'. By 1918 a generation of labour politicians had been produced who saw their role in these terms. They were resistant to any proposal to use extra-parliamentary action such as strikes, boycotts or the 'blacking' of goods, in support of political aims, which Conservative and Liberal MPs denounced as unconstitutional. In the earliest years, moreover, few Labour MPs had either the educational or theoretical background to enable them to develop even a comprehensive set of reform proposals.[3]

The lack of a mass membership base outside parliament also gave the early Labour MPs greater autonomy. Although the authority of the party's Annual Conference (consisting of delegates of the trade-union and other organisations which had affiliated to the LRC) and of the National Executive Committee (chosen by the Conference) was acknowledged, the MPs demanded, and were in practice allowed, a good deal of freedom to go their own way. This was rationalised by saying that they must decide the 'timing and method' of implementing conference decision in parliament: they alone, they argued, could judge the practical possibilities for action in the light of the party balance in the House of Commons, and electoral considerations. This freedom was contested from the first, but it was only after 1979 that the Labour left directed their efforts to changing the constitution so as to oblige the Parliamentary Labour Party (PLP) to carry out the policies adopted by the party Conference. Before 1918, however, the question of whether the parliamentary party's *de facto* autonomy was compatible with socialist objectives did not arise, as socialism was not then the aim of the party, even in theory. By 1918 a large measure of autonomy for the parliamentary party had become established practice, however much it continued to be questioned.

One more development on the party's earliest years also had a major influence on later events. In 1903 the Social Democratic Federation withdrew from the LRC because of the LRC's reformist policy. At this time the SDF was a significant force, with forty-three branches and a cadre of tireless propagandists who enjoyed considerable respect among trade unionists. But the Marxism of the SDF was of a highly sectarian brand, and its leader Henry Hyndman had stamped on the organisation a highly autocratic mode of operation. In separating itself from the LRC, the SDF separated itself from the mainstream of working-class politics. The result was that it remained 'chronically unable to break out of its isolation, or to influence the course of history', although it continued to form an important pole of attraction for left-wing activists who became frustrated by the Labour Party's parliamentary and reformist limitations.[4] In 1913 the SDF merged briefly with some of these elements to form the British Socialist Party, and in 1920 the Communist Party of Great Britain was formed, inheriting the role, and many of the personnel, of the SDF and BSP. The Communist Party's existence divided the left wing of the labour movement and strengthened the hand of Labour Party leaders who adopted right-wing positions by enabling them to appeal to anti-Communist sentiment.

This factor was already significant in the Labour Party's response to the wave of industrial militancy which developed from 1908 to 1913. Prices were rising while wages stayed constant (or in some industries were even cut). Trade-union membership increased rapidly: more people joined unions between 1900 and 1914 than in all previous years combined, reaching a total of 4.1 million in 1914. Strike activity rose dramatically. In 1912, 40 million working days were 'lost' in stoppages, more than any year since except for 1921 and 1926, the year of the General Strike. To many contemporaries it was an extraordinary and frightening development, as the working class expressed its resentment and seemed to feel its potential strength in a way not seen since Chartism.

The Labour Party, however, and the ILP (which retained its separate existence as an organisation affiliated to the Labour Party) opposed the strikes, criticising them as 'undemocratic' – i.e., as expressing grievances which should be settled through parliamentary action. The SDF, on the other hand, declared that the strikes were a distraction from the task of organising a party with a revolutionary programme. The political initiative among the strikers passed by default to the syndicalists – advocates of the direct seizure of economic control by the workers in factories. This helped to spread socialist ideas and to popularise unionism. But syndicalism had no organisational base, and the only long-run beneficiaries were the leaders of the established trade unions whose membership increased.

A few years later, during the First World War, when the trade-union leadership agreed to an 'industrial truce' (i.e., no strikes) without first securing guarantees from the employers on job security and price controls, this was exploited by employers to raise profits at the expense of wages. As a result, the leadership of the workers' resistance (especially in the munitions industry) fell to the shop stewards in the affected factories, and a nation-wide Shop Stewards' Movement developed. Its inaugural conference, held in Leeds in 1916, called for the formation of soldiers' and workers' councils (Soviets) on the Russian model. The movement collapsed, however, with the end of the war, the rise in unemployment (as soldiers were demobilised), and the end of the industrial truce. The radical impulse imparted to the labour movement by the pre-war crisis and the upheavals of war-time was thus contained and limited by the early evolution of the Labour Party and its relationship with the Marxist left.

Party Structure

The Labour Party thus emerged from the First World War with a potential mass base that had been greatly extended, even if many of the party's own leaders had not supported the popular movements which had helped to accomplish this. It was now essential for the party to take advantage of the base which had been developed. The new constitution adopted by the party in February 1918 grafted a mass individual-membership, organised in 'Constituency Labour Parties', onto the structure of affiliated labour organisations created by the LRC, creating a unique party structure which was to persist, virtually unchanged, until the present day.

The Annual Conference of the party was made formally sovereign. In contrast to the Conservatives' annual conferences it formally determines the policies which the PLP is supposed to implement. Within the Conference the balance of power rests with the trade unions, because delegates' votes are weighted according to the number of members in the organisations they represent. In 1982 the General Secretary of the Transport and General Workers' Union cast a 'block vote' of 1,250,000, this being the number of TGWU members whom the union had 'affiliated' to the party as having paid the voluntary 'political' levy (in addition to their

Table 10.1 Votes at the 1982 Labour Party Conference

Transport and General Workers Union	1,250,000
Amalgamated Union of Engineering Workers Engineering Section	850,000
General and Municipal Workers Union	650,000
National Union of Public Employees	600,000
Union of Shop, Distributive and Allied Workers	418,000
National Union of Mineworkers	225,000
Union of Construction Allied Trades and Technicians	200,000
Union of Communication Workers (formerly Post Office Workers)	194,000
Electrical, Electronic, Telecommunications and Plumbing Union	180,000
National Union of Railwaymen	170,000
Total vote of 10 largest unions	4,748,000
Total vote of all other (38) unions	1,534,000
Total Constituency Parties vote (579 organisations)	602,000
Total Socialist and Co-operative Societies Vote (10 organisations)	66,000
Total Conference Vote	6,950,000

Source: Labour Party Information Department; through the courtesy of L. Minkin.

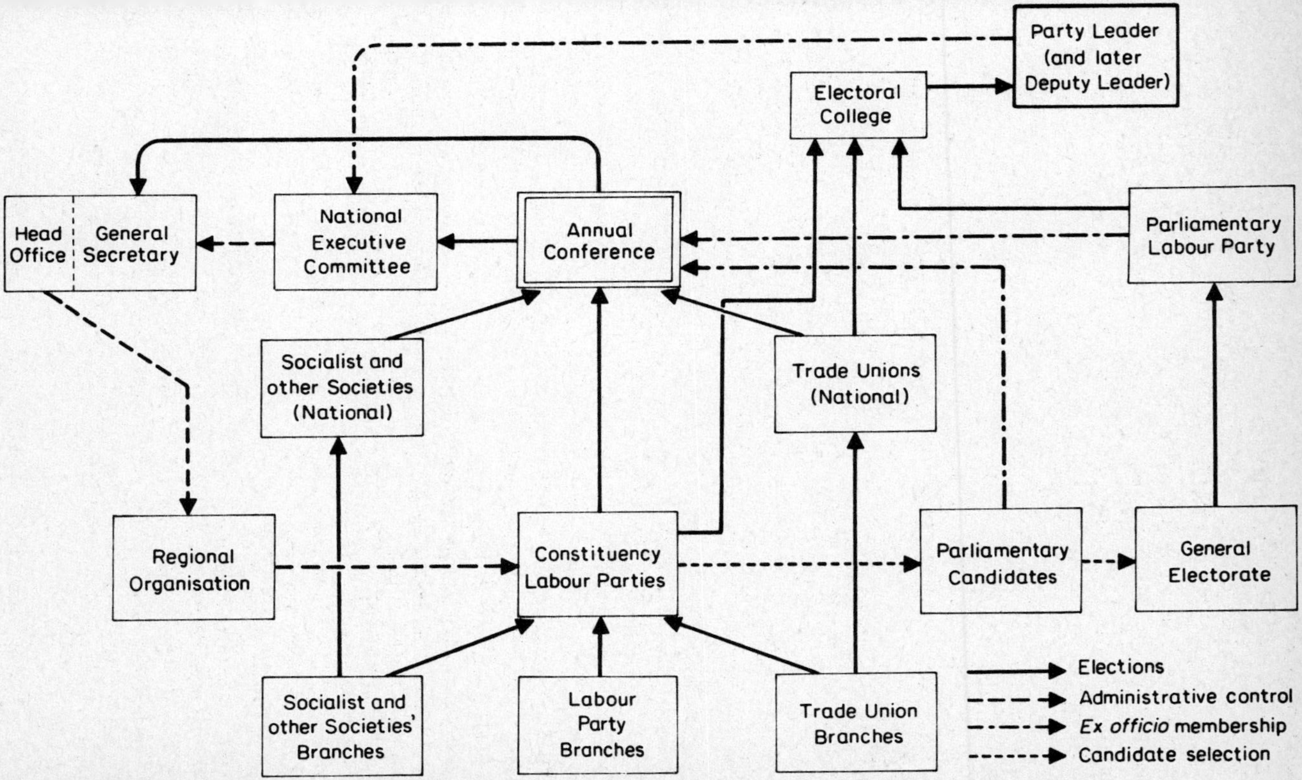

Figure 10.1 *Labour Party Structure*

Source: Adapted from L. Minkin *The Labour Party Conference*, Manchester University Press, Manchester 1980.

union subscription).[5] By contrast the delegates from a constituency party might cast as few as 256 votes.[6]

The National Executive Committee is elected by the Conference. Constituency Parties' delegates vote separately from the rest of the Conference to fill seven of the 29 NEC seats. One more member is chosen by the Young Socialist organisation and another by affiliated socialist, co-operative and professional organisations, and the party's Leader and Deputy Leader are members *ex officio*. The remaining 18 seats, however, including the five reserved for women, are voted for by all the delegates, so that the NEC's composition also reflects trade-union predominance.

Before 1981, the formal sovereignty of the Annual Conference was not supported by any organisational control over the parliamentary party. If anything, power ran in the opposite direction. Constituency selection committees chose candidates for election, subject to 'official' endorsement by the NEC (which was rarely withheld), but once elected the Labour MPs alone chose a Leader, who was, in practice, automatically the Leader of the party as a whole, and who exercised great influence on all its parts. By 1981, however, the 'Labour left' had secured three changes.

First, sitting MPs were henceforth obliged to submit themselves for re-selection prior to the next general election, rather than to be automatically re-selected as in the past. The aim was to make them more representative of, or responsive to, changing sentiment within their Constituency Parties. By the end of 1981 the results were still rather inconclusive. Some right-wing MPs had been reselected in spite of strong opposition within their local parties (two were even re-selected on the eve of joining the SDP); others declined to submit to re-selection and either left politics or joined the SDP. In all, seven had sought and failed to secure re-selection.

Second, the Leader would in future be chosen by an electoral college in which MPs would have only 30% of the votes, with 30% allocated to delegates of the Constituency Parties and 40% to those of the trade unions. The new procedures came into force after Michael Foot had been chosen by the PLP under the old system in November 1980, but they were applied in September 1981 to the election to the (largely symbolic) office of Deputy Leader, for which Tony Benn challenged the incumbent, Denis Healey. On this occasion the constituency parties' vote was overwhelmingly cast for Benn, the union vote was divided, and the outcome was settled in favour of Healey by a margin of less than one per cent of the total electoral college vote, primarily by the abstention of a group of MPs who were considered part of the parliamentary party's left wing but who opposed Benn and were anxious to prevent a further defection of MPs to the SDP.

Third, the final approval of the contents of election manifestos would lie with the NEC after a draft had been prepared jointly by the PLP and the

NEC. In 1979, those responsible for drafting the Manifesto felt that at the last minute Callaghan had arbitrarily diluted Conference commitments which had been included in the draft.

While the evidence is too limited to permit a very definite assessment of these changes, they tilted the balance of power more towards the party outside parliament, though with no decisive or early advantage to the party's left wing.

The real structure of power within the party cannot, of course, be read off from its formal constitution alone. Three other considerations are especially important. One is that the party's funds come overwhelmingly from the trade unions, partly in the form of the levy already mentioned, but also in voluntary contributions. These are of two kinds: sums donated from time to time to support the party's headquarters, and especially to meet election expenses, and funds given by individual unions to cover the constituency expenses of individual Labour MPs.[7] The unions' financial support for the party underwrites their dominant position in the party's Conference.

Second, to be elected even to a Constituency Party seat on the National Executive Committee it is necessary to be well-known, which means that most NEC members are MPs. The PLP is thus heavily represented in the extra-parliamentary party's chief policy-making organ.

Third, and most important, most trade-union delegates to Labour Party Conferences are activists; some are active in their Constituency Labour Party as well as in trade-union politics. Their political outlook is affected by events in a similar way to the outlook of other constituency party activists who, though almost always trade-union members, are active primarily in their local parties. The difference lies in the fact that trade-union delegates to the Conference are elected by a rank and file most of whom are chiefly concerned with their unions' industrial aims, and only secondarily with the political aims of the Labour Party. This often produces union leaders who are militantly labourist, and lukewarm or even hostile to radical proposals for social change. But it does not exclude the election of officials who believe that their members' interests demand social change, or possibly even revolution.

The workers' experience of the vicissitudes of the British economy has led them to oscillate between faith in labourism and disillusionment with it. This is reflected, though in a very delayed and mixed fashion, by changes in the character of the union leadership, and changes in the power of individual leaders of the big unions. By the mid-seventies these changes had led to a radical shift in the internal balance of forces in the Labour Party, although its effects were temporarily held in check by the appeal for loyalty to the Labour Government between 1974 and 1979.

Also important for any analysis of the Labour Party over the years, and for assessing its future potential, are the attitudes, conceptions, myths and feelings that make up what Drucker has called the party's 'ethos'.[8] Drucker identified four elements in this ethos: intense loyalty to leaders, a demand for personal sacrifice on the part of both leaders and minor party and trade-union officials, an irrational attitude to funds (meanness and hoarding), and a deep faith in written rules. All these traits exist, albeit to arguable degrees, and are traceable to the distinctive historical experience of the British working class – a long and bitter series of lessons in the essentials of class solidarity and self-help. Drucker also notes an 'oppositional' mentality, reflecting the workers' acceptance of their 'underclass' status, and a distrust of their own party leaders in office, and this is also true.

But Drucker's list is incomplete, and perhaps slightly dated. For instance, there was also an anti-intellectual tradition in the Labour Party, reflecting distrust of the middle class from which virtually all the party's intellectuals and most of its leaders have been drawn. In 1981 it was still there, but a considerable proportion of the 'doctrinaire', 'polytechnic Marxists' who had been pushing the party to the left over the previous decade were of working-class origin. So far from becoming irrelevant, as Drucker predicted, intellectuals were becoming more effective in the party than, perhaps, at any previous time in its history.[9] Another aspect of Labour's ethos not stressed by Drucker is the concept of the labour 'movement', i.e., the whole range of organisations and institutions through which the workers have historically expressed their interests, including not only organisations affiliated to the party but also such institutions as working men's clubs and colleges, the Workers' Educational Association, the Institute for Workers Control and even international organisations such as the Socialist International. The Labour Party has always been thought of as the political wing of this wider movement, whose traditions it shares, especially those of fraternity and democracy. This aspect of the party, it could be argued, helps to explain the strength of the swing to the left within the party after 1979, following two periods of Labour government which did not seem to have accomplished much in the interests of the labour movement.

Milestones 1918–45

Besides these structural and cultural features the Labour Party was also the product of certain deeply formative historical experiences. The first was the formation in 1924 of Labour's first minority government, with Liberal support. In the December 1923 elections the Conservatives emerged as the largest party but with no overall majority; Labour was the larger of the two other parties which had both defended free trade, the main issue in the election campaign. In agreeing to form a government

Ramsay MacDonald, the Labour Leader, set three precedents: he alone chose the cabinet; he chose a strategy of trying to prove that Labour was 'fit to govern' rather than bringing forward socialist measures which the Liberals would not have supported, and then calling an election on them – i.e., an educational and mobilisational strategy for socialism; and again, he alone called an election in October 1924 on the issue of Labour's opposition to communism, not its opposition to capitalism.* All three precedents were consistent. MacDonald wanted to prove that the Labour Party was in every respect as 'constitutional' as the Conservatives and Liberals, so that middle-class voters should feel safe in voting for it. What was forfeited was the opportunity to use office to encourage the working class to believe that the 'new social order' envisaged in the party's 1918 policy statement was something which the party could and would achieve.

The second formative event was the General Strike of May 1926, called by the TUC in support of the coal-miners, who were faced with a 13% wage cut and an extra hour on the working day. The Conservative government had prepared for the strike and indeed finally provoked the TUC into calling it. The TUC had no plans for sustaining a strike, let alone for seizing power if the government collapsed, and called it off unconditionally after nine days. The miners stayed out for six months, but were totally beaten. The Conservatives passed a new Trades Disputes Act in 1927 which outlawed 'sympathy strikes' and strikes intended 'to coerce the government'. They also cut at the trade unions' financial support for the Labour Party by requiring that union members should explicitly declare their wish to pay the political 'levy' to the Labour Party ('contracting in') rather than have the option of explicitly declaring their wish not to ('contracting out') as was previously the case. The Labour leaders, who had at first given lukewarm support to the TUC, and then counselled retreat, were reinforced in their fear of the consequences of extra-parliamentary action. The TUC, whose membership fell sharply, resolved in 1928 to avoid, in future, all industrial action going beyond immediate industrial disputes and to co-operate positively with management.

The third event was the collapse of the second Labour government in 1931. Once more heading a minority government with Liberal support (though this time Labour was the single largest party in the House of Commons), the Labour leadership, still under MacDonald, had no conception of a socialist approach to the economic crisis in which they found themselves after the Wall Street crash of 1929. Still obsessed with being

* The issue concerned the Attorney General's decision to withdraw the prosecution of the editor of a communist newspaper for sedition. MacDonald chose to treat the Conservatives' and Liberals' decision to set up a parliamentary enquiry into the case as an issue of confidence.

'responsible', they ignored the Keynesian proposals of the Liberals and of their own left wing. Instead, they accepted the need to balance the Budget by cutting unemployment benefits in order to create enough confidence among foreign bankers, to whom the government looked for a loan to stem a run on sterling. After much agonizing, the General Council of the TUC finally declined to endorse the cuts, and the Cabinet split. MacDonald resigned, but immediately agreed to form a 'National Government' instead. Nominally this included all the parties but it actually consisted overwhelmingly of Conservatives and contained only three Labour members besides MacDonald himself. This government imposed a ten per cent cut in unemployment benefits, devalued the pound by 29% (a course which the Labour government had been advised was unthinkable), and called an election in which MacDonald appealed for a 'national' vote against his own former party. The Labour vote fell by 20%, and the party was reduced to 52 seats in parliament, exactly equal to its position after 1906.

This traumatic experience, followed as it was by eight years of high unemployment, had an ambivalent effect on the party. The 1933 Conference resolved that the formation, composition and programme of any future Labour Government should be subjects for determination by the party as a whole, not just the PLP or the Leader; and a more explicit programme of socialist measures was adopted as party policy. But the chief political lesson drawn by the leadership (as opposed to the rank and file) was that they must, above, all, become competent to master the existing system, which had twice mastered them. They found an opportunity to do this during the Second World War. As Drucker remarks, the years of the war-time coalition in which the Labour leadership held office without fear of elections, and without the need to prove anything but their own competence (in a war economy over which the government had taken comprehensive powers), were an 'ideological holiday' for the party.[10]

As a result, the leadership was able to forget some other lessons which might have been drawn from the inter-war experience. There was no disposition on the part of most of them to envisage their next period in office as a step towards a new socialist order.[11] There was no reconsideration of the use of industrial action as an instrument to complement electoral politics. On the contrary, the party's official hostility towards communism, muted between 1941 and 1945, reached new heights with the advent of the Cold War after 1946, and this included a blanket opposition to the political use of industrial action such as the communists then advocated. The Labour Party became even more purely parliamentary. Furthermore, having come to think of itself as a 'natural' party of government, it increasingly lost the educational or evangelical conception of its role, which had previously been central to its tradition. By the 1950s most of the leadership had adopted the 'reactive' conception of policy-making of the older parties, posing the question, 'What will the voters vote for?' rather than 'What might they be persuaded to want?'.

The Nature of the Labour Party

In spite of its earlier failures, the Labour Party found itself in 1945 in a position of enormous strength. Its voting support, though not its share of seats in parliament, had recovered from the 1931 debacle as early as the election of 1935. But, in 1945, after five more years of slump and five of the People's War, its share of the total vote rose from 38% to 48%. By 1945, trade-union membership was also back to over eight million, a figure last achieved in 1921; and the party's broad programme of economic and social reforms had been legitimised by the war years. But after enacting these measures, the leadership abandoned the initiative and there followed more than a decade of opposition (1951–64) in which the party was wracked by the bitter struggle between its left and right wings, culminating in the qualified victory in 1961 of the 'revisionist' right led by Gaitskell (see Chapter 4).

The revisionist victory seemed to confirm the long-standing pattern of power inside the party, whereby the trade-union leadership, through its 'block vote' on the floor of the Annual Conference and its dominance of the NEC, consistently sustained the parliamentary leadership in its resistance to left-wing pressure for more socialist policies. It strengthened the view, originally propounded by R. T. McKenzie and popularised by subsequent commentators, that the Labour Party's formal constitution, which made the Annual Conference sovereign over the parliamentary party, was incompatible with the British Constitution. On this view, MPs are responsible to their constituents, not to their party. But, it was held, the real distribution of power inside the party fortunately contradicted the formal party constitution, and made the PLP in practice as free from control by the party outside parliament as the Conservative parliamentary party was.[12]

Later events were to show that this view was doubly wrong. In the first place, the 'British Constitution', being unwritten, has no immutable clauses but only habitual practices with greater or less moral force, all of which are susceptible to change. If MPs became accountable to their parties outside parliament it would change the existing system but no more so than when MPs became elected on party tickets at the end of the nineteenth century.

Secondly, the support given by the trade unions to Labour's parliamentary leadership from 1945 to the end of the fifties proved to have been the product of special circumstances. The biggest unions, those of the transport workers and the engineers, were led at that time by men who endorsed the most limited version of labourism and who were also very strongly anti-communist – Arthur Deakin and William Carron. They supported first Attlee in resisting left-wing pressure for more radical policies, and then Gaitskell in moving official party policy away from its traditional commitment to socialism based on public ownership. They also supported tough procedural measures against the left wing in the party. In 1956, however, Deakin was succeeded by Frank Cousins, and in 1967 Lord Carron (as he had then become) was replaced by Hugh Scanlon. Both these new leaders were left-wingers.

Under Cousins' leadership, the Transport Workers' block vote was no longer automatically cast for the right-wing policies of the PLP; in 1960 this led to a Conference decision, carried by a small majority against the leadership's bitter resistance, in favour of a policy of unilateral nuclear disarmament. A year later Gaitskell succeeded in getting this vote at least partly reversed, and meanwhile the Transport Workers had not opposed the adoption of a policy statement which in effect abandoned nationalisation as a goal. But '... much more than was seen to be the case, the victory of revisionism was achieved by a combination of procedural manipulation and the winning of strategically placed supporters rather than by mass persuasion of the majority of the active rank and file of the unions and the Party'.[13] The Transport Workers' vote now began to swing more and more against revisionism and, after 1967, with the leadership of the engineers, the miners, the shop workers and the post office workers also moving to the left, block votes at the Conference could no longer be relied upon to support the PLP on fundamental questions of party policy.

The response of Harold Wilson, as Prime Minister after 1964, was to ignore Conference decisions, with less and less pretence that he 'accepted' their authority even 'in principle'. After 1974, as the government progressively abandoned the substance of the 'social contract' in favour of deflation (see Chapter 6), Conference support became less and less reliable, culminating in the rejection of Callaghan's proposed five per cent pay 'norm' at the 1978 Conference, and the call (after the 1979 election) to make the Leader and MPs more accountable.

In the light of these changes, people who had formerly celebrated the 'good sense' of the major union leaders who had protected the party's leaders against the left wing, executed a volte-face. They suddenly discovered that the block vote was undemocratic. Union leaders, they reported, were elected by a small minority of their members but cast their entire union block vote in favour of policies which they personally favoured, regardless either of minority views or of the fact that many of their members took no interest at all in politics. The Labour Party was now urged to sever its links with the unions and the call went out for trade unions to be forced to be more democratic.

The work of Lewis Minkin put a long overdue end to this transparently ideological line of commentary. He showed that the changes in the unions' leaderships resulted from long-term shifts in rank and file opinion, which had begun to be registered at party Conferences well before the leadership changes occurred. Carron, for example, who had been notoriously apt to cast the engineers' vote in favour of the party leaders' position even when a majority of the engineers' delegates opposed it (this was ironically called 'Carron's law'), was less and less able to do so in the final years of his presidency, as the left-wing tide rose. Cousins, on the other hand, did not cast the transport workers' vote against a single 'platform' position for two years after his election. When he finally did so for the first time, in 1958, it was because his personal position had by then come to be shared by a majority of his union's delegates. After 1978 the trend in union leadership elections seemed to have moved back again towards candidates of the right; but Conference decisions continued to move leftwards, because the affiliated membership of several left-oriented unions rose while that of several right-oriented ones declined.

In other words, the relation between the PLP and the party outside parliament was determined by long-term trends in which the election of particular individuals sometimes played an important part, but no more than that. It was true that only a minority of union members took part in votes for their national leaders (30%–40% was common) and that certain powerful individuals – a Carron, a Scanlon or a Scargill (the left wing miners' leader who became President of the Mineworkers' Union in 1981) – could make a major impact. But the unions were not very different from most other political organisations in being run by their active minority, and those elected to leadership positions were aware of the need to stay in tune with a wider body of union opinion if their electoral base was to be kept secure. The influence of individual leaders had actually been greater in the days of Deakin and Carron, when delegates tolerated more autocratic leadership than they did later.

So the idea that the Labour Party's 'proper' fuctioning consists of a 'moderate' parliamentary party, sustained by 'moderate' union leaders against an 'extremist' minority, must be abandoned. The party's character has always reflected, and been a focus for, the changing relations between capital and labour. It has no immutable 'structure'; its complex organisation means that the evolving political struggle is registered in it in complex ways, after delays which vary according to the level or nature of the influence reaching it. A strong leader like Carron could delay the impact on the party of a leftward shift in a major union, while economic policies such as those of the sixties, and changes in the structure of employment, rapidly altered the voting balance by dramatically increasing the membership of some unions and reducing the membership of others.* The rhythm of change in constituency representation was different again. Individual membership declined disastrously in the disillusioning years of 1966 to 1970†; but the weakened constituency organisations were then more susceptible to being 'captured' by left wing activists who moved back into party work from the early 1970s onwards.

How then should we understand the Labour Party? What determines these shifts in the balance of forces inside the party and what are their long-term implications? The interpretation of such a complex pheomenon must be tentative, but a historical view suggests the following.

The history of the Labour Party is – contrary to the hopes of the McKenzie school and the fears of many left-wing commentators – the history of the gradual radicalisation of the labour movement. This process has not been smooth or linear. At times the movement has relapsed into, at most, a polite labourism, such as the 'welfare capitalism' propounded by the revisionists in the late 1950s. But over the long run it has been propelled away from its liberal–labourist starting point, towards the point where its commitments are less and less compatible with capitalism. The evidence of opinion polls suggests that most members of trade unions did not yet approve of all the policies adopted by their leaders at union conferences and at the Labour Party Conferences of 1980 and 1981.‡ The fact remains that a large majority of the people they elected, or did not trouble to oppose, had reached the conclusion that these policies were necessary and in their members' interests. The preoccupation of the press with the degree of rank and file approval for these policies was motivated partly by a concern to know how far the shift of opinion in the union leaderships was reflected among the membership, but also by an awareness that, with these policies, the labour movement seemed for the first time to be potentially on a collision course with British capital.

* For example there was a rapid growth in the membership of the National Union of Public Employees and the Association of Scientific, Technical and Managerial Staffs, but a large drop in the membership of the National Union of Mineworkers and the National Union of Railwaymen.

† Individual membership was believed to be one million in 1952. By 1979 it was thought to have fallen to 250,000–300,000, though some observers thought even this figure was too high. The decline in membership was accompanied by a severe erosion of local party activities too (see R. Borthwick, 'The Labour Party', in H. M. Drucker (ed.), *Multi-Party Britain*, Macmillan, London 1979, p. 63).

‡ By 1981 the party Conference had adopted the following policy resolutions: unilateral nuclear disarmament and the closure of all nuclear bases in Britain; withdrawal from the EEC; an Alternative Economic Strategy including reflation, restrictions on capital exports, import controls, and a 35-hour week; extensions of public ownership and planning agreements with large private firms; the introduction of industrial democracy; repurchase at a discounted price of council houses sold to their tenants by local authorities; abolition of private schooling and private medicine; subsidised low fares for public transport.

This did not mean that the movement would follow that course to the end. It had backed away from it at the time of the General Strike in 1926, and part of the point of publishing the polling evidence of members' views was to encourage the leadership to retreat again. However, the crisis was forcing the party as a whole – not just the TUC, as in 1926, nor just the constituency activists, as critics tended to imply – to adopt a more comprehensive and consciously anti-capitalist programme than at any previous time in its history.

Although it could be readily predicted that in the medium run the leadership would moderate the programme adopted by Conference, and although the popular support that would be needed for its implementation was far from having been mobilised, both problems were being more openly confronted at the end of 1981 than ever before.* The changes in the party's constitution which had made the leadership more accountable were primarily aimed at ensuring that more uncompromising leaders would be elected in the future, while some new initiatives also tackled the task of mobilising popular support for the policies adopted at the party Conferences of 1979 to 1981.† It was true that most of these new policies – with the notable exception of the party's opposition to Cruise nuclear missiles – did not yet have majority support among the public. On the other hand, media preoccupation with the conflict between the right wing of the PLP and the party majority outside parliament, and with the rise of the SDP, tended to obscure the fact that these policies were decisions of the whole Conference, not the work of an unrepresentative minority of constituency activists. They expressed the fact that those most responsible for both the unions and the party had come to see the 'centrist' options pursued by Wilson and Callaghan in the past as no longer credible, however much most Labour MPs (not to mention the SDP) still wished they were.

Circumstances had thus propelled the Labour Party in a gradually more radical direction. From 1900 to 1918 it saw itself as a mere 'voice of

* The issue came sharply in focus in the controversy surrounding Peter Tatchell, adopted in 1981 by the Bermondsey Labour party as their parliamentary candidate to succeed the retiring right-wing Labour ex-Whip, Robert Mellish. Tatchell had written an article calling for extra-parliamentary action to complement parliamentary politics. At the instigation of the right wing of the parliamentary party, the NEC refused to endorse his candidature, initiating the most intense internal conflict over the definition and limits of parliamentarism since 1932–3.

† These initiatives were still modest and tended to be overshadowed by the internal struggles over re-selection, the deputy leadership, etc. They included the launching of a new semi-popular journal, *The New Socialist*, in the summer of 1981; and the decision of the Labour Co-ordinating Committee, which had been responsible for the success of the campaign to change the party's constitution, in the autumn of 1981, to shift its activities towards popular education and agitation and to work with other movements and organisations in a variety of campaigns.

labour' within a capitalist parliament; from 1918 to 1979 it aspired, with greater or less seriousness, to institute 'socialist' reforms within capitalism; after 1979 the question was posed – though no more than that – of whether it should (or must) aim to replace capitalism. But the party's progress through these stages was contradictory and erratic. Periods of radicalisation were followed by periods of deradicalisation, due to the oscillations of the economy, political victories and defeats, and the deradicalising pressures experienced by all political movements which have to exist for a long time within the system they aim to replace.

To illustrate these points, in the period after 1906 the economic crisis gave rise to unprecedented industrial militancy, while the PLP's success in securing the passage of the Trades Disputes Act of 1906, combined with the Liberal outlook of most of the Labour MPs of that time, their inexperience and their concern for respectability, led in the opposite direction (a tendency in which they were reinforced by an influx into the new party of ex-Liberal intellectuals). The 1918 Conference represented an attempt to bring these divergent tendencies together again. Conversely, the TUC's defeat in the General Strike, high unemployment and the collapse of the Labour government in 1931 led to a period of industrial quietism:* whereas these were also years in which Labour Party Conferences adopted more comprehensive and specific socialist policy pronouncements than ever before.† Experience of office during the war brought to bear on the Labour leadership the deradicalising influence of participation in the management of the capitalist state.[14] But the long-term effects of the slump and the war had made the labour movement and a significant part of the middle class more radical, to the point where the Labour leaders were obliged to commit themselves to the reforms of 1945–8.

In the 1950s, for the first time the influence of all three factors ran in the same direction – the direction of quietism. The economy enjoyed its brief post-war respite from the international effects of industrial decline, while full employment, the fruit of working-class strength due to war-time mobilisation and resentment of the slump, meant that the workers enjoyed a significant share of the resulting economic gain. There was no compulsion on trade-union leaders to preoccupy themselves with far-reaching radical political proposals. Increasingly severe electoral defeats in 1951,

* The average number of 'days lost' annually through strikes during the six years 1933 to 1938 inclusive was 1.9 million, compared with 4.7 million during the six years 1927 to 1932 inclusive.

† The 1934 Policy statement, *For Socialism and Peace*, called for the 'drastic reorganisation', in most cases involving nationalisation, with a measure of workers' control, of banking and credit, transport, water, coal, gas, electricity, textiles, chemicals and insurance; and for the abolition of the House of Lords.

1955 and 1959 also led to a deradicalisation of the parliamentary leadership, who after eleven years of office (1940–5 in the wartime coalition followed by the Labour government of 1945–51) had absorbed a 'governing party' perspective, primarily concerned with returning to power, and hardly at all with long-term social transformation, or the long-term task of political education which that would require.

McKenzie saw this combination of effects as the normal and proper situation of the Labour Party; left-wing party critics saw it as the culmination of the party's degeneration into a party of 'bourgeois politicians, with, at best, a certain bias towards social reform', who had 'no intention whatsoever of adopting, let alone carrying out, policies which would begin in earnest the process of socialist transformation in Britain'.[15] This was Miliband's judgement in 1960. In 1972 he reinforced his opinion, and concluded that Labour could *never* turn into a socialist party.[16] The reasons he advanced were elaborated by others, notably David Coates, who in 1974 also predicted quite correctly that the new Labour government would once again subordinate the party's promise of social reform to 'the more powerful imperatives of economic growth, capital accumulation and international payments'.[17] These judgements are evidently at odds with our general interpretation, according to which the Labour Party has undergone a long-term process of radicalisation, the latest stage of which brought it closer to a definite break with its parliamentarist and reformist history. Why should the negative verdict of these authorities not be accepted?

One reason is that in politics few verdicts are ever final or complete. Miliband's pessimism in 1972 seemed justified at the time, but in 1981, with the advantage of hindsight, his 1960 verdict seemed more accurate: *either* the Labour Party would become an effective socialist party, *or* it would decline. In the 1960s it did decline; but in response, a new movement developed to try to convert Labour into a socialist party. In reaction to this movement a segment of the party finally left to join the SDP, and in 1981 the SDP–Liberal Alliance appeared to have a good chance of capturing the political centre. Yet, unless the Alliance, with or without Conservative support, could reverse the country's industrial decline, it was hard to foresee a major long-term future for it (see Chapter 11). Meantime, the Labour Party, shorn of many of its non-socialist MPs and members, could well become the socialist party which Miliband had had in mind – though its prospects of subsequently achieving socialism were quite another matter.

Such speculations turn in large part on the question of the effects of industrial decline. Falling real incomes, high unemployment, poorer health care and schools, do not spontaneously give rise to popular demands for socialism. On the other hand they do not leave the political equation unchanged. By the end of the 1970s there were severe limits to how far the Labour Party leadership could go in accommodating the needs of British capital without giving rise to a crisis within the party. These limits were reached in the autumn of 1978. The union leaders could go no further in supporting deflationary policies without losing the support of their own members. Industrial militancy rose, and converged with the rising political militancy of the Constituency Labour Parties, leading to the constitutional changes and radical policy shifts within the party in the years after 1979. On the basis of past experience these initiatives were likely to be subordinated once again to immediate electoral considerations by the ever-powerful appeal for loyalty and unity in face of the Conservative and SDP–Liberal threat.

Yet the circumstances were no longer quite the same as in the past, for two reasons. First, the left had learned some of the lessons of the past, and devoted as much attention to trying to make the PLP itself more left-inclined, as to securing radical policy decisions at Conferences. Second, more members of the unions were being pushed by the crisis to question whether their interests were still compatible with those of the companies which employed – or no longer employed – them. This enabled the left to make greater inroads in the labour movement. It did not mean that the policies pursued by Labour in office between 1966 and 1970, or 1974 and 1979, would not be repeated if the party were to win another election in the 1980s. It was rather that the crisis was gradually changing the balance of forces inside the party in ways not envisaged by Miliband a decade earlier.

None the less, the 'structural' reasons advanced by Miliband and others for believing that the Labour Party is incapable of becoming a socialist party have force – the question is whether they have absolute force. They may be summarised under five main heads.

1 *The parliamentary leaders have become less and less representative of the working class*. By 1974 only just over a quarter of the PLP was of working-class origin. In September 1976 only five members of the Callaghan cabinet had either working-class or trade-union backgrounds.[18] Middle-class leaders tend to acquire middle-class outlooks; their socialism tends to become purely rhetorical.
2 *The parliamentarism of the early leadership, transmitted to later generations by precept and practice, has become an end in itself*. This had two effects. On the one hand it meant opposing and neutralising political activity outside parliament which was judged liable to prejudice the party's electoral image as a constitutional party, or which was liable to weaken the leadership's control. On the other hand it meant assimilating the assumptions on which

parliamentary practice rests – above all, the belief that all MPs are in agreement on certain fundamentals, i.e. on 'liberal democracy', involving an acceptance of the private enterprise economy.

3 *Acceptance of capitalism is reinforced by electoral considerations.* The PLP sees its job in terms of not merely speaking for labour but also defending the interests of labour by holding office. To be elected, the party must win votes from voters who are neither working-class nor socialists. There is therefore a constant tendency to dilute or ignore socialist proposals emanating from the party Conference. The manifesto is drafted so as to give the media as little ground as possible for presenting the party in a light which will frighten the 'floating vote'. This consideration had its most obvious influence under Gaitskell, when political sociologists showed that even Labour's working-class voters were becoming less and less supportive of nationalisation and other socialist elements in the party's traditional platform.[19]

4 *Trade union leaders also see their primary task as the defence of their members' short-term interests,* whatever they consider the desirable long-term goals of the movement. Miliband cautioned against expecting the militancy of unionised workers to translate itself into active pressure from trade-union leaders for a socialist Labour Party.[20] The experience of the years 1974 to 1979 seemed to support his judgement. Not only did 'left-wing' union leaders such as Jack Jones of the Transport Workers support the government through three years of wage cuts and deflation, but some unions began to show signs of a 'business-unionism' hitherto rare in Britain.[21]

5 *There are powerful deradicalising effects of holding office in a capitalist state.* In office, Labour leaders are subjected to still further influences which lead them, consciously or otherwise, to accept the existing state, and the existing structure of the economy, as given. Civil servants, the Bank of England, the Confederation of British Industry, the 'quality press' and the International Monetary Fund all tender advice premised on the necessity of sustaining (or restoring) 'business confidence'. Even if this advice seems interested and partial, ministers may still feel that the immediate interests of the workers call for everything to be done to revive the economy. Although the compromises and sacrifices involved are presented as temporary (until the 'corner is turned' and economic recovery permits socialist goals to be put back on the agenda), in reality they become an end in themselves.

Taking the arguments in turn, the reasons for considering that they do not have absolute force are briefly as follows:

1 The social origins of Labour MPs are undoubtedly important, although as Coates recognised, radical socialists have equally been recruited from the middle class, and many of Labour's most right-wing parliamentarians have been of working-class origin.[22] It is perhaps the middle-class milieu in which all MPs move, rather than their class origins, which matters. Does a parliamentary career *necessarily* 'blunt the edge of dissent' as Miliband argued?[23] Is it impossible to imagine that in changing circumstances – in a prolonged depression, with reselection, and perhaps with proportional representation removing some of the electoral arguments for 'moderation' – a less co-optable kind of Labour MP would become more common? Is it self-evident that the radicalism of some European parliamentary socialist parties could never emerge in Britain?
2 The practice of parliamentarism, with its complex canons of what is 'reasonable', has unquestionably had an important neutralising effect. But these canons were accepted by Labour MPs who saw scope for achieving the party's goals within them. After 1976 it became more and more doubtful if any further reform in the interests of labour was compatible with the survival of British capitalism. One of the reasons for the hostility towards the new Labour left evinced by the media was its rejection of the purely parliamentary canon – its rejection of the existing boundaries of what was reasonable, its literal attitude towards manifesto commitments, its support of industrial action for political purposes, support for civil disobedience, etc. It did not seem out of the question that a growing number of MPs would come to share this perspective.
3 It is true that electoral considerations tend to lead the parliamentary leadership to oppose, dilute or ignore socialist policy commitments which they think will cost votes. Against this, it can be argued that by the mid-1970s the practice had become increasingly self-defeating; the decline in the Labour vote was so serious that the party now needed to create a new electoral majority for socialist policies, something which it had not seriously attempted since 1945. Moreover, if proportional representation were introduced at the instigation of the SDP–Liberal Alliance, even short-term electoral considerations would no longer necessarily tell against the adoption of a more radical programme.

4 Miliband's judgement that trade union leaders cannot be expected to take socialist initiatives turns on the ambivalence of the unions' position in capitalist society, dependent on it at the same time as opposed to it. While this ambivalence is real, it too has limits. If the economy seemed no longer capable of providing the tangible benefits sought by the members there would be no necessary contradiction between the union leaders' industrial roles and their political positions. The greatly increased number of left-wing union leaders in 1981, compared with 1951, was a measure of the effect which the economic crisis had already had. The political context must also be considered. The refusal of Cousins to play an active role in opposition to the Wilson government after resigning from it in 1966 (which Miliband cited as characteristic of trade-unionists even when they have left-wing convictions) must be judged in the light of the paralysis of the left in the party as a whole at that time. As the left grew stronger, the options for trade-union leaders such as Cousins also expanded.

5 The effects of office have indeed been important and would be felt again should the Labour Party once more hold office, alone or in coalition, except to the extent that the party was committed to implement policies which would themselves alter the balance of power in the economy and the nature of the state. If the other deradicalising influences were overcome sufficiently to put a radical Labour leadership into office, this further deradicalising influence would be at least significantly modified.

All of these arguments are highly debatable: but they are perhaps sufficient to induce a degree of scepticism about the thesis advanced by Miliband and others that whatever socialist potential the Labour Party may ever have had, it is irredeemably exhausted. This judgement was a product of the disillusion felt by the left in the labour movement from the late 1950s onwards. By 1981, as the scope for centrist policies narrowed with the continued decline of the economy, it no longer seemed conclusive.

The Extra-Parliamentary Left

It is often said that the Labour Party enjoys a degree of dominance over the British labour movement which is unmatched elsewhere in Europe. Considering that a third of all manual workers (and in 1979 a third of all trade-union members) have voted Conservative this claim must be qualified. What is true, however, is that in contrast to the situation in most other European countries, neither the Communist Party nor any other rival party of the left has ever been able to attract the support of a significant segment of the working class.* The reason is clearly that the trade unions came first and founded the Labour Party; they were not created by previously existing and competing parties of the left.

But the presence of other organisations on the left of the Labour Party has been politically significant, even though they have been electorally unimportant. The tendency of the SDF, and later the Communist Party, to absorb part of the intellectual and organisational talent of the left has already been noted. This has been particularly noticeable at times of disillusion with the pragmatic, accommodating policies of the Labour leadership, for instance in the 1920s when there was a steady trickle of ILP members (the most active socialists in the Labour Party) into the Communist Party; or again in the 1960s, when many activists, especially the young, never entered the Labour Party but instead joined one or other of the Trotskyist organisations.[24] And throughout the Cold War, the left wing inside the Labour Party could often be neutralised by generalised attacks on anyone who had advocated any policies which coincided with those of the Marxist left outside the party.

But the extra-parliamentary left became important in more positive ways as the party system began to break up under the stress of the crisis. Its greater importance was due partly to its near-monopoly of serious analysis of the crisis, the Labour Party having largely abandoned the task of strategic and critical thinking in favour of short-term, sectoral reform proposals.[25] It was also due to the agitational energy of the extra-parliamentary left, which gave them an impact which was 'many-sided and out of all proportion to their actual membership'.[26]

But this was not all. One of the characteristics of any fundamental crisis is that it is difficult to know how to strike a balance between exaggerated ideas of possible change, and a foolish inability to anticipate enough. If the familiar party and electoral system were to change fundamentally in the 1980s, the consequences would be more far-reaching than could easily be imagined in 1981. In a situation of rapid change and uncertainty the influence of the extra-parliamentary left as a whole – its shared view of the necessity for fundamental change, as opposed to its many and often boring differences of opinion about means – could be greater than ever before. For these reasons the 'far left' cannot be altogether omitted from consideration, even though the multiplicity of organisations and the doctrinal differences among them cannot occupy us for long.[27]

The Communist Party of Great Britain (CPGB) declined, from a peak membership of 56,000 in 1942 to 18,500 in 1979, partly due to its support for Soviet foreign policies, partly because of its past tendency to Stalinism,

* The Communist Party had two MPs in the 1945–50 parliament. No MPs to the left of the Labour Party were elected to any subsequent parliament.

and partly because, at least until the late 1970s, its programme seemed far-fetched to most people (it envisaged a Labour Party in power, accepting the CPGB as a 'partner', which would succeed in pushing Labour into carrying out a transition to socialism). The party remained significant mainly because of its strength in some trade unions and because, although it had lost members, it had never split. In its latter-day 'Euro-communist' phase it had also become more flexible and politically creative. It regularly contested 30–40 seats at general elections, but in the 1970s its best result per candidate was in the election of February 1974, when it won 744 votes or 1.7% of the vote cast per candidate.

The Trotskyist or neo-Trotskyist organisations, by contrast, probably accounted, altogether, for as many members as the CPGB, but they were shared by many different groups. Starting from a tiny core of British supporters of Leon Trotsky, in his claim to uphold the true revolutionary tradition of Leninism in opposition to Stalinism, these groups, from the later 1950s, began to attract support from Communists disillusioned by Krushchev's secret speech of 1956 and the Soviet invasion of Hungary, and from radical activists in the Labour Party who were frustrated by its revisionism.

The Socialist Workers Party, with about 4,000 members in 1981, was originally distinguished by some interesting departures from orthodox Trotskyist ideas, and was particularly attractive to intellectuals in the late 1960s. In 1977, however, its leadership determined to convert it into a party of the Leninist type.[28] Subsequently, it contested by-elections with derisory results. Although in 1981 its weekly newspaper, *Socialist Worker*, sold about 30,000 copies, and although it had played an effective part in some important 'common front' movements such as the Anti-Nazi League, it seemed handicapped by centralism and dogmatism.

The Workers Revolutionary Party, with between one and two thousand members, was the most orthodox of the Trotskyist groups. Its distinctive feature was intense activity (including publishing a *daily* newspaper, *Newsline*) and a high turnover of members as they became exhausted by the demands made on them.

The International Marxist Group, the British section of the Trotskyist Fourth International, had about a thousand members; it was the most intellectually creative of all the groupings and perhaps the least sectarian (a judgement which would not, no doubt, be endorsed by the others).[29] By 1980, after an abortive attempt to promote a Socialist Unity front for the 1979 elections, the IMG concentrated on support for the left inside the Labour Party.

So-called 'entryism' proper (entering a social-democratic party to influence it from within) was most successfully practised by the Militant tendency, a Trotskyist grouping of some 5,000 Labour Party members organised around a weekly newspaper, *Militant*. This group, which combined an admirable level of activism with a depressing dogmatism and a strong inclination to manipulation, achieved a dominant position in the Labour Party Young Socialists, thus gaining a seat on the Party's NEC, where the Young Socialists had a reserved place. The Militant tendency was also influential or dominant in some Constituency Labour Parties by the end of 1981, and was the subject of an enquiry initiated by the PLP right wing and endorsed by Michael Foot as Leader in December of that year.

It is arguable that, whatever the significance of these parties and 'grouplets' may be, other 'left-leaning' movements and organisations are equally if not more significant. For example, the Campaign for Nuclear Disarmament and the Vietnam Solidarity Committee were supported on a far larger scale and were themselves important sources of recruitment into the extra-parliamentary left groups in the late 1960s and early 1970s. More generally, new initiatives such as the women's liberation movement, claimants' unions, factory occupations, tenants' associations and organisations to resist plans for new airports or motorways, arguably contributed as much to the development of a 'radical left' culture as any of the left parties or groups listed above.

By the end of 1981 this culture was very much on the defensive. The ideological initiative of Thatcherism was still extremely strong. In the longer run, however, the resources of the extra-parliamentary left were considerable. Many left activists had, it is true, moved (or moved back) into the Labour Party, especially after 1979, and had contributed to the advance of the Labour left within the party in the following two years. But a new socialist impulse corresponding to the gravity of the crisis would require more than committing the Labour Party to the Alternative Economic Strategy and converting the PLP into a body in tune with the party outside parliament. It would require a fundamental rethinking of the meaning of socialism in Britain, and its relation to the many other popular movements that had surfaced in the 1960s and 1970s; a project to which the extra-parliamentary left as a whole would have to make a substantial contribution.

The Future of the Labour Party and the Left

The decline in the Labour Party's share of the popular vote and in its membership, after the peak of 1951–2, has already been noted. The rise of the SDP in 1981 threatened to reduce both still further. Outside London Labour had, by December 1981, only seven MPs south of a line from the Bristol Channel to the Wash. The internal struggle within the party precipitated by the gains of the left further reduced its standing in the opinion polls. The prospect of a Labour majority at the next general election steadily declined.

Given this situation, neither the right nor the left seemed to appreciate adequately the dimensions of the problem. The right wing of the Labour Party seemed still unaware of the extent to which the crisis had by now limited, if not eliminated, the scope for social-democratic reform, or of the seriousness of the gap which now existed between themselves and a majority of the party's active membership. The left wing, for its part, seemed too exasperated with the right's resistance to the implementation of intra-party democracy, and too impressed with the Conference majorities in favour of left-wing policies, to appreciate how badly it needed to convince a majority of the public that left-wing policies had become a necessity.[30]

Among Marxists, the debate still appeared excessively focused on the question whether or not the struggle for socialism should be waged inside or outside the Labour Party. Those inside argued that, so long as the party commanded the loyalty of the labour movement, any attempt to conduct the struggle outside the party was doomed to irrelevance.[31] Their opponents argued that left-wing activity inside the Labour Party always ended by merely conferring a more radical image on a party irredeemably committed to the essential features of the status quo and neutralising extra-party initiatives, not by capturing the party for socialism.[32] On this view the Labour Party's labourist ideology and practice results from an inexorable circular logic. The trade unions' ultimate priorities are their members' jobs and living standards, and their own industrial relations rights. Even when economic conditions are propelling them increasingly to endorse calls for socialist measures, they invariably shrink, in the final analysis, from pressing this to the point where party divisions will make it virtually impossible to win the next election. This is especially true in times of economic crisis when a Conservative government means higher unemployment, lower wages and further reductions in trade-union powers. This fact fortifies the leadership of the parliamentary party in its long-established practice of seeking to channel rank-and-file militancy in 'responsible' (i.e., purely parliamentary) directions and – in the long run – prevents the working class from ever developing a serious belief in the possibility of a socialist alternative to the existing order, or in itself as an historical agent capable of bringing it about.[33]

But the assumptions of both sides in this argument looked less and less obvious. On the one side, the Labour Party's alleged monopoly of working-class loyalty was becoming more and more doubtful; indeed the very meaning of the term, 'the working-class' had become open to question, as we have seen. On the other side, the Labour Party had already suffered a minor but damaging split at the parliamentary level (the formation of the SDP), which might yet be reflected in a serious split within the Labour electorate at the next general election. And the likelihood that a renewed closing of the ranks would enable the party to win the next election – presenting it with yet another opportunity to 'betray' the workers and save British capitalism – seemed to be steadily diminishing. In other words, events had already begun to erode the 'logic' within which the party had long been trapped. Both the risks and the gains of seeking to convert the Labour Party to socialism could now be exaggerated, while the more daunting problem of how a new *popular* majority was to be mobilised for socialism – what elements might compose it and what ideas might inspire it – remained largely unexplored.[34]

In the short run the party's prospects had not looked so bleak since 1931; while with so many shifting variables now at work in the party system – the unknown prospects of Thatcherism within the Conservative Party, the unknown prospects of electoral support for the SDP–Liberal Alliance – the long run became less and less easy to envisage. Of the 245 Labour MPs in Parliament in December 1981, only about 30 or 40 were radical socialists – what the media called the 'hard left' – and even they shared some of the parliamentarist, statist and occasionally even labourist attitudes of the majority of the PLP. The new constitutional rules would alter the internal balance of power only gradually, and in any case not dramatically. Moreover, the trade-union support given to the radical policies adopted in 1980 was primarily support for economic expansion, and could not be counted on to sustain the party in a general and prolonged conflict with capital. The PLP leadership could no longer rely on the trade unions' block votes to prevent Conference adopting radical policies; but they were more than ever aware that the trade-union activists at the Conference did not reflect the views of many, perhaps most trade unionists, just as the Constituency Party activists did not reflect the views of the average Labour voter, and so they were more than ever tempted to ignore both. Consequently, in the short run, 'party unity' meant unity on verbal formulae which obscured the reality of the still-effective autonomy of the PLP, in spite of the now glaring gap between the views of most of its members and those of most Conference delegates.

But 1981 was distinguished from 1973 (when the policies endorsed by Conference had not been very different from those of 1980–1) by the changed political and economic situation. The leadership now strove desperately, in *advance* of any election, to avoid being forced off the 'centre ground' of British politics by the extra-parliamentary left. Michael Foot's election as Leader in 1980 had been seen as a victory for the left, much as Harold Wilson's election had been in 1963. But by the end of 1981 Foot too seemed more and more aligned with the right wing of the party in parliament. The resulting conflict made it look less and less likely that the party would win the next election. If the Conservatives risked losing their role as a 'natural' party of government, Labour did so even more.

11

Beyond The Two-Party System?

By 1974 popular support for the two major parties had been declining for over twenty years (see Table 5.1). Fewer people were engaged in any form of party politics: fewer voted (turnout at general elections declined from 83.9% in 1950 to 76% in 1979, and had been as low as 72.8% in October 1974); and fewer were members of any political party. Political energies flowed out of electoral party politics into various forms of extra-parliamentary politics such as claimants' unions, campaigns against new motorways or airports, or the Campaign for Nuclear Disarmament. Rank and file trade-union activism also rose, drawing in new segments of the labour force, and assuming many new forms. The 1972 'work in' at Upper Clyde Shipbuilders (a complex of four shipyards employing over 8,000 workers), for example, could not have been organised without a high order of political consciousness and local initiative.

But these were not the only alternatives to supporting Labour or the Conservatives. Voters were also drawn towards other parliamentary parties, which tried to exploit the opportunity created by the weakening of the social-democratic hegemony. These were the Liberals and the Social Democrats, the Scottish National Party in Scotland and Plaid Cymru in Wales. There was also the Irish factor. Northern Ireland returned twelve MPs to Westminster. Since the 1880s, all but one or two of the Northern Irish seats had been safe for Unionists who for all practical purposes were members of the Conservative Party. By 1974, however, Unionist opposition to policies designed to conciliate the Catholics in Northern Ireland had forced the Heath government to suspend the Northern Irish Parliament. The Unionists dissolved into three separate organisations, the most radical of which now contemplated independence for a 'six-county' Ulster (i.e., the existing territory of Northern Ireland). In the February 1974 election the main Unionist factions formed an alliance, the United

Table 11.1 The smaller parties 1964–1979

	1964	1966	1970	1974 (Feb)	1974 (Oct)	1979
			Votes at General Elections			
Liberals	3,092,878	2,327,533	2,117,035	6,063,470	5,346,754	4,313,811
Scottish Nationalists	64,044	128,474	306,802	632,032	839,617	504,259
Plaid Cymru	69,507	61,071	175,016	171,364	166,321	132,544
Northern Irish Parties[1]	–	–	–	717,986	702,094	695,889
Others[1]	214,354	232,681	421,481	163,800	98,653	152,987
			Average Percentage of votes cast per opposed candidate			
Liberals	18.5	16.1	13.5	23.6	18.9	14.9
Scottish Nationalists	10.7	14.1	12.2	21.9	30.4	17.3
Plaid Cymru	8.4	8.7	11.5	10.7	10.8	8.1
			Seats Won			
Liberals	9	12	6	14	13	11
Scottish Nationalists	–	–	1	7	11	2
Plaid Cymru	–	–	–	2	3	2
Northern Irish Parties[1]	–	–	–	12	12	12
Others[1]	–	2	6	2	–	–
Total	9	14	13	37	39	27

Note: [1] Before 1974 Ulster Unionists are included with the Conservatives, and dissident or anti-Unionist candidates with 'Others'.

Source: D. Butler and A. Sloman, *British Political Facts 1900–1979*, Macmillan, London 1980

Ulster Unionists, which won eleven seats, but they no longer accepted the Conservative whip in the House of Commons. This remained the case after the October election, when the alliance again broke up.[1] By this time, no less than 25% of the votes cast throughout the United Kingdom were for parties other than Labour or the Conservatives. Together these parties accounted for 39 seats in the House of Commons, and after March 1977 (when by-election losses had destroyed Labour's slender majority) they held the parliamentary balance of power (Table 11.1).

In the 1979 election, the combined Conservative and Labour share of the vote recovered to 80.8% and the number of seats won by other parties fell back to 27. But in March 1981 the formation of the Social Democratic Party (SDP) again altered the situation. By the end of 1981, 27 former Labour MPs and one former Conservative had joined the SDP; the SDP and Liberal leaders had formed an electoral Alliance which had already won two formerly safe Conservative seats at by-elections; and public opinion polls suggested that popular support for the Alliance was greater than for either the Labour or the Conservative parties. And while the Scottish Nationalist vote in Scotland had fallen sharply in the 1979 election its 1974 successes had taken observers by surprise after a worse electoral performance in 1970. The possibility existed of a radical change in the party system – and one which the Liberal–SDP Alliance would seek to make permanent by introducing proportional representation if it could gain sufficient parliamentary leverage to do so.

The prospects for such a change were hard to assess. The results of elections held under the existing 'first-past-the-post' electoral system are highly unpredictable when more than two parties have substantial support widely distributed in the country, and public enthusiasm for the Alliance was very volatile, declining early in 1982 almost as suddenly (though not so far) as it had previously risen. It was also quite uncertain how far this support would be translated into nation-wide support in a general election. None the less the long-term pressures on the Labour and Conservative parties would remain. The chance that one, if not both of them, would be reduced, split or even displaced by some combination of other parties remained a significant one. These parties must, therefore, be briefly examined.

The Liberal Party

Formed (according to convention) in 1859, the Liberal Party, after presiding over the greatest era of Victorian reform and having enlisted the support of the bulk of the newly-enfranchised working class, was destroyed by the contradiction between the interests of labour and those of the middle classes which it represented. After 1918, its collapse was painfully complete. By 1950 it was said that the whole parliamentary Liberal

Party could go to work in a taxi. Yet even at the nadir of their fortunes in 1951, when they contested only 109 seats, the Liberals won nearly three-quarters of a million votes: at the peak of the subsequent revival, in February 1974, they won six million votes (19.3% of the total). In 1979 the Liberals still won 4.3 million votes (14.1%). And throughout the post-war period about a third of the electorate regularly told pollsters that they would be likely to vote Liberal 'if [they] thought they would obtain a majority'.[2] Just what this means is doubtful; but there can be little doubt that the Liberals would have polled more votes at general elections had it not been for the electoral system, which reinforced the dominance of the two leading parties, and made voters feel that a vote cast for a party that could not form a government (or part of one) was wasted. Hence the Liberal Party's devotion to proportional representation.*

Down to 1956 the Liberals' survival as a parliamentary party depended importantly on an understanding with the Conservative Party. This dated from the period of 'National Liberal' participation in the Conservative-dominated National Governments of the 1930s, and during the 1950s the Liberals were indeed not easy to distinguish from the progressive wing of the Conservative Party. From 1956, however, a new leader, Jo Grimond, responding to the decline of Labour in the elections of 1950, 1951 and 1955, set the Liberal Party on a new course designed to make it once more into the new 'radical' party of the day, capable of displacing the Labour Party as the major party of opposition. He sought to appeal to voters who seemed increasingly to reject nationalisation, collectivism and bureaucracy, but who remained interested – as the Conservatives under Macmillan clearly were not – in further domestic reform. To implement this project the Liberal Party itself had to be radically transformed.

> Grimond encouraged the 'radicals' in the party and gave them their head, without worrying too much whether the party or he himself would agree with all they said and did. After all, there was no immediate prospect that he would have to put policies into practice; the main thing was to generate some excitement, give the impression that a new movement was growing and attract people with ideas and enthusiasm.[3]

The results were encouraging. In the 1964 election, with 361 candidates (compared with 216 in 1959) the party won 11.4% of the vote and nine seats. But Labour's second election victory in 1966 made the project of displacing the Labour Party seem unrealistic (even though the Liberals won 12 seats in that year). In 1967 Grimond retired and was succeeded by Jeremy Thorpe, who saw that the Liberals' next step must be to become

*In 1929 the Liberals made the introduction of PR a condition of their support for the minority Labour Government, but it was soon clear that resistance within the Labour Party, as well as on the part of the Conservatives, would have blocked the change even if the Labour Government had not collapsed in 1931.

'credible' as a political force capable of influencing policy. This meant the pursuit of virtually any strategy that seemed capable of broadening the party's electoral base, most notably a policy of wooing 'moderate' trade unionists and – in some urban constituencies – the pursuit of so-called 'community politics', i.e., a tireless devotion to local and personal campaigns and issues. Thorpe personally (like most of the Liberal MPs, many of whom owed their seats to their success in attracting support more from the Conservatives than from Labour) was not radical in either outlook or style, but he accepted the radicals as necessary – even when the Young Liberals went so far as to adopt positions on race, the Vietnam war, withdrawal from NATO and worker control of nationalised industries, which had more in common with the left wing of the Labour Party than with orthodox Liberalism.

In February 1974 (after a set-back in 1970) the Liberals polled their highest post-war vote and, in the south of England outside London, won more votes than Labour; but the electoral system yielded them only 14 seats. Thorpe, although invited by Heath to form a coalition against Labour, declined – Heath would not agree unequivocally to introduce proportional representation, and without this the more radical Liberals would not support Heath – and called instead for an all-party government of national unity which, however, was spurned by Labour. But in 1977, when the chance occurred to make terms over the Liberals' continued support for the Callaghan government, David Steel (who had succeeded Thorpe as leader when Thorpe was forced to resign after a scandal) exploited the opportunity by making a 'pact': Callaghan undertook to consult with him in advance on all parliamentary proposals, in return for Liberal support in the House of Commons. This policy was unpopular with many Liberals, both those who considered that the Callaghan government was in thrall to the trade unions, and the 'community politics' and Young Liberal radicals who considered the Callaghan government too conservative. The pact became unsustainable when the Labour Party refused to support the introduction of proportional representation for the election of the British members of the new European Parliament. Rank-and-file hostility forced Steel to give notice that the pact would lapse in the summer of 1978. But by now a clear strategy had emerged and Steel was gradually able to win the majority of the party over to it: 'to aim explicitly for the *balance* of power, to be prepared to work with either major party, and to make proportional representation the key to any such arrangement'.[4]

This strategy, with whatever 'credibility' the Liberal-Labour pact of 1976–78 may have given it, maintained the Liberal vote at 14.1% of the total in 1979, with the loss of only three seats (down from 14 to 11). And with the formation of the SDP in 1981 the strategy came into its own. The

SDP quickly agreed to an alliance in which the two parties would share out all the parliamentary constituencies between them, and by December 1981 polling data suggested that as much as 50% of the electorate supported the Alliance.

At this point the fate of the Liberals became bound up with that of the SDP. Both parties had, however, a strong vested interest in remaining separate. Although they competed for votes at the centre, each believed the other capable of drawing votes not necessarily available to itself. In competition, they would tend to cancel each other out; in alliance, they might, the opinion polls suggested, be able to establish a parliamentary bridgehead that could then be permanently widened by proportional representation.

What was the Liberals' chief contribution to the Alliance? Above all, it was the fact that the party had a still potent tradition, a proven core of electoral support, an organisation with some 150,000–200,000 members and exceptionally active local parties in some 20–30 constituencies.[5]

The Liberals' problem was how to expand beyond this base, which had some contradictory elements in it. Thanks to the religious basis of much of the Liberals' nineteenth-century programme, the party's support remained strongest in the non-conformist 'celtic fringe' of Wales and the highlands and islands of Scotland. At its lowest post-war ebb, the party retained three seats in Wales and one in Scotland, besides two in the northern English towns of Bolton and Huddersfield (which were only retained because of electoral understandings with the Conservatives). As the party revived, so it gained additional seats in the 'fringe', and in 'peripheral' rural districts such as south-west England, East Anglia, and the rural areas of Scotland. In its best years, the party also advanced in some suburban constituencies, especially at by-elections. What it failed to do was to make a significant impact in urban, and especially industrial constituencies, when these were contested by both the major parties.

Where no local tradition of Liberal voting survived from the nineteenth century, support tended to be drawn rather evenly from all occupational strata – for instance in 1977–8 about eight to nine per cent of each socio-economic stratum declared themselves Liberal supporters. With this even spread, the Liberals had an acute problem of translating votes into seats. Even with nearly a fifth of the votes in February 1974, they won only 14 seats; in sharp contrast with the Labour Party, with its massive concentration of working-class votes in industrial constituencies, and the Conservatives, with their almost equally massive support in most rural and suburban seats.

Even if the Liberal vote had been better rewarded in terms of seats, the party would still have faced difficulties in maintaining its vote because it was composed of three distinct and rather contradictory elements: a more or less constant 'core' (perhaps ten per cent of the electorate) of committed Liberals, and a 'floating' or 'protest' vote, intermittently detached from the Conservative and Labour parties, which was itself divided into two rather incompatible components.

The Liberal 'core' vote was 'radical', humanitarian, libertarian, internationalist, environmentalist and particularly interested in constitutional questions . . . ; the other side of the coin was its relative indifference to the major economic questions of the day'.[6] This core of voters was heavily concentrated in the middle classes, who also provided almost all the Liberals' activists, as well as almost all Liberal candidates (in 1970 there was only one working-class Liberal candidate out of 332; in October 1974, there were 25 out of 619).

The rest of the Liberal vote – its 'floating' component – tended to be much more varied in character. Steed identifies two distinct elements – 'centre' voters and 'anti-system' voters – who were apt to shift their votes towards the Liberals out of frustration with one or other of the two major parties, and especially, at least before 1974, when the Conservatives were in power. 'Centre' voters tended to be refugees from the too-explicit class character of the policies adopted by their 'normal' party – Conservatives upset by the 'unacceptable face of capitalism' (as Heath once called it) and Labour supporters upset by trade-union power or state bureaucratism. 'Anti-system' voters voted Liberal 'as a generalised protest against the operation of the political system', seeing the Liberal candidate as an apparently radical alternative. Some voters of this type would even vote for the National Front (far right) or the Workers Revolutionary Party (far left) if no Liberal candidate was standing.[7]

The problem was how to retain the 'core' Liberal vote while also developing a more durable appeal to these additional elements whose outlooks appeared to be so different – both from the 'core' and from each other. The most distinctive Liberal policies reflected the traditions and interests of the party's activists, who were distinguished less by being almost exclusively 'middle-class' – though that is what they were, in the sociological sense of the term – than by their dislike of being categorised as belonging to any class, and their hostility to class politics. When asked about their own social class, they tended to assign themselves to the most 'neutral-seeming' category (e.g., 'lower middle class') or said that they did not know what class they belonged to. Typical comments were: 'I do not believe in class'; 'classes are something I have never understood'; 'I don't think there is any class structure in this country except in the minds of certain politicians who use it for their own aims'.[8] This was the basis of the party's general bias, shared by its 'core' voters, in favour of non-economic policy-issues. Yet it was largely economic issues, and the Conservative and

Labour failures in economic policy, which were propelling the floating voters towards the Liberals.

Appealing more effectively to the 'floaters' was therefore a problem. They seemed relatively uninterested in traditional Liberal policies, remaining more favourable to either Conservative or Labour policies. And, at the same time, the reasons why they turned towards the Liberals were contradictory. The 'centre' voters turned to the Liberals because one or both of the major parties seemed to be abandoning consensus politics, while 'anti-system' voters were looking for a party which would make a still more radical break with the consensus. The most distinctive Liberal policies on economic issues – support for the EEC, an incomes policy and 'industrial partnership' between capital and labour – expressed the middle-class desire for a more harmonious society in a form which might appeal to 'centre' voters but hardly to 'anti-system' voters. The latter were likely to be the voters most attracted by the 'community politics' increasingly endorsed by Liberal conferences. However, as Olive points out,

> ... many [delegates] who vote for it only do so for the electoral success, and do not really accept the approach, which as well as the redressing of grievances, involves for the real radicals encouraging people to take and use power for themselves. Such an approach, if seriously pursued, could raise the possibility of the kind of self-activity and struggle which the Left sees as an essential prerequisite for the establishment of socialism ... some of the radical Liberals argue (in private) that they are not far distant from a kind of libertarian socialism.[9]

So neither the 'centre' voters nor the 'core' Liberal voters could be expected to warm to anti-system policies, and the radicalism of the Young Liberals and the 'left wing' of the community action activists, though endorsed by the party's annual conferences, was largely ignored or diluted in policy statements by the leadership – a situation with obvious similarities to that of the Labour Party, and involving similar costs. The leadership continued to rely on maintaining what Steed calls the 'vague, nice image' of tolerance and social concern that the party inherited from the nineteenth century. In the short run, therefore, the alliance with the SDP, with its origins in the Labour Party's acute conflicts over economic issues, permitted the Liberals to continue their preferred policy of downplaying economic questions. It offered the possibility of increasing the strength of the political centre, without adding still further to the already considerable difficulty of finding common ground on which the very different elements of Liberal support could come together.

The Social Democratic Party

The SDP was officially launched at an elaborately mounted press conference on 26 March 1981, the culmination of a split within the parliamentary party which mirrored the division developing inside many constituency labour parties since the early 1970s.

Two episodes in particular had been formative. One was the issue of Britain's membership in the European Economic Community. Of the four ex-ministers who founded the SDP, Roy Jenkins had left British politics to become the first British President of the European Commission, from 1977 to 1980. David Owen, Shirley Williams and Bill Rodgers were all also leading advocates of British membership. They had led the 89 Labour MPs who defied the party whip to vote for entry in 1971, and in the 1975 referendum campaign on whether Britain should remain a member they found themselves increasingly in a minority in the Labour Party outside parliament, confronting an opposition led by the Secretary of State for Industry, Tony Benn. Their differences from the anti-marketeers proved to be linked to more fundamental differences as well. Jenkins explicitly renounced 'socialism'; the others considered themselves socialists but explicitly favoured the retention of private enterprise and increasingly attacked trade-union powers.

The other primary determinant of the split was the growth of support for the Labour Left in the constituencies and among trade-union activists, resulting in the changes in the party constitution described in Chapter 10. These changes implied a long-term decline in the influence of centrist politicians of the type represented by the 'gang of four' (as the press dubbed the four ex-ministers) and a long-term strengthening of the party's commitment to extend public ownership, take Britain out of the EEC and give up nuclear weapons. According to Ian Bradley, active discussion of the prospects for a new 'social democratic' party began immediately after the 1979 election among three key groups: Jenkins and his personal friends in England; the Social Democratic Association of Labour local councillors which opposed the advance of the Labour left in the constituency parties; and the 'gang of three' ex-Ministers – Owen and Rodgers in parliament, and Williams who had just lost her seat at Hertford and Stevenage. These discussions developed throughout the next eighteen months as the Labour left advance continued, culminating in the decisions of the special party Conference at Wembley in January 1981 which gave the trade unions the principal share of influence in electing future party leaders. The day after the Conference (25 January 1981) the 'gang' issued a statement (the so-called Limehouse Declaration) announcing the formation of a 'Council for Social Democracy'. A further eleven Labour MPs now declared their support, and two months later the Council became a party.

The new party immediately drew into it various right-wing groups inside the Labour Party – the 'Manifesto' group of MPs, the Social Democratic Association and the leading members of the Campaign for a Labour Victory, all of which had been established since 1974 to oppose the advance of the left wing led by Benn. By the end of 1981 the SDP had 27 MPs including Shirley Williams, who had re-entered Parliament in November after a dramatic by-election victory in the formerly safe Conservative seat of Crosby (a suburb of Liverpool). Jenkins had also contested the safe Labour industrial constituency of Warrington, only narrowly losing with 42.4% of the votes (he was later to re-enter Parliament after a by-election victory in Glasgow in March 1982). In the London borough of Islington a group of 26 Labour councillors switched to the SDP and took control of the council. A long list of prominent figures in show business and the media, academics, lawyers, businessmen and even some trade unionists declared their support for the new party, which by December 1981 claimed over 70,000 paid-up members.

Thus, from its earliest days, the SDP had proved a formidable electoral contender on the evidence of both opinion polls and by-elections. However, the nature of the new party posed some problems. As Bradley has pointed out, there were two very different elements in the SDP. One was the ineffably middle-class element epitomised by Jenkins, Owen and Williams, and by the great bulk of the enthusiastic new recruits in the SDP membership, known in SDP parlance as the 'naives'.[10] Socially speaking, these people strongly resembled the Liberals' core supporters (though they may well have been less concerned to deny their own class membership), and some of them (notably Jenkins himself) felt warmly disposed towards the Liberal Party.* The other element was less middle-class and more closely linked to the labour movement. Prominent in this group were MPs and councillors from safe Labour seats where the local party organisations had previously become, to a greater or less extent, the fiefs of small and often ageing coteries of Labour councillors plus the sitting MPs. These were the constituencies prone to be 'taken over' by an influx of young activists whose views were far to the left of the old guard and the incumbent MP. As the SDP established itself, more MPs and councillors of this type – the 'refugees' – joined the new party. The refugees' conception of the party was much more labourist (a 'Mark II Labour Party') than that of the 'naives', both because they had usually

*Among SDP members polled in November 1981, 57% were in professional and managerial positions, while 7% were in working-class jobs and 10% in 'lower middle-class clerical and sales occupations. As yet it looks a distinctly middle-class club' (*The Times*, 30 November 1981). Among SDP supporters in the electorate the middle-class preponderance was less marked but they were older than the members; whereas most SDP members were aged 25–34, most SDP voters were aged 35–44 – the age group 'too young to have experienced the depression and too old to have been radicalised in the late 1960s and early 1970s', as one activist shrewdly suggested (Bradley, *Breaking the Mould?*, Martin Robertson, Oxford 1981, p. 112).

been in the Labour Party for a long time and because they mostly came from Labour electoral strongholds. Some had joined the SDP in anticipation of not being re-selected by their local parties, and hoped to remain MPs or councillors on the new party ticket. There was a wide gulf between this group and the 'naives', who seemed to constitute the majority of the SDP's activists, and had not belonged to any other party before. It was unlikely that the euphoria of the early months, when the party was the darling of the media, would survive when these contradictory components became better acquainted.

The special role of the media in promoting the SDP also made it difficult to assess the party's longer-run significance. Its popularity was partly a result of the enthusiasm felt by so many journalists for a group of politicians who were so much like themselves – well-educated, reasonable, and equally hostile to both Thatcher and Benn.[11] The effects on the SDP of its prompt alliance with the Liberals were also hard to determine. It undoubtedly helped Shirley Williams to win a by-election at Crosby in November 1981, just as it had helped the Liberal candidate, William Pitt, to win Croydon North-West as an Alliance candidate in October. But it was not certain whether Liberal voters would all vote SDP in constituencies where a Liberal had been asked to stand down in favour of an SDP candidate; or, when the reverse was the case, that ex-Labour voters would be prepared to vote Liberal at a general election, and for mostly unknown candidates. Moreover, tensions within the Alliance over the allocation of constituencies came into the open towards the end of 1981 and resulted in some loss of popularity.* This suggested that its instant appeal was due to dislike of Thatcherism in practice, and of the Labour Party's internal divisions, and to wishful thinking that the career politicians at the head of the SDP, whom the media now represented as born-again radicals, offered a new alternative. In April 1981, between 34% and 68% of SDP supporters polled did not know what the party stood for on any given issue. As Bradley remarked, the SDP was

> in many ways a wish-fulfilment party; many of its supporters see it not as what it is but as what they think it ought to be . . . Amid the platitudes, and given the lack of hard, specific policy statements, it was easy for many voters to regard the Social Democrats as their sort of people.[11]

But, in spite of (or because of) its vagueness on the crucial economic issues,

*The Alliance share of popular support fell from 44% in November 1981 to 34% on 1 April 1982 (MORI poll data reviewed by David Butler in *The Times*, 29 May 1982). The problem was that the Liberals were reluctant to stand down for SDP candidates in areas of traditional Liberal strength; whereas areas of traditional Labour strength, which it might seem logical to allot to SDP candidates, were less likely to be winnable, thanks to Labour's large majorities in such areas. By September 1982 a Gallup poll reported Liberal support at 12% and SDP support at only 8.5% (Peter Jenkins, *Guardian*, 23 Sept. 1982).

a large part of the SDP's appeal consisted in seeming to hold out a hope of returning to a more harmonious past, free from class struggle. The key elements in SDP economic thinking were the maintenance of a 'mixed economy' combined with industrial democracy, an incomes policy coupled with curbs on union powers, and a policy of gradual but steady reflation with, perhaps, a special fund to channel North Sea oil revenues into new (private) industrial investment. There was, besides, a commitment to decentralisation; this would be difficult to reconcile with an effective national incomes policy, or with equality – for instance, in the provision of local services – which the SDP also stressed. The economic policy to which the SDP was most committed, continued membership of the EEC, was one which a majority of voters opposed.

These policies might not look very convincing as a solution to the 'politics of power' – given their limited scope and their broad resemblance to measures that had already been tried unsuccessfully, or rejected, in the past – but they could easily be underestimated as a solution to the 'politics of support'. As David Currie pointed out, the key elements in the SDP's economic thinking were likely to be those intended to bring about a 'fundamental reform' in wage bargaining. Whichever of the schemes proposed by SDP economists was finally adopted, the SDP was clearly going to be committed to imposing on the labour movement some system of controls aimed at preventing wage demands from fuelling inflation, whereas the Labour Party's Alternative Economic Strategy seemed to reject controls without putting forward any concrete alternative for preventing inflationary wage settlements. Faced with a choice between Thatcherite deflation and Labourist inflation, voters could well feel that the SDP's approach was a new initiative which deserved a chance.[12]

None the less, gauging the electoral prospects for the SDP–Liberal Alliance was difficult. Bradley's judgement that 'it [seemed] safe to assume that the SDP/Liberal Alliance [would] do at least as well as the Liberals did in February 1974' seemed reasonable, but as he also pointed out, given the handicap of evenly distributed support (which the SDP shared with the Liberals) the Alliance would need over 30% of the vote to gain a substantial number of seats.[13] A large SDP–Liberal vote, which was nevertheless below 35% of the total, could even result in a Labour victory by taking crucial votes away from the Conservatives. It would also be likely to put more Liberals into parliament than Social Democrats, assuming that Liberal candidates would generally be standing in seats in which they had come second in previous elections. Of all the short-term possibilities, the most likely was that the SDP's emergence would improve the *Liberals'* chances of achieving their goal of holding the balance of power.

Scottish and Welsh Nationalism

Nationalism in both Scotland and Wales corresponds to the perception by some of both countries' elites that development within the British state no longer holds out hope of progress for these 'peripheries'.[14] Instead, they propose a course of autonomous development, seeking to mobilise the Scottish and Welsh nations under their leadership.

Wales and Scotland were culturally and politically autonomous prior to their incorporation into Great Britain under English hegemony in 1536 and 1707 respectively. In both cases the landed classes moved to London and progressively lost their place in Welsh and Scottish national life. This break was especially complete in Wales, where Welsh was universally spoken (as late as 1850, 90% of the population was still Welsh-speaking).[15]In Wales especially, but also to some extent in Scotland, a more democratic, more widely educated and more egalitarian society emerged than in England. Increasingly, the landowners were English, from outside local society, as were a growing proportion of industrialists, especially in the twentieth century.

Scotland, united with England later and on more equal terms than Wales, retained a substantial measure of legal, educational and religious autonomy, reinforced by a largely separate media system, football league, and other spheres of cultural independence. This was cemented by the creation, in 1885, of a Scottish Office, under a government Minister (the Scottish Secretary) at Westminster; the office was elevated to the status of Secretary of State, with cabinet rank, in 1926. By 1981 the Scottish Office was located in Edinburgh and was responsible for the administration, in Scotland, of health, agriculture, prisons, education, trade, industry and economic planning. In addition, a Scottish Grand Committee of all Scottish MPs had been established in 1895, to which all measures exclusively affecting Scotland were referred. Later, two Scottish Standing Committees were set up to consider the implications for Scotland of all other legislation, and later still a Select Committee on Scottish Affairs was created to monitor administrative policy and performance in relation to Scotland. This complex of structures catered to, and helped preserve, the distinctiveness of Scottish culture, and partly explains the relative ease with which the SNP was able to mobilise nationalist support from 1960 onwards, as the British crisis took its toll of Scotland's obsolescent textile, engineering and coal industries. A distinctive Scottish identity, once associated with Scotland's successful participation in the industrial revolution, remained intact and could be appealed to again for an independent initiative when the rewards of the industrial revolution appeared to have been exhausted.

Wales, by contrast, had been united with England earlier, a century after the defeat of the Welsh national leader Owen Glendower. What maintained a distinctive Welsh identity was not separate institutions but only the Welsh language, reinforced by the mass conversion of the Welsh people to Methodism under the impact of the industrial revolution. Between 1850 and 1901, however, compulsory primary education in English (and no compulsory education in Welsh) had reduced the proportion of Welsh-speakers from 90% to 50%; by 1971 the proportion had fallen still further, to 21% (and only 13% of Welsh people under 30). Welsh nationalism, therefore, developed as a movement to try to arrest the decline of Welsh as a spoken language, Welsh culture, such as choirs, the literary culture of Eisteddfodau, Welsh libraries, and so on. The movement was not originally concerned with self-government, let alone Welsh independence, but with trying to prevent the disappearance of the basis of a national identity. Thus it was unlike Scottish nationalism, which took the continued existence of a Scottish national identity as its starting-point and sought to harness it to a new national political project. In electoral terms Welsh nationalism started out with the radical disadvantage that, by the 1920s, only a minority of Welshmen still spoke Welsh, let alone were interested in Welsh poetry. The other side of the coin of the decline of the Welsh language was the rise of the Welsh industrial working class. The vast English-speaking majority were also overwhelmingly part of the labour movement; they belonged first and foremost to the *British* working class, and less and less to the Welsh nation.

By the late 1960s, however, the economic decline of the industrial valleys and towns of South Wales, coinciding with the nation-wide reaction against bureaucracy in all spheres, stimulated a new interest in economic and administrative decentralisation. The growth of tourism was another factor; the rapid increase in the purchase, by prosperous Englishmen, of 'second homes' in impoverished Welsh villages symbolised Welsh economic and cultural deprivation. At the same time, the Labour Party's traditional strength in South Wales had been weakened, not only by the record of policy failure on the part of successive Labour governments, but also by the existence of too many conservative, and corrupt, party oligarchies in safe industrial seats (a factor also present in south-west Scotland). These trends converged with the nationalists' growing awareness that a large measure of political autonomy was essential if Welsh culture was to be protected.

An additional factor was also at work: the 'dissolution' of the traditional working class took a particularly acute form in Scotland and Wales. Heavy dependence on the old staple industries of coal-mining, steel-making, shipbuilding, engineering and (mainly in Scotland) textiles, meant that Scotland and Wales suffered more than England from the crisis of the economy. Unemployment rates there were 30–50% higher than the British average.

In Scotland the sixties saw the start of dramatic changes in employment: ten thousand jobs disappeared every year. Out of a population of 5.1 millions, nearly 300,000 emigrated during the sixties, most of them overseas; by 1981 421,000 had left within two decades, a massive share of the younger generation. For those who stayed, there was a major shift of employment into services or into new, largely foreign-owned and very large-scale consumer goods industries (some of which would also later collapse).[16]

Wales, which had enjoyed some industrial diversification during the 1940s after the catastrophe of the slump, had persistently lower living standards than England but did not experience the same degree of industrial upheaval as Scotland until the new catastrophe of the late seventies and early eighties. But for both countries the contemporary crisis was a period of accelerating disruption. Old ties of culture and place were progressively weakened.

In these conditions Scottish and Welsh voters' allegiances to the two major parties were strained too, and the appeal of an alternative *national* solution, combining economic and cultural aspirations, grew stronger. Disaffected Labour and Conservative voters, who in England gravitated towards the Liberals, tended instead to move towards the nationalists, especially in Scotland. The SNP pre-empted Liberal gains in Scotland almost completely. In Wales, the nationalist electoral achievement was much more modest, but the political potential of Welsh nationalism had probably not yet reached its full potential.[17]

The Scottish National Party

The origins of the SNP go back to the 1880s, when the Scottish economy was showing early signs of weakness. The example of the Irish nationalists led to the formation of a Scottish Home Rule association, to which both Keir Hardie and Ramsay MacDonald belonged; MacDonald was actually its secretary and London-based lobbyist. The central role later played by these two men in the Labour Party explains why Scottish nationalism did not then become a serious force: the Scottish working class, like the Welsh, played a leading, not a supporting role in the development and eventual triumph of the Labour Party. The SNP itself was formed in 1934, in the middle of the slump and after the Labour Party's crushing defeat in 1931, but it did not become a significant electoral force for another thirty years. A fresh groundswell of sentiment in favour of Home Rule arose in 1948–9, during the Labour government's 'austerity' programme. It took the form of a mass campaign to get signatures to a 'Covenant', in effect a petition for Home Rule. But the failure of this project eventually produced a reaction. In the late 1950s the SNP passed under a new leadership who were committed to the idea that Scottish independence could and must be obtained by electoral organisation.

From that moment the party increased its number of candidates, and its share of the Scottish vote, at each successive election until October 1974. Then, with 30% of the Scottish vote and 11 seats at Westminster, the SNP found itself in a position to force a reluctant but thoroughly alarmed Labour government to introduce legislation for an elected Scottish Assembly with devolved powers. This was in no way a measure of independence – on the contrary it was intended to forestall further nationalist advance – but the gradualist wing of the SNP saw it as a step forward. However, opponents of devolution in the Labour Party succeeded in inserting an amendment to the Bill, which provided that the government would only be obliged to implement it if 40% of the entire Scottish electorate (as opposed to a simple majority of those voting) supported it. In the referendum, held in March 1979, only 33% (52% of those voting) did so, and the government felt unable to proceed further. The 'gradualist' strategy had failed and the SNP MPs in frustration voted with the Conservatives to bring the government down. They paid a heavy price. In the May 1979 elections the SNP vote fell to 17.3% of the Scottish total, and its parliamentary representation fell from 11 to 2. In its turn the SNP Annual Conference reacted by reverting to a policy of campaigning for complete independence or nothing. The 'home rulers' in the party's hierarchy were replaced, and the left wing, who wanted to commit the party to a socialist brand of nationalism, were also rejected. In May 1980 the party also lost two-thirds of its district councillors in local government elections throughout Scotland.*

The SNP might therefore seem a spent force. But the rate of decline of the Scottish economy, in combination with the appeal of nationalism, contained a permanent political potential, and the SNP seemed likely to revert, in due course, to a strategy of electoral gradualism. As Jack Brand commented (before the 1979 setback): 'there is no doubt that the SNP will have its ups and downs, but every downturn in the Scottish economy will turn Labour voters, and perhaps Conservative too, into the arms of the SNP'.[18] It is therefore necessary to consider briefly the support which the SNP proved capable of attracting in its electoral heyday.

SNP candidates were predominantly middle-class, not unlike Liberal candidates. SNP activists, however, were predominantly self-employed, or were white-collar employees of small concerns. Like the SDP's new activists of 1981, most were new to politics when they joined the SNP, and as Kellas observed, such recruits tend to lack staying-power.[19] There was also a small element of left-wing activists, who in England would have been in the Labour left or one of the extra-parliamentary groups, and who

*Prior to the May 1980 elections the SNP had controlled two of the 53 district councils and had been the largest party in another. It lost these positions and was reduced to 56 councillors out of a Scottish total of 1,121.

contributed greatly to the party's intellectual calibre.

SNP supporters resembled the floating 'centre' voters who were attracted to the Liberals in England. They were largely refugees from one of the major parties, and rather evenly drawn from all social strata.[20] Apart from by-elections, where the SNP briefly took industrial seats from Labour in the late sixties, the party was most successful in rural constituencies and in semi-urban constituencies where only a minority of the work-force was unionised, especially in the north-eastern seats of Moray and Nairn, Banff and East Aberdeenshire. The Scottish electoral map after October 1974 showed the SNP seats distributed around the periphery, very much like Liberal seats in Britain as a whole.

SNP social and economic policies also bore some resemblance to those of the Liberals, and reflected similar tensions between 'left' and 'centrist' elements. Within an independent Scotland the SNP called for decentralised government, more democratic government and more 'open' government. On the economy, the party favoured worker 'participation', but maintained that it had 'no objection in principle to either private or public enterprise', believing that 'all contributions to the success of an enterprise including capital, expertise and labour, should have a fair reward and have an effective voice in policy making'.[21]*

Unlike the Liberals and the SDP, however, the SNP had a solution to the problem of the Scottish economy – 'Scotland's oil'. In the run-up to the two 1974 elections this theme was stressed almost to the exclusion of any other. If Scotland were independent, then under international law, the SNP argued, most of the oil in the British sector of the North Sea would belong to Scotland. The government in London was extracting the oil as fast as possible, so as to maintain living-standards in England above the level that the English could afford on their own; an independent Scottish government would husband the reserves and plan their extraction in such a way as to endow Scotland with a modern industrial base.

There can be little doubt that the oil issue played a large part in the SNP's 1974 election successes; but the subsequent decision to support Labour's devolution Bill meant that the oil theme had to be played down, because the devolution proposals left London in full control of the oil in the North Sea (and of all other revenues too, for that matter). The 'hawks' in the SNP drew their own conclusions from the result. The new SNP leader chosen in 1979, Gordon Wilson, had been closely identified with the 'Scotland's oil' strategy, and in the long run, as the life of the oil

*Compare the SDP in 1981: 'The Party . . . is committed to fostering a healthy public sector and a healthy private sector . . . it recognises the need for the innovating strength of a competitive economy with a fair distribution of rewards. It seeks to encourage competitive public enterprise, cooperative ventures and profit-sharing' (Bradley, *Breaking the Mould?*, p. 121).

reserves was gradually seen to be longer than originally supposed, this strategy might once again come to have considerable appeal – especially if neither of the major parties seemed capable of arresting the decline of the Scottish economy.

Plaid Cymru

The Welsh (National) Party was formed in 1925 under the leadership of Saunders Lewis, a philosopher and leader of Welsh literature. For Lewis, the new party's task was to fight for Welsh culture, but not for Welsh independence; he envisaged a world of free but federated nations. This formula had little electoral appeal. In 1945, however, the leadership passed to Gwynfor Evans, who began a gradual transformation of the party into a serious political organisation. In the early 1950s it followed the Scottish Nationalists' 1948 example, of trying to mobilise national sentiment through petitions; and in this case too, failure prompted a new, pragmatic brand of activist to try electoral organisation, concentrating especially on by-elections (at which the pull of majority-party allegiances is weakest).

The PC share of the Welsh vote grew from 0.7% (for only four candidates), in 1951, to 11.5% in 1970, when the party ran candidates in all 36 Welsh constituencies and won three seats. In the 1974 elections there was a slight decline (to 10.8% of the total in October) but no loss of seats, and in the district council elections of 1976 the PC went on to capture control of Merthyr in the Labour-dominated industrial heartland and made significant gains throughout the mining valleys.

The growing PC threat prompted a series of administrative reforms which ultimately endowed Wales with a system of devolved administration bearing some similarity to that of Scotland. In 1964 a Welsh Office under a Secretary of State for Wales was created in Cardiff. Within six years, and in face of considerable Whitehall resistance, it had assumed responsibility for health, education and agriculture throughout Wales, and established a Welsh Planning Board and an Economic Council. Welsh trade unionists, too, set up a distinctively democratic Welsh TUC (in spite of resistance from Congress House – the headquarters of the British TUC) and the Welsh Labour Party was also eventually prodded into attempting to come to terms with Welsh sentiment.[22]

These changes had a cumulative effect. The case for a more comprehensive measure of local autonomy was thrown into prominence by the inability of the Welsh people to control the branches of central government that now operated from Cardiff, and by the well-publicised findings of the Welsh Economic Council on Wales's continuing economic decline. The Labour government's Wales Act of 1978, passed simultaneously with the Scotland Act, provided for an elected Welsh Assembly with a committee system to make policy over a wide range of devolved responsibilities. However, in the March 1979 referendum provided for under the Act, only 20% of those voting (11.9% of all Welsh voters) cast their votes in favour of the new Assembly. It was clear that, to the great majority of Welshmen, the Welsh language and Welsh self-government were irrelevant issues.

Plaid Cymru itself had not been strongly committed to the Assembly; its cultural wing had long argued that self-government under a predominantly non-Welsh majority in Wales would be more damaging than favourable to Wales's culture.[23] Perhaps, as a result, defeat was less damaging to Plaid Cymru than it was to the SNP. In the election of May 1979 the PC vote declined from 10.8% to 8.1%, with the loss of one seat; similar losses were experienced in the local elections held at the same time. But the strength of the cultural basis of Welsh nationalism remained, exemplified in the PC leader Gwynfor Evans's successful use of the threat to fast to death in order to force the Thatcher government to honour its 1979 election pledge to establish a Welsh-language TV channel in Wales.

With unemployment in Wales rising sharply from 1979 onwards (the official figure was 16% in December 1981), the long-run possibility of a renewed nationalist advance could not be ruled out unless governments in London showed themselves able and determined to rejuvenate the Welsh economy. Plaid Cymru's advance had paralleled the economy's decline, as well as the continuing encroachment of English culture through education, the mass media, urbanisation, tourism and the decline of church-going.[24] Even among the non-Welsh-speaking population, the appeal of Plaid Cymru, especially as it became more oriented to radical economic demands, remained potentially significant.

In certain respects Plaid Cymru resembled the SNP and the English alternative parties, especially in its broad appeal to all socio-economic strata of the population. Also, like the SNP, (though unlike the English alternative parties) it appealed particularly to young voters, and even more to young activists, a very large proportion of whom were students or even school children.[25] Its leaders were, also overwhelmingly professional people, as were its candidates. Plaid Cymru, at least in the sixties, was 'a party strongly dominated by the middle class in Wales, with a leaven of non-manual workers drawn from the stratum of post-mistresses'.[26]

The point about these people, however, was that they were Welsh-speaking, and moreover the leaders were 'the sons and daughters of coal-miners, steel-workers, shopkeepers and minor civil servants, but overwhelmingly of coal-miners'.[27] Unlike the new Labour MPs from Wales, who tended to move with their families to 'prosperous parts of London', the educated miners' sons who led the PC wanted to mobilise the Welsh masses in a combined cultural and economic revival in Wales. The party's advance in the South Wales valleys testified that this dream was not wholly unrealistic. The cultural dimension and the class origins of many of the party members distinguished their position from that of their less highly-educated, primarily self-employed or small-business counterparts in the SNP.

Yet in the short run, at least, the PC leadership's characteristics were also a source of weakness, compared with the SNP. 'The SNP was guided, if not dominated by men of business and commercial experience. Anyone could see that they could run an establishment. Bardic poets may lack this quality'.[28] And the PC's electoral success was indeed limited. Its vote was strongly related to the proportion of Welsh speakers in every constituency, the three PC victories in 1970 having occurred in Caernarvon, Carmarthen and Merioneth, three of the four most Welsh parts of 'Welsh Wales'.*

Like the SNP and the Liberals, Plaid Cymru tended to be strongest at the periphery. In 1979 it lost most of the ground it had gained from Labour, and the Conservatives also won seats in parts of rural Wales which they had not held since the turn of the century. The scale of the PC threat was highly unlikely to lead to any new devolution measures for Wales in the foreseeable future. On the other hand, the PC vote had not collapsed, any more than the determination of its activists. Plaid Cymru also benefited from the militant actions of the Welsh Language Society, who agitated on the language issue, through calculated attacks on property and other forms of direct action, and so publicised the nationalist cause without compromising Plaid Cymru's reformist image.

Moreover, the party's policies had evolved considerably. From its early concentration on the language issue, to the exclusion of all else, it had, by 1980, evolved elaborate economic policy proposals for Wales. Its language policy had been modified to a call for bi-lingualism (rather than for Welsh only), and the themes of decentralisation and democratisation fitted naturally into its communitarian philosophy, and had particular appeal in Wales. Electorally, Plaid Cymru might still be a force to reckon with.

The Significance of the Alternative Parties

The most obvious common feature of the alternative parties was their 'middle-class' character. Yet, although the term has been used throughout this chapter, its limitations could hardly be more obvious. Between the Welsh-speaking university lecturers and post-mistresses of Plaid Cymru in Merioneth, the pragmatic small businessmen of the SNP in East Fife, and

*But it should be noted that PC support was also relatively strong in some constituencies, such as Caerphilly, Rhondda East and Aberdare, where Welsh-speakers were relatively few, and in a 1968 poll 9% of non-Welsh-speaking voters declared support for PC. (A. Butt-Philip, *The Welsh Question*, University of Wales Press, Cardiff 1975, p. 152).

the Oxford-educated 'gang of four' planning the formation of the SDP in weekend cottages near London, there was in some ways little similarity. Many SDP activists may have had more in common with their Liberal counterparts, though they mostly lacked the Liberals' sometimes earnest sense of being heirs to a distinct tradition, whereas the new entrants to political activity in the SDP gave the impression of having a technocratic and somewhat superficial conception of politics.[29] Yet in their different ways each did express an aspect of the 'new middle class' as a political factor in British politics. (Another aspect was expressed by the Labour left, the so-called 'polytechnic Marxists' from whose political machinations the former Labour MPs and local councillors in the SDP considered themselves to be refugees). This social stratum was undoubtedly playing a central role in attempts to reconstruct parliamentary party politics, though its real importance was difficult to assess.

The class character of the Liberal Party had been its Achilles' heel in the past. The refusal of the middle-class members of Liberal constituency associations to adopt more working-class 'Lib-Lab' candidates had, at the end of the nineteenth century, helped to push the labour movement to seek independent representation, leading ultimately to the Liberals' eclipse. The modern Liberal Party had not entirely surmounted this weakness. The problem was not that middle-class Liberals lacked sympathy for the workers but that they tended to lack empathy with them.

> One ALTU [Association of Liberal Trade Unionists] leader commented, not without bitterness, that while Lady Violet Bonham Carter – Asquith's daughter and a party stalwart throughout her life – had always shown concern for the problems of the working class person as an abstract part of mankind, she had never been willing to have much to do with him as an individual.[30]

It was not difficult to predict that the activists of the SDP would have the same problem. The apparent tendency of the Alliance to draw more votes from Conservatives than from Labour was consistent with this. Of course the Labour Party itself was not immune to this difficulty. The increasingly middle-class character of the parliamentary party was probably responsible for the loss of some of its members and votes after 1951. It was not just the views of the left-wing constituency activists, but also the educated middle-class tones in which they were sometimes expressed, which had – ironically perhaps – precipitated the movement of some of the older working-class members out of the Labour Party into the SDP. But the Labour Party's links with the unions, which the Labour Left took very seriously, made an important difference. In the Labour Party the working class still had a massive and constitutionally guaranteed presence through the trade unions.

The nationalist parties had some advantage in this respect, in that they explicitly appealed to a national identity common to all classes. The PC leadership's background, and the fact that it was so heavily involved in teaching (rather than in commerce or industry), gave it the fewest problems in this regard, either in relating personally to Welsh workers or in adopting broadly 'democratic-socialist' economic and social policies calling for an active and expanded – though more democratic – state sector. The SNP, by contrast, was divided into left and right wings. The party's left wing, contemplating the heavily working-class character of south-west Scotland where the population was concentrated, believed that the party must adopt democratic, socialist policies if it was ever to win power; while the right wing was opposed to socialism in principle and also judged that social-democratic policies would alienate middle-class support. Like most Liberal activists Gordon Wilson, the SNP leader from 1979, 'refused to acknowledge the existence of class problems'.[31] The SDP's early pronouncements did not deny the existence of classes, but scarcely mentioned them either, except to say that the party existed 'to create an open, classless and more equal society'.

The ambiguities of all the alternative parties on the issue of class (with the partial exception of Plaid Cymru) expressed the classical middle-class ambivalence towards both capital and labour – dazzled by capital but resentful of it, sympathetic to labour but fearful of it. Yet with the break-up of so many of the traditional connotations of capital and labour – and especially the gradual disappearance of the small industrial boss and the cloth-capped worker – it could well be that this ambivalence would not matter electorally. In the short run it might even be an asset. Critical commentators on the SDP in 1981 pointed to its lack of rank and file activists to get out the vote among the workers in industrial areas. They tended to forget that Labour Party activists had also become scarce, that television had become the prime medium of political communication, and that more voters than at any time since 1945 had ceased to have a routine attachment to any party.*

In any case, the class character of a party must not be identified with the social background or even the felt interests of its activists. The phenomenal response to the Liberal–SDP Alliance was due largely to the fact that they succeeded in articulating new interests and appealing to new sentiments that had been emerging in Britain during the 1960s and 1970s and were partly independent of class interests and sentiments. The SNP

*This was specially true of the working class. By 1979 fewer voters were strong supporters of Labour than of the Conservatives, and support for Labour had declined most of all among working-class trade unionists. Social class (in the sense of socio-economic stratification) correlated less and less strongly with voting for the two major parties, and by 1979 Labour's lead among manual workers who consider themselves working class was only 20% compared with 42% in 1964 (R. Rose, 'Class Does Not Equal Party', *Studies in Public Policy* **74**, Strathclyde University, 1980).

and Plaid Cymru had also attracted a substantial block of votes. To call all these votes 'protest votes' understates their significance by seeming to imply that these voters were only making a gesture *against* Labour or the Conservatives, whereas they were also registering a positive response to some element or elements in the 'images' they had of these alternative parties. The new 'political subjects' to whom these parties' programmes were addressed, and to whom the parties appealed in their campaigns, were still rather vague and certainly rather contradictory. The call made to them was unlikely to take effect quickly, given the pull of much older identifications. But, as the crisis deepened, it seemed likely that disaffection from one or both of the major parties would grow. In spite of the unpredictability of the electoral process in the short run, the chances of the alternative parties being able to capture the parliamentary balance of power had never been higher.

Moreoever, the Liberals and the SDP were both committed as a matter of priority to the introduction of proportional representation, which was also supported by the SNP and a significant minority within the Conservative Party. The introduction of virtually any system of proportional representation would encourage more 'centre voters' to abandon the Conservative and Labour parties (their votes would no longer seem wasted) and give rise to permanent and substantial representation for the parties of the centre. With proportional representation, neither the Conservatives nor Labour would be likely to win outright parliamentary majorities again.

It is idle to speculate on the effect which this might have on these two parties – on the relation of the Conservatives with capital or of Labour with the trade unions – or on other aspects of the party system and the state. Yet, in a more fundamental sense, the significance of such a change can be understood in terms of two broad possibilities: either it would yield a viable 'centre strategy' for dealing with the crisis, or it would lead to a 'government of national unity' serving as a transition to the imposition of a right-wing authoritarian solution to the crisis.

The former possibility was hard to discern in the policy statements of the Liberals and the SDP (or for that matter the SNP). Continued membership of the EEC, maintaining the mixed economy, and the introduction of an incomes policy, industrial democracy and apprenticeship schemes – there was nothing that had not been proposed before, nor was there any indication of a serious analysis of the nature of the crisis, or the way in which these familiar ideas could be expected to resolve it. Bradley summarises the SDP's formula as follows:

> Social democracy... is less an ideology and more a particular approach to dealing with society and its problems. It is an approach that has worked rather well in Europe, particularly in West Germany and Scandinavia, where it has

> helped to produce societies which are more prosperous, less class-ridden, and perhaps also more fraternal than our own. If we ask what a Social Democratic Britain would be like, we will find an answer by looking at those countries. It would have proportional representation, state-funding of political parties and possibly a federal system of government. There would be more worker participation in industry, some kind of annual agreement on incomes and more small businesses and co-operatives. Our schools and hospitals would be more autonomous and more open institutions. Above all, perhaps, our perspective would be less insular and more enthusiastically European and internationalist.[32]

The question was whether this conception seemed to be an answer to the problem of continuing competitive decline, increasingly inadequate investment, growing technical and educational backwardness, mounting unemployment, falling real incomes and deteriorating public amenities and social services – in short the comprehensive, fundamental reality of the economic crisis as it had been developing for over a century.

Although these policies might appeal to voters anxious to return to the 'middle way' of thirty years earlier, they were largely policies which had already proved inadequate (where they had not proved impracticable in face of political opposition – for instance, capital's opposition to industrial democracy and labour's opposition to wage controls). It was difficult to believe that in the hands of a new government of the 'centre' – in all probability a coalition of divergent elements – they would provide a formula capable of arresting and reversing economic decline and of overcoming the general crisis which this had produced.

The alternative possibility was outlined in 1979 in an important article by Tom Nairn. What, he asked, was the significance of the fact that for so much of the twentieth century Britain had already had 'national' or coalition governments – from 1915 to 1922 and 1931 to 1945, a total of twenty-one years? Nairn's answer was that it had been an historically crucial device whereby the established social order had undertaken limited, 'restorative' reconstructions of the economy and the state so as to deal with problems posed by the weakness of the economic and political order, while preserving the old balance of social and political power. National governments had been necessary to effect the transition from the old Liberal hegemony to the Keynesian social-democratic order, and to secure the safe incorporation of the labour movement into the state. But a new national government, constructed around a coalition of the centre (such as the Alliance, formed three years after Nairn's article was written) could no longer perform a successful *restorative* function.

> National government regimes promise to be both radical and restorative; but the whole point of the crisis conditions that have accumulated over the past 20 years is that restoration is impossible. The actual undertaking of renovation has become inevitable.[33]

A *renovation* would have to break up the established social and political order, which was a basic cause of the crisis; so a new 'national' government would be bound to fail in its 'restorative' mission. The most likely result would be that it would make way for a leadership sufficiently unscrupulous, innovative and adventurous to break up the established socio-political order – most probably a 'strong man' of the far right:

> A transitional government might open the door to him, both by its general incompetence and its destructive effect on the cohesion of the old parties... And the resulting movement... would 'normalize' UK politics with a vengeance.[34]

It may sound far-fetched to suggest that this might be the ultimate historical function of the 'vague, nice' parties of the centre reviewed in this chapter. If so, two questions should be considered. First, whether these parties share a realistic understanding of the fundamental gravity of the crisis, and have a credible solution to it. Second, whether there are reasons to think that the role which similar 'centre' parties have played in crises elsewhere could never be repeated in Britain – for Nairn's scenario is not a pure figment of the imagination, but reflects some of the most painful episodes of modern history.[35]

PART IV

12

The British State

Until the mid-1970s few books on British politics, and virtually no textbooks, referred to the state. This was because the most influential theories of the state were incompatible with the tenets of pluralism. Hegel had seen the state as the embodiment of the ethical and rational principles of the nation and glorified the Prussian autocracy as its supreme expression, while Marx, on the contrary, understood it as the embodiment of the interests of the dominant class. Pluralists rejected the concepts of both nation and class. For them, 'western' societies were systems of constantly changing combinations of groups competing to control the 'institutions of government' through electoral and pressure-group activity. The 'institutions of government' were, moreover, diverse and neutral. They did not constitute a structure exerting a systematic force of any kind on political life; they were a 'dependent variable'.

The concept of the state was, however, resurrected by both left and right thinkers as a result of the crisis. On the left, in 1968 Nicos Poulantzas inaugurated a radical critique of Marxist ideas about the state from which a much more complex and subtle theory eventually emerged, and the following year Miliband published a definitive critique of the pluralist conception of the state.[1] Soon afterwards, on the other hand, neo-liberal theorists identified the 'social-democratic state' as a threat to the interests of capital. While viewpoints of left and right theorists were diametrically opposed, they agreed in recogising what popular opinion had in any case never doubted for a moment – that the state was a massive and problematic reality.

To take Miliband first, he demonstrated that the pluralist conception of the state (shared by most social democrats) as a neutral apparatus, reflecting the changing balance of competing political forces, was untenable. He showed that in capitalist societies the state's directing echelons were staffed by people whose social background and milieu, and whose training within the state apparatus, made them see their task as that of serving the interests of capital. Moreover, even social-democratic ministers invariably saw the health of the capitalist economy as necessary to the achievement of practicable social reforms. He also showed that the pluralists' world of free and equal political competition was another myth. The independent command of economic resources by private capital made it hard if not impossible for the state apparatus to control effectively. The withdrawal of 'business confidence' from a government that threatened business interests was frequently decisive (as in 1931 or 1964–6), and it was reinforced by the dependence of governments on external capitalist interests such as foreign banks or the International Monetary Fund. Furthermore, *vis-à-vis* organised labour, capital was more comprehensively organised, less divided, better endowed, ideologically more confident, and closer to the state apparatus. The state was not neutral and the political struggle between labour and capital was not equal.

Whereas Miliband showed that the state was not neutral, Poulantzas addressed himself to the fact that it was not a mere tool of capital either. The famous dictum of Marx and Engels that the state was 'but a committee for managing the common affairs of the bourgeoisie' had long been taken by Marxists to mean that it was an agent or instrument of the bourgeoisie. This meant interpreting every state action which appeared not to be in the interests of the bourgeoisie, such as the extension of the franchise, as somehow 'in the last analysis' *really* in its interests. Poulantzas initially argued that this must be taken seriously, and advanced the idea that the state was 'relatively autonomous'.

First, he pointed out, it was evident that the state needed a degree of independence from the dominant class if it was to maintain the latter's long-term *political* dominance. Major concessions to working-class political strength, such as the trade-union rights legislated and re-legislated in Britain in 1871, 1875, 1906, 1946 and 1974 were necessary at the time in order to preserve capital from a more fundamental threat. In effect, the most important 'common affair' of the bourgeoisie was the preservation of its political power, and to 'manage' this the state needed enough autonomy *from* the bourgeoisie to be able to override its immediate economic interests if need be. Second, Poulantzas pointed out that the economic interests of different fractions of capital often conflict with each other. To reconcile, and if necessary arbitrate between them, the state must also be independent of the control of any one fraction (for instance the British state had to be able to abolish Resale Price Maintenance, which hurt many small retailers, or to take Britain into the EEC, which hurt many smaller manufacturers).

Poulantzas also suggested that the interests of the dominant class were expressed primarily in the way the state was structured and organised. He criticised Miliband for seeming to say that what makes a state capitalist is the class origin or class ties of its senior personnel. Miliband replied that Poulantzas was attributing to the structure of the state an efficacity which was ultimately mysterious. We shall comment briefly on this exchange later (see pp. 244–5); in the event Poulantzas subsequently shifted his position. In his last book, he abandoned the notion that the state is in fact always functional for capital, either in its actions or in its structure.[2] Instead he developed the idea that the state is a product – a 'condensate', in his words – of class struggles (echoing Marx's dictum that the state is an 'official résumé of civil society'). This implies not only that the structures of the state may not be functional for particular elements of capital: they may not be altogether functional for any of them. But this does not mean that the state in a capitalist society may work systematically against the interests of capital and in favour of the workers; if it did, the society would hardly remain capitalist for long. What it means is that nothing *guarantees* that the state serves the interests of capital consistently, through all changes in the nature and needs of capital, in face of all challenges – an insight of particular relevance to the British state, as we shall see.

Also of importance is the implication that the state is itself a *field of struggle*. The Leninist tradition tended to regard the state as something to be 'seized' (and then 'smashed') by the workers. Poulantzas regarded it rather as a 'field of power relations' in which elements opposed to the dominant class were also engaged. As the state had expanded, this field had been greatly enlarged, offering new opportunities to turn the state's operation against the interests of capital. A good example of this, which is very relevant to the British experience, is 'corporatism', discussed, later, in Chapter 13.

In short, what these and other theorists did was to suggest how the state – whose political significance had become such a central fact of life in the post-war period – might be analysed without falling into the trap of reducing it to a mere reflection of the relative influence of competing groups (as the pluralists supposed) or of the interests of the dominant class (as traditional Marxists had imagined). At the same time, the new way of looking at the matter also made it clear that there is no such thing as *the* 'capitalist state'. There are only the states of particular capitalist societies, the 'condensates' of highly specific historical struggles. Once again, therefore, it is a question of trying to understand British politics – in this instance the British state – in terms of its distinctive historical development.

The Development of the Contemporary British State

The most suggestive recent work on this topic is that of Tom Nairn.[3]

Nairn argued that the essential characteristics of the modern British state could be traced to the social and political context in which the industrial revolution occurred. Because the British industrial revolution was the first such revolution, the state which presided over it could be very different from those which presided over subsequent industrial revolutions in other countries. The latter all faced a common problem: how to make 'space' for, and how to protect and nurture, their countries' new industries in face of Britain's naval power and technical and quantitative superiority in the market. This demanded a high-profile, centralised, rationalised form of state, actively clearing the way for the growth of domestic industry – a type of state which the circumstances of post-Napoleonic Europe fostered, in different ways, in both France and Germany.

By contrast, the modern British state originated in the dominance of the unique 'landed-capitalist' class which emerged from the English revolution of the seventeenth century. This, numerically small, 'patrician' class largely *was* the state – furnishing its parliamentarians, its magistrates, its militia, its policy-making bureaucracy, its military officer corps, and the clergy of its established Church. As a direct emanation of this class the British state could be highly decentralised and 'low-profile', based on strong intra-class personal ties rather than on formal and impersonal rules. In the course of the late eighteenth century, and throughout the nineteenth, this governing 'patrician' class merged with the rising class of commercial and industrial capital. As a result, the rising class had no need to attack the state; it could always be reformed to meet their needs. Steadily, corruption was reduced, and utilitarian principles were gradually extended into the staffing of the civil service and the armed forces and into the organisation of the fiscal system and the poor law. But the essential character of the state – its informal, patrician, decentralised and above all *reactive* character – remained unchanged.

The result was a state capable of superintending the transition to commercial and industrial capitalism in the first country to make this transition: and capable of forging a new hegemony over society at large, which proved strong enough to withstand the social and economic dislocations of the transition with only a minimum resort to force. But when the industrial challenge of more-efficient industrial capitalisms was encountered, the same state was ill-adapted to respond as an agent of industrial reconstruction.

> The fact is that emergence from the crisis demands a political break: a disruption at the level of the state, allowing the emergence of sharper antagonisms and the will to reform the old order root and branch. But in this system, possibly more than in any other, such a break has become extremely difficult. The state-level is so deeply entrenched in the social order itself, state and civil society are so intertwined in the peculiar exercise of the British

> Constitution, that a merely 'political' break entails a considerable social revolution.[4]

Nairn's thesis is much richer than any summary, even though it is itself presented only in broad terms: a critical history of the modern British state does not yet exist.[5] But to understand the character of the British state today we need a sketch, however provisional, of the main stages of its development.

The first period, from 1832 to 1867, is, least controversially perhaps, the period of the liberal representative state. From 1832 onwards the middle classes were increasingly represented in the House of Commons, which as a result became less and less 'manageable' by the magnates of the Tory and Whig parties. The way was open to a reconstruction of the state to meet the needs of the new middle classes, including some provision for the needs of their employees. Municipal government was put on a new footing in 1835, and central administration substantially rationalised between 1853 and the 1870s. Reform of the judicature was initiated with the establishment of County Courts in 1846, and carried further (after a long resistance) in 1876. The reorganisation of the labour supply was put in hand with the 1834 Poor Law (enforced more or less generally from the mid-1850s), supplemented by a series of Factory Acts. The fiscal system was reconstructed with the abandonment of protection and the switch from tariff revenue to income tax; the Bank Act of 1844 established a central bank, and Joint Stock Company Acts of 1856 and 1862 created the legal framework for limited liability and the efficient centralisation of capital.

But the liberal-representative state was not only undemocratic, it was firmly opposed to democracy. By the 1860s, however, the growing strength of working-class organisation made a partially democratic franchise a risk which had to be taken. Thanks to the acceptance of liberal ideas among the leaders of the labour movement at that time, it was an acceptable risk, and the next fifty years saw the construction of a liberal-*democratic* state. This second phase was decisive in the development of the contemporary state: the 'historic bloc' of dominant classes and their allies now expanded and by 1918 embraced at least the male working class. The work of liberal reform was consummated in the civil service, the courts, the army, municipal and county government; and there was a great expansion of the state apparatus to meet the needs of capital as it entered the phase of monopoly and rising foreign competition (for example, to provide it with a more literate labour force) and to meet social demands from the working class.

The shift from the 'negative' or 'night-watchman' liberal state of early competitive capitalism to the 'positive' state of monopoly capitalism was, however, not effected through consensus but through political struggles. The propertied classes remained nervous about what the workers might do with their vote ('a political combination of the lower classes', Bagehot had remarked, 'as such and for their own purposes, is an evil of the first magnitude'). The guiding principle of state development was the need to make those concessions to the workers which could 'safely' be made – a 'passive revolution', in Gramsci's terminology. Safety was ensured, above all, by restricting popular power to the single channel of parliamentary and local elections; by progressively neutralising the independent power of the House of Commons that had been the hallmark of the liberal representative state; and by excluding the principle of democracy from all other spheres. At the same time, the power relations between the classes were reproduced with great precision inside the state apparatus. As a 'terrain' for working-class struggle, the apparatus of the liberal-democratic state was made as unpromising as possible.

This state entered into a general crisis from about 1910 onwards, a crisis resolved by the First World War and then by a transition, begun during that war, to a third phase – the Keynesian, and, eventually, social-democratic state of the post-1945 era. Apart from the reduction in the powers of the non-elected House of Lords (in 1911 and 1949) and the extension of the franchise to women (in 1918 and 1928) this phase was not marked by any major changes of formal structure. Its main features were:

1 The integration of the Labour Party into the state, on the basis of a narrowly-defined parliamentarism, through the 'controlled experiments' of the inter-war minority governments, sandwiched between two periods of 'national government'.
2 The extension of the structure of state-organised social security begun by the Liberals (old age pensions in 1908, and sickness, disability and unemployment insurance in 1911). The Welfare State established by Labour in 1946–7 made comprehensive and more generous a system which had been gradually enlarged by successive governments since that time.
3 The enlargement of the state's apparatus for economic intervention in response to the growing problems posed by declining industries and the slump. Between the wars this branch of the state expanded fourfold.

From about 1960, however, as the new crisis set in, the state apparatus entered a fourth phase in which it once more began to undergo further modifications. On the one hand attempts were made to improve the performance of its existing functions – to expand its apparatus for social security, to improve its capacity to 'manage' the economy, to formalise and stabilise the 'incorporation' of organised labour and to enhance the state's popularity by means of various reforms. On the other hand, steps were taken to narrow the scope for popular control over the state; and from the mid-1970s there began a movement towards a new state-form, based less on consent and more on coercion – the 'exceptional' or crisis state.

In what follows, only the second and fourth of these phases will be examined: the creation of the 'liberal-democratic' state and the way in which its adaptation to civil society entrenched so many of the characteristics that are central in the present crisis; and the response of the state to the contemporary crisis. The first of these subjects occupies the rest of this chapter; the second is the concern of Chapters 13 and 14.

The Liberal-Democratic State

By 1900, the propertied classes' fear of democracy had been largely allayed. The labour movement had been willing to accept Liberal or Conservative leadership and to confine its demands to a relatively limited range of purely economic issues concerned with pay and working conditions. The proposition that 'a democratic political system will always seek, in the long run, to become a democratic society' did not seem to be borne out by experience.*

The middle classes were consequently all the more disillusioned and alarmed at the apparently sudden emergence of an independent Labour Party in parliament in 1906, and more so still at the mass unionisation which followed, and the explosive industrial conflict of 1911–13. Yet matters had not been left entirely to chance: the earlier fears had engendered a highly restricted conception of the political democracy, which it was now felt necessary to concede. The state apparatus was reorganised on lines which made it as far as possible immune to radical impulses of the popular will.

The 'Class-ification' of the State

After 1870 the state began what was probably the most rapid peacetime expansion in its history (before or since), dictated by the growing complexity of the economy and its growing vulnerability to German and American competition, especially with the onset of the Great Depression;

* The quotation is from Harold Laski's *Parliamentary Government in England.* Marx defined the problem in 1850 in a famous passage in 'The Class Struggles in France': '... the most comprehensive contradiction in the constitution consists in the fact that it gives political power to the classes whose social slavery it is intended to perpetuate ... and it deprives the bourgeoisie, the class whose old social power it sanctions, of the political guarantees of this power ...' (D. Fernbach (ed.), *Karl Marx, Surveys from Exile,* Allen Lane/New Left Review, London, 1973, p. 71).

and by the need to meet, as far as possible, working-class demands for improved living and working conditions and a degree of security in face of sickness, disablement, unemployment and – as life-expectancy among workers gradually rose – old age. The need to rationalise urban growth and increasingly deficient public health services, for example, led to the creation of a Local Government Board (a central government ministry) in 1871; the collapse of British agriculture from the 1870s onwards led to the formation of a Board of Agriculture in 1889. Similarly, it became clear that modern workers had to be literate and that only a national system of education could achieve this: a Board of Education was finally established in 1899. In 1873 the Board of Trade had sixty 'clerks'; by 1914 it had over 3,000. In 1871 there had been some 55,000 employees in the central civil service as a whole; by 1914 there were 280,000.[6]

Those responsible for the machinery of state during this period were fully aware of the implications of these changes, occurring simultaneously with the enfranchisement of working men. The state had to be protected from the dangerous influence of the masses. They laid great stress on 'the increasing need of voluntarily submitting the impulse of the many ignorant to the guidance and control of the few wise'.[7] Both the state apparatus and the new educational system were designed with this in view.

Robert Lowe, the politician mainly responsible for the famous Order in Council of 1870 which introduced competitive examinations for entry into the higher civil service, recognised that splitting the service into two separate 'classes', one to make policy and the other to implement it, would be inefficient. But he believed it was necessary. With the rationalisation of the service and the abolition of patronage, increasing numbers of capable lower-class personnel could be expected to enter the middle and lower ranks of the service. Closing the policy-making ranks of the service to them, Lowe judged, was vital to secure 'that sort of free masonry which exists between people who have had a certain grade of education' and 'whose associations and ideas should belong to the class with whom they will have to deal', i.e., the propertied class.[8] Consequently a policy-making 'first Division' of the 'clerks' was created, and effectively reserved to the sons of propertied families by basing the entry examinations on subjects which formed the core curricula of the universities of Oxford and Cambridge.

The new educational system was conceived in similar terms. It was necessary for the ruling class to 'educate its masters' (as Lowe also remarked), but not in an uncontrolled fashion. The Education Act of 1870 which laid the basis of a national system of primary schools was, as H. G. Wells put it, 'an Act to educate the lower classes for employment on lower class lines', and secondary education was almost exclusively reserved for the children of the middle and upper classes. Some of the locally-elected

School Boards, however, began to establish 'Board Schools' which gave a few years of secondary schooling to the ablest working-class children leaving primary school.

> A witness before the Royal Commission on Education in 1887 suggested that Board Schools were likely to foster socialism. Asked what he meant by socialism, he replied: 'the state of things in which there is not the respect for the classes above the children that I think there ought to be'.[9]

Concern about Britain's technological and scientific backwardness eventually prompted the Education Act of 1902, which abolished the local Boards of Education (and the Board Schools) and provided government grants to (mainly church-controlled) secondary schools. But these schools charged fees; they were not envisaged as a normal continuation of the education of children leaving primary school.

In 1906, however, the Liberals abolished fees for up to 25% of the places in state-aided secondary schools, with a view to opening them up to the ablest working-class children. And in 1912 a new Division of the civil service was created, the 'Intermediate Class', in between the First and Second Division 'clerks', in order to recruit 'from among the ablest pupils of the secondary schools who, for economic reasons, could not go to a university' (the idea of making university places free for such pupils was, of course, not entertained).[10]

In other words, by 1914 the essentials of a three-tiered structure in both the educational system and the civil service had been established: what would later be called the 'Administrative Class', drawn from the upper and middle classes via the public schools and Oxford and Cambridge; an 'Executive Class' drawn mainly from the lower-middle class, with some working-class admixture, via the state grammar schools; and a 'Clerical Class', drawn originally from the elementary schools, and later from the grammar schools, with less emphasis on academic achievement. (Below even this tier, of course, there was yet another – the large, minimally educated stratum of messengers, filing clerks, secretaries, etc.)

This structure, mirroring the class structure as the policy-makers understood it, is one of the most characteristic legacies of the state-making of that period. It was replicated, with various nuances, in almost every branch of the central state apparatus. Down to 1871, army officers were commissioned on the basis of their ability to pay a substantial sum to the regiment concerned. A system allowing the appointment of wealthy incompetents was clearly inadequate, but the abolition of the purchase of commissions in 1871 did not throw open the officer corps to competitive examination. Instead, recruitment switched to the public schools, where 'volunteer corps' were established for boys with army careers in mind. In 1909 these became the Officer Training Corps (which have survived with various changes of nomenclature and organisation to the present), channelling boys to the Royal Military Academy at Sandhurst. Similarly for the judicial system. Solicitors, recruited through the open examinations of the Law Society, were permitted to appear in the County Courts set up in 1846, but barristers, trained in the more socially exclusive Inns of Court, retained their monopoly of the right to appear in the Crown Court, the High Court and all Appeal Courts, and only barristers could become judges.

Among the principal arms of the state only the police did not conform to the class-structured pattern. It had been laid down by the founder of the Metropolitan Police, Sir Robert Peel, that senior posts should be filled from the lower ranks in order that an adequate calibre of recruit should be attracted to what had formerly been a low-status employment. This led to a shortage of adequately educated candidates for appointment as Chief Constables, and a substantial minority of Chief Constables, and all Metropolitan Police Commissioners, were recruited from outside (normally from the armed forces). Most Chief Constables, however, had come up through the ranks and had working-class or (more often) lower middle-class backgrounds.

The class-structuring of the state apparatus established before 1914 has survived in essentials, despite many changes of detail.

Administrative, Executive and Clerical classes were formally abolished after 1971, following the recommendation of the Fulton Committee in 1966. Like Lowe, the Committee felt that the division of the service into separate classes was inefficient, but by now the crisis led them to give priority to efficiency over the 'freemasonry' of class and education. They recommended the abolition of the system of Classes; much greater recruitment of specialist civil servants into policy-making posts, in place of the inherited practice of relying almost exclusively on arts graduates; and the regular interchange of civil servants with business executives, especially to give civil servants more experience of the economy and society they administered.

Ten years later, the evidence suggested that the system established by Lowe and his successors was powerfully resistant to change. The number of general classes had been reduced and the Administrative, Executive and Clerical classes nominally abolished. But it was clear that no great change of practice had occurred. Graduates, predominantly with arts degrees and even more predominantly from Oxford and Cambridge, still formed the main source of recruitment for senior posts. The system of recruitment, training and promotion ensured that the class-structured character of the service remained; it is possible that it became stronger by becoming less rigid.*

The record on the other Fulton recommendations was remarkably similar. No appreciable increase in 'lateral' movement of specialists into policy-making posts seemed to have occurred by 1978; nor any significant increase in the secondment of policy-makers into jobs outside the service.[14] The special advisers appointed by Ministers in the 1974–9 government were effectively 'frozen out'; the new Civil Service Department established in 1968 was first deprived of real power and finally abolished in 1981.

Information on the recruitment of army officers is hard to come by.[15] If the evidence of Simon Raven is accepted, the army-officer class structure survived whatever pressure there may have been for more respresentative recruitment, with little modification, at least until the 1950s.[16] Entry from state schools had been accepted (in 1960 only 51% of Sandhurst entrants were from public schools) and it seemed probable that the intellectual quality of recruitment had been raised, but an elaborate social hierarchy of regiments, and the operation of social criteria in the promotion process, appeared to have preserved the class exclusiveness of the senior ranks. In 1959, 83% of the 36 most senior army officers had been educated in public schools;[17] in 1981 the proportion was 80% of the most senior 50.

The social composition of the judiciary also remained impressively constant. In 1967, 80% of all judges and Queen's Counsel (senior barristers from whom judges are recruited) had attended a public school;

* Kelsall's work on recruitment to the higher civil service is illuminating. In 1955 he showed that the gradual shift, after 1945, from competition for entry by means of a written examination plus an interview ('Method I') in favour of a competition consisting only of a battery of skill tests and several interviews of different kinds ('Method II') had markedly shifted the balance of applications, and even more the balance of those who were accepted, away from lower-class candidates, in favour of candidates from the upper and middle classes. He also showed that in 1938 (the one year for which he was given access to the data) the effect of the final interview in 'Method I' had been that 24% of the candidates who would have been admitted on the basis of their examination results alone, were replaced in the final list of those accepted by lower-scoring candidates of higher social status.[11] Kelsall's findings had no effect on policy and, in 1967, when another study, carried out for the Fulton Committee, showed similar results, history, as Kelsall remarked, repeated itself: a committee of enquiry of civil servants was set up and reported in 1969 that there was no 'acceptable evidence of social bias' in the selection procedure. Indeed, after 1969 'Method I' was abolished and was entirely replaced by 'Method II' which, as Kelsall observed, lacks 'any rigorous testing of intellectual ability in which the identity of the candidates is unknown to the examiners'.[12] An interesting footnote is provided by *The Times* of 1905 on the selection of boys for cadetships for the navy. Lord Selbourne's new system, consisting of an interview of candidates at age 12½ (confined in practice to candidates from fee-paying 'preparatory' schools), followed by a non-competitive qualifying test, was hailed by *The Times* as 'a real and very valuable discovery', though it would not satisfy the 'democratic purists'. A letter from Admiral Penrose-Fitzgerald however, considered Lord Selbourne's 'discovery' a retrograde step which had replaced a system of competitive exams taken at a later age, a system which, he said, would be restored if and when the democratic purists returned to power.[13]

only 12% had been to a state school. In 1978, 75% of High Court judges (i.e., not counting judges of the Appeal Courts), were public-school educated, while a study of County Court judges suggested that a similarly high proportion of them had also been to public school.[18] In 1971 the law was changed to permit a very limited eligibility for solicitors to be appointed as judges, while in the meantime the social background of lay magistrates (dealing with minor offences and committal hearings) had been gradually modified so as to include a small proportion from working-class backgrounds (see Table 12.1). Here too, the class structure of the state apparatus had become more subtly graduated, without changing its fundamental character.

The police continued to provide an interesting exception to the general pattern. Between the wars there was anxiety about their political loyalty, as well as their efficiency, and from 1934 to 1939 an attempt was made by Lord Trenchard, a former Air Marshal, to introduce a class-structured system into the Metropolitan Police by recruiting university graduates earmarked for rapid promotion via a new Police Staff College. The resentment in the Police Federation against these entrants, and the outbreak of war, brought the scheme to an end. After the war a new scheme of giving university education to capable officers rising through the ranks was introduced instead. The police force remains, as a result, the branch of the state most open to talent regardless of class origin.

Meantime, large changes had, of course, occurred in the system of education. In 1944, secondary education up to the age of 14 became compulsory, and by 1973 the permissible leaving age had been raised to 16. The 1944 Act embodied the Victorian class-structuring principle by establishing, in effect, a new kind of school for the bulk of working-class children (who would now no longer leave school at age 11 or 12) – the so-called Secondary Modern schools from which most children left with few if any formal qualifications.

A small minority of working-class children were selected to join a much

Table 12.1 The social background of magistrates 1966–67

	% of magistrates	% in general population
Higher professional	21.7	
Managerial and other professional	55.2	3.9
Clerical	9.7	14.4
Skilled manual	12.1	49.9
Semi-skilled manual		19.9
Unskilled		8.6

Source: R. Hood, *Sentencing the Motoring Offender*, Heinemann, London 1972, p. 51.

larger proportion of middle-class children in the state 'grammar schools', but the great majority 'failed' their '11-plus' examination and entered the new Secondary Moderns, which fulfilled the same role at the secondary level as the elementary schools had been intended to fulfil at the primary level in the previous century: that of providing a form of schooling adapted to the needs and expectations of manual workers.

By the end of the 1950s, however, this system no longer met the aspirations of growing numbers of 'new middle-class' parents who also saw their children 'failing' at age 11 to enter a school which afforded any prospect of going on to higher education – the key to new middle-class status. Growing evidence was adduced of the wide margin of error involved in selection by the 11-plus examination, and this, combined with the general meritocratic thrust of the Wilson government, led to a decision in 1965 to replace the segregated secondary school system by a single system of all-ability or 'comprehensive' secondary schools.[19]

Several features of this change should be noted. First, it was undertaken on a gradual, negotiated basis, so that the new schools would reflect the balance of opinion among local politicians, school governors and staff. This permitted prolonged resistance to the change, especially in many Conservative strongholds. As a result grammar schools survived in many places, 'creaming off' the ablest children, so that the new 'comprehensives' in these places were not really all-ability schools. It also meant that within the comprehensive schools the class structure of the wider society tended to reproduce itself, assisted in many cases by the separation of pupils into different 'streams', nominally according to ability but also according to social class.[20] Although the ideal of greater individual mobility for children between streams, compared with what was formerly possible between schools, had been partly served, for most working-class children neither personal mobility nor their general view of the system was altered.

> In the comprehensive school, as in the tripartite schools [the former division between grammar schools, secondary modern schools and a limited number of technical schools], children learn early what level they can expect to achieve in the occupational structure . . . their perceptions and evaluations of class remain unaffected by comprehensive education. There is no evidence that children come to think of the stratification system as a fluid legitimate hierarchy, rather than an inevitable and illegitimate dichotomy, as a result of comprehensive schooling.[21]

The proportion entering university from all state schools remained modest. Few university places were available (equivalent to about one for every nine school-leavers) and pupils from fee-paying schools (which by 1977, as more middle-class parents lost the option of the old grammar schools, had expanded to account for over five per cent of all children at school) took a disproportionate share of them.

There was no reason, of course, to have expected the post-war changes in the educational system to have had any other effect. It was pre-figured in the state and educational system established at the turn of the century. It should have come as no surprise when Halsey and Goldthorpe found that whatever increase there had been in the number of working-class children reaching professional-level employment in the post-war years, it had been entirely due to the growth in such employment, and owed nothing at all to changes in the system of education.[22] The system had been made more flexible; it offered less obvious resistance to individual advance; but it effectively preserved the social hierarchy in education.

The structure of the state established at the turn of the century thus proved extremely durable. In retrospect we can see that the reforms of the Victorians, sweeping as they seemed to contemporaries, actually served to preserve many aspects of the earlier state – above all, in reproducing within it the relationships of power and class in society at large. In a celebrated image, Gramsci compared the state to a possibly vulnerable outer rampart of defence against popular power, behind which lay the

Table 12.2 The educational system in 1977

England			
State primary schools			4.5 million pupils
State secondary schools			3.8 million pupils
of which, comprehensives	3.0 m		
grammar, secondary modern and technical	0.8 m		
Direct Grant schools[1]			0.1 million pupils
Independent schools ('public' and private primary and secondary)			0.4 million pupils
United Kingdom			
School leavers from state schools	880,000		
of whom, entering university	49,000	(5.5%)	
entering other further education	37,000	(4.2%)	
leaving with secondary school qualifications	463,000	(52.6%)	
leaving with few or no secondary school qualifications[2]	425,000	(48.3%)	

Notes: [1] Fee-paying schools financed and inspected by the state. After 1976 they were absorbed into the state system or (in most cases) became wholly independent, relying solely on fee income and endowments.

[2] Includes 146,000 (16.6%) leaving with no qualifications at all and 279,000 (31.7%) with too few qualifications for admission to any form of full-time continuing education.

Source: *Education Statistics for the United Kingdom* 1978, HMSO, London 1978.

tougher in-depth defences of civil society: 'when the State trembled a sturdy structure of civil society was at once revealed. The State was only an outer ditch, behind which there stood a powerful system of fortresses and earthworks . . .'[23] In Britain one might say that the late Victorian state was less a distinct outer rampart than simply the forward line of civil society itself.

The 'Establishment'

In the late 1950s exasperation at the immobility and complacency of the senior levels of every sector of British society inspired Henry Fairlie to coin the expression 'the establishment'. Troubled by the seeming aptness of this label, pluralist writers subsequently devoted a lot of energy to the problem of whether there was a 'ruling elite' which governed or controlled Britain. The question was supposed to be whether they shared, and conspired to achieve, a common aim distinct from that of the rest of society, and if so, whether the evidence showed that their aims prevailed. If this could not be shown, it was argued, the term 'establishment' was no more than a pejorative word to denote those who merely happened to occupy the top places in the social, political and economic hierarchies of which any society is composed.[24] The evidence, they found, did not show the existence of a conspiracy to achieve a separate aim, and hence it followed that the 'elites' did not rule the country independently of the popular will. Yet the term stuck: it denoted something real. The problem needed to be formulated differently: i.e., what was the distinctive feature of the relation between the state apparatus and 'civil society' in Britain, which people intuitively acknowledged by persisting in the use of the expression 'the establishment'?

The question is, how many of the occupants of the top levels of non-state hierarchies have come from the same social class, have had the same socialisation, and are integrated in the same social, economic and political milieu as the occupants of the top ranks of the state hierarchy. What the term 'the establishment' suggests is that in Britain, state and non-state elites are particularly closely integrated in all three dimensions.

The evidence is fragmentary (and it is interesting to speculate why no comprehensive study based on direct observation has appeared). There are studies of the social backgrounds of particular 'elites', mostly relying on education as an indicator of social origin. Given that the cost of sending a boy (much more rarely a girl) to a public school has generally been equivalent to nearly half the average annual income of a manual worker, that the governors of public schools are drawn more or less exclusively from the higher reaches of the propertied classes, and that only some five per cent of the population attend such schools, the indicator is not inappropriate. What Table 12.3 shows is that the majority of both the state and the non-state elite are drawn from the same extremely limited social strata.

Although the 'density' of privilege is greater in some sectors than others, it does not correspond to the state–non-state distinction. There is rather a functional division; as more weight is given to intellectual or practical achievement, the more entrants from state schools are accepted. But nowhere do the latter predominate. Moreover, public-school background is a very conservative measure. An additional proportion of both state and non-state elites have been educated privately (e.g., by private tuition or at profit-making fee-paying schools); while on the other hand, the great majority of recruits to the elite from state schools are also from 'middle-

Table 12.3 Social background of state and non-state elites

			educated at public schools (%)
Conservative cabinet	1979	(1)	86
Conservative MPs	1979	(2)	78
Labour cabinet	1979	(1)	17
Labour MPs	1979	(2)	17
Higher civil servants	1976	(3)	69
Senior army officers	1981	(4)	80
Judges (High Court and Appeal)	1971	(5)	80
Ambassadors	1980	(6)	70
Governors and Directors of the Bank of England	1967	(7)	76
Chairmen of leading companies	1971	(8)	74
Directors of leading financial companies	1970–71	(9)	80
Directors of leading industrial companies	1970–71	(9)	66
Church of England Bishops	1960–62	(10)	85

Sources: (1) *Dod's Parliamentary Companion.*
(2) D.E. Butler and D. Kavanagh, *The British General Election of 1979*, Macmillan, London 1980, p. 286.
(3) (Permanent and Deputy Secretaries) *Who's Who*, 1981.
(4) (50 most senior Generals) *Whitaker's Almanack* and *Who's Who*, 1981.
(5) I. Reid, *Social Class Differences in Britain*, Open Books, London 1977, p. 184.
(6) T. Blackstone in BBC programme on the public schools, 1 December 1981.
(7) The Public Schools Commission, in Urry and Wakeford, *Power in Britain*, pp. 230–1.
(8) Stanworth and Giddens, in *Elites and Power in British Society*, p. 90.
(9) R. Whitley in ibid., p. 70.
(10) K. Thompson in ibid., p. 202.

majority of recruits to the elite from state schools are also from 'middle-class' backgrounds.[25] The overall result is that the class background of the state- and non-state elites is extremely homogeneous and extremely narrow.

This is reinforced by the socialisation process of public school and university. Two points only need be made. First, the essentially closed nature of the public school world both creates social distance between its occupants and the rest of society, and creates an alternative society whose rules are familiar and to which all who have been educated to understand them automatically belong. Anthony Sampson's summary is hard to improve on:

> The Victorians used the public school to remove the sons of tradesmen from the taint of trade; and it is still often true, as G. K. Chesterton put it, that 'the public schools are not for the sons of gentlemen, they're for the fathers of gentlemen'. Most of the boarding schools were set up in the railway age, far from the main centres of population, so that the boys spend eight months a year for five years in the exclusive company of other boys; sometimes this weaning starts at preparatory (prep) schools at the age of seven . . . It was by uprooting boys from their parents and forging them into a tough society that imperial leaders were created; a boy could pass from Eton to the Guards to Oxford to the Middle Temple and still reamin in the same male world of leather armchairs, teak tables and nicknames. They never needed to deal closely with other kinds of people, and some still do not.[26]

Second, the smallness of the alternative world of the privately educated deserves emphasis. In 1967, for example, there were about 10,000 pupils aged 17 or over in the private-sector schools. Of these, about 1,500 would go on to Oxford or Cambridge, forming about 25–30% of all entrants. Although they would perform less well there than their state-school contemporaries, their public school background would help those who did reasonably well to more than hold their own in the subsequent competition for jobs.[27] And within this cohort the influence of a few particularly exclusive public schools would continue to be felt in the later promotion process. In a famous 1959 study of the financial establishment, Upton and Wilson demonstrated the remarkable dominance of a mere six schools and two universities. Theirs was an extreme case, both in its focus (the City) and its timing (at the height of the Macmillan era), but as figures for 1971 (included in Table 12.4) show, a diminution of the influence of these schools in this sector seems to have been compensated for by an increase in the influence of Oxford and Cambridge.

What such data indicate is that the experience of schooling and university education is highly focused, and transcends the occupational divisions between those who have shared it, as well as the division between those in the state and non-state sectors.*

The internal relations of this world are maintained in later life by a variety of devices, such as the 'old boys' associations (Eton's had 12,000 members in 1971), interlocking directorships, membership of London clubs, intermarriage and the honours system.[28] It is no longer true to say, as Nairn did of the early nineteenth century, that the ruling class *is* the state. The state has outgrown the ruling class; the working and middle classes are not excluded from the state apparatus, but their access is progressively attenuated at each step up its hierarchy, while the operation of the 'establishment' guarantees an exceptional degree of harmony between the personnel at the top of the state apparatus and the representatives of capital, as well as of the media and other organs of class power.

This distinctive feature of the British state may well have been the root cause of one of the most celebrated features of the theoretical debate between Miliband and Poulantzas.[29] Miliband laid heavy emphasis on the

Table 12.4 The influence of six schools and two universities

	% Eton		% Eton and 5 Other Schools		% Oxford and Cambridge	
	1959	*1971*	*1951*	*1971*	*1959*	*1971*
All government ministers[1]	32.4	20.0	50.0	40.0	71	70
The 54 most senior civil servants	4.1	3.4	19.2	22.7	68	80
Directors of the Bank of England	33.3	5.5	66.6	38.9	50	61
Directors of the 'Big Five' banks	29.7	26.9	48.0	46.9	50	52
Directors of 14 major merchant banks and discount houses	32.7	23.7	43.0	36.5	35	42
Directors of 8 major insurance companies	30.7	27.3	47.0	39.8	38	39

Note: [1] Cabinet and non-cabinet ministers of the Macmillan and Heath governments.
Source: Upton and Wilson, 'The Social Background and Connection of Top Decision Makers', *The Manchester School* 27/1, January 1959, pp. 30–51; R. Whitley, 'The City and Industry', in Stanworth and Giddens, *Elites and Power in British Society*, p. 70; *Dod's Parliamentary Companion 1971*; *Who's Who 1971*.

* 'Those who govern it [the British Civil Service] belong, effectively, to the same class that rules the House of Commons. Largely, they go to the same schools and universities; after admission to the same clubs. Their ideas, or rather, the assumptions upon which their ideas rest, are the same as those of the men who own the instruments of production in our society. Their success, as a Civil Service, has been mainly built upon that fact' (Harold Laski, *Parliamentary Government in England*, Allen and Unwin, London 1938, p. 316). If Laski had lived to prepare a new edition of this book in 1978 he would have had to make remarkably few changes in this argument.

bourgeois social origin and social milieu of the higher civil service, leaving himself open to the interpretation that he thought that this was the reason why the state was not neutral. Poulantzas declared that the state's bourgeois character was given by its 'objective' function in any capitalist society and that, on the contrary, 'the capitalist state best serves the interest of the capitalist class only when the members of this class do not participate directly in the state apparatus, that is to say when the *ruling class* is not the *politically governing class*'.[30]

But if Miliband was too much influenced by the British experience, Poulantzas did not take it sufficiently into account. Poulantzas's generalisation seems far-fetched in relation to Britain, while Miliband's stress on the ties between the state bureaucracy and the capitalist class probably reflects unduly the British, rather than, for example, the continental experience. It is not that the connections he presents do not exist elsewhere. What is distinctive about the British situation is the directness and informality of the links, unmediated by, for example, the development of the distinctive bureaucratic professionalism and *esprit de corps* characteristic of the French or German state bureaucracy. As Armstrong has noted, in Britain, in contrast with the continental experience,

> what stands out in this initial confrontation of the recruit with his new career was the continuity, the lack of traumatic new experiences . . . bucolic style, aristocratic attitude, corporate loyalty combined with easy intercourse with the general elite – all reinforced preservice socialisation patterns instead of interrupting them, as did the ENA [the École Nationale d'Administration in France] and even the *Referendar* stage [in Germany]. For administrative recruits from lower-middle-class backgrounds, adjustment to the service was no doubt difficult, although their Oxbridge college experience had provided an introduction.[31]

And Griffith made the same point forcibly when comparing the British and continental judiciaries. He showed that however much the 'objective' relationship between these branches of the state apparatus and capital might be considered the same in, say Britain and France, significant differences flow from the uniquely homogeneous 'class situation' (i.e., class origins, class milieu and class identification) of the judicial branch of the British state. In Griffith's words:

> The protection of the public interest in the preservation of a stable society is how judges see their role. The judges define the public interest, inevitably, from the viewpoint of their own class. And the public interest, so defined, is by a natural, not an artificial, coincidence, the interest of others in authority, whether in government, in the City or in the Church. It includes the maintenance of order, the protection of private property, the promotion of certain general economic aims, the containment of the trade union movement, and the continuance of governments which conduct their business largely in private and on the advice of other members of what I have called the governing group.[32]

The higher civil service fits into this pattern through the same 'natural coincidence' which the Victorian state-builders were at pains to assure.*

The Circumscription of Democracy

An elective element in parliament goes back to the thirteenth century. In the nineteenth century new voters were admitted to elections for MPs, and at the same time the representative principle was applied to one new state activity after another at the local level. But this was not democracy; it was a method of including the urban middle classes in the process of managing the state.

The enfranchisement of male workers after 1867, however, altered the significance of elections. It promised to give power to the demos. From then on, the tendency in local administration increasingly ran the other way. By 1940, locally-elected bodies which had been established to operate schools, hospitals, poor-relief and gas and electricity supplies had all been replaced by non-elected agencies, and still further functions had been removed from the general-purpose elected local councils. Parliament also ceased to be the effective determinant of policy that it had been in the 1850s. This change was brought about by the organisation of mass parties and the imposition of discipline on MPs, and reinforced by changes in parliamentary procedure. Parliament gradually ceased in practice to belong to the 'efficient' part of the constitution. The people never in fact became 'sovereign'; they remained 'subjects'. In Britain the term 'citizen' never acquired its continental connotation of equality and political efficacy.The state remained largely non-elective, unrepresentative, unaccountable and secret.

In the first place, the elective principle was entirely confined to the House of Commons and local government. There were, and are, no elections for the Upper House of parliament, or for judges, magistrates, public utility commissioners, or school boards, as there are in the USA, nor is there any popular 'initiative' as there is in Switzerland. No popular voice is heard in the selection of the board of any nationalised industry, the

* In the 1970s the higher civil service found itself obliged to defend policies it considered 'sound' against those it considered 'dangerous' by deploying its internal network of power against radically inclined Labour MPs more openly than before. Benn's Parliamentary Private Secretary Brian Sedgemore wrote an interesting commentary on the use of secrecy by civil servants and Cabinet ministers to mislead MPs (see *The Secret Constitution: An Analysis of the Political Establishment*, Hodder and Stoughton, London 1980), and Benn later gave numerous examples of civil service efforts to substitute its policies for his own (*Manchester Guardian Weekly*, 10 February 1980). The English Committee (a sub-committee of the House of Commons Expenditure Committee named after its Chairman) seems to have been inclined to agree that civil servants had been taking liberties: see the *Eleventh Report from the Expenditure Committee* (note 14 above), pp. iv–lxiii. It was obvious that some incoming ministers of the Thatcher government shared this suspicion of civil service manipulation, from the opposite end of the political spectrum.

board of governors of the BBC or the Independent Television Authority, or of any Regional or District Health Authority, the Arts Council, the University Grants Commission or The Science Research Council.

The *appointment* of such 'representatives' is not peculiar to Britain in its principle, but it is in its extent, and in the unmediated way in which it works. Numerous and powerful branches of the state apparatus have, at their head, people who are co-opted or appointed by secret processes which are informal and, it appears, subjective and arbitrary. The operative criteria of suitability and 'soundness' reflect the social and political standpoint of the co-opters or appointers as well as their professional task as state officials.* The effect is to give an appearance of representativeness – in the usual sense of reflecting the characteristics of society at large – to much of the state apparatus while actually ensuring that the real balance of experience, interests and opinions present in the community is *not* represented there. What is well represented are the characteristics and attitudes of the professional and propertied class.[33]

The secret, informal and subjective process of co-option/appointment also extends in Britain to the judiciary. Not only is 'the reliance on a very small specialist Bar for judicial candidates . . . unparalleled in any other country',[34] but those appointed are neither professionally vetted by their peers (as happens in the USA) nor given professional training as judges (as they are in most European countries); British judicial conservatism is not unconnected with this fact. Even the country's 18,000 lay magistrates are appointed, nominally by the (non-elected) Lord Chancellor, in reality by his civil servants, on the recommendations of local committees of existing magistrates – with the result that the magistracy is only slightly less unrepresentative of the population it regulates and disciplines than the judges

* The Treasury and the Lord Chancellor's Office, and no doubt other departments, maintain lists of potential appointees whose names and records are supplied to them from their informal contacts throughout the country. The flavour of this process as it works in relation to the quasi-judicial branch of the state which applies and interprets administrative law is conveyed (though somewhat uncritically) by R. E. Wraith and P. G. Hutchesson in their book *Administrative Tribunals* (Allen and Unwin, London 1973) Chapter 4, and in W. E. Cavenagh and D. Newton, 'Administrative Tribunals: How People Become Members', *Public Administration* **49**, Summer 1971, pp. 197–218. In this sphere, the ideology in terms of which establishment criteria of 'soundness' are expressed is judicial: for example, people were excluded from becoming members of the Rent Tribunal on the basis of such comments as 'might be a tenant's man', 'inclined to be true blue', 'anti-authority?: not objective', 'no standing', 'profession would resent' (ibid. p. 201). Obviously each branch of the state has an appropriate ideological repertoire of this kind – administrative, political, social, aesthetic, etc. – to which the responsible officials must be attuned. For some light relief the reader is recommended to consult Joe Haines's excellent account of his experience as Harold Wilson's Press Secretary from 1969 to 1976, when he gained some interesting insights into the appointment/co-option process as it operated in relation to the honours system: see *The Politics of Power*, Cape, London 1977, pp. 146–9.

(see Table 12.1 above).*

Secondly, there is virtually no accountability in any part of the state. One of the six Chartist demands of the 1830s and '40s was for annual elections; yet significantly this is the only one that was not subsequently accepted, as it reflected the 'delegate' principle of democracy then current in France, and implied a degree of real answerability to the electors. 'Representative' government was not, and was not intended to be, self-government, even when it became 'representative democracy'. As for the executive, the only mechanisms of accountability were Parliamentary Questions, the limited and *ex post facto* enquiries of the Estimates and Expenditure Committees, and certain other Select Committees whose lack of efficacy is discussed in the next section. In 1967 the Parliamentary Commissioner for Administration (the Ombudsman) was appointed to investigate complaints of maladministration by the civil service: as will be seen in Chapter 14, this institution was, if not quite stillborn, born severely handicapped.

The case of the police is interesting here. The police used to be thought responsible to the 'watch' or police committee of their local authority (or to the Home Secretary, in the case of the London Metropolitan Police), but they have been judicially held, in fact, not to be. According to the courts, they are responsible to 'the law', which in the circumstances means that Chief Constables have complete discretion in deciding how to enforce the law.[35] After the Brixton riots in the summer of 1981 the accumulating evidence of racial prejudice and aggression on the part of the police became so strong that the issue of popular influence or control over policing-policy came to the fore, and the credibility of police investigation of complaints against themselves, already forfeited among blacks, began to evaporate among the rest of the public. The Police Federation itself was finally forced to abandon its opposition to independent investigation of complaints (though it remained opposed to a restoration of local authorities' powers over policing-policy). The difficulty was that if independent oversight of police conduct was not informed by the same values that inspired the repressive tasks that had increasingly been assigned to the police, it could quickly give rise to a policing crisis. The government searched for a formula which would ensure an 'external element' in investigations of police conduct without actually restricting the exercise of police repression. Lord Scarman's report on the Brixton riots co-operated

* Cavenagh and Newton's study of the similarly-appointed administrative judiciary (the 15,000 or so members of Britain's administrative tribunals) in two systems of tribunals in the West Midlands found that they were predominantly male (85%), elderly (only 16% were under 45) and Conservative (40%, or two-thirds of those who declared a political orientation) ('The Membership of Two Administrative Tribunals', *Public Administration* **48**, Winter 1970, pp., 449–68).

with this desire by refraining from recommending either a restoration of local authority powers or a wholly-independent process of investigation of complaints.[36]

Thirdly, any kind of popular accountability depends on information and popular understanding, and the British state is also protected from accountability by exceptionally high levels of secrecy. Secrecy is a general feature of states: it is necessary to their existence as organisations separate from civil society and effectively controlling and managing it. But secrecy conflicts with their need for popular consent, and a wide spectrum of different practices exists. At one end is Sweden, where since 1766 all citizens have had a constitutional right of access – more or less effective in practice – to all state documents other than those concerning security; and the USA, with its Freedom of Information Acts. At the other end is Britain, where not only is there no general public right to information, there are no particular individual rights enforceable through any court either. The doctrine of 'Crown Privilege' is used to protect the government and civil service from being obliged to answer any questions or produce any documents they do not wish to. All information (and disinformation) reaching the public from the state is that which the state decides to release and the evidence is that what is released excludes what would enable the public to exercise any effective control over the policy-making process.

This secrecy is justified by the doctrine that ministers are responsible for policy, and that public knowledge of how they make policy, including the information and advice tendered by civil servants, would undermine their responsibility on which the constitution rests. This justification is spurious, because the responsibility of ministers themselves cannot be enforced unless their party in the House of Commons rejects them, which hardly ever happens; and in any case the doctrine of responsibility is lifted by Prime Ministers from time to time for party purposes, without any apparent constitutional ill-effect. Moreover, ministers themselves are sometimes deliberately deprived of information by civil servants; and – the ultimate 'Catch-22' – the fact that the information on which policy is based is kept secret, makes criticism of it – let alone the enforcement of 'responsibility' by any kind of accountability – difficult.

The British obsession with secrecy is relatively modern. Before workers got the vote and could buy daily papers, and while British economic and military pre-eminence was still unchallenged, Victorian politicians and civil servants do not seem to have felt the need to be very secretive.[37] Concern with secrecy developed in the 1870s. It was integral to the class solidarity on which the new state apparatus rested, and was increasingly instilled by precept and practice from the moment a civil servant was appointed or a politician took office. The result was that secrecy eventually became a passion, which stands out strikingly in official memoirs and in the evidence of civil servants to commissions of enquiry.[38]

This passion was, however, not relied upon absolutely. It was reinforced by the Official Secrets Acts. The first of these Acts was passed in 1911 in an atmosphere of fear of German spying, and was loosely worded to make the 'unauthorised' release of any official secret, or its unauthorised receipt, a crime.[39] A former director of MI5, when asked what was an official secret, could truthfully reply: 'It is an official secret if it is in an official file'.[40] Under the Acts a steady trickle of prosecutions of civil servants, ex-civil servants, and members of the public (mainly journalists) has occurred, concerning information usually (though not always) related to security but not in fact jeopardising it. The effect is to make it risky for anyone but a senior official or politician to give information, because only senior officials and politicians can presumably 'authorise' its release. This risk greatly reduces the chances of journalists finding out what the public in a democracy might well think itself entitled to know. For example, although government policy is largely determined by sub-committees of the Cabinet, it is a closely-guarded secret how many Cabinet committees there are, who sits on them and what they are considering.[41] In the British version of democracy not even the core structures and processes of government are revealed to the electorate.*

Another way in which accountability is avoided is through mystification, of which a chief form is archaism. The original archaism is the absence of a written constitution itself, which helps to preserve all the others. It would at least be harder to perpetuate the mockery of democracy just alluded to if the constitution were written. At the very least some of the quaint titles behind which the vulgar business of the state is often hidden could hardly be solemnly incorporated into a written document: for instance, the Treasurer of the Queen's Household, who is actually the government's deputy chief whip, or the Master of the Rolls, who in 1981 was the embarassingly right-wing octogenarian president of the civil Court of Appeal.

An 'unwritten constitution' also affords scope for resistance to reform, since any unwelcome reform can be pronounced 'unconstitutional'. Making Labour Party MPs accountable to their party for pursuing its policies in parliament can be denounced as unconstitutional; making the police responsible to elected local authorities is termed unconstitutional (though Victorian Chief Constables do not seem to have thought it unconstitutional when their employers were Conservatives or Liberals);[42] above all, the withholding of labour by trade unions to achieve political purposes is attacked as unconstitutional, although the withholding of

* On the result of attempts to reduce secrecy see Chapter 14, pp. 284–87.

investment or credit by companies or banks (as in 1964 and 1976, for example) is not. The fact that there is no written constitution allows anyone who is credited with some authority to say what it is – and such authorities concur in saying that what it excludes are actions tending towards a radical assault on private property.

After the unwritten constitution the chief fount of archaism is the monarchy. The 'convenient fiction' that the Queen rules allows the government to hide behind the 'Royal Prerogative' in refusing to give details about a large range of its actions – concerning the civil service, for example, and the conduct of foreign relations – which would hardly be tolerated if the refusal were explained as an exercise of 'Prime Minister's prerogative'. Moreover, the Royal Family and the court, financed out of public revenues on a scale unmatched by other 'constitutional monarchies', legitimate several of the more archaic elements in the culture of the British capitalist class (of which the highly-publicised upbringing and eventual marriage of Prince Charles provides a paradigm): the public schools, expensive leisure activities, the empire, the ancient universities, the armed forces, the honours system and the Anglican Church.*

Next to the monarchy the legal system is the most elaborately archaic branch of the state, helping to protect a judiciary exceptionally united in its 'tenderness towards private property and dislike of trade unions, strong adherence to the maintenance of order, distaste for minority opinions, demonstrations and protests, indifference to the promotion of better race relations, support of governmental secrecy, concern for the preservation of the moral and social behaviour to which it is accustomed, and the rest'.[43] It is hard to imagine that the British judiciary would have remained so singularly free from serious criticism were it not for the archaic and mystifying practices in which the higher courts are saturated.† Even the structure of the British court system is obscure. While most British people can probably give at least a rough account of the parliamentary and cabinet system, it is doubtful if more than a tiny minority could even outline the court system, distinguishing, for example, between the House of Lords (the upper house of parliament), the House of Lords (the supreme court of

* As Nairn also pointed out, the popularity of the monarchy owes little to its antiquity: Queen Victoria was unpopular throughout most of her reign, and her predecessor still more so. Republicanism was then relatively widespread and respectable. The monarchy's modern popularity dates from the age of empire, with which it is strongly identified, and is part of the general imperial legacy 'transmitted in a thousand ways through the capillary vessels of popular culture' (T. Nairn, 'The House of Windsor', *New Left Review* **127**, 1981, p. 100: a choice example of Nairn's polemical style).

† As with secrecy, however, coercion supplements mystification: anyone attempting to do work on the judicial system that is at all critical is liable to prompt judicial repression, as several researchers have found. 'The common law crime of contempt of court – insofar as anyone knows what it is – is a huge, cloudy barrier to the investigation of... the justice system' (D. Leigh, *The Frontiers of Secrecy,* Junction Books, London 1980, p. 71; see also pp. 71–8).

appeal), and the Judicial Committee of the Privy Council (the supreme court of appeal for certain Commonwealth courts); or explain the different functions of the county courts, compared with those of, say, the Queen's Bench Division of the High Court.

Mystification through archaism extends also into the sphere of parliamentary politics, less glaringly perhaps, though not without effect. Here, however, where press attention is closer, a different form of mystification is more important – media collusion with constitutional myth. The basis of this is laid by the general absence of political education in the schools, compared with the practice of more democratic states, compounded by the uncritical approach of so many academic treatments of British politics, and sealed by the intimate dependence of parliamentary journalists on 'sources' within the leaderships of the parties. A myth of parliamentary significance is maintained, even if rather few parliamentary press correspondents believe it.

Parliament

Between the mid-1840s and the passage of the second Reform Bill of 1867 a significant body of MPs ceased to be dependent for their election on the personal influence of a large landowner or employer, but were not yet dependent on a party 'ticket' either.[44] The House of Commons made and unmade governments and policies, and in 1867 Bagehot quite reasonably assigned Parliament to the 'efficient' part of the constitution. In that year, however, the extension of the franchise created an electorate too large to go on being managed by the personal influence and money of a limited number of political magnates. Mass party organisations were formed, and candidates elected with their support soon became dependent on them, as electors increasingly voted for the party rather than the man. As a result, the government could increasingly rely on being able to discipline its MPs.

Parliament thus ceased to be a forum where governments were made or defeated: that function gradually passed – even if in a qualified and 'managed' fashion – to the electorate. Governments also assumed increasing powers over Parliament, partly to combat obstruction by the Irish Nationalist MPs elected from 1886 onwards, and partly to ensure the passage of the growing volume of government business. The parliamentary timetable passed under government control. The power of 'guillotine' was adopted to terminate debates on legislation. The use of 'framework' legislation, leaving important areas of subordinate legislation to be enacted, in reality, by senior civil servants, with little effective parliamentary scrutiny, became standard. The changes were gradual; like so much else, they only began to be fully apparent after the end of the First World War.

After 1906 the parliamentary parties themselves also grew more homogeneous. As the Conservatives increasingly absorbed the right wing of the Liberals, and Labour the left wing, there was less room for inter-party agreement, and so less scope for the sort of exchanges, in or outside Parliament, that had been possible when both the leading parties had primarily represented (in different combinations) the same alliance of propertied classes. Edwardian politicians – Conservative and Liberal, that is – grew accustomed to deplore the decline of 'rational discussion' in parliamentary debates, and its replacement by increasingly heated exchanges of irreconcilable viewpoints;[45] though as Middlemas notes, these exchanges themselves tended to become more and more 'stereotyped' as the Parliamentary Labour Party was, in reality, gradually integrated into the existing state. By contrast, the extra-parliamentary organisations of the parties were explicitly defined as lying outside the state. The reason for seeking to integrate the Labour leadership into the state was, after all, to separate it from the radical wing of the labour movement in the country. So the language of the Parliamentary Labour Party also became increasingly ritualistic, often only seeming to express fundamental class differences. At the same time there was a growing use by governments of mass communications to manage public opinion, which was increasingly closely monitored by opinion polls.

Parliament was thus placed in a paradoxical position. On the one hand it gradually ceased to be the real scene of decision-making. Even the function of representing public opinion was being usurped by opinion polls and by the government's exploitation of the mass media. Governments also declined to let parliamentary committees be built up, with effective powers of scrutiny, which might hold up the government to obloquy for inefficiency or arbitrariness, or play an active part in the formation of policy. And few MPs with ministerial ambitions – that is to say, few MPs – ever seriously disputed this.

On the other hand, parliament remained the *apparent* focus of political life, and necessarily so, since it was – apart from local government – the only democratic element in the state. Its function was to convey the illusion of self-determination by the electors, legitimating their actual non-participation in government and screening out the reality of class conflict and inequality.* It is impossible to account otherwise for the phenomenal

* 'Parliament, elected every four or five years as the sovereign expression of popular will, reflects the fictive unity of the nation back to the masses as if it were their own self-government. The economic divisions within the 'citizenry' are masked by the juridical parity between exploiters and exploited, and with them the complete *separation* and *non-participation* of the masses in the work of parliament. This separation is then constantly presented and represented to the masses as the ultimate incarnation of liberty' (P. Anderson, 'The Antinomies of Antonio Gramsci', *New Left Review* **100**, 1976–77, p. 28).

effort in text-books and the media to reproduce the myth of parliamentary power when it is so clearly known to be a myth. This effort has some effect. Middlemas notes that in 1977, '49% of [a] sample of secondary school leavers believed that the House of Commons made all important decisions about the running of the country', and Dix is probably still right in saying that 'politics, to most people, is what goes on in the House of Commons'.[46] But in spite of these efforts the myth has been increasingly undermined.

This is partly due to the incapacity of governments of either party to fulfil their economic promises, leading to a general scepticism about the efficacy of parliamentary politics as a whole. The imposition of 'incomes' policies in the sixties and seventies, followed by the monetarist policies of the Thatcher government after 1979, also tended to discredit the idea that the political and economic spheres are separate. During the seventies the close relations between governments and the CBI and TUC also tended to cast doubt on the idea that parliament had a monopoly of the representative function. It was also clear that most people now followed political events primarily on television, which was excluded from parliament.* The central institution of liberal democratic politics was thus being marginalised and ignored at the same time as the need for popular consent to government was becoming more acute.

Moreover, by 1979 the House of Commons had become almost as unrepresentative of the population at large (in terms of social background) as it had been before 1900. The Labour Party had initially returned a large contingent of MPs from working-class backgrounds – an average of 72% of all Labour MPs between 1918 and 1935.[47] By 1945, however, the proportion of manual workers among Labour MPs was only just over 25% (107 out of 400) and by October 1974 the proportion was less than 12% (38 out of 319), while the Conservatives throughout the whole post-war period never had more than one ex-worker in Parliament.[48] By 1974 the proportion of manual workers in the population as a whole was about 54%; in the House of Commons it was 6.3%.[49] The House of Commons had thus largely reverted to being the club of more or less exclusively middle and upper-middle class career politicians that it had been before the advent of the Labour Party. (The average MP served more than ten years between 1945 and 1974, compared with 6.3 years between 1918 and

* The House of Commons rejected the televising of its proceedings twice, once in 1978 and once in 1981, by majorities of 20 and 18 respectively. The main reason for the negative decision seems to have been a fear that a discussion of 'serious issues' would be subordinated to playing to the gallery, and that television editors would be able to 'interpret' the proceedings by the way they edited what appeared on television screens. The difference between being interpreted by television editors and parliamentary press correspondents is that a) the latter interpret parliamentary proceedings in the light of their personal relationships with MPs – i.e., 'responsibly'; and b) the popular press rarely reports debates anyway.

1951, and two-thirds of all MPs in the post-war period served more than 10 years.)[50] But this presented a problem because the working class was not the inarticulate and deferential mass that Bagehot had allowed himself to imagine.* That this House of Commons 'expressed the mind of the English people' (as Bagehot put it) was unlikely. As the crisis raised the political stakes, these middle-class politicians, queuing – either on the government back-benches or in opposition – for their turn to hold office, were all visibly doing little else.

This was the context within which a group of mainly younger MPs elected in the 1960s joined forces with a succession of sympathetic academics to promote parliamentary reform through a Study of Parliament Group. Their objective was to restore to the House of Commons some of the political centrality it had enjoyed before the age of mass parties. Most of the recent literature on parliament is directly or indirectly the product of this initiative. At its best, it presents clearly, judiciously and meticulously the facts about Parliament's negligible powers of either legislation or control of the executive, and its amateur knowledge of, unsystematic approach to, and prevailing lack of interest in, the detailed scrutiny of public expenditure and administration, in all their considerable tedium.

There is no point in rehearsing all the details so conscientiously and clearly established by the specialists. In summary, 'the House of Commons spends at least half its time talking about legislation'; but 'today's conventional wisdom is that ... Parliament has relinquished any capacity for legislative initiative it may once have possessed to the executive...' and 'in this instance conventional wisdom does accord with the facts of life'.[51] Legislation is *government* inspired (i.e., largely civil-service-inspired); and, while it may be improved by the necessity to undergo scrutiny in Parliament, it is seldom significantly modified there – and then only when the government is at odds with its own back-benchers (as for example in 1969, when the Labour Government was obliged to abandon its proposed Bill to outlaw unofficial strikes, and another Bill to reform the House of Lords).

The non-specialist Standing Committees of MPs to which Bills are referred for detailed discussion are as much controlled by the government as is the House of Commons at large. Proceedings in these committees are frequently of a ritual nature.[52] The Minister in charge of the Bill is not infrequently persuaded to reconsider some detail, but rarely to change his mind on any fundamental element in it. As for private members' Bills,

* 'The working classes contribute almost nothing to our corporate public opinion, and therefore, the fact of their want of influence in Parliament does not impair the coincidence of Parliament with public opinion' (W. Bagehot, *The English Constitution*, Collins–Fontana, London 1963, p. 176).

most of them fail to become law. Of the 97 such Bills enacted between 1970 and 1979 (12% of all private members' Bills introduced), most were on narrow and non-controversial questions.[53] The only controversial private members' Bills for which governments agree to provide sufficient time are those on which their own parliamentary party is divided, typically questions of public morality such as divorce or Sunday observance. All in all, the legislative function of Parliament has become largely mythical, even though it remains ideologically central.

As for the 'power of the purse', the famous historical basis of the power of Parliament, 'in the practical sense . . . the House has no power of the purse' and neither debates the government's spending proposals nor shows any serious interest in controlling spending after it is authorised.[54] Uniquely among European parliaments, the House of Commons does not discuss tax proposals and spending proposals together; the Budget is exclusively concerned with revenue so that discussion of it is concerned only with means, rather than their relation to ends. The review of *past* spending, carried out by the Public Accounts Committee on the basis of examinations of the accounts by a large staff of accountants, is relatively haphazard, arouses little interest, and is devoid of any sanctions.

The third general function of Parliament, the enforcement of 'ministerial responsibility', is equally empty. Parliamentary Questions have become a lottery. On average, only some 20–22 questions are answered each day out of 63 put down for an oral reply (plus a further 160 per day calling only for written answers). Only those which are answered orally provide an opportunity for effective pressure on the government (by means of supplementary questions which cannot be quite so confidently turned away with well-prepared answers); and as the choice of which ones are answered is largely accidental, the real function of Question Time is to provide a chance for back-benchers to speak a few words in a relatively full House – in effect to foster the myth of parliament's importance, not its substance.

The main means of control of the Executive, advocated by all reformers since the 1950s, have been specialised select committees. These were introduced in an experimental way in the sixties and seventies, and in 1979 a comprehensive system of twelve committees was established, each dealing with a specific area of administration and having powers to call both ministers and civil servants to give evidence. The reformers, however, had by then discovered that 'select committees have not been and perhaps are not likely to become places where much power resides. They represent predominantly those in the House who do not have much scope for determining what is done'.[55] Their scepticism that the expanded system established in 1979 would subject the executive to a greater degree of scrutiny and control proved well founded.

Behind the apparent failure of parliament to play a significant role in either legislation or the enforcement of ministerial responsibility lay the elementary fact of majority-party government. The operative principle is that elections place a party's leaders in office. Every attempt to enforce accountability when in office is liable to weaken the governing party's electoral prospects and is resisted. Most MPs accept this. They do not protest when ministers, or even civil servants, openly disregard the myth of ministerial accountability. For example, in 1975 Mr Wilson, as Prime Minister, refused to allow the Select Committee on Expenditure to question Mr Harold Lever, the Minister responsible for the Government's decision to give a £162.5 million grant to the Chrysler Corporation, on the grounds that the Committee could only ask ministers questions about their departmental responsibilities, whereas Mr Lever was a 'minister without portfolio'. The Committee made no protest. Nor was there a protest when the Civil Service Department told the Select Committee on Procedure, in 1970, that it would not let the Committee study the process of formal consultation between government and outside bodies in formulating legislative proposals, adding that the Committee in its ignorance ('no doubt because of incomplete information') wrongly believed that such consultations were more important than, in fact, they were.[56] Similarly, no one protested when, in 1966, Mr Callaghan, as Chancellor of the Exchequer, refused to agree to a free vote (i.e., without party discipline being enforced) on the details of the new decimal currency, because various interested concerns 'had already entered into commitments', and, Callaghan said, 'you can't flop around on an issue like this with a free vote' – i.e., on an issue already secretly determined by the Government.[57]*

The Study of Parliament Group finally concluded that only a multi-party system could restore any credibility to Parliament, and turned hopeful eyes on the prospects for the new alliance of the centre represented by the SDP and the Liberals, and the possible introduction of proportional representation. One may doubt, however, if their belated recognition of the political nature of the problem was yet adequate. Their ideal of a parliament having substantial legislative power and enforcing effective ('savage') control over the executive was the American system, 'undistracted by questions of ideology . . . a constantly self-renewing and self-adjusting set of majority coalitions . . . resulting in a government much more sensitive to fine representative tuning than the British system and

* The meaning of the Labour Party's devotion to 'parliamentarism' deserves to be pondered in the light of Callaghan's remarks. It was evidently not to preserve the *power* of Parliament that in 1981 Michael Foot, the party's Leader, refused to endorse Mr Peter Tatchell as Labour Candidate for Bermondsey, on the ground that he advocated extra-parliamentary political action by the labour movement.

marked by a capacity to produce constructive unity rather than chronic division in the governmental process'.[58]

Many Americans might, to say the least, have difficulty recognising their political system in this description. The key item, however, was the vision of a legislature free from the pressure of *class parties*. Behind the detached tone and scrupulous attention to detail of the work of the Study of Parliament Group, it turned out, lay a political viewpoint which had a very familiar ring when it was finally made explicit. On this view, what reform of Parliament requires is the relegation of any party of the working class to a position of marginal significance, which, it is hoped, the introduction of proportional representation could achieve. This seems to be the meaning of the Group's vision of' a *more representative* Commons [which] could provide the forum for a *genuine* and *more broadly-based* debate on the narrowing options which now *present themselves*, which is badly needed to off-set the *wilder solutions* now being canvassed' (italics added).[59] One may doubt whether in the context of the British crisis this dream, if realised, would be likely to prove more stable and enduring than the Fourth Republic of France, or even the Weimar Republic in Germany.

In face of so much disillusionment on the part of those who know Parliament best, it is perhaps surprising that the public at large are not more cynical about it. If fewer people believed that the laws carried some sort of moral sanction, the cost of enforcing them could quickly become prohibitive; the Provisional IRA Campaign in Northern Ireland and even the Transport Workers' resistance to the Industrial Relations Act in 1973 show what can happen. 'Respect for the law' is a constant theme of the comment by editors and judges on militant actions by trade unionists, local councillors and others who find particular laws inequitable. Part of the effort that goes into maintaining the myth of parliament can be attributed to anxieties about what would happen if more people were to make their support for the law conditional on its merits, rather than on the fact that Parliament is supposed to have made it.

The myth is also refreshed by the electoral process itself, which appears to place the determination of both law and administration in the hands of the electorate. At election times, the complex reality of political power – the interposition between the voter and policy-making of the independent power of MPs and the higher civil service, the Royal Prerogative, the management of news and opinion by the state and the media, law-making by non-elected judges, law-vetoing by the non-elected House of Lords, the extra-parliamentary power of the City, CBI or the IMF – is all dissolved, leaving in sharp focus only the image of the voters, arbiters of their own fates, as they decide how to cast their votes. And the myth draws strength from the fact that people know that even this largely fictive power is better than none.

13

The State and the Economy

The same circumstances that made it necessary to extend the franchise – leading to the circumscription of democracy described in the previous chapter – also necessitated the continuous growth of the state. This growth persisted and reached its apogee in the 1970s. The economic role of the state became so large that its policies profoundly affected the economy whether it sought to 'manage' the economy or not. Before 1939, economic orthodoxy in Britain largely rejected the implications of this fact. After the slump, Keynesian ideas of 'demand management' gradually gained credence and the state came to accept, in theory, responsibility for 'steering' the economy by what were seen, at least from about 1950 onwards, mainly as gentle touches on the accelerator or brakes (more often the brakes) through changes in taxation, state spending and the control of credit. As executive dominance replaced parliamentary sovereignty the 'interventionist' state replaced the 'nightwatchman' state.

In the 1960s it gradually became clear that the economy needed radical repairs, not just steering (it was in any case doubtful whether the earlier attempts at steering had done more good than harm). Meanwhile the state began to expand again, at a rate not equalled in peacetime since before 1914. Labour accepted this growth and sought to make the state into a lever of economic reconstruction. But the state apparatus, a 'condensate' of the class struggle at the turn of the century and since, was not capable of playing this role. The continued growth of the state, on the other hand, depended on continued economic growth. As economic growth declined, right-wing Conservatives responded by attacking the enlarged state itself as the prime cause of the crisis.[1] Their reasoning was faulty, but there certainly was a contradiction between a continuous rise in state spending and a continuous decline in the relative productivity of industry. The mid-1970s saw, in fact, a striking example of what James O'Connor, in a study of the American state in 1973, had identified as the 'fiscal crisis' of the state.[2]

The Fiscal Crisis of the State

O'Connor wanted to explain why on the one hand state expenditure constantly rose, while on the other hand people became less and less willing to pay taxes. The capitalist state, he suggested, spends money on two main tasks, supporting the private accumulation of capital, and maintaining popular consent to the capitalist system. These expenditures constantly expand, partly to keep pace with ever-expanding capital (more growth requires more 'infrastructures'); partly to pay for rising unemployment and absolute poverty in the 'competitive sector', caused by the introduction of labour-saving technology in the 'monopoly sector';[3] and partly because productivity in the state sector itself increases slowly or not at all, compared with the large-scale corporate or monopoly sector, whereas state sector wages tend to keep pace with those of the monopoly sector, so that the *relative* cost of state activities constantly rises. Consequently the share of GNP passing through the state's hands constantly grows.

Even in a period of boom the political system may fail to allocate either these expenditures or the taxes to pay for them in a sufficiently acceptable way, tempting the state to bridge the revenue gap by inflation. In times of depression, the problem becomes worse as few of the expenditures can be reduced, and the tax burden becomes even more politically sensitive. Companies can no longer safely pass corporate taxes on in their prices, and so they seek to transfer the tax burden to the workers, at the same time calling for more subventions for business; on the other hand the tax base is narrowed by falling production, while mounting unemployment raises the state's social security bill. The result – as events in the USA after O'Connor's study was published demonstrated – is a growing ideological attack on 'state spending', though actually only in its 'welfare' components, not on those that benefit capital, while popular support is enlisted by holding out the promise of reduced personal taxes.

The relevance of this analysis to Britain is clear. As Table 13.1 shows, by 1975 almost 58% of the national income was being appropriated by the state. Half of this was 'transfer spending' – taken by the state through taxation but handed over to other individuals or companies to spend in the form of pensions, investment grants, etc. The other half was spent by the state, partly on procurements from the private sector (especially for defence, housing and the health service), and partly on the wages and salaries of state employees. Almost one person in three worked for the state (see Table 13.2). This situation had come about in three successive 'jumps' – in each of the two world wars, and then again from 1960 onwards.

Table 13.1 State expenditure as a percentage of National Income (1910–1980)

									New Basis[1]	
	1910	1921	1931	1937	1951	1961	1971	1975	1975	1980
% of GNP at factor cost:										
All Social Services	4.2	10.1	12.7	10.9	16.1	17.6	23.8	28.8	28.1	28.9
Social Security		4.7	6.7	5.2	5.3	6.7	8.9	9.5	9.3	11.5
Welfare						{0.3	0.7	1.1	1.0	1.1
Health		1.1	1.8	1.8	4.5	{4.1	5.1	6.0	5.8	6.2
Education		2.2	2.8	2.6	3.2	4.2	6.5	7.6	7.2	6.5
Housing		2.1	1.3	1.4	3.1	2.3	2.6	4.6	4.7	3.7
Infrastructure	0.7	0.6	1.0	1.0	3.6	4.8	6.3	6.8	5.8	4.0
Industry and Employment	1.8	4.5	3.2	2.8	6.9	4.9	6.5	8.3	5.9	4.2
Justice and Law	0.6	0.8	0.8	0.7	0.6	0.8	1.3	1.5	1.5	1.7
Military	3.5	5.6	2.8	5.0	10.8	7.6	6.6	6.2	6.1	7.0
Debt Interest and Other	1.9	7.7	8.2	5.2	6.9	6.3	5.9	6.3	5.5	6.8
Total State Expenditure	12.7	29.4	28.8	25.7	44.9	42.1	50.3	57.9	54.2[2]	53.6[2]
Total State Revenue	11.0	24.4	25.0	23.8	42.7	38.5	48.6	46.6	45.1	47.7
Borrowing Requirement	1.7	5.0	3.8	1.9	2.2	3.6	1.7	11.3	9.1	5.9

Notes: [1] 'New Basis' for calculating public expenditure involves the following major changes:

(a) Only government lending to nationalised industries included, instead of their total capital expenditure under the old basis.

(b) Only that part of debt interest financing non-trading 'social capital' such as roads, schools and hospitals included, instead of total debt interest under old basis.

(c) Non-trading capital consumption (i.e., wear and tear of social capital such as hospitals) excluded from individual categories of social services; under old basis this was included as 'imputed rent'. Now added at end to total state expenditure.

[2] Including non-trading capital consumption not shown in above figures.

Source: I. Gough, based on Gough, *The Political Economy of the Welfare State*, Macmillan, 1979, Table 5.1, and *National Income and Expenditure*, 1981.

Table 13.2 State employment in the United Kingdom (1951–1979)

	1951[1]	1961	1971	1979
			(millions)	
Central government	1.9	1.8	1.9	2.3
(H.M. Forces)	(0.8)	(0.5)	(0.4)	(0.3)
(Civilians)	(1.1)	(1.3)	(1.6)	(2.0)
Local government	1.4	1.9	2.7	3.1
Public corporations	2.7	2.2	2.0	2.1
Total public sector	6.1	5.8	6.6	7.5
Private sector	17.7	18.6	17.8	17.6
Total employed labour force	20.5	24.5	24.4	25.0

Note: [1] Great Britain only – excluding Northern Ireland.
Sources: *Social Trends*, HMSO London 1981, Table 5.8; *British Labour Statistics: Historical Abstract*, Department of Employment, HMSO 1971, Tables 121 and 152.

Military spending accounts for rather little of the long-term increase in state spending; direct aid to industry, and infrastructure, account for rather more; but the really major growth was in social services – welfare, health, housing, education and social security. With each World War, the state was obliged to go further to meet working-class needs for social services in order to maintain popular support for the war effort. After the Second World War the need for industrial and infrastructural reconstruction caused wartime spending levels to be maintained. However, in the case of both World Wars, there was, after some time, a tendency for state spending to grow less fast than national income and so to begin to decline again as a share of the total.

What is striking is that, in the sixties and seventies, without any war, the state again expanded dramatically. Gough analysed the causes of the social service component of this as: rising relative costs (for instance housing costs grew 41% faster than prices generally, health and personal social service costs 13% faster); demographic changes (a smaller working population relative to the number of children, and especially relative to the growing number of very old people); rising needs (for instance higher unemployment, more single-parent families depending on state assistance); and improved, or new, services.[4] Gough concluded that there had been some improvement in the quality and range of services, but that it was uncertain whether these improvements had kept pace with newly-emerging needs. The expansion of the Welfare State in response to political demands generated (originally) in the years of the depression and the Second World War, and kept alive subsequently by electoral competition between the parties, had been resumed in the 1960s and 1970s mainly as a result of its own built-in logic, without necessarily giving added satisfaction. Rather the contrary: the chronically ill, fatherless families and the unemployed understandably found the level of state provision painfully inadequate as it fell further and further behind the standard set elsewhere in Europe.

At the same time the state was increasingly drawn into efforts to make British capital more competitive, or at least to halt its relative decline. This was reflected in the rise of state spending on industry through regional investment grants, subsidies to assist mergers, export assistance, industrial training, etc. It was also reflected in the less visible, but probably even more important 'tax expenditure' on industry (i.e., revenue foregone as a result of tax concessions) as the crisis worsened; this reached a point where, for instance, by 1977 'for the "average" industrial company main-stream corporation tax [had] effectively been abolished'.[5] Tax expenditure, of course, severely restricted the state's revenues, and the scale of tax expenditure in Britain meant that successive governments had to raise more and more tax (directly or indirectly) from personal incomes. The 1970s saw the income tax 'net' being lowered until it caught almost the whole working population, however poor – the point where even workers who received Supplementary Benefit from the state, because their earnings were below the poverty line, still paid income tax on their earnings.[6] This was done by keeping the lowest tax 'thresholds' fixed while money wages rose with inflation, an inflation which was itself aggravated by government borrowing.[7]

This 'fiscal crisis of the state' – culminating in the exchange crisis of 1976 – led to the programme of expenditure cuts inaugurated by Denis Healey as a condition for the IMF loan, and to the anti-tax, anti-state reaction championed by Margaret Thatcher.*

State Economic Management

Even if the Conservative attack on state spending were maintained well into the 1980s it was improbable that the state's share of the economy would be more than marginally reduced (it was already significantly below the share taken by the state in most other major European economies). The effects of state policies could not be anything but decisive for the economy as a whole, and the 'market-oriented' economic strategy of the Thatcher government was, in many respects, a reaction to the fact that the state had already proved incompetent to steer the economy, let alone

* The cuts begun by Healey are difficult to assess. The most succinct review of the period down to 1979 shows that real cuts were made in 1976–7, but that a modest growth in state expenditure was resumed in 1978–9. However, the renewed growth was increasingly due to social security payments to the growing number of unemployed and low-paid victims of the earlier cuts, a vicious circle that was also to make the Thatcher cuts largely self-defeating (see T. Millwood, 'State Expenditure in the 1970s', *Socialist Economic Review, 1981*, Merlin Press, London, 1981 pp. 151–65).

reconstruct it. In this respect Thatcherism made a virtue of necessity by adopting an economic policy in line with the balance of forces within the sectors of the state concerned with economic policy-making.

Before 1939 not even the Labour Party questioned, in practice, that the chief economic role of the state was to balance its own income and expenditure. Keynes's idea that the state could maintain effective demand by expanding its own spending out of borrowing, to compensate for falling private demand in times of depression, repaying the loans in the subsequent years of boom, was adopted more readily abroad than in Britain. Only some Liberals, by then a dwindling minority, and Oswald Mosley, who left the Labour Party and later formed the British Union of Fascists, seriously embraced Keynes's views. By 1944, however, Keynesianism had become the new orthodoxy. Both the major parties committed themselves in a White Paper of 1944 to maintaining full employment. It was also accepted – even by a significant element within the Conservative Party – that the task of economic reconstruction could not be left to market forces. The wartime system of economic controls was kept in being for most of the period 1945–50 without occasioning much controversy.

However, subsequent events make it clear that these developments did not represent a radical or permanent change in the state's relation to the economy. Full employment was maintained after the war by the pressures of both domestic and foreign demand; there was no need to engage in deficit financing, which was fortunate since the record of post-war economic policy-making does not suggest that the Treasury or the Bank of England would have allowed deficit financing on any significant scale or for any significant length of time. The portrayal of the Treasury as predominantly 'neo-Keynesian', down to 1976, refers primarily to its acceptance of the view that it should regulate the economy, and to the periodic illusion that it did so, not to any commitment to full employment, let alone planned development.[8] The postwar apparatus of controls was seen as transitional; it began to be dismantled by the Labour government as early as November 1948 (the celebrated 'bonfire of controls' announced by Harold Wilson as President of the Board of Trade) and was finally scrapped by the Churchill government of 1951–5. The long-term economic policy pursued by state policy-makers during these years was the restoration of Britain's pre-war economy, and notably the re-establishment of overseas assets by investing British capital abroad. A good indicator of their outlook is their attempt to maintain an unrealistically high exchange-rate for the pound until devaluation was forced upon them in 1949.

Under the Conservative governments of 1951–64 the state's economic role was minimised. As the recurrent balance of payments crises, which announced the return of Britain's long-term crisis of production, began to intensify during the late 1950s and early 1960s, the response of the State consisted primarily of a corresponding series of reductions in public and private demand.[9] The resistance of the Treasury to devaluation after 1964 was matched, logically enough, by the tacit abandonment of the 1944 all-party commitment to full employment; unemployment began the long upward climb which brought it to 12% in 1981. In other words, state economic policy after 1945 showed an underlying continuity with the past, which was reflected in the fact that, down to 1961, virtually no organisational changes were made in the economic branches of the state apparatus, except to undo the changes made in wartime.

In 1961, however, there began a series of innovations intended to deal with the re-emerging economic problem. A National Economic Development Council (NEDC) was established, representing the government, employers and unions, with a permanent staff, the National Economic Development Organisation (NEDO).* There was also a set of committees for particular industries, the so-called 'little Neddies'. This was a conscious imitation of the French planning machinery which was then being credited with much of the French economy's dynamism. The idea was to achieve higher economic growth by making quantitative estimates of the implications of a higher growth target, identifying obstacles in each sector and consulting about the best means to overcome them. With Labour's return to office in 1964, on a platform of growth through modernisation and technology, this machinery was supplemented, if not eclipsed, by the creation of a new ministry, the Department of Economic Affairs (DEA), nominally charged with 'responsibility for the management of the national economy as a whole', which immediately set about producing a National (five-year) Plan. Meantime new offices were established to control wages and prices, the National Incomes Commission (NIC, 1961–4) and its successor the Prices and Incomes Board (PIB, 1965–70). There was also a new Industrial Reorganisation Corporation (IRC, 1966–70) to supervise and subsidise mergers in the supposed interest of achieving economies of scale.

The outcome of all these initiatives has already been discussed in Chapter 5. The Treasury lost its responsibility for long-term economic strategy to the DEA but remained in charge of short-term policy. On this division of responsibility Roger Opie, an economist who worked with the DEA, cites a civil service colleague's remark, in another context, that 'no-one bothered to decide *important matters* – what always received prior attention was what was *urgent*'. Opie comments: 'The division between the Treasury and the DEA . . . exactly paralleled the division between the

* The NEDC contained six employers' and six trade-union representatives, two nationalised industry representatives, two academics, three economic ministers and the Director of NEDO.

"urgent" and the "important" '.[10] The DEA was abolished in 1969, its purpose having already been abandoned in 1965 when growth was sacrificed to the maintenance of the exchange rate. Most of its staff were transferred to the Treasury's revived Central Economic Planning Staff, from which many of them had originally come. The PIB and the IRC were abolished by the incoming Heath administration of 1970. Of all the innovations, only the NEDC and NEDO still survived after 1979 – a testimony to the embarrassment of abolishing such a public token of the government's presumed interest in consultation.

The importance of this episode is that it shows why the British state could not serve as an independent lever for capitalist reconstruction. The subordination of growth to maintaining the value of the pound was not a mistake, but the outcome of a sharp struggle within the state apparatus. Opposition to reversing the priority given to free trade, overseas investment and the City's interest in a strong pound was encountered at every level. Outsiders brought in to help to implement the Wilson strategy met with a solid wall of resistance, reinforced by ignorance of economics and an indifference to numbers or even factual evidence, erected in defence of the trade-and-finance definition of the national economic interest permeating the Treasury, the Board of Trade and the Foreign and Commonwealth Office, not to mention the 'nationalised' Bank of England.[11]

Having lost an initial battle to devalue the pound, the advocates of industrial reconstruction sought to gain the necessary relief from the balance of payments crisis, which expansion would undoubtedly produce, by introducing a temporary surcharge of 15% on all imports, a tax rebate on exports of goods, and restrictions on exports of capital. These measures were unpopular abroad, but in the opinion of their advocates they could be successfully defended if they led ultimately to a growth in the British economy, and they were certainly essential to growth if devaluation was ruled out. But by 1966, all these measures had been abandoned.

> The new Government, and its new economic advisers, were defeated by the sterling lobby. They were not defeated in the battle to control the deficit, but in the primary battle to decide how to control it...once the decision not to devalue had limited the room to manoeuvre drastically, each alternative measure was either destroyed where it outraged the overseas lobby, or emasculated where that lobby had to operate it.[12]

How far the failures of the 1960s, and the effects of the Fulton reforms in civil service recruitment and training, led subsequently to changes in the state apparatus that would make it less ill-adapted to the task of economic reconstruction is still unknown; apart from the indications that the Fulton reforms were largely neutralised (see pp. 236–7), two considerations must be borne in mind.

First, the state apparatus registers the balance of social forces, which has certainly not tilted in favour of industrial capital at the expense of commercial and financial capital since 1970. The Thatcher strategy had the support of industrial capital, but not because it was seen as giving priority to industrial recovery rather than to the interests of commercial or banking capital; it was rather that industrial capital again chose the path of deflation, with a view to reducing the strength of the trade unions and the risk of further nationalisation.

Secondly, since 1970 the state has not been seriously engaged in any effort at industrial reconstruction. After Edward Heath's U-turn, there was a revival of some of the institutional innovations that had been abolished in 1970 – a new Prices Commission (1973–9) and a new Pay Board (which, however, was quickly abolished by the Labour Government in 1974); there was also a new Industrial Development Executive, which performed some functions of the recently-abolished Industrial Reorganisation Corporation, and this Labour replaced in 1975 with the National Enterprise Board (NEB) whose functions were extended to include selected nationalisation and planning agreements. But all these institutions suffered the same fate as their predecessors; they were largely or wholly ineffective, either because their powers were whittled down at the moment they were established, or because they were subsequently rendered marginal by the continued commitment to deflation. The fate of the NEB and of planning agreements has already been described. This time the civil service did not need to put up a strong resistance, as the Labour leadership itself evinced little enthusiasm for either.[13]

In retrospect, the 1970s appear as a period of relatively consistent retreat from the initiatives of the 1960s, directed at state-led economic reconstruction, towards a policy of reducing the state's economic role and allowing the fate of British industry to be determined as far as possible by the forces of the international market. This policy would no doubt have been impossible but for the discovery and exploitation of North Sea oil. Coinciding with its coming into full production, the Thatcher government was able to revert much more thoroughly to the initial policies of the Heath administration in the period 1970–2, and even to abolish exchange controls for the first time since 1945 without running into a politically-unacceptable balance of payments crisis. Monetarism – carried out by public expenditure cuts and the management of interest rates – reduced the task of state economic management to one quite compatible with the organisation and orientation of the state apparatus as it had crystallised at the turn of the century, and in particular with the special place of the Treasury.

Although revenue-raising, co-ordination of the state apparatus and long-term policy-making for the economy are also united in one department in some other states, the centralisation of these functions in the British

Treasury is peculiar in two main respects. First, Treasury control of the expenditures of other departments is exercised in such a way as to make Treasury officials quite intimately responsible for the evolution of their policies – a practice which, incidentally, was established between 1868 and 1914, as spending on social services proved impossible to control by means of purely financial limits.[14] All policy decisions, however minor, that may entail new expenditure, must have prior Treasury approval, which is granted if they conform to principles that the Treasury judges sound. A minister must seek cabinet support for any policy opposed by the Treasury, which in practice gives the Treasury effective policy-making power on all but the most contentious issues. The Treasury's 'co-ordination' is thus not a question of seeing that the spending departments keep within their approved estimates; it is a matter of determining the content of all future estimates, as these result from the continuous evolution of policy.

Second, the Treasury is not only, like all treasuries, hostile to increases in state spending because it is responsible for finding the revenue to pay for it; it is also hostile (for reasons we have already considered) to policies that would give manufacturing priority over trade and banking. The influence of the Treasury throughout the state apparatus reflects this bias, and is reinforced by the Treasury's control of the promotion and appointment of senior personnel in all departments (a power restored to it in 1981 with the re-absorption of the functions of the separate Civil Service Department set up in 1968). The hegemony of banking and commerce in the economy is thus reflected in the hegemony of the Treasury in the state apparatus.

The successive spending cuts after 1976, and again after 1979, and the contraction of the industrial economy under the strategy of monetarism, were policies to which the British state was well adapted.* Yet, in 1981, it was by no means clear that the state was any more successful in achieving the limited goals set for it by monetarism than it had been in achieving the more ambitious goals set by governments in the sixties and seventies. In December 1969 the Bank of England and the Treasury admitted that over the previous ten years

* This was conspicuous in the implementation of 'cash limits' from 1976 onwards, which made expenditure cuts much more effective than earlier public spending cuts had been. The state apparatus as a whole cannot be held responsible for all the illusions of monetary theory, but there is ample evidence of the growth of enthusiasm for monetarism in the Treasury which Keegan (the economic Editor of the *Observer*) described in 1979 as having an 'obsession . . . with financial targets as the criterion of economic rectitude' (W. Keegan and R. Pennant Rae, *Who Runs the Economy?*, Temple-Smith, London 1979, p. 209).

> economic policy may be said quite simply to have failed in that none of the major problems facing the UK in 1959 can be said to have been solved and some of the most important of these have become more severe.[15]

Much the same could have been said in December 1979 – or in December 1981.

The Nationalised Industries

The state-owned sector of industry, besides being an important element in the expansion of the state, also provides a useful insight into the character of the British state's relationship with the economy. What was the meaning of the 'nationalisation' of industries? How has the state dealt with these large extensions of its domain?

By 1976, state-owned corporations accounted for some 11% of total GDP and 8% of total employment; the nationalised industries proper – i.e., public corporations (or publicly-owned enterprises) producing all or a large proportion of the output of particular production sectors of the economy – accounted for 9.6% of GDP and 6.9% of employment. As Table 13.3 shows, nationalisation took place in three broad phases – before the Second World War, immediately after it, and in the 1970s.

The first phase comprised industries considered to be strategic at the time of their first appearance – the Post Office, electricity supplies and international air services. The last phase also included a similar industry – the ownership and distribution of the newly-discovered oil resources of the North Sea – but otherwise comprised industries or companies that would have collapsed but for massive injections of public funds, eventually necessitating full state-ownership (Rolls Royce, British Leyland, and the shipbuilding and aircraft industries). These nationalisations were far from being inspired by socialist goals; Rolls Royce was even nationalised by the Conservative government in 1971. The industries of the second phase, however, were taken into state ownership by the Labour government of 1945–51 (steel was de-nationalised by the Conservatives in 1953 and re-nationalised by Labour in 1967) as a result of strong rank-and-file pressure within the Labour Party. This group of nationalisations is, in consequence, usually seen as falling in a different category, i.e., as a step towards the 'common ownership of the means of production, distribution and exchange' envisaged in Clause 4 of the Labour Party Constitution.

But this is a misunderstanding. The nationalisations of 1946–51 were, with the partial exception of steel, as much responses to the problem industries which could no longer be run profitably in their existing form. They were run down, partly as a result of wartime exigencies but mainly due to fragmented ownership, lack of integration and a vicious circle of declining profitability and under-investment stretching over many decades (in the case of coal, for almost half a century). Left in private

Table 13.3 Major nationalised industries and enterprises

	Shares in total UK economy in 1975 % of total			
	Output	Employment	Investment	Domestic Market
Nationalised before 1945				
Post Office & Telecommunications [1](1635–1710)	2.8	1.8	4.5	100
Electricity Board (1926)	1.5[2]	0.7[2]	2.9[2]	100[3]
British Airways[4] (1939)	0.3	0.2	0.4	76
Nationalised 1945–64				
National Coal Board (1946)	1.5	1.2	0.9	96[3]
British Railways Board (1947)	1.2	1.0	1.0	8[5]
National Bus Company (1947)	0.2	0.3	0.1	34
National Freight Corporation (1947)	0.2	0.2	–	10
British Gas Corporation (1948)	0.8	0.4	1.7	100[3]
British Steel Corporation (1951, 1967)	0.8	0.9	2.0	56
Nine major nationalised industries	9.2	6.7	13.6	
Other nationalised industries	0.4	0.2	0.8	
All nationalised industries	9.6	6.9	14.4	
Other public corporations	1.4	1.1	4.6	
All public corporations	11.0	8.0	19.0	
Nationalised after 1970				
Rolls Royce (1971)[6]				
British Leyland (1975)[6]				
British National Oil Corporation (1976)				
British Shipbuilders (1977)				
British Aerospace (1977)				

Notes:
[1] British Telecommunications became separate corporation in 1981.
[2] England and Wales only.
[3] In 1975 gas accounted for 22%, coal 19%, electricity 13% and oil (then still imported) 46% of final consumption of energy.
[4] British Overseas Airways Corporation formed 1939; British European Airways 1946; merged 1972–74.
[5] Of total passenger/km: 47% of freight tonne/km.
[6] Limited liability companies wholly owned by the state.

Source: (for industries nationalised before 1970) NEDO, *A Study of UK Nationalised Industries*, HMSO, London 1976, Appendix Volume.

hands they could only have been restructured by widespread bankruptcies, contraction and mergers. It was no longer possible to force down wages, as had been done in the coal mines in 1926; and, significantly, it was the industries dominated by the Triple Alliance of mine-workers, railwaymen and transport workers (whose solidarity had led to the General Strike) which formed the core of the 1946–8 nationalisations. In the political climate of 1945 no government could have accepted either the political cost of confronting these unions, or the economic dislocation which would have resulted from the unplanned reconstruction by 'market forces' of these basic industries. The main 1946–8 nationalisations, then, actually belong to the same category as those of the 1970s: they represent the state intervening to prevent the market from re-organising – or in some cases perhaps eliminating – weak sectors of production, because of the economic, social and political costs this would have implied.

Once this is recognised, the subsequent history of the nationalised industries become more comprehensible. The state's intervention followed a fairly clear pattern. The coal industry and the railways were re-organised and drastically contracted; the simultaneous nationalisation of road passenger and freight transport permitted railway re-organisation, like that of the coal mines, to be accomplished in a planned fashion, avoiding redundancies (though road freight transport was partly de-nationalised in 1953 by the Conservatives). Tax revenues were used to compensate the former owners on generous terms and to finance large-scale new investment. Then, a process began of re-assimilating the nationalised industries to the norms and requirements of the market.

This has been obscured by a large and somewhat uninspiring literature concerned with the issue of the control and accountability of the nationalised industries. This literature starts out from a distinction between 'public' and 'private' which the nationalised industries are seen as infringing. The problem is then posed as being one of how to ensure that they are accountable to parliament, since they are *publicly* owned, without this adversely affecting their performance as *businesses* (i.e., as organisms operating in the 'private' sphere). The solutions proposed concern how the chairmen of the boards of nationalised industries are appointed, what directions ministers should be able to give them, what information Parliament is entitled to receive about them, what financial targets or controls should be applied to them, and so on. The distinction between public and private, however, is largely ideological. Many 'private' industries are almost wholly dependent on the state as a customer (e.g., armaments), many more have been the recipients of large grants from public funds, and virtually all have received large tax expenditures from the state. What really matters are the principles on which an industry is run, not its juridical ownership. In this respect, the history of nationalisation is relatively clear.

In the first place, the boards of directors of the nationalised industries were constituted so as to provide 'the best possible collective leadership' and not, 'as in the case of comparable boards in certain other countries, to secure the representation of... workers and consumers'.[16] In practice, managment continued to be recruited as before: there was no element of industrial democracy.* Then in 1961, when the reconstruction of coal-mining and the railways was well advanced, a White Paper drew a distinction between those nationalised industry activities which were undertaken to meet 'social service' obligations, and which would be subsidised from tax revenues, and the rest, which should be made to pay for themselves. In 1967 this policy was tightened by requiring nationalised industries to charge prices equal to marginal costs and to use a test discount rate for proposed investments, to try to secure a rate of return comparable with that of other 'private' industries. In 1976 the nationalised industries' investment budgets were made subject to 'cash limits' imposed by central government – i.e., they were no longer able to spend more on capital projects than had been approved by Whitehall. From 1978 the rate of return to be sought was laid down, and financial targets based on a three- to five-year period were required.[17]

These increasingly specific assertions of capitalist norms took place in a context of rapidly declining employment in the nationalised coal-mines and railways. The number of National Coal Board employees fell from 749,000 in 1950 to 304,000 in 1977; membership of the National Union of Railwaymen (which included all the railway manual staff other than footplate workers) fell from 392,000 to 180,000 in the same period. In combination with large investments (and in spite of government-imposed additions to costs and limits on prices) this contraction increased the nationalised industries' overall productivity (measured by conventional criteria) faster than in manufacturing as a whole and, it seemed, faster than in comparable nationalised industries in other countries – in striking contrast to the view constantly reiterated in the media that the nationalised industries were inefficient.[18]

The main targets of this propaganda were the workers in the nationalised industries, who were accused of 'feather-bedding' behind the

* From 1935 onwards the Labour leadership, conceding to rank-and-file pressure, had accepted a commitment to have worker representation on the boards of future nationalised industries, though only on the basis that the trade unions would be legally entitled to *nominate* representatives from among whom the Minister responsible would appoint *some* board members. At the persistent instigation of Herbert Morrison even this minimal commitment was abandoned prior to the 1945 election (see R. A. Dahl, 'Workers' Control of Industry and the British Labour Party', *American Political Science Review* **41**, 1947, pp. 875–900).

protection supposedly offered by the industries' monopoly positions in their markets. There was high absenteeism among underground mine-workers and there was some over-manning on the railways, but the evidence suggests that the initial debt-burdens imposed on the nationalised industries for compensation payments, and government-imposed constraints on investment and pricing policies, played a more significant role in lowering morale and limiting productivity growth.[19] The propaganda had, however, the effect of legitimising the re-establishment of market norms for the nationalised industries. Especially after 1979, such propaganda served to justify a much narrower definition of the social costs that nationalised industries should seek to avoid – the 70,000 redundancies made at British Leyland or the 100,000 at British Steel would not have been accepted twenty or ten years earlier. It also justified the de-nationalisation or 'privatisation' of selected nationalised industries or parts of industries.

The subordination of the nationalised industries to the general interests of private capital also had a broader aspect, and other costs. Because they needed large-scale investments, there was constant anxiety in the Treasury lest they pre-empt investible funds, making investment more expensive for private enterprise; and in the 1960s their investment spending also began to be curtailed as part of the government's increasingly strenuous attemps to deflate the economy. They were only permitted to borrow from the Treasury, which placed them under non-market financial controls and led to successive cuts in their investment plans, in spite of the new policies which were supposed to put the nationalised industries on a more 'market' footing. The effect was to create deficits for the gas and electricity industries and the Post Office, and to increase the deficit of the railways. Then, after 1979, as part of the Thatcher government's policy of reducing state expenditure, subsidies which had been given to the nationalised industries to enable them to keep their prices down were rapidly removed so that nationalised industry prices rose much faster than the average, curtailing demand.

Meantime the nationalised industries, besides remaining subject to central government financial controls, unlike private corporations, also remained prohibited from expanding, like private companies, into other profitable activities.[20] This meant that the nationalised industries were under constant pressure to contract, rather than expand, as the only practicable means of meeting their ever-receding financial targets. Fine and O'Donnell argue that this has complemented, and perhaps accelerated, domestic de-industrialisation generally, as compared with European countries whose nationalised coal, steel and transport industries have been heavily subsidised out of general revenues as part of a strategy for industrial expansion.[21]

The trend of state policy towards nationalised industries after 1979 was dramatically illustrated by the contraction of British Leyland and British Steel. The steel industry is particularly revealing because, out of all of the nationalisations immediately following the Second World War, it was the only one that had been resisted because parts of the industry were still profitable. However, by 1953, when the Conservatives sought to return steel production to the private sector, many of the former owners realistically declined to re-purchase their plants. Many of the plants which were re-purchased were once again neglected, so that, by 1967, the re-nationalisation of the industry 'brought to BSC [the British Steel Corporation] a large number of works with obsolete technology', as well as a large new compensation bill.[22] There then followed an attempt at reconstruction, based on a ten-year expansion plan (1973–83), which was riddled with serious management errors. The plan envisaged production of 36–38 million tonnes of steel per annum by the mid-1980s, but by 1980 the Corporation was incurring large and rapidly growing losses (for which both management and the government blamed the workers).

Instead of writing-off the mis-investment, the Conservative government brought in a new chairman from an American finance company, with instructions to close down plants until BSC could break even and, in addition, meet the charges on its debt. The result was to reduce the Corporation's capacity to 14.4 million tonnes, which would entail new imports of steel to meet any significant domestic economic expansion in the future:

> The legacy is the worst of both worlds: a high interest burden on the investment which has taken place; no funds for investment in improving quality; and the closures which reduce capacity to dangerously low levels . . . [23]

It is difficult not to believe, when contemplating such cases, that almost any measure of workers' participation in management would have been more valuable from a national standpoint – however capitalist – than the successive and much-discussed changes in the arrangements for control by the executive branch of the state, and supervision by parliament, which produced no apparent benefits at all.

The primary significance of most of the post-war nationalisations was thus to secure the re-organisation, in several cases through drastic contraction, of declining sectors, without incurring political instability. The principles of private capitalist organisation and production were progressively asserted, not least with regard to management – but not to the point where state-owned industries were allowed to borrow, spend or expand their sphere of activities like any privately-owned capitalist enterprise. On the contrary, after 1979 they were obliged to divest themselves of whatever profitable assets and activities the private sector was willing to buy. Not surprisingly, the economic results were frequently mediocre, where they were not altogether disastrous.

Politically, however, nationalisation was successful. Apart from the coal industry, which had a high level of industrial conflict throughout most of the 1950s, nationalisation permitted contraction to be imposed without significant challenge from the labour movement during the years when full employment made the movement strong. By the end of the 1970s, on the other hand, contraction could be imposed (notably in BL, BSC and shipbuilding) much more rapidly, thanks to high unemployment and declining trade-union strength. In this way, major casualties of Britain's industrial decline were prevented from becoming the focus of a potential radicalisation during the period of the labour movement's ascendancy.

Corporatism

But the state could not ignore the contradiction between capital and labour, even if nationalisation proved capable of neutralising some of its most acute manifestations. The power of organised labour and large-scale capital in the years after 1918 forced the state to deal with them more and more directly. The CBI, the National Employers' Federation, the TUC and major individual unions such as the AUEW and the TGWU became more than 'pressure groups' seeking to influence policy. 'Parliament *appeared* to be the home and parties the source of political power', but in truth 'great areas of national policy tended to become the prerogative of ministers and civil servants' dealing directly with the organisations of the employers and the workers.[24] This was the reality, and in the 1970s the oscillation of policy between an ever more desperate search for consensus on economic and social policy and the increasingly sharp rejection of consensus, led to a literature which for the first time tried to portray the working of the state in relation to the economy as it actually was, rather than as liberal theory imagined it to be.

What had emerged had obvious affinities with the doctrine of the 'corporate state' advanced by conservative thinkers in the nineteenth century and later adopted by Fascist regimes in Italy, Spain and Portugal. According to this doctrine the state recognises the different interests of which society is composed by fostering their organisation in separate nation-wide institutions which both represent and control their members, and then provides a forum within which their mutually complementary needs are harmonised. But since in reality the interest of capital and labour conflict, 'harmony' has in practice to be imposed. Actual corporate states have always been authoritarian. However, the dream of harmony has inspired 'corporatist' ideas among representatives of both capital and labour in liberal states too, including Britain.[25] What developed in Britain in practice, however, was a 'corporatist' system of economic and social policy-making and industrial conflict-management – a 'corporate bias' grafted onto the parliamentary structure.[26]

Before the 1960s, however, the graft remained relatively inconspicuous, for three reasons.

First, it was largely a product of the two world wars, which called for a national economic effort for which the labour movement's co-operation was indispensable. During the First World War the sacrifices called for from the workers – the ban on strikes, the 'dilution' of labour, wages which did not keep pace with prices, and the appalling losses on the front – were not matched by adequate control of either prices or profits. Consequently, the Shop Stewards' Movement flourished and radical and revolutionary socialist ideas spread. By 1916,

> the TUC had . . . become the Government's only lasting insurance against the Shop Stewards' Movement and the terrifying combination of industrial and political unrest in wartime, clearly visible in Germany, Italy and France.

As a result,

> by the middle of 1916 a new conception of trade unionism was becoming current in England in which responsible and representative leadership was seen to merit a role in the country's political life.[27]

This was indeed a major change, though its implications were not thoroughly accepted until much later – no doubt because the origins of corporatism had an 'exceptional' character, like so much else in wartime. The peacetime continuation of the relationships established in the war years, after much of the rest of the wartime machinery of Government had been dismantled, was seen as nothing remarkable.

Second, during most of the inter-war period the labour movement was relatively weak. Between the 1926 General Strike and the general election of 1935, trade-union leaders adopted a broadly co-operative attitude towards capital. In 1928, following the General Strike and the Trade Disputes Act of 1927 (see Chapter 4), Sir Alfred Mond, an industrialist and former Minister of Health, held talks with Ben Turner, the Chairman of the TUC, which culminated in a proposal for a consultative Industrial Council representing workers and employers. This appealed to neither the employers nor the TUC, but in subsequent meetings the TUC and the National Confederation of Employers' Organisations 'set themselves to build their own form of industrial co-operation – corporatist in a far more subtle and flexible form'.[28] This was, essentially, a relationship of consultation which enabled both sides to discover where conflict was likely to occur and how it could best be avoided. It was not the sort of arrangement to cause much anxiety to strict constitutionalists, but it laid the basis for a much more significant joint exercise of power when prosperity returned.

The third reason why corporatism remained relatively inconspicuous was the modesty of trade-union demands. Until the 1970s these were almost wholly confined to wage levels and hours of work. British unions were much slower than unions elsewhere to include even so-called 'fringe benefits' among their demands, let alone demands such as participation in management or specific investment policies on the part of the employing companies. This reflected in part what Crouch calls 'the Compromise':[29] in spite of their unique freedom from statutory regulations (by comparison with other countries) British trade unions did not challenge 'management prerogatives' (at least not officially, even though plant-level bargaining from the 1950s onwards undermined many management prerogatives in practice); and they also accepted a strict separation between industrial action (the unions' prerogative) and political action (the Labour Party's).

Nonetheless the machinery, and even more the informal practices, had been put in place. When the Labour Party joined the war coalition in 1940, Ernest Bevin, the General Secretary of the TGWU, became Minister of Labour and secured trade-union agreement to another ban on strikes, supported this time by effective controls over profits and prices. The TUC and the employers formed a Joint Consultative Council which acquired 'the status of an unofficial Government department'.[30] The years 1945–51 saw a partial rift when the unions seemed, in the eyes of capital, to have acquired a privileged position, since 'their' party now had a large parliamentary majority. But this proved much more apparent than real, and after 1951, helped by historically high rates of growth, Conservative governments encouraged the restoration of the earlier informal triangular relationship.

From now on, 'what had been merely interest groups crossed the political threshold and became part of the extended state'.[31] But this only became *obvious* with the renewal of the crisis. Now governments sought to control wages in peace-time. In return they once again had to try to control prices and profits, but now – in contrast with the war years – they had also to convince both unions and employers that the sacrifices were worthwhile. This meant inviting them to participate, or seeming to invite them to participate, in economic policy-making. This was the primary reason why, in 1962, the Conservative government under Macmillan established the NEDC. Its purpose was to plan economic development; its political significance lay in giving a formal role in long-term economic policy-making to these non-party, non-parliamentary organisations.

The pressure of the crisis quickly revealed the limits of corporatism, however. In 1916, under the exigencies of war, Lloyd George had been able to rely on TUC and Labour Party support when he suppressed the ILP newspaper and used force to break up the left-wing leadership of the Clydeside engineering workers. It is doubtful if this could have been repeated during the Second World War and it was certainly out of the question by the 1960s and 1970s. The trade-union rank and file had become too confident and militancy was too widespread. Although wage controls were imposed by Labour in 1966 with TUC support, the government's abandonment of its plans for expansion and the ineffectiveness of price controls quickly led to mass discontent, culminating in the abortive effort to bring in legislation to control strikes in 1969. There followed the initial effort by Heath to dispense with corporatism; tripartite meetings of government, unions and employers largely ceased, except for the meetings of the NEDC (which had become somewhat ritualistic with the abandonment of Labour's planning initiative after 1966). Strikes were allowed to run their course without state intervention.

But the collapse of the Heath strategy, itself due to the advanced debility of British industry, inaugurated not merely a revival of coporatism but a fundamental change in its nature. By July 1972 Heath had decided that wages could not be left to the determination of the market in Britain – not even with the help of the Industrial Relations Act, which in any case threatened industrial conflict on an unacceptable scale. The TUC and CBI were once again summoned to Downing Street. This time, however, the unions had understood that if they were to give up their freedom to bargain for wage increases, they should demand substantial compensation in terms of social and economic policy. The TUC therefore 'put nearly every issue of socio-economic policy on the agenda'.[32] Their demands included reversing, or at least mitigating, the effects of most of the government's tax and social policies of the previous two years. This, of course, was a lot more than Heath was prepared to concede, and, besides, he was in a hurry. In November 1972 he introduced a statutory wage-freeze and followed it up with new legislation for long-term controls, resulting in a confrontation with the miners in the autumn and winter of 1973–4.

The next phase of 'bargained corporatism' (to use Crouch's term) was the 'social contract' of 1974–5, in which the unions not only obtained from the Labour government a significant quid pro quo for wage restraint *before* they began to restrain wage demands, but were able to have included in the 'contract' a broad range of social as well as economic policies. What is more, these policies included some which bore directly on the relationship of the unions to the state. The Trade Union and Labour Relations Act and the Employment Protection Act, passed in 1975, did not refer explicitly to the corporatist structure itself but they consolidated its base by strengthening the legal position of labour *vis-à-vis* capital. On the other hand, they did not increase the political *power* of labour, which had always rested on solidarity and on the unions' autonomy from the state, not on legislative provisions. This became very clear when, in 1980, the

Thatcher government passed a new Employment Act which removed some of the unions' long-established legal immunities without encountering any effective political opposition from the labour movement.*

In other words, 'bargained corporatism', while making the corporatist character of the state quite visible, also disclosed the real limits of corporatism. As in 1966, so in 1976 the Government again abandoned the policy of economic expansion which had been central to the social contract, and in 1978 the unions abandoned wage restraint, ushering in the anti-corporatist government of Margaret Thatcher. The TUC – but not the CBI – was thereafter excluded from the councils of state.

However, the government – significantly – did not dismantle the institutional apparatus of corporatism. The NEDC continued to meet, and the state-financed but theoretically 'independent' Arbitration and Conciliation Advisory Service, set up by the Labour government in 1975, was kept in being. Although the new government ostentatiously declined to intervene in major strikes in the engineering and steel industries that occurred early in its life, it intervened dramatically to avert a miners' strike early in 1981. And, by the end of that year, not only were the Liberals and Social Democrats committed to the idea of the need for wage controls (an 'incomes policy') but the Labour Party's Alternative Economic Strategy and the economic views being urged by the 'Keynesian' wing of the Conservative Party all implied the need to re-establish the tripartite relationship between the State, the CBI and the TUC. Even a 'negotiated' *decline*, let alone any strategy for economic recovery, required co-operation from organised labour, if it was not to generate political instability and risk radicalising the labour movement as a whole. It is true that:

> In the absence of the underlying social harmony which is needed if trade union leaders are not to be repudiated by their members for their voluntary co-operation in wage restraint, corporatist structures and policies have proved difficult to establish in the first place and much more difficult to protect from breakdown once established.[33]

But, by the end of 1981, it also seemed that there was no alternative – short of authoritarianism, or a transition to socialism – but to try and constantly re-establish them.

* The Act outlawed sympathy strikes, secondary action and flying pickets. It also put in question the legality of pickets of more than six people. In 1981 further legislation was announced to cut back the number of closed shops; to make unions liable for civil damages up to £250,000 for unlawful actions by their officials or members; to allow strikers to be dismissed selectively; and to make illegal industrial action motivated by political considerations.

14

Consent and Social Control

The state is 'hegemony protected by armoured coercion': a combination of measures, both ideological and practical, to secure popular consent, and measures of social control.[1] In times of prosperity consensual themes come to the fore and little force is needed; in hard times a different range of themes is resorted to, some popular, some authoritarian and – eventually – there is more reliance on coercion.

In the 1950s and early 1960s 'consumerism' served as a powerful general ideology which obscured economic inequality and legitimated the state. But even in the 'age of affluence' other contradictions emerged and other ideological themes were taken up to validate the state's activities. For example, economic growth, as interpreted by the nuclear power industry, the automobile industry, transport engineers and the airlines, obliged the state to build nuclear power stations and expropriate land for motorways and airports in hitherto middle-class 'green' areas, giving rise to new demands for 'participation' in planning and a new concern for the 'environment'. Uneven growth brought about new demands for local control, or even independence, in backward regions, leading to the issue of 'devolution'. Simultaneously, new spheres of state bureaucracy – for example, in post-secondary education, social work and health services – led to demands for 'open government' and for machinery for the redress of grievances.

As the crisis set in, some of these themes became even more prominent, but they were gradually superseded by an alternative ideology of 'toughness', backed up by a franker reliance on force. Measures to strengthen social control were justified in terms of the need for 'discipline', 'the smack of strong government', and so on.

Legitimation – Redress of Grievances and Official Secrecy

In the Wilson era – including both the 1964–70 and the 1974–6 administrations – the rhetoric of reform stressed the need for popular 'access' to and 'participation' in the state's activities, as well as the need for efficiency. As the economic crisis deepened, and as reforms aimed at efficiency seemed less and less likely to be effective, the stress on 'participation' grew. Reforms in the committee system of the House of Commons in the 1960s (to give MPs more access to government information and a sense of efficacy in making government 'responsible' to parliament) had strong overtones of both efficiency and participation. So did the measure of devolution offered – however unwillingly – to Scotland and Wales in 1979. The Fulton proposals for reform of the civil service also equated a less exclusive administration with a more efficient one, and explicitly called for more 'openness' in public administration; and Margaret Thatcher – ironically, in view of her subsequent position on official secrecy when Prime Minister – made her parliamentary debut in 1960 by securing the passage of a Private Member's Bill to make local government meetings open to the public.

The weakness of all these measures was, however, that while they reflected a climate of criticism of established institutions, they did not correspond to a widespread popular demand. At most, they reflected the concern of strong minorities (such as the ecology lobby or the student movement), a concern shared by a section of the press and the liberal intelligentsia and by a varying number of MPs – so long as they remained on the back benches. They were opposed by most ministers and ex-ministers, civil servants and some back-benchers as well. Predictably, the result was a series of reforms which it would be an exaggeration to call half-measures. Thatcher's Public Bodies (Admission to Meetings) Act of 1960 is a good example. She was 'persuaded to accept a provision allowing secrecy if the council thought it would be "prejudicial to the public interest"' to meet in public, with 'no machinery to enforce the measure and no penalties for its evasion', with the result that many councils evaded it.[2] The fate of parliamentary reform, the Fulton reforms and the devolution bills has already been discussed. To bring out the common pattern, we will briefly consider here two more examples from the sixties and seventies – the redress of grievances and the issue of state secrecy.

Unlike the French, with their comprehensive system of administrative justice, or the Scandinavians, with their ombudsmen, British citizens before 1967 who felt that they had been unjustly treated by the ever-expanding bureaucracy often had no effective means of redress. In 1967 the office of Parliamentary Commissioner for Administration was established. The model was the Scandinavian ombudsman, and the initiative came from a quarter not too far removed from the establishment: Justice, the British section of the International Commission of Jurists. When the Macmillan government flatly rejected Justice's extremely cautious proposals, the Labour Party took up the idea and legislated on it in 1967. A Health Service Commissioner was added in 1973, and Commissioners for Local Administration in 1974 (as part of the reorganisation of local government carried out in that year).[3]* On paper, then, a comprehensive mechanism for investigating complaints of injustice by bureaucrats had been created.

But the jurisdiction and powers of the British ombudsmen (and one ombudswoman) were astonishingly limited – and even these powers were exercised, in crucial respects, in such a way as to reduce still further the usefulness of the institution. First of all, in deference to the supposed anxiety of MPs that their position *vis à vis* their constituents would be undermined (whether many MPs really felt anxiety was never actually tested) the Parliamentary Commissioner for Administration was only allowed to investigate complaints submitted to him through MPs. As Marshall remarks, this means that

> citizens of the United Kingdom are, in lacking direct access for complaint, denied a facility that is provided by Ombudsmen in Sweden, Norway, Denmark, New Zealand, Alberta, Ontario, New Brunswick, Quebec, Manitoba, Saskatchewan, Nova Scotia, South Australia, Western Australia, Victoria, Queensland, New South Wales, Alaska, Nebraska, Iowa and Hawaii, not to mention Uttar Pradesh and Jackson Missouri.[4]

The Parliamentary Commissioner regularly received more complaints directly, which he could not investigate, than he did from MPs (for instance in 1980, 1,194 compared with 1,031).[5]

Secondly, of those complaints passed on by MPs a high proportion fell outside his jurisdiction. The Parliamentary Commissioner was not allowed to investigate anything to do with the staffing of the civil service itself, anything to do with the nationalised industries, any contractual or commercial activities of the state, or any action involved in a police or security investigation.† Similarly, the Commissioners for Local Administration could not investigate complaints about personnel matters in local government, or about any contractual or commercial transactions by a local authority except those relating to land. 'This means that no complaint can be investigated, for example, against the bus services run by local authorities . . . Nor can they investigate complaints about the internal management and organisation of schools or colleges'.[6] A court decision further ruled that a local authority could refuse to disclose any document to the Local Commissioners. The Health Commissioner likewise might not investigate complaints concerning the professional medical judge-

* A Parliamentary Commissioner for Northern Ireland, and a Northern Ireland Commissioner for Complaints (against local authorities and various other public bodies) were established in 1969.

† A Police Complaints Board was later established to monitor the results of the police's investigations of complaints against themselves, but it was not a success.

ments of doctors, dentists, etc., or concerning the work of the Service Committees (which consist of doctors, dentists, etc., and hear complaints by patients). The areas – and the personnel – made immune to the new machinery were thus remarkably numerous.

Thirdly, the Commissioners' powers were limited to reporting on cases of maladministration. They were expressly forbidden to comment on the reasonableness of decisions. Later holders of the office of Parliamentary Commissioner have interpreted 'maladministration', on which they may comment, so as to include gross unreasonableness, and not just bad procedures. But they have done so very warily, and without any firm conviction. The ombudsmen could not say that, in their view, a civil servant had simply made a wrong or bad decision, even if he or she clearly had.

Fourthly, the ombudsmen were not entirely independent of the administrations they were supposed to investigate. They were not elected – the 'Parliamentary Commissioner' was not even elected by parliament, as he is in Sweden, but appointed, in the usual British fashion, nominally by the Prime Minister. The first three Parliamentary Commissioners were, moreoever, all former civil servants, and the first three Local Commissioners were, respectively, an ex-government minister (Lady Serota, a Labour life peer), a former civil servant and a former Town Clerk. One wonders whether such appointments, supposedly to serve as public watchdogs over the executive, would have been politically credible in any other country. What is more, all the Parliamentary Commissioner's staff were civil servants too, on secondment from their various government departments!

Fifthly, and following from this, Parliamentary Commissioners, especially, were hardly aggressive on behalf of citizens aggrieved by bureaucrats. They did not interpret their powers – though they might have – in such a way as to seek primarily a quick change of decision, where this seemed prima facie reasonable. Instead, they preferred to emphasise meticulous '*ex-post facto*' reports. However, they were unwilling to name names in their published reports on selected cases; and as 'anonymised' reports naturally do not get much attention from the press the only effective weapon placed in the Commissioners' hands – publicity – was severely blunted.

Not surprisingly, in view of all these limitations, the public did not make much use of the ombudsmen. They – and especially the Parliamentary Commissioner – were too inaccessible.* The Parliamentary

* The Health Commissioner, however, may be complained to directly. The Local Commissioners may also consider a complaint direct from the public if they are satisfied that a local councillor has been asked to submit it and has failed to do so. About half of the complaints submitted directly to the Local Commissioners for England and returned with a request to submit through a councillor have subsequently been so submitted.

Commissioner, moreover, did not actively advertise his services. Their jurisdiction was heavily restricted and they did not use the powers they had very energetically. Consequently, in 1971, the ombudsman for Denmark, with 5 million inhabitants, investigated more than twice as many cases as the ombudsmen of Great Britain, with a population of 55 million. It is unlikely that the British are twenty-times better administered. But the Parliamentary Commissioner 'has scored one major success', Stacey noted in 1975, 'in that he has been accepted by the Civil Service'.[7] Comment on this would be superfluous.*

Only slightly later than the establishment of the ombudsmen, there developed a parallel concern with state secrecy. The Fulton call for more openness was part of a gradual build-up of concern, fuelled by party rivalry and some back-bench frustration, with the way the Official Secrets Act was used simply to conceal state policy-making (and incompetence) from parliament and the public, rather than to protect national security.[8] The instinct of conservatives (with a small 'c', notably including James Callaghan, Prime Minister from 1976 to 1979) was to leave the situation alone. The scope of the Act was so broad that the courts were unwilling to enforce severe penalties against journalists for 'receiving' unauthorised official information that did not in fact harm state security, even though this was illegal under the Act. But they were willing to jail civil servants, particularly junior ones, who 'leaked' any official information, however harmless to security, that their superiors wished to conceal; British judges were intrinsically indisposed to back 'whistle-blowers' within the civil service. So the Act reinforced discipline within the state apparatus without, on the whole, constituting a severe threat to the press. Reformers wanted information that really related to security to be more clearly defined so that other official information could be made more freely available; while, at the other extreme, there was a call for less information to be released, a strengthening of the Act, and a more rigid enforcement against offenders.

In 1972 the Heath government, fulfilling an election pledge, appointed a Committee to review Section 2 of the Official Secrets Act (the section which made all unauthorised transmissions of official information illegal).

* However, it should be added that the Local Commissioners operated under legislative provisions which went much farther than the Parliamentary Commissioner Act in making case reports locally available to the public, although their annual reports were 'anonymised' like those of the Parliamentary Commissioner. In 1980–81, 9% of all complaints investigated by the Local Commissioners for England disclosed some maladministration. They received 2,434 complaints referred by local councillors in that year, compared with 1,031 complaints referred to the Parliamentary Commissioner by MPs. Of the latter, 225 were the subject of completed investigations, of which 47% disclosed maladministration (*Your Local Ombudsman: Report of the Commissioners for Local Administration*, London 1981, and Parliamentary Commissioner for Administration, *Annual Report for 1980*, HMSO London, 1981).

Its recommendations included a more restricted definition of what could not be divulged.[9] But, by the time it reported, the parties had become preoccupied with the economic situation to the exclusion of almost anything else, and no action was taken.

In October 1974, however, the Labour Party adopted – through the efforts of a small group of enthusiasts – a policy pledge which went much further: 'to replace the Official Secrets Act by a measure to put the burden on the public authorities to justify withholding information' – i.e., a British version of the Freedom of Information (or 'right to know') legislation passed by the US Congress in 1966 and greatly strengthened in 1974. Meanwhile, yet a further issue became entwined with that of preventing the improper disclosure of necessary secrets or the improper concealment of facts to which the public should have access. This was, how to protect individuals' 'privacy' against invasion by the owners (state or private) of computerised data banks.[10] The stage was set for a classic exercise in the neutralisation of democratic initiatives.

Roy Jenkins, Labour Home Secretary from 1974 to 1976, visited the USA in 1975 and was readily persuaded by US officials that a Freedom of Information Act would be impossibly costly. Moreover, he subsequently declared his own opposition to conducting decision-making 'under a public searchlight'. Protagonists of change persevered, however, working on back-benchers in the House of Commons. It was difficult for the Labour government, with its rashly-adopted election pledge and its growing dependence on the minority parties in parliament, to reject too openly a series of 'freedom of information' bills introduced by private members. Indeed, in 1975 the government had promised specifically to 'prepare proposals to amend the Official Secrets Act and to liberalise practices relating to official information'. As a result, one of the Private Members' Bills, introduced by the Liberal MP Clement Freud in 1979, passed the committee stage without being wholly emasculated by government amendments. It is unlikely that the Bill would have become law, especially in view of Callaghan's personal dislike of the idea, but the question was pre-empted by the government's fall from office in April 1979.

As an incoming Prime Minister Mrs Thatcher was even less sympathetic to 'open government' than Callaghan (her 1960 concern for open government in local affairs did not extend to central government in 1979). The Conservatives now introduced a Protection of Official Information Bill which had been prepared by the civil service. This said nothing about the public's 'right to know'. On the contrary, so far from limiting the scope of what information it would be a criminal offence to transmit, the Bill extended it. The Bill also allowed any minister to determine – after the event, and beyond any enquiry by the courts – whether a given piece of information was 'likely to cause serious injury to the interests of the nation'. Criticism of the Bill was widespread, but what stopped it was not criticism but the simultaneous publication of Andrew Boyle's book, *The Climate of Treason*. The facts disclosed in the book forced the government to admit that it had done a deal with a well-placed former Soviet spy who had later become Keeper of the Queen's Pictures and received a knighthood. Under the new Bill, Boyle would have been liable to a jail term for publishing his book. In the circumstances the government could only withdraw its Bill.

Still, the initiative had been decisively recaptured by the executive. The operations of the British state remained as secret as ever. An official circular of 1977 from Sir Douglas Allen, Head of the Civil Service, nominally laying down a policy of making more information available to the public (at the state's discretion), actually made it very clear that the object was to help forestall the introduction of legislation (such as 'the formidably burdensome Freedom of Information Act in the USA' as Sir Douglas called it) which would oblige the state to disclose the processes through which decisions were arrived at.* In practice, government departments persistently refused to make available to enquirers even the purged, sparely factual background documents envisaged in the circular, saying that there were none.[11]

Publicity for the processes of decision-making in government would, civil servants all agree, make their work more difficult:

> not necessarily produce worse decisions . . . but cause inconvenience . . . The unspoken heart of the argument for closed government is that private debate among civil servants and ministers produces more *rational* policies, freed from public pressure, which is assumed to be irrational.[12]

But, as Kellner shows,

* As J. Michael has shown, this was a canard whose presence in Sir Douglas Allen's memorandum (known later as the Croham memorandum, when Allen became Lord Croham on his retirement) is exactly the sort of thing the reform is aimed to prevent. At the time when the memorandum was written there was already good evidence that the costs of the US legislation had been greatly exaggerated in the forecasts made by US civil servants before it was introduced. A year later, two civil servants from the Civil Service Department visited the USA and reached the reasonable conclusion that no one really knew what the costs of the legislation were, noting that the early estimates seemed to have been exaggerated. Had the Croham memorandum been publicly available, this inaccurate information on which its main argument turned could have been exposed. Its contents are only known because it was leaked to the press. As regards the CSD report, Michael calls it 'balanced' but later adds: 'Turning from financial costs of the US laws to other costs and benefits, the CSD report shows that impressions depend even more on who is quoted. In its balanced way, the report gave about three times as much space to those who think the laws have been a bad thing [as] to those who are in favour of them' (J. Michael, *The Politics of Secrecy*, Penguin, Harmondsworth 1982, p. 145).

> Far from producing more rational government, the evidence suggests that secrecy produces more manipulative and arbitrary government... Officials are often ill-informed about the real world; ministers are often inaccurately advised by officials; Parliament often receives too little information too late from Ministers.[13]

As Lord Armstrong, another former Head of the Civil Service admitted ('candid in retirement'): 'it [secrecy] obviously is comfortable, convenient, and one has to say it allows mistakes to be covered up'.[14]

Donald Rowat, a Canadian specialist on government secrecy, concluded that in a country without a strong tradition of openness government can only be expected to become more open if a radical law is passed requiring disclosure of information as the rule rather than exception, with narrowly defined exceptions, and effective enforcement by appeals to some independent arbiter. Quite apart from the unlikelihood of a measure meeting these requirements emerging from the configuration of British parties in 1981, there is the more general question of how to find an independent arbiter, given the British tradition of the appointment by the state of 'independent' arbiters – whether for industrial disputes, on committees of enquiry, or as ombudsmen or judges – from within the establishment. It is difficult to share Michael's faith that either the British courts or the British ombudsmen would prove the champions of openness that judges and ombudsmen have been in the USA and Sweden respectively.[15] In short, it is difficult to see how British government can be made much more open without the British state becoming much more democratic.

To sum up what has been said in this section: it would be an exaggeration to claim that no progress whatever was made in the sixties and seventies in providing for the redress of grievances or in opening up the working of the state. However, as with parliamentary reform, civil service reform and, most visibly, devolution, the real thrust of the reformers was deflected, absorbed or in some way neutralised. What is more, in the increasingly important sphere of local government the tendency ran in the opposite direction, despite this being an area where great play was made with the idea of 'participation'. Here, a process of state centralisation and bureaucratisation was completed, which from the standpoint of Whitehall, was already seriously overdue. In contrast to the initiatives just discussed in relation to 'open government', these initiatives came mainly from within the state, and, again in contrast, they were largely successful.

The Local State

The problem of the local state – to give 'local government' a more accurate name – is that it was a good deal more democratic than the central state. As

Dearlove has pointed out, the fundamental problem was that local government (here referring explicitly to its elective component, the local councils) enjoyed a

> relative autonomy from both the concerns of the central state and the impact of dominant classes. Related to this, local government is especially vulnerable to working class demands, pressures and even control.[16]

Once again we are dealing with the legacy of the informal, patrician state of pre-capitalist Britain. In most European countries which experienced the centralising and rationalising impact of the Napoleonic order, a strong measure of central control was maintained over local administration. But in Britain, as local administration in the nineteenth century outgrew the capacity of the local gentry to oversee it in their capacity as magistrates, it was generally entrusted to locally-elected *ad hoc* commissions and boards, alongside the new municipal corporations, which were representative of the limited electorate of that time. There were elected boards or commissioners for cleaning, paving or lighting the streets, for road-building, for slum clearance, sewers, burials and water supply; as well as for administering public assistance, building and maintaining highways, and building and running primary schools.[17]

When, in 1888, a rationalised system of elected County and County Borough Councils was created, with property taxes (the rates) as their independent source of revenue, no general system of central supervision was placed over them.* Parliament, at the centre, established local councils by law, and by other laws laid a growing number of duties on them, and prescribed how they were to be performed; but the local accountability of locally elected councils, and a measure of financial independence, were clearly established.

> Parliament might have decided that local authorities should be elected but not have rate-raising powers, or that they should be able to raise rates without being elected. In fact Parliament has clearly established local authorities as bodies with independent sources both of democratic power and of finance.[18]

The effect was to create a potentially democratic component of the state that was to prove peculiarly susceptible to working-class influence – an influence which could not be as easily circumscribed as in the central state itself.

The majority of the working-class were concentrated in the towns and cities. Nationally, this preponderance was offset by rural and suburban

* County Councils were made responsible for most local administrative functions, except that towns with more than 50,000 inhabitants had 'County Borough' Councils which enjoyed the same powers as County Councils and were fully independent of them. 'Non-county' boroughs had fewer powers; the County Councils of the counties within which they were situated also exercised some functions in relation to their inhabitants.

constituencies, where the middle classes were more numerous. However, once workers could vote, urban councils fell increasingly under their influence and eventually under Labour control. This was by no means universal, but as early as 1919 half the Metropolitan (London) Borough Councils created in 1899 were under Labour Party control, and by 1934 even London County Council was too – this at a time when the Labour Party in parliament had been reduced to a small minority. By 1939 Labour controlled, in addition, 18 County Borough Councils, 4 County Councils, and 100 District Councils (a further Act of 1894 had created a 'second tier' of Urban and Rural District Councils alongside the 'non-County' Borough Councils).

Labour control of city government was also strengthened by the exodus of the middle class into the suburbs from the end of the nineteenth century onwards, and the exodus of industrial and commercial men of property from provincial cities into the countryside. Owners of urban industrial and commercial property remained urban ratepayers and so still had votes in the towns, but they were too few to retain real power. Thus, there developed a powerful tradition of 'municipal labourism' and a significant measure of Labour moral and ideological hegemony in many cities, also reflected in a 'labourist' outlook among council employees, whose entire careers might be spent working for a Labour-controlled authority.

In addition, local authorities did not lend themselves to the absorption of real power into the hands of an executive more or less immune to democratic control. This was partly because their functions were primarily to administer laws made by Parliament, and only secondarily to pass by-laws for their areas (a fact reflected in the committee system whereby councils operated largely through committees of councillors, each committee being responsible for a separate area of administration and working directly with the responsible officials). It was also partly because the laws they administered and the services they provided dealt with local things which people experienced at first hand, and so were on the whole in a position to understand; and partly because raising revenue by rates, whatever its faults (such as that it is inelastic, uneven and regressive), is a form of taxation which, unlike the national Budget, directly relates the amount of revenue demanded to the expenditure proposed, and is therefore more comprehensible.

For these reasons, Labour control of a council meant a real degree of control over the local state. The limitations of labourism itself, combined with the limited powers given to local authorities by Parliament, circumscribed the political impact of this state of affairs. But as they acquired confidence, Labour-controlled councils began to exploit the powers they had been given, in addition to fulfilling the functions required of them by law: building houses for workers and undertaking various kinds of 'municipal trading', i.e., enterprises such as public transportation, gas and electricity services, entertainments, telephone systems, docks and crematoria.

So long as central government remained under the effective control of the Conservative Party, Labour control of many of the country's city and town councils was an irritant, but not a critical one. Any new functions assigned to local authorities were determined by the central state. Extensions of municipal trading were resisted.[19] The one notable power which presented a problem during the inter-war years, the administration of the poor laws (including unemployment relief), was transferred to the central state (in the shape of a non-elective Unemployment Assistance Board) in 1934.* There were complaints about the 'calibre' of local councillors in the cities (a coded way of regretting that they only had the education provided for the working class, and were prone to set the standard of municipal services, such as council housing, above the level which middle-class ratepayers thought appropriate for workers).[20] But the problem was not a major one.

After 1945, however, the consolidation of the expanded Welfare State greatly extended the role of the local state, since much of the expansion was in services that were already administered by local government, or led to the creation of new services that clearly ought to be. The new National Health Service was an exception; control over it was given to non-elective Regional Hospital Boards controlled by doctors, in order to help overcome their opposition to the scheme, and some 1,700 hospitals were transferred to these from local council control.[21] But the growth of the state, as measured by expenditure, was growth of the local state almost as much as of the central state. In the last pre-war year, 1938–9, local governments spent £782.8 million out of a total state expenditure of £1,801.8 million (43.4%). In 1977–78 they spent £24,017 million out of a total of £68,007 million (35.3%).[22] By that time they were also employing some 2½ million people, about ten per cent of all employees. The local state had become an immense social and economic presence. The control by Labour majorities of a large part of it was one source of the rise of anti-state sentiment in the Conservative Party in the 1960s. Labour councils spent more on housing, education and personal-health services than non-Labour councils in areas with similar needs.[23]

This spending was covered partly by local rates, partly by revenues from services provided by the councils (e.g., rents from council-house tenants) and partly by grants from the central government to meet the cost of nationally-required services administered by local authorities, and to

* Down to 1930, poor relief in England and Wales was administered by locally-elected Boards of Guardians, also often Labour-controlled in urban areas. From 1930 to 1934 it was briefly entrusted to County and County Borough Councils.

Table 14.1 Sources of local government income 1960–61 and 1976–77

	1960–61		1976–77	
	£m	%	£m	%
Rates	696.7	33.3	4,151.0	23.8
Grants	755.9	36.2	8,639.8	49.6
Other	638.3	30.5	4,638.6	26.6
Total	2,090.9	100.00	17,429.4	100.00

Source: T. Burgess and T. Travers, *Ten Billion Pounds*, Grant McIntyre, London 1980, p. 34.

equalise the burden of local rates between councils with differing property bases and differing social needs. By 1976–7, out of total local authority spending of £17,429 million, central government grants covered nearly a half of that sum (Table 14.1). Meanwhile, ratepayers were complaining bitterly about their sharply-increased rate demands.* In this context the scale and spirit of the expenditures of many Labour-controlled councils seemed ever more unacceptable. As the fiscal crisis of the state developed, the 'accumulation function' of the state, which was seen as calling for reduced state spending, and the 'legitimation function', which called for its maintenance, came into conflict in the local sphere.

The problem was both delicate and complex. It was delicate, partly because a solution meant reducing the degree of effective local democracy – an explosive issue given the ideological importance of democracy in general – and partly because any such scheme promoted by a Conservative government would affect Conservative-controlled councils as well as Labour ones. On the other hand, the Labour leadership was also less than enthusiastic about local democracy because of its potential for generating more radical, extra-parliamentary forms of action.

What the Labour leadership opposed was commonly known as Poplarism. In 1921 the Mayor and 29 Labour councillors of the East London Borough of Poplar went to prison for refusing to collect rates, as required by law, for any services other than those operated by themselves and the Poplar Poor Law Guardians (also controlled by Labour and largely the same people). This was a gesture aimed at forcing the govern-

* It is important to avoid mystification here. 'Grants' should be put in inverted commas because the term tends to connote something for nothing. 'Grants' to local government are primarily central government expenditures on nationally-required tasks which are carried out locally, such as education or road-works, for which policy is almost wholly laid down in Whitehall. Similarly with the term 'ratepayers'. It is not generally realised that tenants, including council-house tenants pay rates just as owner-occupiers do. Commercial and industrial ratepayers, moreover, are major users of council services, contrary to the impression often given in the media.

ment of the day to legislate so as to redistribute the cost of unemployment relief, which at that time was all borne locally. Thus, ratepayers in Poplar, a poverty-stricken dockland area with 15,000 unemployed out of a total population of 160,000, were expected to pay more than twice as much as the prosperous ratepayers of Westminster, where there was virtually no unemployment. In the event, the persistent and overwhelming support of the Poplar electorate over the years 1919–25 obliged successive governments to secure the release of the Mayor and councillors, after a month's imprisonment, to equalise the burden of unemployment relief, to introduce a more humane system and level of poor relief, and – as a result of the gathering momentum of the cause of the Poplar leaders and the backing they received from their council employees – to accept some improvement in the real wages paid to council workers.[24]

In 1934, nine years after this protracted struggle, in which one impoverished borough forced fundamental policy changes on unwilling governments, the administration of public assistance was removed from elected councils altogether. Also significantly, the Labour Party leadership was unhappy at the way the Poplar radicals had conducted their campaign. The Labour Government of 1924 had been attacked in the House of Commons for supporting 'unconstitutional' action, and the leadership saw this as partly to blame for Labour's defeat in the 1924 election.

Fifty years later, the Labour leaders were caught in exactly the same trap. In 1972 the Labour-controlled Urban District Council of the mining town of Clay Cross in Derbyshire, confronted with unemployment approaching 20% due to pit closures, refused to collect an additional £1 per week in rent from the tenants of its Council houses, as required by the Conservatives' new Housing Finance Act. On this occasion the government carefully avoided enforcing the law in such a way as to risk having the eleven rebel councillors sent to prison, and for two years the Clay Cross Council successfully resisted the government's efforts to collect the increased rent directly. They also raised the pay of council manual workers above the limits prescribed in the 1973 wage controls. The basis of their success was the same as that of the Poplar leaders: the solid support of a large majority in a distinctive, somewhat isolated and densely working-class area.[25]

What was significant was the reaction of the Labour Party leadership. The 1972 Labour Party Conference resolved to support any council which refused to apply the new rents, and to indemnify councillors against disqualification from office, and against any 'surcharges' which might be made on them (under the law, councillors judged by the District Auditor to have spent council funds improperly could be disqualified and billed personally to recover the sums in question). In 1924 the Labour minister concerned had promised to remit any surcharges made on the Poplar Poor

Law Guardians for exceeding the legally-permitted rates of relief, and this had been attacked as unconstitutional. In the Clay Cross case the Labour leadership refused to give any such promise, although without it the Conference's declaration of 'support' for councils opposing the Housing Finance Act was distinctly hollow; and after Labour won the 1974 elections six of the Clay Cross councillors were allowed to be bankrupted (a lesson which was not lost on the Labour Group of the Greater London Council in their fight with the Conservative Government over their cheap fares policy for London Transport in 1981 – see pp. 297–8).

The problem of Clay Cross was only resolved in a permanent manner by the abolition of Clay Cross Urban District and its absorption into the new, and much larger, District of North-East Derbyshire during the local government re-organisation of 1974. This formed part of a comprehensive re-organisation of local government, endorsed in its essentials by both parties, and designed to reduce if not eliminate the difficulty presented for the state by local democracy.

By 1961 the system of local government had remained virtually unchanged for sixty years while the social and economic structure of society had changed a great deal. However, neither party cared to impose a reform over the vociferous opposition of the members and officials of the existing local authorities (both Labour and Conservative). The most obvious anomaly was that some large and growing cities were still subordinate to County Councils while others which had declined, and were much smaller, retained their autonomous 'County Borough' status and had full responsibility for all local government functions. At the same time, it was argued that many functions could now only be efficiently performed on a larger scale than that of any existing county. But none of these arguments had been enough to carry the first proposals for change, presented by a commission in 1947.[26]

In London, however, where the anomalies were among the most severe, an opportunity to make a change independently of the rest of the country existed. Moreover, London County Council and the majority of London's Metropolitan Boroughs were Labour-controlled, while a Conservative government was in power at Westminster; a change could be imposed in London that would benefit the Conservatives without hurting Conservatives elsewhere. In 1963, therefore, following a special Royal Commission, the LCC was merged into a new Greater London Council (GLC) covering most of the built-up area (the LCC's boundaries having long since been outgrown), with responsibility for planning, transport policy, main roads, fire and ambulance services; while a few greatly enlarged London boroughs were made responsible for the rest (except for education in the Inner London area, which was left in the hands of an Inner London Education Authority jointly responsible to the GLC and the London boroughs).

The enlarged GLC included much more of the suburbs. This dramatically altered the electoral balance, as the Conservatives had expected. Labour continued to control the solidly working-class borough councils of East London and most of the 'inner city', but in 1967, the GLC itself and, in 1968, 27 out of the 32 new London Boroughs passed under Conservative control, giving them overall control of London again for the first time since 1934.[27]

The example of London played an obvious part in the solution ultimately found for re-organisation elsewhere. The official argument was that larger units were much more efficient (though this was shown to be not merely not proven, but fallacious).* The tacit reasoning was that combining towns and cities with peri-urban and rural areas would also dilute areas of working-class concentration with middle-class areas. In the coded language of establishment social science, commentators noted that 'by creating areas which are rather more functionally united, but socially heterogeneous, the [proposed] structure will mean that there are fewer councils in England which are politically and socially unbalanced' – i.e., (in Dearlove's translation) 'it would reduce the unfettered control which working-class voters and Labour dominated councils have over the affairs of the central city'.[28]

It was again the Conservatives who, in 1972, implemented the long-delayed reorganisation. As a result, the number of counties was reduced by mergers to 47, with 333 much-enlarged District Councils within them. The conurbations outside London followed the London model, with six Metropolitan Councils – Greater Manchester, West Midlands, Merseyside, West Yorkshire, South Yorkshire and Tyne and Wear – and 36 lower-tier District Councils within them. In Scotland nine regions were created, with 53 districts within them, and three virtually single-tier island councils.† The new authorities were so much larger that few voters any

* The way in which the Radcliffe-Maud Commission on Local Government tried to discredit all research findings which led to this conclusion (including its own) should be an object lesson for all those who are tempted to think that making social science useful means conducting investigations into questions of interest to, or at the request of, state agencies (see Dearlove, *The Reorganisation of British Local Government*, Cambridge University Press, Cambridge 1979, pp. 68–78).

† In the 1973 elections for the new councils in England and Wales the results in terms of party control were as follows:

	Conservatives	Labour	No clear party control
Metropolitan Counties	—	6	—
Other Counties	18	11	18
Metropolitan Districts	5	26	5
Other Districts (England)	86	73	137
Other Districts (Wales)	1	19	17

longer had first-hand knowledge of their overall problems.

Besides the enlargement of local authority areas, two other major changes also curtailed the scope of local democracy. One was the drive to assimilate local authority administration to the 'corporate' model – i.e., the model of management advocated for companies. How this drive was transmitted from the sphere of private enterprise to local administration is an important and still only partially-explored story.[29] But it was actively encouraged by the central government through two enquiries, the Maud Committee of 1964–7, and the Bains Working Group of 1972.[30] The change however, was also the product of a convergence between a new kind of councillor (Labour as well as Conservative) coming to the fore in the 1960s, and a new kind of local government official who emerged at about the same time; both were responsive to the ideology of planning, economies of scale and efficiency which was then being promoted by academic social scientists and business consultants who played an active part in local government reorganisation.

Under this initiative, virtually all local authorities abandoned the practice whereby department heads (Directors of Education, of Housing, etc.) were separately responsible to corresponding committees of councillors. This was judged incompatible with integrated planning and efficient management of the councils' work considered as a whole, and – not least – considered in relation to the needs of the businesses located in their areas. Instead councils, like companies, now appointed Chief Executives, who unlike the old Town Clerks had formal authority over the Department Heads or Directors. The latter could, in consequence, now be grouped in a Committee of Officials (the Directors' Board was the name given to it in Lambeth, for example) who prepared agendas for an, equally new, Policy Committee, chaired by the elected Leader of the Council and consisting primarily of the chairmen of the various council committees. Although the committees still met, these changes, whatever else they accomplished (and this has still to be seriously analysed) shifted effective power out of their hands and lodged it with the Policy Committee and the Directors Board.[31] In effect, the local state was brought more into line with the structure of the central state.

The executive had been strengthened and concentrated, and the equivalent of a cabinet under the control of the Leader had been created. Information was now increasingly controlled by the officials and the inner leadership of the majority party on the council, at the same time that the larger areas reduced the independent knowledge which any councillor was likely to have of the detail of any question before the council.

The second change which helped to roll back local democracy was increased financial control by central government. It had always been necessary for local councils to secure Treasury permission to borrow for capital expenditure, and as the crisis developed during the 1960s and 1970s severe cuts in the building of schools, roads and houses were imposed. Local authorities were now also required to furnish estimates of their long-term future recurrent expenditure for inclusion in the annual projections of the Treasury's Public Expenditure Survey Committee. When monetarist policies began to be enforced from 1976 onwards, local recurrent spending also fell under the axe. 'At constant prices local authority capital expenditure was halved between 1974 and 1978, and the cuts in current expenditure have probably hit the local government sector harder than any other part of the public sector'.[32]

This was accomplished by changing the terms on which the central government supplemented local councils' income from rates and other local sources. In 1958, central government grants were consolidated into a single Rate Support Grant, calculated on a very complex formula. From 1977–8 this was sharply cut back and, at the same time, any over-spending in one year was to be compensated for by a corresponding cut in the grant in the following year (the so-called 'cash limits'). The effect was to shift the burden of maintaining services onto the rates.[33] Rates had already risen sharply in the immediately preceding years, as a result of the rapid growth in the demand for social services and their above-average cost increases (see Chapter 13, p. 262). They now rose even more sharply, leading to a 'ratepayers' revolt' and to Conservative victories in local elections. In effect, officials in Whitehall were now able to control in considerable detail the whole range of local government spending, and hence local government policy too.

This process reached its logical limit in 1981 when Michael Heseltine, the Conservative Environment Minister (who was responsible for local government), took a further step and announced that any council proposing to spend above the limits approved by his department would have its grant *reduced* by a corresponding sum. In effect, ratepayers would have to be asked for twice the proposed additional spending – the extra spending plus the same amount that would be subtracted from the central government grant. The aim was to force councils to cut spending by making the electoral price too high. Even so, faced with increasingly acute needs, some councils preferred to ask for even bigger rate increases rather than close schools or clinics, eliminate bus services or dismiss staff. Heseltine's strategy also had the disadvantage that commercial and industrial firms contributed 50–60% of rates in many areas so that at least half of the extra burden appeared to fall on the Conservatives' natural supporters. In the autumn of 1981, therefore, he proposed new legislation which would forbid local authorities to levy any supplementary rates.* What remained of the financial independence of local government was thus close to being removed altogether along with much of the reality of local democracy. 'The comparison between local authorities today and their self-confident predecessors at the end of the last century is very striking'.[34]

The difficulty with all these measures, justified in the name of efficiency and of the need for central government to control all public spending as part of its responsibility for managing the economy, was that they destroyed whatever lingering sense of personal responsibility many people had for what local government did. The legitimacy of the local state declined and, with it, some of the legitimacy of the state as a whole. Two illustrations of this will suffice.

One concerns the GLC's attempt to reverse the decline of London's public transport system. In May 1981, the Labour Party won control of the Council from the Conservatives on a platform of which a central plank was a commitment to a 25% reduction in fares. This, it was expected, would produce a 7–10% recovery in passenger use, at a cost of £125 million in the first full year of its operation. Whitehall disapproved of the scheme, and cut the GLC's grant by an equivalent amount, so that, altogether, the GLC would have to find an extra £250 million from the rates. The fares scheme was introduced in September 1981, leading to an initial passenger increase of 7% on the underground and 11% on buses. The Conservative-controlled London Borough of Bromley, however, brought a court action against the GLC on the grounds that it lacked the authority to subsidise fares out of the rates. The case finally went on appeal to the House of Lords who found in favour of Bromley. According to the five judges concerned, the GLC had a 'fiduciary duty' to the ratepayers, which meant that it could not do anything which was not reasonably in their interest; and, they held, the London Transport Act did not envisage the subsidisation of fares out of the rates except to cover *temporary* deficits on fare revenues.†

* Supplementary rates usually had to be levied where councils proposed to spend more than Whitehall wanted because councils could not know how much more money they would finally need from the rates until the level of the central government grant, after the penalties had been deducted, was known. Initially, Heseltine had proposed a bill which would have allowed the minister (himself) to call a referendum in any local area in which the Council proposed to levy a supplementary rate to cover any spending not approved by Whitehall. This was abandoned in face of back-bench opposition within his own party, prompted by Conservative councils which were unwilling to hand over the appearance as well as the reality of local fiscal power to central government.

† This is a rough summary of a judgement which even the establishment press found it impossible to admire (see the *Sunday Times*, 20 December 1981). The judgement implied that the subsidies given to London Transport every year in the recent past by the GLC under Labour and Conservatives alike had also been illegal, and also that Whitehall already had powers to enforce any veto it wished on any local government spending.

The Conservative government expressed its satisfaction with the judgement and refused any further financial assistance, other than a loan spread over five years to recoup the money which the GLC had hoped to get from the rates to meet the deficit caused by the cheap fares policy to date. To close the deficit for the future, fares had to be increased by 96%, leading to an expected passenger loss of 18% and inevitable cuts in services. The interesting question was whether Londoners in general would agree with the judges, and Conservative policy, or conclude that the existing network was necessary and that the policy for which they had voted in May 1981 had been more reasonable. If the latter, the long-term costs for the legitimacy of the state could be considerable. If the Law Lords' decision, and central government's domination of local government, were eventually to be identified with a discredited economic doctrine and an unpopular government, both the judicial system and the centralisation of the state might be questioned in a novel way.

A second example of the costs of the bureaucratisation of the local state was the frustration of local groups faced by the unresponsiveness to their needs of the enlarged, more remote, local authorities. This was not confined to groups confronting Conservative councils. Some of the worst problems were in areas where Labour had been unchallenged for so long that the party's grass-roots organisation had atrophied – often in decaying inner-cities with severe housing-problems and poor social amenities. These were the areas where Constituency Labour Parties, from the mid-1970s, tended to be taken over by left-wing activists. They were also the areas where the problems of poverty and deprivation had 're-emerged' most acutely when the Wilson government embarked on the deflationary policies which, with the brief exception of the years 1970–2, have prevailed ever since. The spirit of activism which this produced was particularly strong at the local level. Tenants' rights associations, squatters' organisations, claimants' unions and ethnic community groups sprang up or expanded.

Protagonists of local government reorganisation, seeking efficiency through larger areas and corporate management, foresaw the need to deal with the problems that would arise when council policy became less amenable to working-class influence. The reforms were accompanied by a strong rhetoric of public 'participation', and led to a series of experiments and projects designed to secure public support for the policies of the local state, by 'associating' the public with local government planning – though not, of course, in such a way as to determine the content of the plans.

It is difficult, as Cockburn pointed out, to keep firmly in view the co-optive, manipulative intentions and effect of this aspect of local state policy in the 1970s, because of the 'fine humanitarian and radical motives' of so many of the people who were involved in it.[35] But the thinking of the proponents of 'participation', official and unofficial, was unequivocally managerial and paternal.[36] There is a profound difference between 'participation' and democracy. Burgess and Travers's remarks are justified:

> It has to be recognised that consultation is always undertaken for the benefit of those consulting, not of the consulted. It alerts the former to what they cannot get away with, but does not give the consulted any genuine opportunity for sharing in the making of the decisions . . . The whole process does not mitigate but, rather, increases the evils of ignorance, incompetence and dependence.[37]

The penalty, however, may be long-delayed: the immediate costs are borne by the 'public'. 'Cost-efficient' policies led to the further destruction of local urban communities and the creation of soulless – and, as it later emerged, often unsafe and ultimately extremely expensive – factory-built housing. Under the continued impact of spending cuts, services were 'consolidated' and 'withdrawn'. Day nurseries were closed, school meals abolished; refuse collection deteriorated, the redevelopment of urban wasteland created by 'slum clearance' was postponed indefinitely. 'Participation' made no difference; it was not meant to. The result was to compound alienation and anomie, especially among young people in inner-city areas. When they took to the streets in July 1981 it was significant that some of the worst rioting was in Brixton, in the enlarged London Borough of Lambeth, a pioneer of both corporate management and 'community participation' throughout the 1970s.[38]

Law and Order

The general cause of the riots, which sociologists and community workers had been expecting for several years, was the alienation of young people, especially blacks, caused by very high unemployment, a deprived and depressed environment, and lack of hope for the future. The proximate cause, however, was the impact on these communities of a new style of policing. What the riots threw into prominence was how the state had responded to the national crisis by radically strengthening its repressive capacity.

Besides Brixton (south London) and Toxteth (Liverpool) – where the rioting was the most intense and prolonged – there were also major riots in Southall (London) and in Moss Side (Manchester). But that was not all. The weekend of 10–12 July 1981 saw disturbances in more than thirty British towns and cities. In April of the previous year, too, there had been a serious riot in the St Paul's district of Bristol. What Brixton, Toxteth and St Paul's had in common was not just inner-city deprivation and substantial black minorities, but also a recent history of exposure to the new kind of policing. They rarely, if ever, saw a local uniformed 'bobby' on a regular 'beat', who was known to and familiar with the local residents, someone who could rely on them for information and a degree of support and who was subject – even if only indirectly – to the influence of local councillors on the local police committee in matters regarding policing policy. Instead, policemen in cars and vans, acting on information from informers or from suspects' answers to questions, or on no information at all, were apt to stop and search people in social centres, such as youth clubs, discos and pubs, or on the streets. Sometimes this was done on a massive scale as part of the 'saturation policing' of an area (as happened extensively in Brixton before the riots).

Consequently, relations between the police and the local populations of these areas altered. Policemen were encountered less as 'helpers' and more as an arbitrary and often aggressive outside force, who tended to see all those who were unemployed or black, especially the young, as actual or potential trouble-makers who must be kept in their place. The evidence collected by the Commission for Racial Equality in Bristol, the Working Party on Police–Public Relationships in Toxteth and the Scarman inquiry in Brixton all showed that these confrontations were precipitated by incidents which brought hostility to the police to boiling point.[39]

The developments which lay behind this go beyond policing in the narrow sense. During the 1960s and 1970s the coercive arm of the state as a whole – the organisation and practices of the police, the secret police and the army – underwent a qualitative change. This can be summarised as follows:

(a) the bureaucratisation of the non-secret police and the elimination of popular control over it;
(b) the change from 'community policing' to 'fire-brigade policing' based on the doctrine of the 'pre-emption' (as opposed to prevention and detection) of crime;
(c) the development of new police technology, especially computers;
(d) the expansion of secret police surveillance of political opposition;
(e) the conversion of the army into an instrument of domestic political control.

The background to these developments (which are dealt with under separate headings below) was partly a rapid growth in crime rates. In 1900 there were 78,000 indictable offences, or 250 per 100,000 people. In 1967 there were over 3,000 offences per 100,000 people, and in 1977, 4,000 offences.[40] Such figures should be treated with great caution. Part of the increase was due to new legislation (for example, most traffic-related crimes). More importantly, reported crimes constitute such a small proportion of all crimes committed (according to all research on this question) that increases in recorded crime-rates usually tell us more about changes in reporting, recording or policing than about changes in criminal behaviour (for instance, the jump from two cases of male importuning recorded in Manchester, in 1958, to 216, by 1962, was due to an increase in police attention to the crime, ordered by a new Chief Constable, not an increase in male prostitution).[41] None the less, it seems clear that the incidence of crimes against property, in particular, did increase substantially. Small rural police forces, with as few as 20 or (in one case) 10 officers, were increasingly inadequate for the job of crime prevention and detection in the age of the motorway and computer fraud. Greater centralisation, specialisation and the use of new technology were necessary. It is also clear that one or two policemen on the beat were unequal to dealing with gangs of motor-cyclists involved in mass brawls, crowd violence and damage to property at football matches, or large-scale direct political action by groups such as the Committee of 100 (a section of the Campaign for Nuclear Disarmament).

However, this factor is hard to separate from at least two other developments. One was the general movement for bureaucratisation of the local state, and the elimination of control by elected local authorities. This was very clear in the attitude of Chief Constables towards local authority police committees, an attitude supported by Home Secretaries of both parties and by the judiciary. The other was a growing concern about the state's capacity to deal with extra-parliamentary political opposition, which was partly an anxiety about the growth of trade-union militancy. The confrontation between 6,000 workers and 700 police at the Saltley coke depot in Birmingham during the 1972 miners' strike was a turning-point here. The police were obliged to concede to numbers and give up their attempt to protect lorries crossing the picket line. Later changes in the law on picketing (in the Employment Act 1980) were one reaction: drastic changes in the state's capacity to deal directly with industrial mass action were another, starting immediately after the Saltley incident.

At the same time, there was a growing anxiety about 'subversion'. This was partly a response to the IRA Provisionals' bombing and shooting campaigns both in Northern Ireland and (from time to time) in England. But it was also a response to the growth of extra-parliamentary radical politics generally, after about 1960: the multiplication of Marxist 'grouplets' on the left, the large increase in unofficial strikes and the emergence of community action groups of all kinds who were prepared to act directly in spheres where the parliamentary parties seemed impotent or uninterested.

Faced with these developments, successive governments expanded the definition of 'subversion'. In 1963 Lord Denning (in his report on the Profumo affair) said a subversive person was someone who 'would contemplate the overthrow of government by unlawful means'.[42] This made 'subversion' a matter of someone's ideas, but seemed to confine it to ideas about unlawful means of political action. In 1975, however, a Labour Minister of State at the Home Office said 'subversion is defined as activities threatening the safety or well-being of the state and intended to undermine or overthrow parliamentary democracy by political, industrial or violent means'.[43] This definition referred to activities, rather than ideas, but defined them so broadly or vaguely as potentially to cover almost any political action considered hostile by those in charge of the state. It remained only for a Labour Home Secretary, Merlyn Rees, to bring the two definitions together when he said in 1978 that 'the Special Branch collects information on those whom (*sic*) I think cause problems for the state';[44] and the evidence makes it clear that this was indeed the increasingly large task that the secret police had set themselves by this time.*

These institutional and policy changes, reflecting broader social and political developments, were also influenced by the political campaign for 'law and order' mounted by the Conservative right from the late 1960s onwards (see Chapter 6). In 1975 the Police Federation (the policemen's lobbying and negotiating organisation) broke with tradition and launched an extensive public campaign for 'law and order' as part of its efforts to raise police pay and recruitment and to make the task of the police easier. Sir Robert Mark, Metropolitan Police Commissioner from 1972 to 1977, began a new tradition of police chiefs engaging in public political discussion, with a series of attacks on the jury system and the rules of evidence. This agitation reinforced a policy trend which had developed with the support of both major parties throughout the sixties and seventies.[45] The main elements within this trend, which were listed earlier, are now considered in turn.

(a) *The bureaucratisation of the police and the elimination of democratic control*

The movement to enlarge local authorities in the name of efficiency was preceded by a movement to enlarge police authority areas, which had similar motives. In 1918 a brief police strike for recognition of the Police Union frightened the authorities (Lloyd George's later remark that 'it was the nearest the country ever came to Bolshevism' shows how the strike was

* And not the secret police alone. One of the most prominent of the new 'political' Chief Constables, James Anderton of Great Manchester, said on television in 1979 that he thought that for the next ten to fifteen years 'basic crimes as such – theft, burglary, even violent crime – will not be the predominant police feature. What will be the matter of greatest concern to me will be the covert and ultimately overt attempts to overthrow democracy, to subvert the authority of the state and, in fact, to involve themselves (*sic*) in acts of sedition designed to destroy our parliamentary system and the democratic government in this country' (BBC-1 'Question Time', 16 October 1979, cited in *Review of State Security*, 1980, p. 34).

viewed, fantastic as the idea may be).* After the strike, the Desborough Committee initiated a process of standardising police recruitment, pay, training and organisation throughout the country, under Home Office supervision, beginning with the Police Act of 1919. The Committee also recommended abolishing all police forces of non-county boroughs with less than 15,000 inhabitants. This was successfully resisted by local authorities, however – a measure of their vitality and strength at that time – and the amalgamation process only began as a general policy with the Police Act of 1946. A Royal Commission on the Police in 1960–2 recommended carrying the process further by amalgamating the remaining smaller forces, but at the same time resisted proposals to create a single national police force. A new Police Act of 1964 allowed the Home Secretary to impose amalgamations even on forces serving populations of over 100,000. Between 1946 and 1969, the number of forces in England and Wales was reduced from 159 to 49. In 1974, with the reduction in the number of counties, the number was reduced still further, to 43 (including the Metropolitan and City of London Police forces). In Scotland, 33 forces in 1950 had been reduced to eight by 1980. Northern Ireland (the model of 'pre-emptive' policing from the moment of partition) had only one force.

Meantime the 1960–2 Royal Commission had also redefined the power of the once-powerful police committees of local councils as consisting of appointing and removing Chief Constables (subject to the Home Secretary's approval) and thereafter 'giving advice and guidance to the Chief Constable about local problems'. This change was reflected in the 1964 Police Act.

> Thus the idea of local control . . . was set aside in a way that would have been totally incomprehensible to most 19th-century watch committees and county justices.[46]

On the other hand, the Home Secretary was not made formally responsible for the police outside London, except in having to approve the appointment or removal of Chief Constables, and in overseeing the general standards of recruitment, training and efficiency. As a result, the Home Secretary declined to answer parliamentary questions about the conduct of provincial police forces; he also declined to answer questions about the conduct of the Metropolitan Police, for which he was formally responsible. With these changes, the new enlarged police forces thus

* The strike was settled with a large pay increase and an apparent agreement to recognise the Police Union when the war was over. When this recognition was later withheld the Union was skilfully divided and a second strike was quickly broken. The Police Federation, with no right to strike and with heavy over-representation of senior officers, was established by the government in place of the Union.

became, for all practical purposes, immune from any control except the private influence of the Home Secretary and his officials.[47]

(b) *The shift to 'fire-brigade' and 'pre-emptive' policing*
By 1979, after large pay increases and large-scale expenditure on equipment, the new police forces had grown to a total of 126,500 officers and 47,500 civilians.[48]* As the Chief Inspector for Scotland remarked in his 1978 report, 'in effect our police force has more than doubled in the last forty years . . . and one could well ask where all the policemen have gone'.[49] The answer was that they had been reorganised into specialised roles and into formations capable of being quickly deployed to meet threats to public order, such as from strikers or demonstrators, which were beyond the capability of the traditional police on foot patrol. The reason usually given for the absence of policemen from the streets (Whitaker records that in 1975 'there were times when none of the six stations in London's E Division could spare any man to put on the beat') was that crime-rates were outstripping police resources, but the truth was that police resources had been deliberately deployed off the streets.[50] 'Command and control' techniques, utilising computerised information on the whereabouts of the force on duty, and radio communication, imply that most policemen are in mobile units and specialised squads of various kinds. As one Chief Constable (a critic of the trend) summed it up, 'The car, the radio and the computer dominate the police scene. The era of preventive policing (by patrolling) is phasing out in favour of a responsive or reactive police'.[51]

By 1980 at least 27 police forces in the United Kingdom had Special Control Groups (under one name or another) trained as riot control units, and all the forces had Police Support Units, notionally prepared for special security duties in the event of a nuclear attack. It is estimated that at least 11,000 police had been specially trained in riot control, and all forces had 'mutual aid' arrangements for this purpose. In addition, many more police had been trained in the use of firearms (an estimated 10%), although it should be stressed that by international standards British policemen remained mainly unarmed.

The point is that police work in general had undergone a marked change. The new concept of policing had reinforced the distancing from the community caused by larger local authority and police force areas and the elimination of local democratic control. The outlook and experience of

* Excluding Northern Ireland. It is difficult to compare this with the figures for other countries. Whitaker (*The Police in Society*, Methuen, London 1979, p. 116) gives a figure for England and Wales in 1978 of 423 people per policeman, compared with 702 in the Netherlands, 533 in Canada and 323 in Belgium. The latter figures, however, are for 1972; on the other hand the British figures omit auxiliary forces such as the British Transport Police (1,900 in 1980) and the Atomic Energy Police (400).

policemen trained more to 'contain' crime than prevent it, to deal with disorder and 'subversion' more than crime detection, tended to involve a self-fulfilling prophecy. The new 'squads' could not be put on the beat but they could be used to 'saturate' or 'swamp' a so-called 'high crime area' such as Brixton or Huyton with police for a day or a week, stopping and searching hundreds of young, unemployed or black people on the streets; or used to make 'fishnet sweeps', ostensibly to catch illegal immigrants in London, or arsonists in Wales, but actually as much to gather information and discourage or intimidate potential wrong-doers.[52] The racist attitudes which policemen in these formations tended to exhibit were in part a product of the situation into which they had been thrust by the concepts of 'pre-emptive' and 'reactive' policing and the organisation and training which this entailed.

(c) *The development of new technology*

Apart from new weapons of crowd control, the prime innovation was the computer.[53] A Police National Computer (PNC), with a capacity for 40 million records, could store information on stolen or suspect vehicles, all vehicle-owners, fingerprints held by the police and the names of criminals, wanted or missing persons and disqualified drivers.

The nature of this computer facility was supposed to be a matter of public record. The Metropolitan Police 'C' (Criminal) Department Computer, by contrast, was secret. It contained the records of the Central Drugs Intelligence Unit, the National Immigration Intelligence Unit, the Criminal Investigations Department and the Special Branch (the political police). Moreover, by 1981, computers had been or were to be installed by sixteen local police forces, with facilities for exchanging information with each other and with the PNC. Besides the local records that were held on these computers there was also 'intelligence'. This consisted of both factual information and hearsay and subjective speculation about individuals that had been compiled by officers designated as 'collators'. Five of these computers, following Northern Ireland practice, had or would have comprehensive street registers, listing every house and its occupants. The evidence suggests that by 1979 the PNC alone contained 'intelligence' (not confined to details of car ownership) on more than one-fifth of the adult population.* Telephone tapping, bugging and photo-

* This estimate is based on 'jury-vetting' data handed to the defence in a trial held in 1979. Of 93 on the jury panel, intelligence data had been provided to the prosecuting counsel on 20, of whom less than half had criminal records. The data included items (in several cases false) such as being 'believed to be a squatter' (occupying empty premises illegally) or having made a complaint against the police. The data given to the defence did not, moreover, include whatever intelligence had also been collected by the Special Branch (D. Leigh, *The Frontiers of Secrecy*, Junction Books, London 1980, pp. 171–6).

graphic and video technology all expanded as well during these years. The evidence also suggests that it had become standard practice to tap the phones of left-wing organisations and *ad hoc* radical organisations such as strike committees and to photograph all participants in demonstrations.[54]

(d) *The expansion of political surveillance*

The Special Branch (originally the Special Irish Branch, having been, like many of the repressive aspects of the contemporary state, a response to the Irish anti-colonial struggles of the late nineteenth century) grew to a strength of 1,608 officers (about one per cent of the total police force). Half was in London, with the rest attached to local forces round the country.[55] The Special Branch maintained an index of some three million people, of whom files were kept on all those considered to be activists or important members of left-wing or extreme right-wing groups; and attended, or received reports from other police officers or informers about, all political meetings (apart from those of most MPs and councillors, or candidates for election to parliament or councils). The Branch aimed to have informers in as many political organisations, and on as many university campuses, as possible. Agents provacateurs also were employed to try – though not always successfully – to implicate 'subversives' in criminal acts.[56] The military secret service concerned with counter-espionage, MI6, worked with the Special Branch but its work overlapped that of the Special Branch and even included spying on trade unionists during strikes. At one time MI5 even put some MPs under surveillance.[57]

(e) *The use of the army for domestic political control*

By 1981 most infantry units of the British Army had been stationed for a period of duty in Northern Ireland at some time during the past twleve years, so that the military control of civilians within the UK had been their main operational experience. The lessons of this (and of earlier colonial operations) had been generalised into a doctrine of 'low-intensity operations' whose potential application on the mainland for dealing with 'nationalists' or 'industrial subversives' played an increasingly explicit part in training exercises.[58] In 1974 the army and the police jointly occupied London Airport and the surrounding area in four successive exercises. The real object, critical commentators concluded, was 'to accustom the public to the reality of troops deployed through the High Street'.[59] The army was also brought into industrial disputes in new ways, once to provide fire services during a firemen's strike in 1977–8, on another occasion to guard prisoners during 'industrial' action by prison warders in 1980. An organisational structure was created which would enable the army and the police, aided by a network of volunteer reserves totalling some 8–900,000, to operate independently in controlling the country. As the State Research group commented,

> Since the early 1970s, planning for war and 'emergencies' has been treated as one problem – how to maintain law and order and the status quo *inside* Britain (whatever the source of the threat). These plans have now been far advanced with little or no democratic knowledge or debate . . .[60]

The results of so many far-reaching developments were complex. Civil liberties were the most obvious casualty. In 1967 the unanimity of jury decisions had already been abandoned by a Labour Home Secretary (Jenkins) in favour of majority verdicts (ten votes out of twelve became sufficient to convict). At the same time, and unknown to the public, the prosecution began 'jury-vetting' – i.e., weeding out jurors they thought likely to be sympathetic to the accused – using police, Special Branch and MI5 intelligence records.* Justified as a measure against 'disloyal' jurors in political trials (though this justification should itself be challenged), the practice was soon extended to 'major criminal' cases. The 'Judges' Rules' governing the protection of suspects' rights during police interrogation were increasingly ignored. A disturbing volume of evidence indicated that the detention and interrogation of subjects without cautioning them or informing them of their right to communicate with a solicitor was common, that those asking to speak with a solicitor were commonly refused, and that violence was not infrequently employed. Between 1970 and 1979, 245 people died in police custody, the numbers rising in every year but one during this period; 66 of these died from 'natural causes' and 36 were suicides.[61]

Arrests for being 'suspected' of intent to commit a crime became common, especially in relation to black youths. The Police Federation was authorised to use its funds to enable policemen to sue anyone who made a false complaint against the police, while the police were left in charge of investigating such complaints and so determining their truth or falsehood. Not surprisingly, the number of complaints withdrawn rose dramatically, but not public confidence in the police.[62] Evidence obtained by illegal means was ruled juridically admissible by the courts. No controls existed over the use of the new police computers, and information was exchanged

* The familiar pattern of retreating from democracy as the franchise gradually widened to include the working class was also at work here. Rate revaluations resulting from inflation gradually lowered the property qualification for jury service, leading to an almost fivefold increase in the number of eligible people between 1955 and 1964. In 1974 property qualifications for jury service were finally abolished and all voters became eligible unless they had served a prison sentence. The police and right-wing lawyers called it a lowering of standards, just as right-wing ratepayers complained of a decline in 'councillor calibre' (see *Review of Security and the State* 1980, p. 43, and P. Kellner, 'Deemed Unfit to Serve', *New Statesman*, 2 July 1982).

between them despite earlier assurances to the contrary by the government. Cases also brought to light the fact that purely speculative and sometimes false data were held on the computers, and in other cases supposedly confidential data were found to have been given out to private individuals. Telephone tapping, bugging and camera surveillance intruded increasingly on individual privacy. No laws prohibited or regulated any of this. The 1972 Younger Report on Privacy was ignored and no action on the 1978 Lindop Report on the control of computerised data had yet been taken by the end of 1981.[63] A White Paper of 1980 on phone tapping revealed nothing, proposing a non-accountable judicial review which in practice left tapping, like mail opening, as legal and as uncontrolled as before.[64]

In 1981, following the riots, the Scarman Report recommended, as we have seen, the introduction of an 'independent element' in the procedure for complaints against the police, and the restoration of some effective links between the police and local communities. A Royal Commission on Criminal Procedure had also recommended, in 1980, changes in investigation and prosecution procedures which, while controversial, were intended to strike a 'rational balance' between the need for efficiency and the need to protect civil rights in an area that had become essentially anomic. By the end of 1981, however, it seemed likely that even on these issues, where recent events, especially the riots, had produced a substantial consensus that reforms were needed to restore civil liberties, the government would make only minimal changes, if any.* A similar consensus, that 'community policing' should be revived, was contradicted by the organisational reality of the new police forces. The chief exponent of 'community policing', John Alderson, Chief Constable of Devon and Cornwall, resigned, expressing pessimism about the prospects for change.[65]

Politically, the changes had led to a serious alienation of an important minority of the public from the police, especially among young people and blacks. As unemployment and public-spending cuts aggravated living conditions in the inner cities, it was difficult to see this situation being radically altered without major reforms which the police themselves, apparently with Home Office support, almost always opposed (and which, incidentally, the left had only belatedly advocated). As for the wider development of the 'law and order' state, it seemed very unlikely to be reversed without a radical change in the political situation. It would be

* This was notably true in relation to local democratic control of the police. A Labour MP, Jack Straw, had introduced Private Members' Bills in both 1979 and 1980 seeking to give local authorities, including the GLC, powers to give general directions to their Chief Constables on policing policy. The Conservative government proposed only to impose a statutory obligation on Chief Constables to 'consult'.

misleading to present Britain as a state primed for the suspension of the democratic process, but the extensive and largely secret reorganisation that had occurred in the police, secret police and army, and the significant erosion of civil liberties that had taken place, had unquestionably shifted the balance in the direction of social control and the capacity for repression.

PART V

15

Conclusion

Unless a solution is found to the problem of production in Britain it is obvious that the political system will be radically altered: and a solution will also require political changes no less profound. But what solution can and should be sought, and how, cannot be deduced from the trajectory of past events; nor is it the purpose of this book to provide ready-made answers to these questions. The proper aim of political enquiry is, rather, to try to grasp the underlying tendencies at work in a society, to try to shed light on what is possible and what is not.

In one sense a period of crisis implies that the options have narrowed: society cannot go on in the old way. But in another sense, wider possibilities than ever open up. One indication of this is the proliferation of alternative visions of the future such as have been appearing in Britain since the mid-1970s; and it is quite instructive to look at some of these, not as glimpses of what is likely to happen – they largely cancel each other out – but, on the contrary, as indications of the scope that exists for human agency, the challenge to men and women in Britain to make their own history as the country approaches the end of the twentieth century.

But this raises the fundamental question of the issues that are at stake in exercising the options that are open. A systematic consideration of these issues would require a text of political philosophy and ethics. In the medium run they include, as a minimum, two issues which are momentous enough: whether the problems now confronting advanced capitalist economies can be resolved under either capitalism or socialism (as it has so far been conceived), and whether democracy can be preserved while *this* question is being answered. In the final section some questions are raised which touch on these issues.

Foreseeable Futures?

Some of the 'scenarios' of Britain's future that were prompted by the crisis were acute and plausible, others were more or less apocalyptic visions intended to frighten readers into accepting the author's usually reactionary panaceas. Most of the latter date from before the 1979 election. They appealed to a rising middle-class hysteria about inflation and industrial militancy in order to enlist support for an anti-democratic programme.

In 1975, for example, Robert Moss presented a scenario of corporatism finally resulting, in 1985, in a communist state.[1] In this vision, Scotland and Northern Ireland had left the United Kingdom, while England, with Wales, had become a grey, bureaucratic and totalitarian society where individual movement was controlled and there were only two daily papers, *The British Times* and *The Morning Star*. Farms had been collectivised, and personal wealth expropriated ('inspectors from the... Ministry [of Equality] went from house to house assessing, and often impounding, paintings, furniture, jewellery and other "anti-egalitarian" possessions'), the TUC had replaced the House of Lords, and a gin-and-tonic cost £250. This state of affairs had come about because the Communists cleverly worked through the Labour Party and the trade unions, hand-picking union officials and MPs, taking advantage of the unlimited sovereignty of Parliament to legislate away freedom by apparently democratic means. They were aided by the Conservatives' loss of nerve – their failure, when returned to power in the late 1970s, to restore a market economy and curb union power; by the failure of the middle class to mobilise itself against the unions; by the failure to prevent left-wing infiltration of the police, the armed forces and 'a certain department of the Home Office'; and, in general, by the failure to take the communist threat seriously.

Moss's fantasy (as he himself called it) was, he urged, not entirely fantastic: there was a 'real enough' danger that something similar would happen by 1985, unless parliamentary sovereignty was curtailed by entrenched clauses in a Bill of Rights, and trade-union powers and the size of the state were reduced. Moreover – since 'only perennial optimists and soggy thinkers in either of the two major parties seemed [in 1975] to believe that the British crisis would be solved without a fairly momentous social confrontation' – it was necessary also to think about an authoritarian regime of the right as an alternative to, and as a lesser evil than, left-wing totalitarianism.

Anthony Burgess, writing in 1978, offered a 'remake' of Orwell's *1984* called *1985*.[2] His 'clockwork orange' society is half-recognisably still the Britain of 1978. As in Moss's nightmare, the TUC has become all-powerful, but the multinationals live, and Arab oil-interests (to whom North Sea oil has been mortgaged to pay off another IMF loan) increasingly own everything (including all the major hotels in London – Al-Dorchester, Al-Klaridges, etc.), permitting the economy to stagger on. Burgess's inflation is only the 1978 variety: according to him, in 1985 a cauliflower costs £3.10 – perhaps more unpleasantly plausible. His hero lives on the fringes of society with other 'anti-state' outcasts who refuse to conform, and eventually witnesses a crisis in which a right-wing private army with Arab backing attempts to seize power after provoking a general strike with police connivance. The situation is saved – whether permanently or not is unclear – by King Charles III, apparently dispensing with parliamentary government and skilfully exploiting nationalist and monarchist sentiment (in his Trafalgar Square speech he announces the birth of a son to the Queen – 'I think we might call him Bill').

Burgess, a novelist and critic, did not spell out the policies which in his opinion were needed to avert this scenario, though he did not leave the reader in any doubt as to who the villains were. Brian Crozier, however, a friend of Robert Moss and a fellow right-wing activist, was more than willing to fill the gap in his book *The Minimum State*, published in 1979. Crozier too offered a scenario – world-wide, for good measure: according to him, it is only a matter of time before democracy, in the shape of party politics, leads to either authoritarianism or totalitarianism everywhere. Using France as an example, Crozier imagined that instead of the Gaullists, the Socialist-Communist alliance had won the 1978 elections. A 'predominantly Marxist government would have come to power with six or seven portfolios in the hands of Communists. There would have been a programme of sweeping nationalisation, leading to a grave crisis'. The army could then be expected to take over. Crozier imagines the military coup as incomplete, however, with the unions responding by calling for a general strike, and the government appealing to the USSR for 'fraternal assistance'.

> Then one of the following alternatives would have been in prospect:
> 1. Soviet forces land at key points, counting on American apathy, and get away with it. Collapse of NATO.
> 2. Soviet intervention sparks a nuclear war.
> 3. More likely, the Soviet Union decides on balance that it is unwilling to risk war and with it, the lucrative 'detente' relationship with the United States.
> If the third alternative prevailed, the army would have its victory with the collapse of the general strike and the surrender of the ministers. Thereafter, the real question would be what to do with the successful *coup d'état*?[3]

In general, says Crozier, 'the authoritarian interlude could be used (if the strong man or woman has wisdom as well as strength) to think, and to prepare for a restoration of liberties with a suitable residue of authority to avoid a return to the inherent chaos and vulnerability of the unsatisfactory present'.[4] What he has in mind is a constitution which outlaws any extension of the state sector, forbids the raising of personal taxes above a fixed minimum, and forbids political parties to compete for office, allowing them to function only as pressure groups. Parliament would be filled from a College of Politicians selected on the basis of merit and impeccable right-wing convictions. State expenditure having been reduced to a minimum by privatising nationalised industries and dismantling the Welfare State, there would be abundant funds for increased spending on internal security, including the 'elimination of Marxist-Leninists and other extremists, whose influence on the content of [media] programmes, in Britain and other countries, is grotesquely disproportionate'.[5]

So much for the vision of the right – one would like to say the 'far right', except that many of its ideas were shared by the Thatcher wing of the Conservative Party, not to mention the armed forces, the police, and a significant segment of the middle class. With Mrs Thatcher in office and giving every indication of not being likely to lose her nerve ('the Lady's not for turning'), the need for scenarios to frighten people into the neo-liberal (or neo-Hobbesian) fold abated, temporarily at least. Now it was the turn of the left, though less colourfully.

In his remarkable book *Britain in Decline*, published in 1981, Andrew Gamble briefly contemplated a number of possible twists of an increasingly inscrutable fate. Thatcherism might be defeated by strikes and disorder, leading to the formation of a National Government (combining, presumably, Conservatives, the SDP–Liberal Alliance, and the right wing of the Labour Party):

> If armed with a clear strategy, such a government might introduce major changes. These could be in the direction of a social market economy and indeed only such a government might be able to create the political conditions for a prolonged experiment of this kind. But it is likely, given the political elements from which such a government would be formed, that it would lean towards a revival of the old modernisation strategy, of incomes policy, and of tripartism between government, industry and unions, and, if the situation were desperate enough, it might well implement parts of the alternative economic strategy, particularly controls on imports and capital movements, and direct investment in industry.[6]

But in reality,

> There are few signs that such a government would be better equipped than its predecessors to bring about modernisation and industrial recovery. What is to prevent it merely presiding over further decline and rising unemployment, since it would be caught within the same field of constraints and pressures? National governments in the past have often been excuses for inertia and reaction, and a Centre government would not necessarily be any different[7]

– an opinion shared, as we have seen (pp. 223–4), by Tom Nairn.

Alternatively, Gamble suggested, Thatcherism could survive strikes and avoid disorder but become unpopular and succumb to defeat in an election, most probably at the hands of the Liberals and Social Democrats. This would give rise to a centre government with an agenda of 'radical bourgeois policies'. Success would depend on the degree of popular support for these policies, the degree of resistance encountered, and the coherence and determination of the government.

Gamble did not rate the chances of success highly. The most lasting result might, he thought, be 'quite novel openings to the Left through the emergence of a clear socialist opposition', but he was not optimistic about this either. To be able to implement a socialist strategy a Left Labour government would need the sort of mass popular support that is only given to a government in an emergency. None the less, 'If such a national emergency did arise it seems very unlikely that the Labour Left would be entrusted with the leadership of the coalition'.[8] Somewhat more likely, was that a Left Labour government might come to power through an election, following yet another failure of 'centre' government. But the resistance to any attempt to implement the Alternative Economic Strategy would be immense, and an election victory of the kind which has formed the usual basis of recent British governments (such as the 44% of the vote won by the Conservatives in 1979) would not be enough: 'the present party and electoral system is not intended to give mandates for policies that radically challenge the existing state... but only for policies that administer it'.[9] So, such a government would need allies in the state machinery and among capitalists themselves. This would mean emptying the Alternative Economic Strategy of its socialist content and turning it into a strategy merely for saving 'national' capitalism. In any case,

> Why... should the alternative economic strategy prove any easier to implement than the social market strategy? Everything indicates that it would be more difficult.[10]

The result of failure implied in this case could only be, presumably, an authoritarian regime.[11]

Gamble offered two more scenarios, perhaps the most interesting ones in the long run. One was that,

> If the Thatcher government, aided by recovery in the world economy, moderates its policies and holds firm, then the British political system could well be stabilised under Conservative leadership for a considerable period.[12]

But this could only lead to continued industrial decline:

> Unemployment would rise more slowly and would be confined as far as possible to particular regions and disguised by ameliorative measures of all kinds. Rentier incomes from overseas investments would be steadily enlarged, trade-union membership and industrial employment would dwindle, and strong internal security forces and adequate welfare benefits would be first charges on the Exchequer to maintain reasonable stability.[13]

This 'rentier option' is plausible, if only because it is so clearly foreshadowed in the recent past, especially in the first two years of the Thatcher government. It is a scenario envisaged by Tom Nairn as well:

> Ultimately this must lead to the internationalisation of the United Kingdom economy, leaving the City-dominated, gentrified south-east as a permanent off-shore service-station for global capital, and a handy resort for itinerant capitalists... The implacable corollary of this south-eastern ascendancy is the internationalisation of the rest of the economy, the river-valley relics and their people. For a few United Kingdom monopolies (already 'internationalised' as multinationals, and producing overseas) this presents no problem. But for the others, the only viable solution is to sell out, to whichever foreign giants may be interested in opening branches here.[14]

As Nairn noted, 'Hobson saw this coming 80 years ago' (actually 90). It was in 1891, not 1981, that Hobson argued that unless measures were taken to compel British capital to continue to invest in Britain, it would eventually go elsewhere, in pursuit of cheaper labour or some other combination of circumstances permitting a higher return.

> Should we decline to protect our country against the alienation of capital... another century may see England the retreat for the old age of a small aristocracy of millionaires, who will have made their money where labour was cheapest, and return to spend it where life is pleasantest. No productive work will be possible in England, but such labour as is required for personal service will be procurable at a cheap rate... Thus, without any wild stretch of the imagination, we may look forward to a revived feudalism, in which the industrial baron will rule with that absolute sway which wealth must exercise over poverty...[15]

If then, the historical mission of the Conservatives is not to preside over the death of industrial Britain – or at least over Britain's demotion to the 'fourth division' of the international industrial league, making low value-added goods for low wages – then they must, as Gamble's final scenario suggested,

> turn... towards the full implementation of the social market strategy, starting with a major cutback in the public sector and an open confrontation with the unions... securing a new legitimacy for the market order, by compelling all individuals to relate as individuals to the market and to their work, and no longer to seek protection in collective organisation.[16]

By the middle of 1982 this was what the Thatcher wing of the party was proposing, though it was not clear that the rest of the party would agree, or that it contained a formula for economic recovery.

Questions

However illuminating, or at least entertaining, scenarios may be, they are fictions. The agenda remains always open. People do not follow a script; real life is always more complicated and surprising. Within limits, what people want always remains to be struggled for.

Even the soberest of Gamble's scenarios may be radically challenged. Is it really plausible, for example, that a thoroughgoing neo-Conservative 'social market' economic strategy could work, even if we imagine the labour movement permanently broken? Gamble suggests that

> A successful implementation of the social market strategy, pushed to the limit of destroying the power and independence of the organised working class, might eventually lay the foundations for a revival of British capitalism.[17]

The difficulty with this proposition is that it seems to assume away the complexity of the factors which in combination give rise to the lack of competitiveness of British industry. The 'market strategy' ultimately comes down to saying that competitiveness will be restored when the price of 'labour' is right. Yet it seems less and less likely that it is the 'sovereign market', which, in modern times, has produced the various 'regimes of accumulation', the particular combinations of cultural, psychological, social, organisational, technical and political forces, that have permitted certain countries at various moments in the twentieth century to compete successfully in the international market for industrial capital. One may doubt whether a British working class whose 'power and independence' had been destroyed, no better educated and less socially and politically 'competent' than now, would be the kind of workforce towards which international industrial capital would gravitate; or that managers, designers, technicians and civil servants under this dispensation would exhibit the necessary qualities of creativity and technical rationality that have been so conspicuously lacking hitherto. It seems improbable, furthermore, that the British ruling-class tradition (of which Thatcherism is no more than a late suburban variant) contains the potential to generate all these missing elements. The economic prospects for even a radical Thatcherite strategy, then, are not self-evidently good. If it were to be attempted, the prospects would be at least as good for the 'novel openings to the left' to which Gamble refers.

The Labour left's Alternative Economic Strategy, on the other hand, was also very much a strategy for economic expansion, and it too seemed to presuppose a 'productive culture' in Britain. That is, it assumed that given a larger state sector, higher investment, and more industrial democracy, the conditions would be fulfilled for a rapid expansion to which the workers, as well as managers, technicians and the rest could be expected to contribute their ingenuity, skills and enthusiasm. But generally speaking, British workers' interest in work was modest, compared with that of workers in many of Britain's major industrial competitors, for reasons some of which were mentioned earlier (see Chapters 3 and 7). In some respects this is an attractive quality. However, Shadwell's judgement of 1909 remains valid, disagreeable as it may be: 'the nation which aspires to a place in the industrial race must whirr and whiz with the best'.[18] Since the 'best' – given the nature of capitalism – are constantly improving, a left strategy for arresting Britain's industrial decline, let alone of engineering an industrial revival, cannot ignore the question of how personal motivation and technical proficiency equal to that of competing work-forces can be secured. Hitherto, the British labour movement has been primarily concerned with reducing the hours and intensity of labour, and suspicious of proposals for raising productivity, thanks to the historical resistance of British employers to sharing the rewards of increased productivity with the work-force. Transforming this outlook seems likely to prove a more difficult and protracted task for even a left-oriented development strategy than has been generally recognised.

This problem is, of course, closely related to the issue of unemployment. The trade unions' fear of labour-saving innovations was aggravated by rapidly rising unemployment, and Thatcherite propagandists made things worse by blaming unemployment on technological advance itself rather than on government policies. According to them, technological innovation would eventually create more jobs by making British firms more competitive, and by making goods cheaper and so releasing more spending power. The trouble with this argument is that it was only convincing on a national scale if most sectors of the economy as a whole could be expected to move forward rapidly to match 'best practice' elsewhere. Otherwise, it was bound to seem more certain that jobs would be lost than that new ones would be created.

So while the trade unions might be forced, by the threat of still more unemployment, to acquiesce in labour-shedding technological innovation, they were unlikely to enthuse over the prospect. What is more, one effect of justifying high unemployment in terms of the need to accept new technology was to draw attention to the basic irrationality involved. Slowly, it dawned on people that less and less work would, in fact, be needed; that science and technology had finally brought us within reach of the 'emancipation of labour' (from the need to toil for survival) foreseen by Marx and other nineteenth-century thinkers. This idea is quite subversive. It is not absurd that the result of arriving at the threshold of abundance should be a growing mass of unemployment, detested by those condemned to idleness and dependence and resented by those who 'pay for' it out of their earnings? If the way out of Britain's decline in productivity relative to other economies has to be a wave of technological innovation the essence of which would be to reduce the number of workers required, can capitalism be relied on to ensure that the result will benefit these workers?

The new right sees the danger. In order to prevent the existing order being called in question great efforts are made to preserve the illusion that the problem lies with individuals rather than social arrangements. Society is presented as being divided into two elements, one 'productive' (and *hence* employed) and 'law-abiding' (i.e., conforming), the other 'unproductive' (and *hence* unemployed), a more or less tolerable outer layer who must live on welfare 'handouts' under the eye of the police.

Peter Laurie, in the concluding chapter of the 1979 edition of his book *Beneath the City Streets*, has sketched a scenario for this, too. The full application to industry and commerce of existing micro-processor technology, he suggests,

> will split the population into two sharply divided groups: those who have intelligence or complicated manual skills that cannot be imitated by computers, and those – a much larger group, who have not. In strict economic terms, the second group will not be worth employing. They can do nothing that cannot be done cheaper by machinery. They cannot contribute their own intelligence, because the machines will have enough of their own. The working population will be reduced to a relatively small core of technicians, artists, scientists, managers, surrounded by a large, unemployed, dissatisfied and expensive mob. I would even argue that this process is much farther advanced than it seems, and the political subterfuges necessary to keep it concealed, are responsible for the economic malaise of the western nations and their galloping inflation . . . To cope with millions of unemployed and unemployable people needs – in terms of crude power – greatly improved police and security services. It demands that factories and computers should be put out of cities, preferably where they are inaccessible to the mob or the saboteur. It suggests that the unemployed should be concentrated in small spaces where they can be controlled, de-educated, penned up . . . The useless masses gravitate to decaying cities like New York: one can foresee a time when the rest of America will put barbed wire across the bridges and throw enough supplies over them to keep the mob quiet.[19]

Such a fantasy is of course as absurd as Robert Moss's. Or is it? Presumably no one in the USA, let alone in Britain, wants this. Yet the evidence is that, by 1982, policy-makers were beginning to think in these terms. 'Managing unemployment' was becoming a routine policy concern. £15 billion a year was being spent on unemployment benefit and foregone taxes. A comprehensive Youth Training scheme for all school leavers was being introduced at an annual cost of another £1.1 billion. Another scheme, costing £150 million, was being prepared to give 130,000 part-time temporary jobs to the long-term unemployed. A new programme of 'voluntary adventure training' with the armed forces had been started for 7,000 young people, and a larger scheme to combine new forms of military service with other approaches to the 'youth unemployment problem' had been mooted. The Department of the Environment none the less feared that the inner cities would become centres of chronic violence by the middle of the decade, and a conference of local government officials was reported, in June 1982, as having under serious study 'the possibility of a Britain wracked by urban devastation with unemployment topping 4.5 million and riots commonplace'.[20]

Laurie's scenario could, it seems, be the result towards which incrementally accumulating policies were tending – and who would halt the process? How, in general, did policy-makers imagine that the contradiction between the phenomenal productive capacity finally attained by capitalism, and the way in which it distributes the capacity to consume, could be resolved? Were the trade unions so wrong, after all, in suspecting that capitalism had no answer to this question?*

These reflections could be formulated in another way. Perhaps, in the final analysis, Marx was right when he argued that democracy and capitalism were fundamentally incompatible. For some time now, it has been held that this was one of his mistakes: that capitalism has the capacity to direct enough of the growing mass of surplus value – the growing volume of output in excess of subsistence needs – into the hands of the workers, so as to secure their continuing consent to capitalism. It is argued that this capacity also extends to dealing with the problem of rapidly growing unemployment due to productivity increases, not only by means of unemployment benefits but also by devices like earlier retirement, prolonging the years spent in formal education, and so on.

This argument tends to forget the decisive role played by the two world wars, both in temporarily solving the problem of over-production and in clearing the way politically for new approaches which subsequently enabled more surplus value to be transferred to the workers – i.e., Keynesianism. It is doubtful whether a third world war would serve either function. Yet, without a catastrophe, what political circumstances would permit increasing amounts of surplus to be diverted into the hands of the workers? Would these circumstances in any event seem attractive to international industrial capital? It is difficult to imagine that this would be so in Britain: much more likely, it may seem, that the outflow of capital will continue while domestic investment stagnates, so long as workers still have votes and votes have any influence on state policy – unless, that is, workers come to look at things very differently from the way they have in the past. If Marx was wrong, and capitalism and democracy are not ultimately incompatible, then they should go on voting for capitalism even through a long period of high and rising unemployment, declining real

* Laurie ends by speculating that a nuclear war, which would destroy the cities but which many of the employable minority, living and working in the rural areas, might survive, could come to seem less than totally unacceptable to policy-makers once both the superpowers were equally beset by the problem of an unemployable majority. The same line of reasoning is pursued in Giles Merritt, *World Out of Work*, Collins, London 1982.

personal incomes, declining social services and increasing inequality. To expect so much is to put great faith in the power of ideology. It is to assume that the advocates of a return to *laisser-faire* – from the theologists of the neo-conservative 'think-tanks' to the vulgar right-wing press – will be capable of keeping a majority of the population convinced that this process is inevitable, and ultimately benign.

True, the ideological achievements of the right since the 1970s have been very considerable. By 1980 the weakening, if not yet the complete destruction, of the social-democratic 'common sense' established during and after the Second World War was an accomplished fact of immense importance. But there was not yet a new 'common sense' which positively reflected the *laisser-faire*, anti-democratic philosophy of the new right. The kind of nationalistic, racist, and traditionalist populism invoked so effectively by the Conservatives in the Falklands war could be used to weaken people's attachment to social-democratic ideas; but did it contain an adequate rationale to ensure their acquiescence in the long-term re-imposition of a capitalist order based on low wages and permanent unemployment of over twelve per cent?* The middle class, who were largely unaffected, might agree, but it was doubtful if enough of the working class could be persuaded over the long run. Social reality *is* 'socially constructed' – i.e., the way things seem is a result of the way they are conceptualised – but this does not mean that it is always possible to make what is actually happening seem 'natural' to its chief victims. It still seemed unlikely that a permanent reversion to nineteenth-century values could be achieved by democratic means.

On the other hand, as Gamble pointed out, it was also unlikely that the Labour left strategy, as it stood in 1981–2, would win sufficient electoral support. This was not just because the Labour Party was divided and the crisis was not yet acute enough. It was also because of the theoretical, practical and even moral shortcomings of the ideal of 'socialism' itself. The Labour left version of socialism, as it emerged in the winter of 1981–2, revealed a clear line of tension. On the one hand, it was still quite heavily 'statist' (assigning great weight to *state* ownership, *state* spending, *state* control and *state* initiative), without indicating very clearly why the British state as it actually existed should be more successful in attaining socialist goals in the future than it had been in the past. On the other hand,

* The Falklands war brought out one of the contradictions between the different strands of Thatcherite ideology because of the contrast it demonstrated between the Conservatives' passionate attachment to the military aspect of the state, and their hostility to its civil aspect. The cost of the war, at over £1,600 million (almost £1 million for each resident of the islands), which the government met very willingly and apparently easily, was widely contrasted with the smaller cost of meeting various urgent social needs which the government declared it was 'impossible' to pay for.

it also proposed democratic changes, from abolishing the honours system and the House of Lords, to securing more 'open government' and popular control over the security forces – changes which went well beyond the old 'labourist' conception of socialism and for which the electorate was far from ready. The truth was that the meaning of 'socialism' had been put in question by the experience of the past sixty years in many countries, and this was reflected in conflicts within the Labour left's own thinking, as well as in the conflicts between left and right within the party. By 1981 there was a growing awareness of the need to re-think some of the fundamental conceptions and aims of socialism.[21] But the immensity of this task – and of the task of winning popular support for new conceptions of socialism and democracy – was still only partially perceived. Would Hegel's owl of Minerva yet again spread its wings only when night had already fallen?

A major consequence of the crisis was a widening of the gap between the experiences of the classes. The 'two nations' were again becoming as separate, for most practical purposes, as they had been when Disraeli coined the term. The gap was partly bridged by the 'new' middle classes, pulled in contradictory directions by economic pressures and aspirations, past associations and new fears, but none the less was growing wider and more ominous. Working-class life on a northern – or East London, West Midlands or South Wales – council estate, or in any inner city, was again becoming so different from middle-class life in a southern suburb or commuter village that policy made by the upper middle-classes for working-class people became ever more colonial in character. Sitting in a field on a Cotswold hillside, or contemplating a Chiltern village green, it was hard to believe that Britain might be entering an age of chronic impoverishment, repression and mediocrity. But it was a fact that Britain's past achievements had rested on a productive base that had finally started to collapse. The Thatcherite answer was to restore the law of the market, the discipline of the dole queue and the culture of commerce. All this was advanced in the name of restoring national greatness. Britain's greatness, in the past, however – its literary and artistic culture, its scientific discoveries, its heritage of architecture and landscape, its liberal political institutions and tradition of social reform – was by no means a product of such values. A true restoration would depend on the reassertion of other values, such as tolerance, fraternity, and a principled opposition to authority, to which Britain's greatness was much more profoundly due.

Epilogue

In her New Year message to the Conservative Party for 1982 Mrs Thatcher declared that the country was 'through the worst' and Treasury ministers spoke of the signs of recovery. In particular, a productivity increase of over ten per cent for the economy as a whole in 1981 was greeted as proof that the government's strategy was succeeding. By the middle of 1982, however, these claims had been abandoned. The productivity increase appeared to be largely a statistical effect of the closure of the least-productive plants and of labour-shedding, and much less due to altered work-practices for those still in work, or to new investment, which on a national basis had fallen below the level needed for capital replacement. Instead the figures showed that net capital outflow had risen to £7.5 billion in 1981 – larger than total investment in domestic manufacturing. Even the government's sympathisers began to withdraw the benefit of the doubt. On January 27 *The Times* expostulated:

> After making every allowance for economic principle and political prudence, the nagging doubt remains that the present economic reality in Britain simply does not make sense. With three million out of work, output below the level of 1974, large chunks of our industry disappearing, our cities crumbling, services deteriorating, the education and training of our children being hacked away, and the financial costs of recession actually raising government expenditure and interest rates, it is not clear that the kind of budget which is being previewed [i.e., continuing the policy of deflation] and indeed heralded as a new dawn is appropriate to the daunting task which faces our rulers. It is devastatingly clear that Britain needs massive investment, private and public, to restore its competitive strength . . .

But the Budget maintained the deflationary strategy (and the redistribution of the tax burden from the rich to the poor). Unemployment continued to increase. An opinion poll on 1 April found that only 33% of voters said they would vote Conservative, and another poll reported that 48% of the population thought that Margaret Thatcher would be remembered as the worst Prime Minister in British history.

The following day, the second of April, Argentine forces occupied the Falkland Islands. Lord Carrington, the Foreign Secretary, resigned. A military task force was assembled and despatched to the South Atlantic. Less than three months later, after more than 1,000 people had been killed, and at a cost to the Treasury of £1.6 billion, the 1,800 residents of the islands were once more subject to British rule. In economic terms it was a Pyrrhic victory. The islands were a colonial company sheep estate, surviving by paying very low wages to the indigenous workforce which was, as a result, steadily contracting (the post-war population was expected to drop to 1,000, and there were already more Falkland Islanders in Argentina than in the Falklands). To defend the islands now required a garrison of 4,000, at an estimated cost of over £400 million per annum (not counting the cost of repairing war damage, or a further £100 million which it was proposed to spend on 'economic development'). The diplomatic costs were also severe: the support obtained from the countries of the European Community had to be paid for (as became clear when the 'Luxembourg compromise' was over-ridden at Britain's expense in May), while Britain's position in Latin America deteriorated to new depths.

But in Britain the result was a dramatic reversal of the Conservatives' political fortunes. In the opinion polls support for the Conservatives rose to over 50% in June. In the local government elections held in May the Conservatives made substantial gains – unprecedented since 1945 for a government in mid-term – followed by an equally unprecedented by-election victory in Mitcham and Morden in south London.

This astonishing reversal of fortune was due to Mrs Thatcher's skilful exploitation of the issues of national sovereignty and the principle of 'self-determination' for the Falkland Islanders. Dipping deep into the well of frustrated national pride and nostalgia for a lost imperial past, the Prime Minister presented herself and her government as the defenders of freedom against tyranny, in the tradition of Churchill. Critics of the war, including Benn and a handful of Labour left MPs (and the two Plaid Cymru MPs), were vilified as traitors, as were television producers who did not identify themselves unambiguously with the cause for which 'our boys' were fighting. Military success gradually overcame an initial public reluctance to endorse the shedding of blood; and, with the final victory, the 'Falklands factor' became a formidable electoral asset. The media obsession with the war was reinforced by a succession of publicity-dramas – official visits from the Pope and President Reagan and the birth of a son to Princess Diana – followed by a series of receptions for returning heroes attended by the Prime Minister and Prince Charles: a protracted visual celebration of nation, church and crown.

To say that Conservative confidence was restored by the Falklands war would be a huge understatement. While dismissing rumours of a snap election (which the evidence suggested would produce a Conservative landslide), Thatcherite leaders talked of 'an irreversible shift in the balance of the economy, as represented by the private sector' which another Conservative victory would now make possible. The Chancellor of the Exchequer foreshadowed a policy of zero pay-increases and a new programme of privatisation including various local government functions and social services, as well as in industry.

Electoral considerations, however, dictated a more cautious approach. Having resisted any temptation to call an election in the immediate aftermath of victory Mrs. Thatcher counted instead on reaping the electoral benefits of declining inflation (it fell just below 7% by the end of the year) and on making the long-promised tax cuts in 1983. But tax cuts meant more spending cuts, and given the constantly rising burden of paying for social security for the unemployed, this meant finding more radical measures. The Central Policy Review Staff produced proposals in September for abolishing the National Health Service and replacing it by private health insurance, and for putting all higher education on a fee-paying basis. The adverse reaction led Mrs. Thatcher to make a public denial of any intention to dismantle the Health Service. Electoral calculations also led to a government decision in December to retain the British Steel Corporation mill at Ravenscraig in Scotland, postponing until 1985 the Corporation's target date for breaking even (at the cost of an estimated further subsidy of £500 million). The government did, however, press ahead with its privatisation measures. Amersham International, a medical technology firm, was sold (cheaply, as it turned out) in January for £70 million; 51% of the shares of Britoil, which owned the government's North Sea oil-producing interests, were sold in November for £550 million (this issue was seriously undersubscribed). Other large sales were planned for British Telecom and British Airways (though in the latter case it seemed that most of the airline's £1 billion debt would first have to be written off by the state).

A tough policy towards the trade unions was also succesfully maintained. The 1982 Employment Act, which outlawed political strikes, curtailed closed shop agreements and removed some of the unions' legal immunities, became law in October; and the Employment Minister, Mr. Tebbit, foreshadowed yet another Bill which would end 'contracting out' of union members from affiliation to the Labour Party (like the Trade Disputes Act of 1927), and would also require unions to ballot all their members for the election of leaders, and on strike action. Selective strikes for a 12% pay increase by nurses and ancillary health workers, starting in the spring, produced only minor concessions from the government in spite of widespread public sympathy for the nurses: as the year ended, the government's offer (by then roughly equal to the rate of inflation) was accepted. Railwaymen (in June) and the miners (in November) drew back from confrontations with the government over pay; and the 27,000-strong train drivers' union, ASLEF, was decisively defeated when it struck in July against the imposition of 'flexible rostering' (a changed distribution of working hours which implied the loss of up to a fifth of ASLEF's jobs) and failed to get the support of the National Union of Railwaymen and other unions.

The general results of the government's economic policy, however, remain unchanged. Official 'crude' unemployment figures rose to over 3.3 million by the end of the year (13.8% of the workforce); manufacturing production fell by 3.1% in the year to October 1982; and the continuing decline in competitiveness was expected to eliminate, in 1983, the current account balance of payments surplus of £6 billion achieved, thanks to oil production, in 1981. Short of an industrial revival that would now have to be considered miraculous, the respite from balance of payments constraints due to North Sea oil would, it seemed, have lasted less than a decade.

As the 'Falklands factor' receded and the economic crisis returned inexorably to the centre of attention, the Labour Party's internal divisions continued to be the main reason why persisting economic failures did not do the Conservatives as much damage as might have been expected. The Labour Leader, Michael Foot, had endorsed the decision to send the task force to the South Atlantic, while calling for a negotiated settlement. This protected the party in the short run from being labelled unpatriotic but did not enhance his reputation for realism. Meantime a special meeting of trade union and party leaders at Bishop's Stortford in January had agreed to a moratorium on leadership or deputy-leadership contests before the next general election; in return, the right wing of the party would not attempt to reverse the changes in the party constitution made the previous year. But the Conservatives' recovery after the Falklands war, which opened up the prospect of a further period of anti-union government, led to a hardening of opinion within the trade union leadership against the Labour left, whom they now began to see as the chief threat to the party's election chances. At the party's Annual Conference in October the balance of power on the National Executive committee was restored to the right wing. Tony Benn and Eric Heffer were replaced as chairmen of the NEC's policy and organisation committees and measures were endorsed to try to expel the chief activists of the Militant Tendency (including eight parliamentary candidates who had been adopted in the course of the previous year).

But the left's support in the party was not confined to constituency activists and the Conference strongly endorsed many of the policies championed by the left, including unilateral nuclear disarmament and the closing of all nuclear bases in Britain (but not a proposal to leave NATO); leaving the European Community; and implementing a strong version of the Alternative Economic Strategy. The picture was complicated, also, by the fact that the Militants, whose expulsion most of the Labour left opposed in principle (in spite of their often strong differences with them), were determined to resist; and the party had never been in greater need of the enthusiasm of its left activists. In all this Foot's leadership, even when the difficulty of his position is taken into account, was lacklustre. The party's opinion poll standing declined to around 30% and its candidates were pushed into third place by the Liberal-SDP Alliance in two by-elections.

But the Alliance was, if anything, a more significant casualty of 1982. Roy Jenkins succeeded in returning to Parliament at a March by-election in Hillhead, Glasgow, and was subsequently elected leader of the SDP by the party members in a contest with David Owen at the end of June. In the local government elections in May, however, the 'Falklands factor' operated to prevent the Alliance from cutting into the Conservative vote as it had been doing at parliamentary by-elections; its gains, more at Labour's expense, were modest. Familiarity, declining media interest, continuing differences over the share-out of parliamentary seats, and the absence of convincing policy alternatives, all took their toll. From the end of May onwards the Alliance's standing in the opinion polls stayed within the range of 23–27%; in September a Gallup poll found it as low as 20.5%, barely above the Liberals' share of the vote in the general election of February 1974. Given the volatility of opinion in the previous ten years, and the relentless pressure of the economic crisis on both Conservatives and Labour, fresh shifts in party support could be expected; but it was no longer clear that the Alliance would be their beneficiary.

References and Notes

Part I

1 British Politics and Political Science

1 H. Stretton, *The Political Sciences*, Routledge, London 1969, pp. 155–7; see also his admirable discussion of 'bias' and 'values' on pp. 412–18.
2 R. Rose, *Politics in England*, 3rd revised edition, Little, Brown, Boston 1980.
3 Ibid., Rose, p. 250.
4 Ibid., p. 42.
5 For an explicit statement of Rose's views, which have affinities with those of the 'new right', see R. Rose and G. Peters, *Can Governments Go Bankrupt?*, Sage, London 1980.
6 J. P. Mackintosh, *The Government and Politics of Britain*, Hutchinson, London, 1977.
7 Makintosh, p. 211.
8 P. Calvocoressi, *The British Experience*, Pelican Books, Harmondsworth, 1979.
9 These quotations are from pages 111–12 and 115.
10 J. Blondel, *Voters, Parties and Leaders: The Social Fabric of British Politics*, revised edition, Pelican Books, Harmondsworth 1973.
11 Blondel, p. 256.
12 'Marxist History, a History in the Making: Dialogue with Louis Althusser', *New Left Review*, **80**, 1973, pp. 104–5.
13 'Origins' was first published in *New Left Review*, **23**, 1964, pp. 26–53; the description is from Thompson, 'The Peculiarities of the English', the *Socialist Register*, 1965, p. 311.
14 The best overall introduction to the question of ideology is perhaps J. Larrain, *The Concept of Ideology*, University of Georgia Press, Athens 1979.
15 For a brilliant example of the analysis of ideology in the British context, see S. Hall et al., *Policing the Crisis*, Macmillan, London 1979.
16 E. P. Thompson, 'The Peculiarities of the English', *Socialist Register*, 1965, pp. 358–9.

2 Britain in Crisis

1 Cited by Asa Briggs in *The Age of Improvement*, Longmans, London 1959, p. 18.
2 Eric Hobsbawm, *The Age of Revolution*, Weidenfeld and Nicolson, London 1962, p. 29; see also p. 52: 'And both Britain and the world knew that the Industrial Revolution, launched in this island by and through the traders and entrepreneurs, whose only law was to buy in the cheapest market and sell without restriction in the dearest, was transforming the world. Nothing could stand in its way.'
3 See Eric Hobsbawm, *Industry and Empire*, Penguin, Harmondsworth 1969, Table 26.
4 For the general importance of the empire, especially the new empire, for the British economy at the turn of the century, see the first chapter of R. D. Wolff, *The Economies of Colonialism*, Yale University Press, New Haven 1974.

5 P. Calvocoressi, *The British Experience*, Penguin, Harmondsworth, 1979 p. 228. The reference to growth as a 'will o' the wisp' is from R. Rose, *Politics in England*, Little, Brown, Boston 1980, p. 4.
6 Bernard Nossiter, *Britain: A Future That Works*, Deutsch, London 1978, esp. pp. 191–201.
7 Malcolm Crawford in the *Sunday Times*, 20 July 1980.
8 *OECD Economic Surveys: United Kingdom*, February 1980, p. 19; *Economic Trends*, No. 214, HMSO, London December 1979, p. 77. The figure of £6.0 bn is approximate and includes the value of natural gas production as well as oil. The actual impact of oil and gas production on the balance of payments is impossible to gauge precisely because so much else would have been different if this production had not existed.
9 *Economic Trends* No. 296, HMSO, London June 1978, p. 75; *Economic Surveys: United Kingdom*, February 1980, p. 19. In 1976 a surplus was achieved in the non-oil trade balance (for the first time since 1971) so the trade deficit was wholly due to oil imports, the need for which was clearly going to be eliminated by 1981 at the latest. The flight from the pound was thus a largely speculative and political movement.
10 *Survey of Current Affairs* 9/4, May 1979, p. 130; *OECD Economic Surveys: United Kingdom*, February 1980, p. 19.
11 T. Nairn, 'The Future of Britain's Crisis', *New Left Review*, **113/114**, 1979, p. 44.
12 J. Habermas, *Legitimation Crisis*, Heinemann, London 1976. A similar general model, richly illustrated from a variety of national experiences, but especially that of the USA, is A. Wolfe, *The Limits of Legitimacy: Political Contradictions of Contemporary Capitalism*, Free Press, New York 1977.
13 A. Gramsci, *Selections from the Prison Notebooks*, (Q. Hoare and G. Nowell Smith, eds.), Lawrence and Wishart, London 1971; see esp. pp. 210, 275–6 for summaries of Gramsci's concept of crisis.
14 Gramsci, p. 276.
15 Gramsci, p. 210.
16 On profit rates see A. Glyn and B. Sutcliffe, *British Capitalism, Workers and the Profits Squeeze*, Penguin, Harmondsworth 1972, pp. 58–69.
17 Hudson Institute, *The United Kingdom in 1980: The Hudson Report*, London 1974, pp. 115–16.
18 According to a contemporary estimate by Sir James Dewar, cited in A. L. Levine, *Industrial Retardation in Britain 1880–1914*, Weidenfeld and Nicolson, London 1967, p. 71.
19 Hobsbawm, *Industry and Empire*, p. 182.
20 G. R. Searle, *The Quest for National Efficiency*, University of California Press, Berkeley 1971, pp. 73–4.
21 R. J. S. Hoffman, *Great Britain and the German Trade Rivalry 1875–1914*, University of Pennsylvania Press, Philadelphia 1933, p. 94.
22 All these quotations from the turn-of-the-century literature are from Levine, op. cit., pp. 58–9 and 73.
23 Searle, esp. pp. 80–3 and 86–92.
24 A. Peaker, *Economic Growth in Modern Britain*, Macmillan, London 1974, pp. 37–8.
25 Ibid., pp. 70–1.
26 E. Hobsbawm, *Industry and Empire*, p. 187.
27 W. A. Lewis, *Growth and Fluctuations 1870–1913*, Allen and Unwin, London 1978, p. 118.
28 Hobsbawm, *Industry and Empire*, p. 192.
29 Ibid., p. 191.
30 Ibid., p. 208.
31 Ibid., p. 218.
32 Ibid., p. 187.
33 Ibid., p. 264.
34 Ibid., p. 270.

35 Ibid., p. 270.
36 For a similar argument see M. J. Wiener, *English Culture and the Decline of the Industrial Spirit, 1850-1980*, Cambridge University Press, Cambridge, 1981, Appendix, pp. 167–70.

3 The First Crisis

1 Raphael Samuel, 'Workshop of the World', *History Workshop*, **2**, Spring 1977, p. 8 and *passim*.
2 Samuel, 'Workshop of the World', p. 21; Neil K. Buxton, *The Economic Development of the British Coal Industry*, Batsford, London 1978, p. 55; H. S. Jevons, *The British Coal Trade*, Kelley, New York 1915, p. 116.
3 Marx, *Capital*, Vol. I, Penguin, Harmondsworth 1976, p. 1,035. Marx's distinction between the 'formal' and 'real subsumption of labour under capital' is crucial to understanding the British experience; see pp. 1,019–38.
4 R. J. S. Hoffman, *Great Britain and the German Trade Rivalry, 1875-1914*, University of Pennsylvania Press, Philadelphia 1933, pp. 114 ff.
5 Cited in Hoffman, p. 97.
6 The average annual rate of growth of the stock of capital per worker for the whole economy of the UK 1870–1970 was 1.0%; the corresponding figures for other countries were France (1913–70) 2.6%; W. Germany 1.9%; Italy (1882–1970) 2.5%; Japan 2.7%; USA 1.8%; see A. Maddison, 'The Long-Run Dynamics of Productivity Growth', *Banco Nazionale del Lavoro Review*, June 1977, cited in A. Glyn and J. Harrison, *The British Economic Disaster*, Pluto Press, London 1980, p. 37.
7 On the availability of capital see W. A. Lewis, *Growth and Fluctuations 1870-1913*, Allen and Unwin, London 1978, pp. 115–16. ('There is no evidence that entrepreneurs experienced a shortage of capital in the home market'). H. W. Richardson, however, in 'Over-Commitment in Britain before 1930' (in D. H. Aldcroft and H. W. Richardson (eds.), *The British Economy 1870–1939*, Macmillan, London 1969) thinks there may have been some shortage, though not a severe one. On the psychology of industrial investment at this time see A. L. Levine, *Industrial Retardation in Britain 1880-1914*, Allen and Unwin, London 1967, pp. 122–5.
8 Lewis, pp. 123–6. 'In the mid-1930s, in boots and shoes, where British and American factories were using almost exactly the same machinery, American output per hour exceeded the British by about 80 per cent' (p. 126).
9 Lewis, p. 127.
10 Arthur Shadwell, *Industrial Efficiency*, Longmans, London 1909, p. 556.
11 P. Anderson, 'Origins of the Present Crisis', *New Left Review*, **23**, 1964, pp. 17, 26–53.
12 E. P. Thompson, 'The Peculiarities of the English', *The Socialist Register 1965*, pp. 311–62, esp. 314–30.
13 D. W. Rubinstein, 'Wealth, Elites and the Class Structure of Modern Britain', *Past and Present* **76**, August 1977, *passim*. Over a third of all millionaires who died in Britain between 1900 and 1914 made their fortunes in the City of London (p. 105).
14 T. Nairn, 'The Twilight of the British State', in *The Break-Up of Britain*, New Left Books, London 1977, esp. pp. 14–32.
15 J. Vincent, *The Formation of the British Liberal Party*, Penguin, Harmondsworth 1972, p. 113.
16 Hoffman, pp. 240–41.
17 Ibid., p. 85.
18 H. Perkin, *The Origins of Modern English Society 1780–1880*, Routledge, London 1969, pp. 225 ff.
19 On 'the gentrification of the industrialist' see M. J. Wiener's survey, *English Culture and the Decline of the Industrial Spirit 1850-1980*, Cambridge University Press, Cambridge, 1981, especially Chapters 2, 5, and 7.
20 Levine, pp. 77–8.
21 Rubinstein, loc. cit., pp. 123–4.

22 J. Foster, *Class Struggle and the Industrial Revolution*, Methuen, London 1974, chs. 6–7.
23 Quoted by Foster, p. 242.
24 Cf. G. Dangerfield, *The Strange Death of Liberal England*, London 1936.
25 Anderson, loc. cit., p. 23.

4 Labour and the New Political Order 1914–1961

1 A. Loveday, *Britain and World Trade*, Longman Green, London 1931, p. 160.
2 Loveday, pp. 170–1 (italics added).
3 E. Hobsbawm, *Industry and Empire*, Penguin, Harmondsworth 1969, p. 218.
4 B. Barker (ed.), *Ramsay MacDonald's Political Writings*, Allen Lane, London, 1972, p. 93.
5 J. Leruez, *Economic Planning and Politics in Britain*, Robertson, London 1973, p. 201.
6 I. Gough, *The Political Economy of the Welfare State*, Macmillan, London 1979, p. 79.
7 J. Westergaard and H. Resler, *Class in a Capitalist Society*, Heinemann, London 1975, p. 66.
8 A. Glyn and B. Sutcliffe, *British Capitalism, Workers and the Profits Squeeze*, Penguin, Harmondsworth 1972, p. 66, Table 33.
9 *National Institute Economic Reviews*, Statistical Appendices.
10 S. Brittan, *Steering the Economy*, Penguin, Harmondsworth 1964, p. 493.

5 The Paralysis of Social Democracy 1961–1970

1 P. Townsend, *Poverty in the United Kingdom*, Penguin, Harmondsworth 1979, p. 273. An even larger proportion were poor, or on the 'margin' of poverty, by the state's own poverty-line criteria.
2 D. Robinson, 'Labour Market Policies', in W. Beckerman (ed.), *The Labour Government's Economic Record*, Duckworth, London 1972, p. 313, Table 9. 1.
3 S. Holland, *The Socialist Challenge*, Quartet Books, London 1975, pp. 49–50. Holland cites a forecast that by 1985 the proportion would be 66%.
4 Holland, p. 76.
5 'Ninety-four firms account for half Britain's exports', *British Business*, 3 July 1981, Table 3.
6 Holland, pp. 77–8.
7 A list of the sources for these views in the sixties and seventies would be very long. Early examples are H. Thomas (ed.), *The Establishment*, Blond, London 1959; B. Chapman, *British Government Observed*, Allen and Unwin, London 1963; M. Shanks, *The Stagnant Society*, Penguin, Harmondsworth 1961; M. Nicholson, *The System*, Hodder and Stoughton, London 1967.
8 R. Bacon and W. Eltis, *Britain's Economic Problem: Too Few Producers*, Macmillan, London 1976.
9 Central Policy Review Staff, *The Future of the British Car Industry*, HMSO, London 1970, p. 83.
10 J. H. Dunning, 'US Subsidiaries in Britain and their UK Competitors', *Business Ratios* No. 1, Autumn 1966.
11 See especially T. Nairn, 'The English Working Class', *New Left Review*, **24**, March–April 1964, pp. 43–57, and 'The Nature of the Labour Party', in P. Anderson and R. Blackburn, *Towards Socialism*, Fontana, London 1967, pp. 159–217.
12 Quoted in A. Sked and C. Cook, *Post-War Britain*, Penguin, Harmondsworth 1979, p. 207.
13 D. Butler and A. Sloman, *British Political Facts 1900–1979*, Macmillan, London 1980, p. 253.
14 V. Bognador and R. Skidelsky, *The Age of Affluence*, Macmillan, London 1970, p. 10.
15 R. Opie, 'Economic Planning and Growth', in W. Beckerman (ed.), *The Labour Government's Economic Record*, pp. 174–5.
16 Opie, loc. cit., p. 177.
17 On price controls see L. Panitch, *Social Democracy and Industrial Militancy*, Cambridge

University Press, Cambridge 1976, pp. 129, 160 and 210; on dividend controls see pp. 114, 140 and 154.
18 B. Chapman, *British Government Observed*, Allen and Unwin, London 1963, p. 56.

6 Into the New Crisis

1 A. Gamble, *The Conservative Nation*, Routledge and Kegan Paul, London 1974, p. 91.
2 D. Butler and A. Sloman, *British Political Facts*, Macmillan, London 1980, p. 254.
3 *The Times*, 8 June 1973.
4 1971 Labour Party Conference Report.
5 On the operation of the IMF see Cheryl Payer, *The Debt Trap*, Penguin, Harmondsworth 1974.
6 See A. Glyn and J. Harrison, *The British Economic Disaster*, Pluto Press, London 1980, p. 121 for an analysis of the figures.
7 See D. J. Smith, *Racial Disadvantage in Britain*, Penguin, Harmondsworth 1977.
8 Notably S. Hall in 'The Great Moving Right Show', *Marxism Today*, January 1979, pp. 14–20; and 'Thatcherism – A New Stage?', *Marxism Today*, February 1980, pp. 26–8.
9 The evidence is summarised by P. Kellner in *Slump '82*, NS Report 6, London 1982, pp. 26–33; see also F. Field, 'The Missing Half Million', *The Times*, 28 January 1982. The Manpower Services Commission broadly accepted the arguments; see *The Times*, 4 February 1982.
10 See e.g., the *Economist*, 4 April 1981, pp. 47–52; or the leading article in *The Times*, 27 January 1982.
11 Kellner, pp. 38–46.
12 That is, not counting Professor Minford's 'Liverpool' model. The next most optimistic was that of the London Business School; see *The Times*, 14 March 1982.
13 See Chapter 14, pp. 299 ff.; and E. P. Thompson, *Writing By Candlelight*, Merlin Press, London 1980, and M. Kettle, 'The Drift to Law and Order', *Marxism Today*, October 1980. pp. 20–7.

Part II

7 Capital and Labour

1 T. Nichols and P. Armstrong, *Workers Divided*, Fontana, London 1976, p. 56.
2 S. G. E. Lythe, 'Britain, the Financial Capital of the World', in C. J. Bartlett (ed.), *Britain Pre-Eminent*, Macmillan, London 1969, pp. 40–1.
3 E. P. Thompson, *The Making of the English Working Class*, Penguin, Harmondsworth, London 1968.
4 S. Aaronovitch *et al.*, *The Political Economy of British Capitalism*, McGraw-Hill, London 1981, p. 267.
5 *Economic Trends*, Supplement 1981, p. 172, and *Business Monitor*, May 1979, p. 85.
6 Lythe, loc. cit., p. 33.
7 F. Longstreth, 'The City, Industry and the State', in C. Crouch (ed.), *State and Economy in Contemporary Capitalism*, St Martins Press, New York 1979, p. 171.
8 The CBI's Discussion Document, *The Will to Win* published in March 1981 could be regarded as an eleventh-hour attempt to outline an economic policy needed for industrial recovery, but it lacked a serious political dimension.
9 C. Crouch, *The Politics of Industrial Relations*, Fontana, London 1979, p. 157.
10 Crouch, pp. 147–8.
11 Longstreth, 'The City', p. 188.
12 Crouch, p. 142.
13 See *Review of Security and the State 1978*, Julian Friedmann, London 1978, pp. 135–45, for an article on the Economic League in which this estimate is cited.
14 See T. Nichols, 'Social Class: Official, Sociological and Statistical', in J. Irvine *et al.*, (eds.), *Demystifying Social Statistics*, Pluto Press, London 1979, pp. 158–9.
15 On this point, see J. Westergaard and H. Resler, *Class in a Capitalist Society*, Heinemann, London 1975, pp. 291–6.

16 T. Nichols and H. Beynon, *Living with Capitalism*, Routledge, London 1977, p. 200; see also H. Beynon, *Working for Ford*, Allen Lane, London 1973 and T. Nichols and P. Armstrong, *Workers Divided*, Fontana, London 1976.

17 E. J. Hobsbawm, 'General Unions in the British Labour Movement', in *Labouring Men*, Weidenfeld and Nicolson, London 1964, p. 181.

18 The Royal Commission on Trade Unions and Employers' Associations *Report*, HMSO, London 1968; Hyman, however, thought that there were about 200,000 (R. Hyman, *Strikes*, Fontana, London 1972, p. 45).

19 H. Beynon, *Working for Ford*, p. 145.

20 Hyman, pp. 33–4. It is also relevant that workers in most EEC countries tend to have longer holidays, besides working shorter hours, than British workers.

21 C. T. B. Smith *et al.*, *Strikes in Britain: Manpower Paper No. 15*, Department of Employment, London 1978, p. 139.

22 R. Maybin, 'NALGO: The New Unionism of Contemporary Britain', *Marxism Today*, January 1980, p. 17; J. Gardiner in S. Aaronovitch *et al.*, *Political Economy*, p. 332; A. Coote and B. Campbell, *Sweet Freedom*, Picador, London 1982, p. 78: on the unions and women generally, see ibid., Chapter 5.

23 R. Miliband, *The State in Capitalist Society*, Weidenfeld and Nicolson, London 1969, Chapter 6, 'Imperfect Competition'.

24 Certification Office for Trade Unions and Employers' Associations, *Annual Report of the Certification Officer 1979*, p. 49. The total was £269.9 million. The total political funds of the unions at the end of 1979 were £4.5 million.

25 P. Anderson, 'The Limits and Possibilities of Trade Union Action', in R. Blackburn and A. Cockburn (eds.), *The Incompatibles: Trade Union Militancy and the Consensus*, Penguin, Harmondsworth 1967, pp. 263–80, reprinted in T. Clarke and L. Clements (eds.), *Trade Unions Under Capitalism*, Fontana, London 1977, pp. 334–50.

26 Glasgow University Media Group, *Bad News* and *More Bad News*, Routledge, London 1976 and 1980.

27 *NOP Bulletin*, March 1969, and the *Economist*, 10 January 1976, reporting a MORI survey.

8 Social Classes and British Politics

1 See R. T. McKenzie and A. Silver, *Angels in Marble*, Heinemann, London 1968, pp. 167–8.

2 The common procedure is to note the 'looseness' of ordinary usage of the term 'class' and then to discuss how it can be made more exact, concluding with the adoption of occupation as the indicator closest to popular usage: see e.g., R. Rose, *Politics in England* (3rd edition), Little Brown, Boston 1980, pp. 156 ff, and J. Blondel, *Voters, Parties and Leaders* (revised edition), Penguin, Harmondsworth 1974, pp. 26 ff.

3 Asa Briggs, 'The Language of "Class" in Early Nineteenth-Century England', in A. Briggs and J. Saville (eds.), *Essays in Labour History*, Macmillan, London 1967, pp. 43–73, and especially pp. 52 ff.

4 W. S. Churchill, *Lord Randolph Churchill*, Odhams, London 1951, p. 565.

5 T. Nichols, 'Social Class: Official, Sociological and Marxist' in J. Irvine *et al* (eds.), *Demystifying Social Statistics*, Pluto Press, London 1979, p. 158.

6 Nichols, loc. cit., p. 159.

7 See e.g., D. Butler and S. Stokes, *Political Change in Britain* (Second College Edition), St Martin's Press, New York 1976, pp. 44–9.

8 V. I. Lenin, 'A Great Beginning' in *Selected Works* Vol II, Foreign Languages Publishing House, Moscow 1947, p. 492.

9 Nichols, loc. cit., p. 165.

10 A. Giddens, *Class Structure of the Advanced Societies*, Hutchinson, London 1973, Chapter 6.

11 Lenin, 'What Is To Be Done?', *Selected Works* Vol I, pp. 167–77.

12 A. Przeworski, 'Proletariat into a Class', *Politics and Society*, 7/4, 1977, pp. 343–401.

13 A. Przeworski, 'The Material Bases of Consent: Economics and Politics in a Hegemonic System', *Political Power and Social Theory*, 1979, p. 133.
14 K. Marx and F. Engels, 'The Manifesto of the Communist Party', in *The Revolutions of 1848*, (ed. D. Fernbach), Penguin, Harmondsworth 1973, p. 80.
15 Giddens, pp. 107 and 110.
16 E. O. Wright, *Class, Crisis and the State*, New Left Books, London 1978, Chapter 2.
17 G. Carchedi, *On the Economic Identification of Social Classes*, Routledge, London 1977.
18 H. Braverman, *Labour and Monopoly Capital*, Monthly Review Press, New York 1974.
19 J. Lindsey, 'The Conceptualisation of Social Class', *Studies in Political Economy*, **3**, 1980, pp. 17–36. For a similar argument see also B. and J. Ehrenreich, 'The Professional-Managerial Class', in P. Walker (ed.), *Between Labour and Capital*, Black Rose Books, Montreal 1978, pp. 5–45.
20 N. Poulantzas, *Classes in Contemporary Capitalism*, New Left Books, London 1975, esp. pp. 209–223.
21 Butler and Stokes, p. 63. 'Middle Class' here refers to the way people described their own class membership.
22 J. Westergaard and H. Resler, *Class in a Capitalist Society*, Heinemann, London 1975. Westergaard's early critique is in 'The Withering away of Class', in P. Anderson and R. Blackburn (eds.), *Towards Socialism*, Fontana, London 1965, pp. 77–113.
23 'Even in the presumably very favourable context of a period of sustained economic growth and of major change in the form of the occupational structure, the general underlying processes of intergenerational class mobility – or immobility – have apparently been little altered, and indeed have, if anything, tended in certain respects to generate still further inequalities in class chances.' J. H. Goldthorpe, *Social Mobility and Class Structure in Modern Britain*, Clarendon Press, Oxford 1980, p. 85. The evidence is summarised in Table 2.3 on pp. 60–1.
24 Westergaard and Resler, *Class in a Capitalist Society*, Part Two, Chapters 5 and 6.
25 Giddens, p. 171.
26 K. Coates and R. Silburn, *Poverty: The Forgotten Englishmen*, Penguin, Harmondsworth 1981, pp. 259–60, and *Social Trends* 1979, p. 112. Using the 'deprivation standard' of poverty Peter Townsend put the number living in poverty at 12.4 m or 23% in 1968–9 (*Poverty in the United Kingdom*, University of California Press, Berkeley 1979, pp. 301–2).
27 The seminal article on this is E. J. Hobsbawm, 'The Forward March of Labour Halted?', *Marxism Today* September 1978, pp. 279–86, reprinted in the book of the same title edited by M. Jacques and F. Mulhern, Verso Books, London 1981. See also J. Clarke, 'Capital and Culture: the post-war working class revisited', in J. Clarke *et al.*, (eds.), *Working Class Culture*, Hutchinson, London 1979, pp. 238–53.
28 *Social Trends 1979*, HMSO, London 1979, p. 15.
29 H. Stephenson, *Mrs Thatcher's First Year*, Jill Norman, London 1980, p. 22.
30 I. Crewe, 'Do Butler and Stokes Really Explain Political Change in Britain?', *European Journal of Political Research*, **2**, 1974, pp. 47–92.
31 G. Bourque, 'Class, Nation and the Parti-Quebecois', *Studies in Political Economy*, **2**, 1979, p. 130.
32 A. M. Schlesinger, Jr., *The Age of Roosevelt* Vol III, Heinemann, London 1961, p. 273, cited in G. Thexborn, *What Does the Ruling Class Do When It Rules?*, New Left Books, London 1978, p. 148.
33 Przeworski, 'Social Democracy as a Historical Phenomenon', *New Left Review*, **122**, 1980, p. 58.
34 See e.g., C. Offe, 'The Separation of Form and Content in Liberal Democratic Politics', *Studies in Political Economy*, **3**, 1980, pp. 5–16.
35 See E. Laclau, 'Democratic Antagonisms and the Capitalist State', paper presented to the ECPR Conference, Brussels, April 1979.
36 On Gramsci's theory, see especially C. Mouffe, 'Hegemony and Ideology in Gramsci', in Mouffe (ed.), *Gramsci and Marxist Theory*, Routledge, London 1979, pp. 168–204.

37 S. Hall, 'The Great Moving Right Show', *Marxism Today* January 1980, pp. 14–20; see also his 'Thatcherism – a New Stage?', *Marxism Today* February 1980, pp. 26–29.
38 A. Coote and B. Campbell, *Sweet Freedom*, Picador, London 1982, Chapter 4.
39 See G. Stedman-Jones, 'Marching into History?', *New Socialist*, **3**, 1982, pp. 10–15.
40 S. Boston, *Women Workers and the Trade Unions*, Davis-Poynter, London 1980, pp. 284–5.
41 B. Campbell, 'Women: Not What they Bargained for', *Marxism Today* March 1982, p. 18.
42 M. Prior and D. Purdy, *Out of the Ghetto*, Spokesman, Nottingham 1979, p. 97.

Part III

9 The Conservative Party

1 N. Harris, *Beliefs in Society*, Penguin, Harmondsworth 1968, p. 99.
2 R. Rose, *The Problem of Party Government*, Penguin, Harmondsworth 1976, p. 309.
3 S. Beer, *Modern British Politics*, Faber, London 1965, pp. 249–51 ff.
4 F. Boyd, *British Politics in Transition 1945-63*, Praeger, New York 1964, p. 760. R. Behrens (in *The Conservative Party from Heath to Thatcher*, Saxon House, Farnborough 1980), comments that while controversy raged between the radical right and the pragmatists in the party leadership, 'there was little disagreement . . . about the importance of the rule of law, wealth and property, and aspects of Conservative policy governed by these immutable glories changed hardly at all' (p. 126).
5 Cited in A. Gamble, *The Conservative Nation*, Routledge and Kegan Paul, London 1974, p. 116.
6 Rose, p. 57.
7 N. Harris, *Competition in a Corporate Society: British Conservatives, the State and Industry 1945-1964*, Methuen, London 1972, p. 259.
8 Gamble, *The Conservative Nation*, Chapter I. Gamble's formulation is more sophisticated, though perhaps somewhat less clear, than the summary presented here.
9 Gamble, p. 5.
10 Gamble himself was momentarily deceived in this respect: see his 'The Conservative Party' in H. M. Drucker (ed.), *Multi-Party Britain*, Macmillan, London 1979, p. 43.
11 Gallup poll reported in *The Times*, 18 December 1981.
12 J. Blondel, *Voters, Parties and Leaders*, Penguin, Harmondsworth 1974, pp. 96 ff and 130 ff.
13 Blondel, p. 135.
14 A. H. Birch, Small-Town Politics, Oxford University Press, Oxford 1959. *The report of the Houghton Committee on Financial Aid to Political Parties* (Cmnd. 6601, 1979), estimated that in 1975 the Conservatives had about $1\frac{1}{2}$ million members.
15 Mrs Thatcher's government of 1979 had 86 MPs and 21 peers in paid government posts, and 20 unpaid Parliamentary Secretaries. These powers, of course, are equally enjoyed by a Labour Leader.
16 This was first pointed out by R. McKenzie in *British Political Parties*, Praeger, New York, Revised Edition 1963.
17 P. Willis, *Learning to Labour*, Saxon House, Farnborough 1978.
18 P. Willis, *Profane Culture*, Routledge and Kegan Paul, London 1978.
19 See Blondel, p. 79.
20 Harris, *Competition in a Corporate Society*, p. 264.
21 J. Ramsden, 'The Changing Base of British Conservatism' in C. Cook and J. Ramsden (eds.), *Trends in British Politics Since 1945*, Macmillan, London 1978, pp. 28–46.
22 A. Gamble and P. Seyd, 'Conservative Ideology and Electoral Strategy in Britain Since 1964', paper presented to the European Consortium for Political Research, April 1979, mimeo, p. 12.
23 Harris, p. 260.
24 W. Grant and D. Marsh, *The Confederation of British Industry*, Hodder and Stoughton, London 1977, pp. 89–90, and CBI Annual Reports.

25 Gamble, 'The Conservative Party', loc. cit., pp. 44–5.
26 N. Nugent, 'The National Front' in N. Nugent and R. King, *The British Right*, Saxon House, London 1977, p. 183. In October 1974 the National Front ran 90 candidates.
27 Ramsden, 'The Changing Base of British Conservatism', loc. cit., p. 43.

10 The Labour Party and the Left

1 Shirley Williams's victory at Crosby in November 1981; by the end of 1982 a further by-election and two more defections brought the total of SDP MPs to 30: see Chapter 11.
2 R. Miliband, *Parliamentary Socialism*, Merlin Press, London 1973, p. 62.
3 H. Pelling, *A Short History of the Labour Party*, Macmillan, London 1965, pp. 19–20.
4 W. Kendall, *The Revolutionary Movement in Britain*, Weidenfeld and Nicolson, London 1969, p. 6.
5 This figure was well below the total number of TGWU members who actually paid the political levy, and substantially below the total membership affiliated to the TUC. Big unions often under-declared their affliated membership to the party, partly so as to be free to use part of their political funds for other political purposes. On the history of the block vote see L. Minkin, 'Politics of the block vote', *New Socialist*, Sept–Oct 1981, pp. 52–6.
6 This was the minimum of delegates which any constituency could declare affiliated in 1980. Estimates for the 1970s suggest an average constituency affiliation of perhaps 500. See L. Minkin, *The Labour Party Conference*, Manchester University Press, Manchester 1980, p. 87; G. Hodgson, *Labour at the Crossroads*, Martin Robertson, Oxford 1981, p. 56.
7 About a third of all Labour MPs have been 'sponsored' by trade unions in the post-1945 period: see D. Butler and A. Sloman, *British Political Facts* (fifth edition), Macmillan, London 1980, p. 146.
8 H. M. Drucker, *Doctrine and Ethos in the British Labour Party*, Allen and Unwin, London 1979, Chapter 1.
9 Drucker, p. 120.
10 Ibid., pp. 106–7.
11 See Miliband, pp. 276–78, on how the party Conference had to force an unwilling parliamentary leadership to adopt the 1945 programme of nationalisation.
12 McKenzie, *British Political Parties* (second edition), Heinemann, London 1964.
13 Minkin, p. 326.
14 See e.g., Minkin, p. 21.
15 Miliband, p. 214.
16 Miliband, Postscript to the 1972 edition of *Parliamentary Socialism*. He also reaffirmed this conclusion in 'Moving On', *Socialist Register 1976*, pp. 128–40.
17 D. Coates, *The Labour Party and the Struggle for Socialism*, Cambridge University Press, Cambridge 1975, p. 214.
18 L. Minkin and P. Seyd, 'The British Labour Party', in W. E. Paterson and A. H. Thomas (eds.), *Social Democratic Parties in Western Europe*, Croom Helm, London 1977, p. 132.
19 Minkin, pp. 274–7.
20 Miliband, *Parliamentary Socialism*, p. 375.
21 The most affected unions were hostile to proposals to nationalise banks and insurance companies in 1976–78 (see L. Panitch 'Socialists and the Labour Party: A Reappraisal', *Socialist Register 1979*, pp. 69–70). The electricians' union also killed a sacred cow by signing an industrial agreement in 1979 which provided private medical services for its members.

22 Coates, p. 133.
23 Miliband, *Parliamentary Socialism*, p. 376.
24 R. Dowse, *Left in the Centre*, Longman, London 1966, p. 206, and G. Thayer, *The British Political Fringe*, Blond, London 1965, p. 169.
25 The most notable exception to this, prior to the new infusion of left intellectuals in the 1970s, was Anthony Crosland's *The Future of Socialism*, Cape, London 1956, which set out the philosophy of 'revisionism'.
26 R. Miliband, 'Moving On', *Socialist Register 1976*, p. 137.
27 The modern extra-parliamentary left in Britain has not been adequately studied. Useful sources may be found in the contributions to the debate on the future of the left in the *Socialist Register 1978*; a typical example of the 'counter-subversion' literature is B. Baker, *The Far Left*, Weidenfeld and Nicolson, London 1981.
28 The name was changed from the International Socialists to Socialist Workers Party at this time. See M. Shaw, 'The Making of a Party', *Socialist Register 1978*, pp. 100–45; also I. H. Birchall, 'The Premature Burial: A Reply to Martin Shaw', *Socialist Register 1979*, pp. 26–50.
29 The *New Left Review*, the most widely read and accomplished left-wing theoretical journal in English, was the work of intellectuals more or less close to the IMG.
30 See M. Rustin, 'The New Left and the Present Crisis', *New Left Review*, **121**, 1980, pp. 63–89.
31 The best formulation of this thesis from within the Labour Left is Ken Coates, 'Socialists and the Labour Party', *Socialist Register 1973*, pp. 155–78. See also G. Hodgson, *Socialism and Parliamentary Democracy*, Spokesman Books, Nottingham 1971, and *Labour at the Crossroads*, Martin Robertson, Oxford 1981; and M. Rustin, 'Different Conceptions of Party: Labour's Constitutional Debates', *New Left Review*, **126**, 1981, pp. 17–42.
32 Miliband, 'Moving On', p. 131; and D. Coates, 'Labourism and the Transition to Socialism', *New Left Review*, **129**, 1981, pp. 3–22.
33 For a vivid formulation of this argument see L. Panitch, 'Socialists and the Labour Party: A Reappraisal' (note 21 above).
34 But see, e.g., M. Prior and D. Purdy, *Out of the Ghetto*, Spokesman, Nottingham 1979; M. Prior (ed.), *The Popular and the Political*, Routledge and Kegan Paul, London 1981; H. Wainwright and S. Rowbotham, *Beyond the Fragments: Feminism and the Making of Socialism*, Merlin, London 1980; and the articles collected in the series *Politics and Power*, Routledge and Kegan Paul, London 1979–81.

11 Beyond the Two-Party System?

1 For an introduction to the politics of Northern Ireland see L. de Paor, *Divided Ulster*, Penguin, Harmondsworth 1970; R. Rose, *Northern Ireland: A Time of Choice*, Macmillan, London 1976; M. Farrell, *Northern Ireland, the Orange State*, Pluto Press, London 1976; B. Probert, *Beyond Orange and Green*, Zed Press, London 1978; P. Bew *et al.*, *The State in Northern Ireland: Political Forces and Social Classes*, Manchester University Press, Manchester 1979; and L. O'Dowd, *Northern Ireland: Between Civil Rights and Civil War*, CSE Books, London 1980.
2 M. Steed, 'The Liberal Party', in H. M. Drucker (ed.), *Multi-Party Britain*, Macmillan, London 1979, p. 84.
3 P. Olive, 'Realignment: The Case of the Liberals', *Marxism Today*, May 1981, p. 14.
4 Steed, loc. cit., p. 105.
5 Olive, loc. cit., pp. 16–17.
6 Steed, loc. cit., p. 86.
7 Ibid., pp. 89–90.
8 A. Cyr, *Liberal Party Politics in Britain*, Calder, London 1977, pp. 247–8.
9 Olive, loc. cit., p. 17.
10 For an insight into this milieu see A. Stephen, 'The Kicking, Squealing Birth-Pangs of the SDP', *Sunday Times Magazine*, 27 September 1981.

11 I. Bradley, *Breaking the Mould? The Birth and Prospects of the Social Democratic Party*, Martin Robertson, Oxford 1981, p. 157. Or, as C. Husbands put it, 'there are numerous voters who wish or hope that there is a political Santa Claus' ('The Politics of Confusion', *Marxism Today*, February 1982, p. 12).
12 D. Currie, 'SDP: A Prop for Profits', *New Socialist*, **4**, March–April 1982, pp. 9–11.
13 Bradley, pp. 155–9.
14 This thesis is argued persuasively in T. Nairn, *The Break-Up of Britain*, New Left Books, London 1977, Chapter 9, 'The Modern Janus'.
15 J. Osmond, *Creative Conflict: The Politics of Welsh Devolution*, Routledge and Kegan Paul, London 1977, p. 92.
16 H. M. Drucker and G. Brown, *The Politics of Nationalism and Devolution*, Longman, London 1980, pp. 35–6, 49–50.
17 The foregoing sketch is intended to provide only the barest account of the background to the rise of the nationalist parties, and makes no pretence to do justice to the complexity of Scottish or Welsh nationalism. The literature on both nationalisms, but especially the Welsh, has lagged behind their development. For recent studies of Wales see the references in Gwyn Williams's savage survey, 'Mother Wales, Get Off Me Back?', *Marxism Today*, December 1981, pp. 14–20.
18 J. Brand, 'From Scotland With Love', in I. Kramnick (ed.), *Is Britain Dying?*, Cornell University Press, Ithaca, New York 1978, p. 182.
19 J. Kellas, *The Scottish Political System* (second edition), Cambridge University Press, Cambridge 1975, p. 127.
20 Kellas, pp. 128, 131.
21 R. Mullin, 'The Scottish National Party', in Drucker, *Multi-Party Britain*, p. 126, quoting an SNP policy document of 1977.
22 Osmond, pp. 115–30, esp. p. 124.
23 D. Balson, 'Plaid Cymru', in Drucker *Multi-Party Britain*, p. 134.
24 For a survey of the economic decline see A. Butt-Philip, *The Welsh Question*, University of Wales Press, Cardiff 1975, Chapters 2–3, and the references referred to in note 17 above.
25 Butt-Philip, pp. 158–9; the data, however, refer to the late 1960s.
26 Ibid., p. 168.
27 Osmond, p. 94, quoting B. Khleif.
28 Drucker and Brown, *The Politics of Nationalism*, p. 44.
29 On the SDP's philosophical claims, and the reality of their politics, see R. Samuel, 'Tawney and the SDP', the *Guardian*, March 29 and April 5 1982.
30 Cyr, pp. 239–40.
31 Drucker and Brown, p. 12.
32 Bradley, p. 137.
33 T. Nairn, 'The Future of Britain's Crisis', *New Left Review*, **113–114**, January–April 1979, p. 62.
34 Nairn, loc. cit., p. 66.
35 See e.g., R. A. Pois, *The Bourgeois Democrats of Weimar Germany*, Transactions of the American Philosophical Society, Vol. 66, Part 4, 1976. Reasons for expecting SDP policies to be inflected to the right under the pressure of events in office are advanced in D. Currie, 'SDP: A Prop for Profits' (note 12 above).

12 The British State

1 N. Poulantzas, *Political Power and Social Classes*, published in English by New Left Books, London 1969; R. Miliband, *The State in Capitalist Society*, Weidenfeld and Nicolson, London 1969.
2 N. Poulantzas, *State, Power, Socialism*, New Left Books, London 1978.
3 Especially his essay 'The Twilight of the British State' (Chapter 1 of Nairn's book *The Break-Up of Britain*, New Left Books, London 1977).
4 Nairn, p. 45.

5 Nairn's thesis has been subjected to extensive criticism on general theoretical grounds; some of the criticism is justified, though without (to my mind) destroying the main force of his hypotheses. See R. Johnson, 'Barrington Moore, Perry Anderson and English Social Development' in S. Hall *et al.*, (eds.), *Culture, Media, Language*, Hutchinson, London 1980, pp. 48–70.
6 K. B. Smellie, *A Hundred Years of English Government*, Duckworth, London 1950, pp. 162, 328.
7 Sir Robert Morant, author of the 1902 Education Act, cited in J. Harvey and K. Hood, *The British State*, Lawrence and Wishart, London 1958, p. 94.
8 Harvey and Hood, p. 191. Similar sentiments among senior officials are recorded in Smellie, pp. 71–74.
9 K. Hutchison, *The Decline and Fall of British Capitalism*, Cape, London 1951, p. 78.
10 Smellie, p. 169.
11 R. K. Kelsall, 'Recruitment to the Higher Civil Service: How Far Has the Pattern Changed?', in P. Stanworth and A. Giddens, *Elites and Power in British Society*, Cambridge University Press, Cambridge 1974, pp. 179–80.
12 Kelsall, loc. cit., p. 180.
13 *The Times*, 25 and 31 March 1905.
14 See the *Eleventh Report from the Expenditure Committee 1976–77: The Civil Service* and *The Civil Service: Government Observations on the Eleventh Report from the Expenditure Committee*, Cmnd 7117, 1978. See also P. Kellner and N. Crowther-Hunt, *The Civil Servants*, MacDonald, London 1980, Chapters 4, 5 and 12; and B. Sedgemore, *The Secret Constitution*, Hodder and Stoughton, London 1980, Chapter 6.
15 A request for information on the educational background of officers commissioned into the armed forces was refused by the Ministry of Defence on the grounds that it would not be meaningful.
16 S. Raven, 'Perish by the Sword', in H. Thomas (ed.), *The Establishment*, Blond, London 1959, pp. 49–79.
17 C. B. Otley, 'The Public Schools and the Army', in J. Urry and J. Wakeford, *Power in Britain*, Heinemann, London 1973, p. 241.
18 J. A. G. Griffith, *The Politics of the Judiciary* (second edition). Fontana, London 1981, p. 30.
19 P. Bellaby, *The Sociology of Comprehensive Schooling*, Methuen, London 1977, pp. 44–5.
20 J. Ford, *Social Class and the Comprehensive School*, Routledge and Kegan Paul, London 1969. After the initial changeover a decline in 'streaming' was reported by the schools inspectorate, but by the end of the 1970s it was increasing again.
21 Ford, p. 120.
22 See Chapter 8, note 23.
23 A. Gramsci, *Selections from the Prison Notebooks*, Lawrence and Wishart, London 1971, p. 238.
24 See e.g., J. Blondel, *Voters, Parties and Leaders*, revised edition, Penguin, Harmondsworth 1977, Chapter 9.
25 For example, in 1967 the proportion of higher civil servants whose fathers had been manual workers was only 17%. At the highest levels the proportion was probably smaller still, as many of the sons of manual workers were men who had been internally promoted and such promotees rarely attained the most senior ranks. See Kelsall, 'Recruitment', (note 11).
26 A. Sampson, *The New Anatomy of Britain*, Hodder and Stoughton, London 1971, p. 132. The portrait needs updating to recognise the later tendency of many public schools to admit girls into their sixth forms.
27 H. Glennerster and R. Pryke, 'Born to Rule', in Urry and Wakeford, *Power in Britain*, p. 221.
28 Upton and Wilson and Whitley looked at the first three of these. The others have been largely neglected.
29 N. Poulantzas, 'The Problem of the Capitalist State', *New Left Review*, **58**, 1969, pp.

67–8; R. Miliband, 'Nicos Poulantzas and the Capitalist State', *New Left Review*, **82**, 1972, pp. 83–92; Poulantzas, 'The Capitalist State: A Reply to Miliband and Laclau', *New Left Review*, **95**, 1976, pp. 63–83.

30 Poulantzas, 'The Problem of the Capitalist State', p. 73.

31 J.A. Armstrong, *The European Administrative Elite*, Princeton University Press, Princeton 1973, p. 209.

32 Griffith, p. 240.

33 On the concept of representation, see A. H. Birch, *Representation*, Macmillan, London 1972; and R. Williams, 'Democracy and Parliament', *Marxism Today* June 1982, pp. 14–21. On patronage see R.S. Goldsten, 'Patronage in British Government', *Parliamentary Affairs* 30/1, 1977, pp. 80–96.

34 C. Campbell, 'Judicial Selection and Judicial Impartiality', *Judicial Review*, December 1973, p. 269.

35 G. Marshall, 'Police Accountability Revisited', in D. E. Butler and A. H. Halsey (eds.), *Policy and Politics*, Macmillan, London 1978, pp. 51–65. The loss of power by local police committees was confirmed by the Police Act of 1964.

36 *The Scarman Report: The Brixton Disorders 10–12 April 1981*, Penguin, Harmondsworth 1982, pp. 149–50 and 187 (paras 5.64–5.66 and 7.28).

37 H. Thomas, 'Towards a Revision of the Official Secrets Act', in H. Thomas (ed.), *Crisis in the Civil Service*, Blond, London 1968, p. 112. See also the Franks Committee Report, Cmnd. 5104, 1972.

38 Also in the views of local government officials. See F. Stacey, *Ombudsmen Compared*, Clarendon, Oxford 1978, p. 209.

39 D. Williams, *Not in the Public Interest*, Hutchinson, London 1965, Chapter 1.

40 D. Leigh, *The Frontiers of Secrecy*, Junction Books, London 1980, p. 202, citing evidence given to the Franks Committee on the Official Secrets Acts in 1971.

41 B. Sedgemore, *The Secret Constitution*, Chapter 1.

42 Marshall, loc. cit., pp. 55–56.

43 Griffith, p. 230.

44 See A. H. Birch, *Representative and Responsible Government*, Allen and Unwin, London 1964, especially Chapter 5.

45 K. Middlemas, *Politics in Industrial Society*, Deutsch, London 1979, p. 309.

46 Middlemas, p. 380; B. Dix, in M. Jacques and F. Mulhern (eds.), *The Forward March of Labour Halted?*, Verso, London 1981, p. 126.

47 W. L. Guttsman, *The British Political Elite*, MacGibbon and Kee, London 1963, p. 105.

48 C. Mellors, *The British MP*, Saxon House, London 1978, pp. 62–6.

49 The latter figure (from Mellors) is for October 1974. M. Rush gives the proportion of workers in February and October 1974 as 13.5% and in 1979 as 14.2%. His definition of 'workers' evidently includes a number of non-manual employees. (M. Rush, 'The Members of Parliament', in S. Walkland and M. Ryle (eds.), *The Commons Today*, revised edition, Fontana, London 1981, pp. 49 and 61.

50 Mellors, pp. 83 and 87.

51 G. Drewry, in Walkland and Ryle, *The Commons Today*, p. 93.

52 See J. A. G. Griffith, *Parliamentary Scrutiny of Government Bills*, Allen and Unwin, London 1974, summarised and updated in his 'Standing Committees in the House of Commons', in Walkland and Ryle, especially pp. 130–1 and 136.

53 P.G. Richards, 'Private Members' Legislation', in Walkland and Ryle, p. 146.

54 A. Robinson, 'The House of Commons and Public Expenditure', ibid., p. 155.

55 N. Johnson, 'Select Committees as Tools of Parliamentary Reform: Some Further Reflexions', ibid., p. 222.

56 Griffith, *Parliamentary Scrutiny*, pp. 255–6.

57 N. Shrapnel, *The Performers*, Constable, London 1978, p. 120.

58 S. Walkland, 'Whither the Commons?', in Walkland and Ryle, p. 296.

59 Ibid., p. 302.

13 The State and the Economy

1 The most sophisticated version of this argument was advanced by R. Bacon and W. A. Eltis in *Britain's Economic Problem: Too Few Producers*, Macmillan, London 1976.
2 J. O'Connor, *The Fiscal Crisis of the State*, St Martin's Press, New York 1973.
3 This aspect of O'Connor's analysis has been convincingly criticised by Ian Gough in 'State Expenditure in Advanced Capitalism', *New Left Review*, **92**, 1975, pp. 53–92, but without detracting from O'Connor's main argument.
4 Ian Gough, *The Political Economy of the Welfare State*, Macmillan, London 1979, pp. 84–94; see also his article cited in note 3 above.
5 S. Aaronovitch and R. Smith, *The Political Economy of British Capitalism*, McGraw-Hill, London 1981, p. 292.
6 F. Field, *Inequality in Britain*, Fontana, London 1981, pp. 105–16. Field's book is also an important source for the scope and scale of tax expenditures.
7 The threshold for the 'basic' rate of income tax was finally 'indexed' – i.e., linked to the falling value of money – as a result of the 'Rooker-Wise amendment' to the Finance Bill of 1977.
8 See W. Keegan and R. Pennant Rae, *Who Runs the Economy?*, Temple-Smith, London 1979, pp. 40–7, 94–6.
9 For this story see S. Brittan, *Steering the Economy: the Role of the Treasury*, Penguin, Harmondsworth 1971.
10 R. Opie, 'The Making of Economic Policy', in H. Thomas (ed.), *The Crisis in the Civil Service*, Blond, London 1968, pp. 60–1.
11 See especially Opie, loc. cit., pp. 53–82; see also D. Seers, 'The Structure of Power', also in Thomas, pp. 83–109. Both authors show surprising faith in the possibility of overcoming the problem by introducing more economists into the state apparatus.
12 Opie, loc. cit., pp. 61–3. The last reference is to curbs on overseas investment which were supposed to be operated by the Treasury and the Bank of England and which proved ineffective in practice.
13 D. Coates, *Labour in Power?*, Longman, London 1980, pp. 86–131.
14 See S. Beer, *Treasury Control*, Clarendon Press, Oxford 1957, pp. 17–18; K. B. Smellie, *A Hundred Years of English Government*, second edition, Butterworth, London 1950; and H. Heclo and A. Wildavsky, *The Private Government of Public Money*, Macmillan, London 1974.
15 'The Operation of Monetary Policy since the Radcliffe Report', Bank of England Quarterly Bulletin December 1969, p. 438, cited in D. C. Cohen, *British Economic Policy 1960–69*, Butterworth, London 1971, p. 263.
16 A. Hanson and M. Walles, *Governing Britain*, 3rd edition, Fontana, London 1980, p. 197.
17 These developments were outlined in successive White Papers, Cmnd 1337 of 1961, Cmnd 3437 of 1967, and Cmnd 7131 of 1978.
18 NEDO, *A Study of the Nationalised Industries*, HMSO, London 1976, p. 16; R. Pryke, 'The Growth of Efficiency', in L. Tivey (ed.), *The Nationalised Industries Since 1960*, Allen and Unwin, London 1973, pp. 21–3. Much of the productivity growth was due to contraction which eliminated branch railway lines and some high-cost pits; and there are serious difficulties involved in using the conventional criteria of productivity in relation to large, semi-monopolistic industries such as these. The international comparisons may have some significance, but to the lay observer the most obvious feature of nationalised industries compared with those of other European countries appears to be the greater capital expenditure undertaken abroad.
19 G. L. Reid and K. Allen, *Nationalised Industries*, Penguin, Harmondsworth 1973, pp. 88–98, 119–29.
20 B. Fine and K. O'Donnell, 'The Nationalised Industries', in *Socialist Economic Review 1981*, Merlin Press, London 1981, p. 272.
21 Fine and O'Donnell, loc. cit., pp. 272–4.
22 *The Ten Year Development Strategy*, British Steel Corporation, 1973, cited in T. Man-

waring, 'Labour Productivity at BSC', *Capital and Class*, **14**, Summer 1981, pp. 61–97. The data in this paragraph are drawn from this source. See also R. A. Bryer and others, *Accounting for British Steel*, Gower, London 1982.
23 Manwaring, loc. cit., p. 77. In mid-1982 a further capacity reduction was being mooted costing 10,000 more jobs.
24 K. Middlemas, *Politics in Industrial Society*, Deutsch, London 1979, pp. 309 and 327.
25 L. Carpenter, 'Corporatism in Britain 1930–50', *Journal of Contemporary History*, **1**, 1976, pp. 3–25.
26 The best definition of corporatism as a structure of political management within advanced capitalism is in L. Panitch, 'Recent Theorisations of Corporatism: Reflections on a Growth Industry', *British Journal of Sociology*, **31/2**, 1980, pp. 159–87. The term 'corporate bias' is from Middlemas (see note 24).
27 Middlemas, pp. 89–90.
28 Ibid., p. 209.
29 C. Crouch, *Class Conflict and the Industrial Relations Crisis*, Heinemann, London 1977, Chapter 3.
30 Middlemas, p. 279.
31 Ibid., p. 373.
32 Crouch, p. 243.
33 L. Panitch, *Social Democracy and Industrial Militancy*, Cambridge University Press, Cambridge 1976, p. 246.

14 Consent and Social Control

1 A. Gramsci, *Selections from the Prison Notebooks*, Lawrence and Wishart, London 1971, p. 263.
2 James Michael, *The Politics of Secrecy*, Penguin, Harmondsworth 1982, p. 25.
3 All these institutions were scrupulously studied and assessed by the late Frank Stacey in *The British Ombudsman*, Clarendon Press, Oxford 1971, and *Ombudsmen Compared*, Clarendon Press, Oxford 1980.
4 G. Marshall, 'Parliament and the Redress of Grievances', in S. Walkland and M. Ryle (eds.), *The Commons Today*, revised edition, Fontana, London 1981, pp. 277–8.
5 *Annual Report for 1980*, Parliamentary Commissioner for Administration, HMSO, London 1981.
6 Stacey, *Ombudsmen Compared*, pp. 200–1.
7 F. Stacey, *British Government 1966–1975*, Oxford University Press, Oxford 1975, p. 190. The reasons for this acceptance are apparent in the establishment prose of the Commissioners' reports, and their constant stress on the difficulties of administering a complex society such as Britain and on the need to avoid wasting 'my valuable resources' on investigating frivolous or vexatious complaints. Lady Serota's annual Reports for the English Local Commissioners, on the other hand, are refreshingly free of these characteristics.
8 Michael, pp. 48–9, 194.
9 *Report of the Committee on Section 2 of the Official Secrets Act 1911*, Cmnd 5104, HMSO 1972 (the Franks Committee).
10 This was the subject of two enquiries: the *Report of the Committee on Privacy*, Cmnd 5012 of 1972 (the Younger report) and the *Report of the Committee on Data Protection*, Cmnd 7341 of 1978 (the Lindop report).
11 A noted enquirer was Peter Hennessy of *The Times*: see P. Kellner and N. Crowther-Hunt, *The Civil Servants*, Macdonald, London 1980, pp. 269–70 and 292.
12 Kellner and Crowther-Hunt, p. 275. Chapter 11 of their book is an exceptionally cogent summary of the secrecy issue.
13 Ibid., p. 281.
14 Ibid.
15 Michael, pp. 177–8.
16 J. Dearlove, *The Reorganisation of British Local Government*, Cambridge University

Press, Cambridge 1979, pp. 244–5.
17 T. Byrne, *Local Government in Britain*, Penguin, Harmondsworth 1981, pp. 27–8.
18 T. Burgess and T. Travers, *Ten Billion Pounds: Whitehall's Takeover of the Town Halls*, Grant McIntyre, London 1980, p. 18.
19 B. Keith-Lucas and P. G. Richards, *A History of Local Government in the Twentieth Century*, Allen and Unwin, London 1978, p. 40.
20 The theme of 'councillor calibre' is central to Dearlove's path-breaking study (see note 16). See especially Chapter 4.
21 See B. Abel-Smith, *The Hospitals 1800–1948*, Heinemann, London 1964; and D. Widgery, *Health in Danger*, Macmillan, London 1979, Chapters 2–3.
22 Burgess and Travers, pp. 24–8.
23 J. Alt, 'Some social and political correlates of county borough expenditure', *British Journal of Political Science*, **1**, 1971, pp. 49–62; other sources are also cited by Dearlove, pp. 234–5.
24 Keith-Lucas and Richards, *A History of Local Government*, Chapter 4; and N. Branson, *Poplarism 1919–1925*, Lawrence and Wishart, London 1979.
25 D. Skinner and J. Langdon, *The Story of Clay Cross*, Spokesman Books, Nottingham 1974. A partisan but vivid account by the leader of the Clay Cross 'rebels'.
26 The Local Government Boundary Commission Report for 1947 (the Trustram Eve Commission).
27 G. Rhodes, *The Government of London: The Struggle for Reform*, p. 108, cited in Dearlove, p. 100. Subsequently, control alternated between the two parties.
28 Dearlove, p. 103, citing M. Steed.
29 See Dearlove, Chapters 5–6, and C. Cockburn, *The Local State*, Pluto Press, London 1977, Chapter 1. See also J. Benington, *Local Government Becomes Big Business*, CDP Publications, London 1976.
30 *Report of the Committee on Management of Local Government*, HMSO 1967, and *The New Local Authorities: Management and Structure*, HMSO, 1972.
31 Cockburn, pp. 27–8.
32 C.S.E., *Struggle over the State*, CSE, London 1979, p. 51.
33 The share of 'relevant expenditure' financed by grants had risen to 66.5% by 1975–6. By 1977–8 it had been cut back to 61%. See Burgess and Travers, p. 46.
34 Ibid., p. 36.
35 Cockburn, p. 112, with particular reference to the 'community work' element in the 'participation' movement.
36 See Cockburn, pp. 103–31 and especially 103–10; also Dearlove, pp. 255–6.
37 Burgess and Travers, p. 7.
38 See Cockburn, Chapters 4 and 5.
39 See also M. Kettle and L. Hodges, *Uprising – the Police, the People and the Riots in Britain's Cities*, Pan, London 1982.
40 B. Whitaker, *The Police in Society*, Eyre Methuen, London 1979, p. 19.
41 Whitaker, pp. 73–8 and 164; see also P. Evans, 'The great myth of the detective', *The Times*, 25 March 1982.
42 *Review of Security and the State 1978*, Julian Friedman, London 1979, p. 33.
43 Lord Harris, quoted in ibid., p. 77.
44 Ibid., p. 80.
45 See M. Kettle, 'The Drift to Law and Order', *Marxism Today*, October 1980, pp. 20–7, for an excellent and balanced overview.
46 T. A. Critchley, *A History of the Police in England and Wales*, revised edition, Constable, London 1978, p. 288.
47 See *State Research Bulletin*, No. 23, April–May 1981: 'Controlling the Police? Police Accountability in the UK', pp. 110–23.
48 *Review of Security and the State 1980*, pp. 146–71.
49 Cited in ibid., p. 147.
50 Whitaker, p. 88.

51 John Alderson, Chief Constable of Devon and Cornwall, 1978, cited in *Review of Security and the State 1980*, pp. 147–8.
52 See *Review of Security and the State 1979*, pp. 130–40 and 1980, pp. 141–2.
53 The following data are mainly drawn from D. Campbell, 'Society Under Surveillance' in P. Hain (ed.), *Policing the Police*, Vol. 2, Calder, London 1980, pp. 65–150.
54 *Review of Security and the State 1980*, pp. 131–6 and T. Bunyan, *The Political Police in Britain*, Quartet Books, London 1977, pp. 196–211.
55 *Review of Security and the State 1979*, p. 8.
56 For examples see Bunyan, pp. 222–5.
57 Ibid., Chapter 4.
58 *Review of Security and the State 1980*, pp. 63–4.
59 The *Guardian*, cited in Bunyan, p. 273.
60 *Review of Security and the State 1979*, p. 23. For a full account of these preparations see P. Laurie, *Beneath the City Streets*, Panther, London 1979.
61 *Review of Security and the State 1980*, pp. 4–5 and 57–8.
62 D. Humphrey, 'The Complaints System', in Hain, *Policing the Police*, Vol. 1, p. 41.
63 The latter report (Cmnd 7341 of 1978) recommended the establishment of a Data Protection Authority to protect individuals' rights not to have either state or private computers secretly accumulate information about them.
64 *The Interception of Communications in Great Britain*, Cmnd 7873, 1980; its successor of the same title (Cmnd 8191 of 1981), by Lord Diplock, merely reported his judgement that tapping was being carried out 'in accordance with the procedures laid down'.
65 His pessimism about the prospects for a reversal of recent trends was expressed in an article in *The Times*, 9 January 1982.

Part V

15 Conclusion

1 R. Moss, *The Collapse of Democracy*, Temple Smith, London 1975.
2 A. Burgess, *1985*, Hutchinson, London 1978.
3 B. Crozier, *The Minimum State*, Hutchinson, London 1979, pp. 210–11.
4 Crozier, pp. 209–10.
5 Ibid., p. 183.
6 A. Gamble, *Britain in Crisis*, Macmillan, London 1981, p. 225.
7 Ibid., p. 226.
8 Ibid., p. 223.
9 Ibid., p. 232.
10 Ibid., p. 234.
11 For a scenario of this see C. Mullin, *A Very British Coup*, Hodder, London 1982.
12 Ibid., p. 237.
13 Ibid., pp. 224–5.
14 T. Nairn, 'The Strange Death of Industrial England', the *Manchester Guardian Weekly*, 19 April 1981. The political scenario which corresponds to this is provided by Ralph Miliband in his excellent book, *Capitalist Democracy in Britain* (Oxford University Press, London 1982), pp. 154–55.
15 J.A. Hobson, 'Can England Keep Her Trade?', the *National Review*, Vol. 97, March 1891, p. 11.
16 Gamble, p. 224.
17 Ibid.
18 A. Shadwell, *Industrial Efficiency*, Longman, London 1909, p. 341.
19 P. Laurie, *Beneath the City Streets* (second edition), Panther, London 1979.
20 G. Merritt, *World Out of Work*, Collins, London 1982, and the *Observer*, 18 July 1982.
21 See e.g. E. Hobsbawm and others, *The Forward March of Labour Halted?*, ed. M. Jacques and F. Mulhern, Verso, London 1981.

Index